F455 .A88 2012
Rebels on the border :
33663004848038
CYP

DATE DUE

REBELS ON THE BORDER

CONFLICTING WORLDS
NEW DIMENSIONS OF THE AMERICAN CIVIL WAR

T. Michael Parrish, Series Editor

REBELS
ON THE BORDER

CIVIL WAR, EMANCIPATION, AND THE RECONSTRUCTION OF
KENTUCKY MISSOURI

AARON ASTOR

LOUISIANA STATE UNIVERSITY PRESS   BATON ROUGE

Published with the assistance of the V. Ray Cardozier Fund

Published by Louisiana State University Press
Copyright © 2012 by Louisiana State University Press
All rights reserved
Manufactured in the United States of America
FIRST PRINTING

Designer: Barbara Neely Bourgoyne
Typeface: Chaparrel Pro
Printer: McNaughton & Gunn, Inc.
Binder: Acme Bookbinding, Inc.

Maps by Mary Lee Eggart

Library of Congress Cataloging-in-Publication Data

Astor, Aaron, 1973–
 Rebels on the border : Civil War, emancipation, and the reconstruction of Kentucky and
Missouri / Aaron Astor.
   p. cm. — (Conflicting worlds: new dimensions of the American Civil War)
 Includes bibliographical references and index.
 ISBN 978-0-8071-4298-1 (cloth : alk. paper) — ISBN 978-0-8071-4299-8 (pdf) — ISBN
978-0-8071-4300-1 (epub) — ISBN 978-0-8071-4301-8 (mobi) 1. Kentucky—Politics
and government—1861–1865. 2. Kentucky—Race relations—History—19th century.
3. Reconstruction (U.S. history, 1865–1877)—Kentucky. 4. Missouri—Politics and
government—1861–1865. 5. Missouri—Race relations—History—19th century. 6.
Reconstruction (U.S. history, 1865–1877)—Missouri. I. Title.
 F455.A88 2012
 976.9'03—dc23

                                                                                                2011039199

CONTENTS

ACKNOWLEDGMENTS

This book is the product of a lot of hearts, minds, and hands. It would not be possible without the material and moral support of my colleagues at Maryville College and Albion College. The encouragement especially from Dan Klingensmith, Nancy Locklin-Sofer, Doug Sofer, Will Phillips, Kim Trevathan, and Susan Schneibel at Maryville and Deborah Kanter and Marcy Sacks at Albion has been more valuable than they could ever realize. The comments and criticisms from dozens of colleagues at numerous conferences have helped me hone the book's argument and style in countless ways. For their support in helping develop a raw text into a book, I especially want to thank Anne Marshall, Diane Mutti-Burke, Stephen Ash, Michael Fellman, Christopher Phillips, Frank Towers, John Quist, Allison Fredette, Matthew Gallman, John David Smith, Luke Harlow, Patrick Lewis, Jacob Lee, Leslie Rowland, Gary Gallagher, Matt Stanley, Christopher Waldrep, Helen Lacroix, Ira Berlin, T.R.C. Hutton, Minoa Uffelman, Mark Geiger, Jim Klotter, Steve Rockenbach, Elizabeth Leonard, Gary Kremer, Edward Ayers, Mike Crane, William Freehling, Jeffrey McClurken, J. Michael Rhyne, Blake Renfro, Fitz Brundage, and Amy Murrell Taylor. I also want to thank Mary Lee Eggart for crafting maps that bring the geographic significance of the study to the fore. These are exciting days for scholars of the border states, and it is an honor to contribute to a promising new subfield in the study of the Civil War and Reconstruction. I also would like to thank LSU Press's Rand Dotson and Conflicting Worlds Series Editor Michael Parrish for their words of encouragement and support for the project from the first time we discussed it.

There are so many graduate students, advisors, and archival experts at Northwestern University who made this project possible from the beginning. First, I want to thank my graduate school advisor and dissertation chair, Stephanie McCurry, who always encouraged me to push the analysis as far as I could and whose feedback on numerous drafts of this and other works helped me to sharpen the argument. Steven Hahn and Josef Barton also helped guide my intellectual process from the moment I arrived in graduate school. Just as helpful were my colleagues and friends at Northwestern University who took time from their own doctoral work to share their thoughts with me on my research and with whom I enjoyed discussing their own work. In particular, I would like to thank Justin Behrend, Jarod Roll, Erik Gellman, David Brodnax, Carole Emberton, Shuji Otsuka, Erik Mathisen, Greg Downs, Erik Taylor, Deborah Cane, Dana Weiner, Owen Stanwood, Katy Burns-Howard, and David Sellers Smith. I would also like to thank Krzystof Kozubski in the history office at Northwestern University for his tireless work organizing my graduate funding and coursework.

While visiting archival sites, a few people were particularly helpful in navigating me through the sources of Kentucky and Missouri, especially Lynn Morrow and Carolyn Collings at the Missouri State Archives, Jim Pritchard at the Kentucky Department of Libraries and Archives, Bill Marshall at the University of Kentucky Library Special Collections, and Mark Wetherington at the Filson Historical Society in Louisville, Kentucky. I would also like to recognize the late Richard C. Brown of Danville, Kentucky, for introducing me to his work on the town's history.

My family gave me the encouragement I needed to pursue this project from the beginning and supported me all the way through. Thank you to my parents, Ronnie and Mark Astor, and my sister, Rachel Snyder. Mary and Siegfried Hausner, also helped with financial and moral support during the lean years of graduate school. Emily, the mother of my children, helped me organize so much material into something meaningful. And finally, to my children, Henry and Theodore, whose patience and love made this whole endeavor worthwhile and enjoyable.

REBELS ON THE BORDER

INTRODUCTION

In a grisly discovery on a cold morning in February 1865, a patrol of Unionist Missouri militiamen found "an old Negro Man" hanging from a tree just
six miles from the city of Columbia, a heavily fortified Unionist stronghold.
Why, the commanding officer wondered, was this man murdered? Surely he
posed no threat to Confederate "bushwhackers" prowling the countryside.
He was too old to fight in the Union army, so his death could not have been
retaliation for taking up the blue uniform. The commanding officer, Captain
H. A. Cook of the Ninth Missouri Cavalry, found a clue, however, in a note
pinned to the corpse's coat pocket. The clue was a cryptic handwritten message declaring, "Killed for knot going into the federal arma, by order of Jim
Jackson."[1] Jackson, a notorious Confederate bushwhacker who had already
warned blacks in the area to leave, had been murdering any African American he and his men could find. But the message confused the officer. Was
the word *knot* a pun to describe the method of the man's death? Was it some
sort of grotesque joke? If it was not a pun and was indeed a misspelling, why
would Jim Jackson, a Confederate bushwhacker and terrorist who hated
black soldiers and reviled Union officers even more for enlisting them, lynch
an African American for not going into the Union army?

Captain Cook conjectured to his lieutenant: Jackson was simply playing
on the tactics of substitute brokers. According to Union military draft policy,
a potential draftee could avoid service by hiring a substitute in his place.
To facilitate this process, thousands of private substitute brokers collected
money from wealthy men unwilling to fight and then scoured the farms
and cities for poor men willing to serve for pay. After paying the new enlistees for their service, the brokers kept a portion of the hiring fee. Many
of these hires in the latter months of the war were African Americans who

had yet to be drafted—or were ineligible for the draft due to age or other reasons. These military matchmakers thus provided two services to the Union cause: they filled the army with African American men, and they relieved disgruntled white proslavery conservatives of their military duties. Although white Missourians had long protested the enlistment of African Americans in the Union army, some conservative, proslavery white Unionists condoned the presence of black soldiers in the final months of war only because they helped fill the draft quota. And so, according to Captain Cook, Jackson mockingly posed as an outraged conservative Unionist who hanged an elderly black man for not relieving fellow white Unionists of their military obligations. The point of the sordid and ironic message: blacks must get out of central Missouri, and whites must stop enlisting them in the army to fight Confederates. Yet Cook was only guessing, as nobody understood Jim Jackson's real motives in pinning this note on the innocent victim's body.

In Danville, Kentucky, a town even more staunchly Unionist than Columbia, Al McRoberts met his death at the hands of a mob on Christmas Eve 1866. On the grounds of the First Presbyterian Church, once the home of an early Kentucky emancipationist minister, two hundred men and women hanged McRoberts, a black man, from an old elm tree just hours before Christmas morning.[2] Unlike the elderly man killed at Columbia nearly two years earlier, McRoberts carried a violent reputation. He and a police officer had shot at each other earlier in the day, and he was known in the community as a "bad man." But why would hundreds of Danville citizens spend their Christmas Eve storming a jail and lynching a man who scuffled with a police officer? It is quite clear that the mob that lynched McRoberts viewed him as more than just a common and violent criminal. More likely, the mob saw in him the peril of general emancipation. In the white imagination Danville and central Kentucky were filled with people like McRoberts who did not "know their place" and refused to bow to the old racial order. To the Danville mob only extralegal community violence could restore the honor and standing of the white population that had been undermined by emancipation, black soldier enlistment, and the potential of black equal citizenship.[3]

The very space where McRoberts met his death held great symbolic value for Danvillians in the decades to come. It is no coincidence that the United Daughters of the Confederacy erected a memorial to the Confederate soldiers of Danville and Boyle County on the exact site of the McRoberts lynching. White conservative Unionists and Confederates fought a bloody war over the fate of the nation. But about white supremacy they agreed: the

United States was a white man's country. And later, as the ex-Confederates frequently reminded their former Unionist foes, the Confederates had known all along that a war for Union would eventually mutate into a war for racial equality and all its attendant evils. The monument, which still stands today on the edge of the Centre College campus, consecrates a dramatic shift in sentiment among white Danvillians. With the old conservative, pro-slavery Union in the dustbin of history, border state white Unionists in the years and decades after the Civil War reconciled their own longings for white supremacy with the emerging "Lost Cause" of Confederate memory. As in much of Kentucky and Missouri, Danville's former Unionists made common cause with their former Confederate foes in the larger fight for white political and social domination.

These three iconic moments—two lynchings and the erection of a Confederate memorial—revealed a common white backlash against black efforts to transform a war for union into a war for emancipation. The enlistment of large numbers of black soldiers from central Kentucky and central Missouri drove a wedge through the white community and stimulated a violent white reaction that would reshape politics in the border states for decades. At the crossroads of antebellum America—a region long defined by mixed free and slave labor regimes, social and kinship ties to both North and South, and westward migration of both agrarian and industrial economic systems—decades of political tension exploded in violence and social revolution. In the wake of war and emancipation border state blacks and whites holding conflicting notions of citizenship, liberty, and democracy fashioned a new politics with broad implications well beyond the region. From the center of the country outward, violent struggles over the shape and nature of the Union radiated into the conservative lower North and into the upper South Confederate states. While Civil War and Reconstruction–era politicians based primarily in New England and the upper Midwest mulled over the fate of the vast plantation belt states of the Deep South, the middle third of the country, from Indiana to Tennessee and especially Kentucky and Missouri, underwent a grassroots political revolution with little guidance from the White House or Congress.

This book tells the story of that struggle among black and white Kentuckians and Missourians to make sense of the Civil War and Reconstruction at America's crossroads. As for African Americans in the border states of Kentucky and Missouri, they gained the rights and responsibilities of full membership in the American Republic in the decade after the war. In doing so, they transformed their informal kin and social networks of resistance against slavery into more formalized processes of electoral participation and institution building in the post-emancipation era. When slaves fled their masters and joined the Union army in the war's latter years, they made an unprecedented bid for the rights of citizenship. As soldiers, they rejected their masters' contention that the Union war effort was designed for the protection of slavery, and they recast the Union cause as a radical project for universal emancipation and racial equality. After the war ended in 1865, these radicalized black Union soldiers built upon their wartime experiences and continued their struggle for equal rights, social and economic auton-omy, and suffrage. In both Radical Republican postwar Missouri and conser-vative Democratic postwar Kentucky, African Americans advanced a coher-ent politics of equal citizenship and social autonomy based on community institutions such as schools, churches, benevolent societies, and grassroots civil rights organizations. When black Kentuckians and Missourians earned the right to vote with ratification of the Fifteenth Amendment in 1870, they relied on other modes of power developed before the arrival of black suf-frage—including the ability to organize for violent self-defense on Election Day—to buttress, and ultimately sustain, the new power of the ballot.

In the meantime white politics underwent a radical shift between 1860 and the early 1870s as the social revolution engendered by war, emancipation, and black military enlistment provoked violent white reaction, electoral re-alignment, and a cultural reinterpretation of regional identity. The vast ma-jority of whites in Kentucky and Missouri fought for the Union in the Civil War. And most did so for conservative reasons: they felt that the perpetua-tion of the Union was the only way to preserve the slave-based social order. These conservative Unionists resisted the secessionist impulse in 1861 and then fought off efforts in Washington and at home to radicalize the war for the "defense of the Union and the Constitution" into a "war of abolition." Their efforts were ultimately in vain, however, as supporters of the Confed-eracy—based primarily in the slave-rich central Missouri region later known as Little Dixie and the equally fertile and heavily enslaved central Kentucky region called the Bluegrass—launched a vicious guerrilla insurgency against the Unionist state governments and the federal government. Ironically, this guerrilla insurgency weakened the patrol system that had once kept slavery intact. With white rebels focused on resistance against the Unionist, albeit conservative, state governments and not on patrolling the highways of the border for runaways, slaves escaped en masse to the freedom of Union lines or to the North.

Conservative white Unionists who fought solely to preserve the "Union, the Constitution, and the Laws" found themselves in a precarious position at the war's end. In the months and years following the Confederate surrender, former white conservative Unionists joined hands with ex-Confederates to fight the Radical tide that had taken over Missouri in 1865 and, at least theoretically, threatened Kentucky. White conservatives, some of whom pledged allegiance to the old Whig Party as late as 1861, now united behind the new "White Man's Democratic Party." White conservatives also responded to black assertions of citizenship with violence. Just as blacks had joined the fight for freedom within the Union army during the Civil War, white conservatives organized shadowy paramilitary gangs in the postwar era to keep the aspirations of black would-be citizens in check. With names like the Regulators, Skaggs's Men, and the Ku Klux Klan, these white paramilitary organizations terrorized black soldiers and their families as well as white radicals who protected them. Both former Confederates and conservative Unionists staffed these organizations, with each holding the emancipated black population in equal contempt. They targeted black soldiers and their families but then unleashed their wrath upon larger segments of the black community, especially those who established any degree of political authority or social autonomy. Al McRoberts was one of their victims.[4]

In a more symbolic mode of protest against black egalitarian claims, conservative whites reimagined their own participation in the Civil War to reflect their disenchantment with the Union's radical course. Although Unionists far outnumbered Confederates in Missouri and Kentucky, the postwar period witnessed dozens of ceremonies, celebrations, and commemorations honoring the Confederate soldiers. Unionists, however, refrained from joining in the great celebratory tradition of the Grand Army of the Republic of the North, choosing to "forget" their whole service to the Union. Most interesting were those former Unionists who symbolically accepted the Confederate cause in the postwar period as the most honorable course. These belated Confederates, as I term them, constructed their own memories of the war based on the deep sense of shame they felt at watching their once conservative Union succumb to radicalism and biracial citizenship. They helped legitimize the construction of a southern regional identity in the postwar border states.[5]

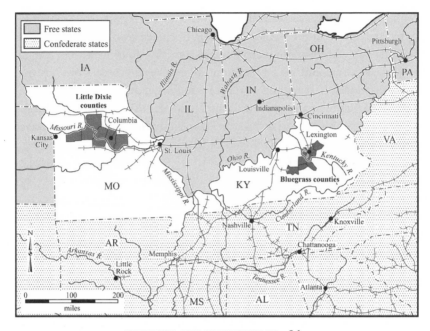

MISSOURI AND KENTUCKY IN 1860

In the end three different kinds of rebels appeared on the border between the free and slave states. In the midst of deepening sectional crisis, border state conservative Unionists rebelled against the Lincolnian notion that the nation could no longer endure "half slave and half free." A tradition of compromise and moderation in the best spirit of Kentucky's own Henry Clay demonstrated for border conservatives that sectionalism itself was anathema to social peace and order. But that conservative Unionist order itself faced two new kinds of rebels from within the border state heartland: Confederates who rejected the federal Union and launched a guerrilla insurgency against the old political order; and African American slaves who rejected the social system of slavery and advanced a very different notion of Union than that propounded by the majority of Kentucky and Missouri whites.

The outcome of this complex border state rebellion forecast the shape of national politics for the next half-century. In what one historian describes as a "rehearsal for redemption,"[6] conservatives in both Kentucky and Missouri showcased for white conservatives in the former Confederacy how they could use political unification, violence, fraud, and a cultural veneration of the

Confederate cause to reestablish moral, and ultimately political, authority within the South. Border politicians and citizens served as ambassadors of the suffering white South—with Kentucky and Missouri women playing a leading part—recounting for a nation the depths of destruction wrought by Union military action and, equally important, Radical malfeasance. As such, the white men and women of the border states provided an example of conservative renewal to inspire the overall South and lent a direct hand in overturning radicalism in postwar America.

Just as important as the "redemptive" lesson for white conservatives was the self-emancipatory experience of black Missourians and Kentuckians for African Americans in the former Confederacy. After 1867 each and every former Confederate state provided black men with the chance to participate in formal electoral politics; with the exception of Virginia, every one of these states witnessed a Radical Republican ascendancy that placed African Americans in positions of state and local authority unimagined before the Civil War. In Missouri, by contrast, a new Radical Republican government established its authority within the state without providing the vote to the state's black population. German immigrants, Ozark Unionists, and northern-born businessmen centered mostly in St. Louis ushered in a radical constitution in 1865 that abolished slavery in the state, provided basic civil rights to freed people, and excluded all Confederate sympathizers from political or civil life. But Missouri Radicals refused to support black suffrage in 1865 and offered only lukewarm support for black suffrage in a statewide referendum in 1868. Kentucky offered far less to black people, refusing even to allow African Americans to testify in court in cases involving whites until 1872. Kentucky's state government remained in conservative Democratic hands throughout the postwar era and resisted all efforts to provide civil or political rights to the state's black population. Yet against this hostility in Kentucky and cynical indifference in Missouri, border state blacks employed multiple tools of power that gave meaning and sustenance to their aspirations for autonomy, justice, and equality.[7]

The border state story that I present demonstrates the peculiar challenges, and prospects, of black politics in a white-majority region where mere numbers militated against black Republican dominance. Blacks in many sections of the former Confederacy—especially those living outside the black belts—would need to rely on these nonvoting notions of power after the overthrow of Reconstruction in the 1870s, and they could look to Kentucky and Missouri for guidance.[8]

That this sort of political transformation occurred in the crossroads of
nineteenth-century America underscores the need to re-center our portrait
of the secession crisis, the Civil War, and Reconstruction. Kentucky and
Missouri were in many ways western replications of what Barbara Fields
once described as the "middle ground—that misty and elusive terrain that
occupies such a place of honor in the geography of American political ideology."[9] Along this middle ground migratory streams of people, ideas, and
cultures traversed the slave-free line, creating a heterogeneous border culture. As the nation—and slavery—extended westward into Kentucky and
Missouri, the middle ground grew along with it. In time, however, secession,
Civil War, and the resulting abolition of slavery effectively destroyed this
middle ground, leaving in its wake a society beset by guerrilla violence and
social instability. As a result, the cauldron of war in the border spilled over
into both sections, launching an early African American "Great Migration"
to such cities as Cincinnati, Evansville, and East St. Louis, even as whites
stayed behind to consolidate political and cultural alliances with conservative Democrats in both the lower North and the former Confederacy.

Another consequence of locating the study in the border states is a reinterpretation of the events that led to the Civil War. The historical debate
over the origins of the Civil War generally breaks down into two camps:
those who identify the social differences between the free North and the
slave South as incompatible, thus leading to an "irrepressible crisis"; and
those who view the onset of Civil War as a result of blundering and self-serv-
ing politicians, propagandists, and ideologues who exploited decades-old
tensions for their own gain. By telling the story of the border states and using this region as representative of larger strains of political thinking in the
middle third of the country, I argue that the heart of antebellum America
despised extremism from both abolitionists and secessionists and viewed
each force as equally culpable for the war. The conservative, proslavery
Unionists who shaped political thought in Missouri and Kentucky also predominated in the lower tier of northern states along the Ohio River and in
the upper South states such as Virginia, Tennessee, and North Carolina. The
politics in this great American heartland that yielded compromise in the decades before the Civil War reflected not only intersectional comity but also
internal social complexities and mixed labor relationships. In cities such as
Lexington, Kentucky, and Columbia, Missouri, resident slaves, hired slaves,
free blacks, and white wageworkers toiled side by side in small factories.

Even in the countryside, many slaveholders employed wageworkers alongside their slaves, thus mixing two forms of labor that most historians char-
acterize as either distinctly northern or southern.[10]

The social complexity of border state life encouraged the dominant white
political class to approach matters of labor and social relations with a heavy
dose of pragmatism. With a labor system that at least partially resembled
that in the Midwest and with extensive kin and social ties to those living
in states such as Illinois, Indiana, and Ohio, Kentuckians and Missourians
rarely viewed the national debates over slavery as irreconcilable. To be sure,
there were some within the border states—especially Missouri's Governor
Claiborne Fox Jackson and his pro-secession allies—who welcomed confrontation with the free North and accentuated social differences for political gain. But I argue that this politics of sectional extremism proved only
fleeting in the border, as the majority of whites sought as long as possible
to remain neutral in the Civil War and only joined in the defense of the
Union—or in rebellion against it—when neutrality proved untenable.[11]

Always central to antebellum border state political culture was the preservation of a racial order that privileged whites in all aspects of social, political, and economic life. The small-scale nature of border state slavery required
both political flexibility and willingness to compromise as well as vigilance
against those within and outside the region who would threaten this order.
But these threats emerged from secessionists just as often as from abolitionists. Although most elites in the Deep South concluded after November 1860
that the Union could no longer protect the plantation-based racial order, the
calculus of antebellum border state whites leaned instead toward a vigorous
defense of slavery within the Union. As Kentucky and Missouri conservative
Unionists correctly prophesied, it would be civil war itself—an inevitable
result of secession—that would undermine this racial order.

On a methodological level this book argues that historians need to rely
on an expansive understanding of "politics" in order to make sense of the
transformations at the heart of border state, and national, society in the
mid-nineteenth century. *Politics,* as I use the term, implies the construction of collectivities based on shared grievances, aspirations, and identities;
the development and articulation of coherent demands that reflect social
and cultural desires of these collectivities; and the employment of multiple
tools of power to actualize the demands. Thus, first, the study examines the
nature of political collectivities in central Kentucky and Missouri. Blacks

living on scattered farms across the border countryside shared news, built institutions, and expressed their political objectives. The process through which antebellum resident slaves, hires, and free blacks formed a racial political consciousness was one of the central political acts in the Civil War and postwar era. Meanwhile, whites, long accustomed to a vigorous two-party political system that reinforced community-wide conservatism and Unionism, gave way to single-party rule based on militant defense of white supremacy and an explicitly southern regional orientation. Old collectivities died with the Civil War, only to be replaced with new and lasting alliances that shepherded both blacks and whites through this revolutionary period.[12]

Second, this book interrogates the cultural and social meanings attached to various forms of political mobilization. Blacks grappled with the meaning of freedom, and ultimately citizenship, at each and every moment in the Civil War and Reconstruction period. Although blacks successfully created collectivities to advance their more general aspirations, they struggled internally to spell out exactly what those aspirations were. Lines of class, previous status, and geographic residence helped define the ways in which border state blacks gave meaning to freedom, equality, justice, and citizenship. For whites the Civil War destroyed one of the nation's longest-standing political traditions—conservative Unionism—which had at one time reflected a pragmatic and traditional political culture that privileged order and stability over sectional extremism. Historians traditionally focused on the former Confederate South tend to highlight the destruction of a plantation aristocracy and debate the extent to which the postwar order differed from that of the antebellum South. But the changes affecting the middle band of the country, which never resembled the sort of seigneurial system that prevailed in the lower South, receive far less attention from historians. This book argues that one of the great political transformations of Civil War America was the death of a decades-old political culture of conservative Unionism, strongest in the border states, and its replacement with belated Confederatism and a new breed of white supremacist militancy. This revolution in white border state society provided substantive and symbolic meaning to larger conservative currents that undermined Radical Reconstruction at the national level.[13]

Third, I explore the ways in which the various historical actors exploited the instrumentalities of power. As members of slave-based societies, white Kentuckians and Missourians regularly used violence to enforce the social order and, by extension, defend the polity itself. In the Civil War and postwar eras violence played an even more pivotal role in resolving political disputes and defining the limits of social power. The guerrilla insurgency launched by white Confederates in Little Dixie and the Bluegrass and the often-clumsy and heavy-handed counterinsurgency led by various state militias and the federal army remain a remarkably under-studied phenomenon, despite the sizable effect this "outrageous" form of warfare had on the American imagination; to a large extent our modern Geneva Conventions regarding treatment of prisoners of war have their roots in the Missouri struggle.[14] Violence also shaped the limits of dissent and political activism in the postwar period, especially with regard to black aspirations for equal citizenship. Black soldiers, by taking up arms against, and often alongside, their masters, fundamentally altered the meaning of the Union cause. Perhaps nothing undermined conservative Unionism in the border states and the nation as a whole more than the presence of black soldiers fighting for the Union and emancipation. Whites—both Unionist and Confederate—employed racial violence in return and engaged in a campaign of intimidation and expulsion that reflected a newer breed of white supremacy. As blacks organized in violent defense of the right to vote in the early 1870s, whites found their worst fears confirmed. No longer interested in merely cowing blacks to remain docile farm laborers, white conservatives now found the black population to be economically unnecessary and socially dangerous.

Violence was hardly the only instrument of power employed by Kentuckians and Missourians. The ballot box was the primary means through which they selected their political leaders, voiced opinion on policy matters, and earned the rewards of patronage. For these reasons, as well as the desire to protect civil rights, African Americans made manhood suffrage a central political demand in the postwar years. But as I argue in the final chapter of the book, other tools proved just as important as the vote; in many ways these other modes of political behavior made suffrage possible. For blacks the construction of community institutions such as schools, churches, benevolent associations, and civil rights leagues reflected the various components of freedom in the black imagination. Whites, divided internally by civil war and the vitriolic politics of Reconstruction, employed ad hoc leagues, aid associations, and cultural institutions to reflect the values of conservative Unionism and its replacement, belated Confederatism.

To explore these transformations in border state political culture, I focus on the most heavily slave-based regions of Missouri and Kentucky. Little Dixie,

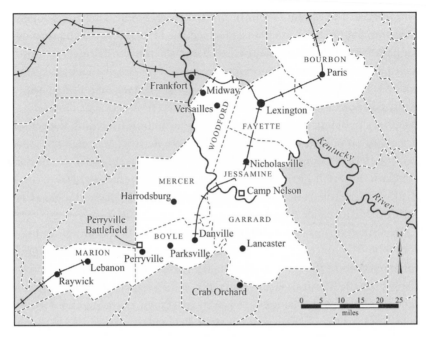

BLUEGRASS COUNTIES OF KENTUCKY IN 1860

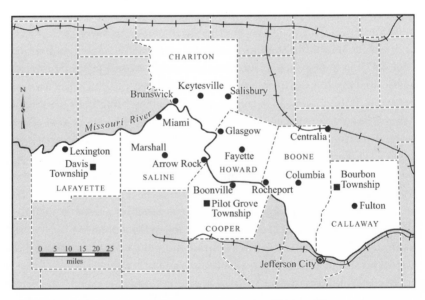

LITTLE DIXIE COUNTIES OF MISSOURI IN 1860

composed of the Missouri counties of Callaway, Boone, Howard, Cooper, Chariton, Saline, and Lafayette, traversed the Missouri River and formed the backbone of the state's slave-based hemp and tobacco culture. Although slaves never accounted for more than 37 percent of the overall population in any Little Dixie county, the political culture of the region reflected a vigorous defense of slavery and the rights of slaveholders.[15] For Kentucky I examine the Bluegrass region surrounding Lexington, including the counties of Bourbon, Fayette, Woodford, Jessamine, Garrard, Mercer, Boyle, and Marion. Here the slave population was greater as a percentage of the overall population than in Little Dixie, though only in Woodford did slaves constitute a majority. As in Little Dixie, slavery played an integral role in the political culture of the Bluegrass.

Nevertheless, it is important to place the slave-based sections of the border within the context of their state politics. In both cases the slave-dominated portions of the states tended to dominate state politics. In Missouri's Little Dixie the "Central Clique" controlled the state's Democratic Party and added a level of sectional militancy to the party not shared by those living in St. Louis or the Ozarks. Thus, if Little Dixie politicians were to pursue a course of moderation or conservative Unionism, nobody in the state was going to push them toward secessionism. The same was true in Kentucky's Bluegrass. A handful of counties in the western part of the state embraced the Confederacy more so than in the Bluegrass, mostly because of river trade to the lower South. But these counties were sparsely populated during the Civil War and held little political power in the state. As a result, Bluegrass politicians felt no pressure from southern militants residing elsewhere in the state. These statewide patterns are noteworthy because in the upper Confederate states such as Virginia and Tennessee, the regions that most resembled Little Dixie and the Bluegrass were not the most pro-secessionist portions of their respective states.[16] White conservative Unionist politicians from Middle Tennessee and Virginia's Piedmont—where slave populations looked quite similar to Little Dixie and the Bluegrass—faced off against militant secessionists in plantation-rich West Tennessee and Tidewater Virginia in the months following Lincoln's election. The coming of war in April 1861 was enough to encourage Middle Tennesseans and Piedmont Virginians to join their more insistent secessionist friends and take their respective states out of the Union. This dynamic, more than anything else, explains why conservative Unionism survived Fort Sumter as a significant political force in Little Dixie and the Bluegrass and not in Middle Tennessee or the Piedmont.

Any study of the border states during the Civil War era leads the historian to some rich sources. First and foremost is the press. Small towns such as Paris, Lebanon, and Danville, Kentucky, and Boonville, Fulton, and Lexington, Missouri, produced semiweekly highly partisan newspapers that covered local events in great detail. Larger communities such as Lexington, Kentucky, tended to have multiple newspapers, with contrasting perspectives and contents. Nineteenth-century newspapers are useful to the historian because of what they report and because of how they report it. Although it is unlikely that readers employed the colorful rhetoric of newspaper editorialists, there is little doubt that newspapers helped mediate the perspectives of ordinary people grappling with the complex and painful events of the Civil War and Reconstruction.

Newspapers were weakest in their coverage of events facing the black community, but federal government documents help to fill the void. The records of the Union army and the Freedmen's Bureau reveal in rich detail the struggles of African Americans to build schools, hold meetings, join the army, and protect themselves from racial violence. Like newspapers, these government documents reflect the political biases of their authors, who were disproportionately Radical Republicans held in low regard by the white communities in which they served. Some of these officers were natives to Kentucky and Missouri, and some were residents of the North. Geographic origin seemed to matter less than political ideology, however, as some of the most radical officers serving Kentucky and Missouri were border state natives themselves. Together, these published and manuscript sources provide a window into a tumultuous and revolutionary moment at the heart of nineteenth-century America.

CHAPTER 1

BUILDING THE WESTERN MIDDLE GROUND

Joseph C. Kennedy, superintendent of the 1860 population census, quoted an old aphorism that aptly described population movement across the border South. "Men seldom change their climate, because to do so they must change their habits; the almost universal law of internal migration is, that it moves west on the same parallel of latitude."[1] The rise of conservative, pro-slavery Unionism in Kentucky and Missouri during the late antebellum era resulted, in many ways, from the transfer of a diversified, small slaveholding class westward from Virginia. What historian Barbara Fields referred to as the "middle ground," a society materially based on small-scale slavery, diversified agricultural holdings, and widespread slave hiring, reemerged in large part in central Kentucky's Bluegrass and central Missouri's Little Dixie and directly informed the development of conservative Unionist political culture.[2] The local tensions and rhythms of border state society and the national political context of late antebellum America encouraged white Kentuckians and Missourians to articulate a specific set of social values that conveyed the fears and aspirations of the border's small slaveholding class. These values privileged stability, pragmatism, compromise, and tradition over ideological rigidity and sectional honor and helped solidify the region's embrace of conservative Unionism with the outbreak of Civil War.

Jefferson's Yeoman Slaveholders Populate Kentucky and Missouri

If Kentucky was an "offspring" of Virginia, as historian E. Merton Coulter wrote in 1926, then Missouri was an offspring of Kentucky.[3] Tens of thousands of Virginians, many of them small or middling farmers, set out through the

Cumberland Gap or down the Ohio River to Kentucky; among them were masses of Revolutionary War veterans due land grants in lieu of war bounties. The sons and daughters of many of these same westward migrants then headed a generation later across the Mississippi River to the newly annexed territory of Missouri.

Consider Edward Darnaby, who left Spotsylvania County, Virginia, for the transmontane Kentucky country with his brother John in 1785. Once there, Edward's youngest son, John H., worked his father's farm in the Bryant's Station area of Fayette County in Kentucky's fertile Bluegrass region, helping to raise horses and tend to the hemp and corn crops. John H. Darnaby later purchased his own farm near Athens, Fayette County, to be worked by his five slaves.[4]

Or Arthur Withers, who moved from his native Virginia to the Bluegrass region of Kentucky as a child in the early 1800s. In 1832 Withers repeated the westward migration his parents had undertaken and pulled up his family for Chariton County, Missouri. One of the earliest settlers in Clark Township of Chariton County, Arthur Withers employed his sons George and James on a farm growing the common Little Dixie staples of tobacco, hemp, and corn; investment in five slaves in the 1850s added additional laborers to work alongside his sons in the field.[5]

Then there was Martin Baker, a wealthy farmer, 64 years of age in 1860 and born in Millersburg, Bourbon County, Kentucky. He probably brought at least one of his seven slaves into Missouri—two older male slaves are listed on the manuscript census of 1860.[6] At his new home outside Millersburg, Bourbon Township, Callaway County, Missouri, Baker attained a veritable fortune worth ten thousand dollars.

Or Daniel Norvell, born in Virginia's Piedmont region, who moved to Kentucky at age 24 and a year later set out for New Frankfort in Saline County, Missouri. A farmer and carpenter by trade, Norvell worked six slaves on his tobacco fields in 1860.[7] Like the other slave families from Virginia, the Norvells carried with them into Kentucky and Missouri the habits and values of a small slaveholding society.

Western migrants from Virginia, like immigrants from Europe, moved in a chain migration pattern, with young adult men establishing homesteads in the newly opened western lands and sending for their families to join them.[8] Some migrants brought slaves with them, as Martin Baker assuredly did.[9] One historian dubbed these emigrants "portable planters" for their tenacious desire to re-create their old Virginia lifestyle in the West.[10] Other migrants hoped to attain the wealth (and slaveholdings) their own fathers had achieved in Virginia but that they could not replicate in the Old Dominion. Still others started out poor, hoping that cheap land and hired slaves would pave the way to a future of prosperity.[11] And if place names and settlement patterns are an indication, western migrants sought to re-create their earlier routines and habitations as closely as possible; considering that the largest town in Martin Baker's Bourbon Township, Callaway County, Missouri, was called Millersburg, the same town in Bourbon County, Kentucky, where he was born, the links between Kentucky and Missouri could not be any clearer.

Census figures in 1860 bear out the larger trend of Virginian expatriation to Kentucky and Missouri, especially to the central portions of each state. An analysis of four jurisdictions across central Missouri reveals nativity patterns for the Little Dixie region as a whole. Tables 1.1–2 show nativity figures for three rural townships—Pilot Grove Township in Cooper County, Davis Township in Lafayette County, and Bourbon Township in Callaway County—and one urban jurisdiction, the city of Fayette in Howard County, by state of birth and by region of birth.

TABLE 1.1. Nativity of white central Missourians by percentage of place of birth

Jurisdiction Name	Missouri	Kentucky	Virginia	Tennessee	Ohio	Pennsylvania	Germany
Pilot Grove, Cooper Co.	49.5	11.6	9.1	2.5	7.5	2.3	5.2
Fayette City, Howard Co.	56.1	10.5	8.1	0.7	2.5	2.5	6.7
Bourbon, Callaway Co.	62.0	21.1	10.8	0.7	0.0	0.5	1.1
Davis, Lafayette Co.	51.9	21.0	18.9	0.9	0.7	0.4	1.7
Missouri statewide	44.5	9.4	5.1	6.9	3.3	1.7	8.3

Source: Eighth Census, Population, 1860.

TABLE 1.2. Nativity of white central Missourians by region of birth

Jurisdiction Name	Missouri	Total North	Total South, excluding Missouri	Total Foreign
Pilot Grove, Cooper Co.	49.5%	13.0	29.4	8.1
Fayette City, Howard Co.	56.1	11.4	21.7	10.8
Bourbon, Callaway Co.	62.0	1.3	34.6	2.1
Davis, Lafayette Co.	51.9	2.5	42.5	3.1
Missouri statewide	44.5	14.4	25.7	15.0

Source: Eighth Census, Population, 1860.

Nativity patterns in central Missouri reveal a sizable portion of non-southerners. Especially in Pilot Grove and Fayette, German immigrants and westward migrants from free states such as Ohio and Pennsylvania populated the community to a significant degree. Caspar Beechler, for example, a 30-year-old immigrant from Bavaria and his Prussian-born wife, Kate, farmed a small plot of land in Pilot Grove. Nearby J. M. Dickey of Pennsylvania worked as a teamster and accumulated a personal estate of one thousand dollars.[12] To be sure, lateral migration from Virginia to Kentucky and on to Missouri clearly prevailed in the overall central Missouri population, but other movement—geographically if not socially "lateral"—lent a cultural diversity to central Missouri that would complicate the region's political response to the sectional crisis.

Although some townships yielded northern-born proportions over 20 percent, other townships such as Bourbon and Davis were almost entirely populated by natives of Kentucky, Missouri, or Virginia. Regardless of these slight variations within Missouri's Little Dixie, however, the vast majority of whites in the region would have considered themselves "southern," especially insofar as they were well accustomed to the habits and social customs associated with slavery. It may be that during the first few decades of statehood central Missourians considered themselves to be "westerners" at heart; as the first state to be populated heavily by eastern whites after the Louisiana Purchase, the moniker aptly applied. But the building blocks to an increasingly southern identity, centered on protection of the peculiar institution associated with the place of birth of most whites in the region, were well in place by the 1850s.[13]

For Kentucky, and the Bluegrass region in particular, nativity patterns were more uniform. In the late eighteenth and early nineteenth centuries thousands of Virginians journeyed through the Cumberland Gap to the "breakaway" state of Kentucky.[14] Bypassing the mountainous region surrounding the Gap, pioneers set up the first, and largest, permanent settlements in the fertile Bluegrass region just to the northwest of the mountains. The Bluegrass resembled the Piedmont of Virginia in physical appearance— broad, rolling hills—but with richer soil and limestone-bedded streams producing high-mineral water for horses and for making whiskey. From wealthy and powerful Virginia politicians such as John B. Breckinridge to farm renters such as John and Lucinda Bailey of Louisa County, Virginia, Kentucky beckoned thousands of westward migrants from all social classes, especially in the years following the Revolutionary War.[15] Philip C. Kidd, who became one of Lexington's greatest horse auctioneers, traced his family roots to King and Queen County, Virginia, where his paternal grandfather had emigrated in the 1780s.[16] But migration through the Gap to the Bluegrass had largely ended by the antebellum era. Whereas Kentuckians once drew heavily from the "mother state" of Virginia, migration to the Bluegrass State was largely complete by the early to mid-nineteenth century. More than eight Kentuckians in ten were Kentucky-born in 1860, whereas less than half of Missourians that year had been born within that state.[17] In the Bluegrass region in-state nativity may have been even higher. In the town of Lancaster, Garrard County, on the southeastern edge of the Bluegrass region, for example, 89.3 percent of all white residents were native Kentuckians, with 3.1 percent coming from Virginia and only 2.4 percent from overseas.[18] In fact, by 1860 Kentucky, particularly the Bluegrass region, exported twice as many whites to Missouri as it imported from Virginia.[19]

The slight demographic variations between Little Dixie and the Bluegrass would have political implications in the years leading up to the Civil War. Missouri's German-born residents and free state natives, though a minority constituting less than a quarter of the population in Little Dixie, nevertheless aroused suspicion in the eyes of many proslavery Missourians. By contrast, the more uniformly southern heritage of the Bluegrass probably limited antebellum anxieties over slavery's destiny in Kentucky. The presence of abolitionist Kentuckians such as Cassius Clay and John Fee certainly provoked hostility and consternation in Bluegrass political circles. But these activists were few and far between; Bluegrass slaveholders never faced the sort of antislavery base that Missouri did, with its German immigrant population. Not surprisingly, these internal differences between relatively heterogeneous Missouri and solidly "southern" Kentucky would influence both antebellum political debates as well as wartime loyalties in the two border states.

Slave-Based Societies in Missouri and Kentucky

Nativity data alone cannot explain the culture, society, and political world that emerged in central Missouri and central Kentucky.[20] Historian Frank Owsley once described the "field crops . . . tillage, habits and marketing" of westward migrants as part of their "mental furniture," which they implanted in their new homes on the westward frontier.[21] A key item of mental furniture for Kentuckians and Missourians was small-scale slavery. Dispersed smallholdings, diversified farming, and slave hiring characterized the central

Kentucky and Missouri countrysides, just as they did in much of colonial Virginia.[22] From the earliest days of white settlement, slavery touched the lives of a large percentage of white Missourians and Kentuckians. In both cases slaveholders brought slaves with them westward into Kentucky's Bluegrass region in the 1780s and the Missouri Boonslick area in the 1810s,[23] often to fell the Kentucky wilderness or plow the Missouri prairie for farming. In some instances slaves played an integral role early on in fending off Indian attacks; Edmund Cabell's slave "Black Sam," for example, saved members of Cabell's family during an Indian raid on the family cabin, rescuing baby Augusta from the burning house.[24] Despite reservations from antislavery advocates, such as the Reverend David Rice at Kentucky's 1792 founding constitutional convention, slaveholders had already established slave-based tobacco and hemp farms across the Bluegrass by the time of statehood.[25] Constitutional sanction of slavery in 1792 ensured that Kentucky's tobacco and hemp farms would continue to define the state's economic and social order.

In Missouri slaveholders from Kentucky and Virginia, along with a sizable number of Tennesseans and North Carolinians, occupied the fertile Boonslick region along the Missouri River in the years following the War of 1812. By 1820 and the Missouri Compromise—the nation's first major constitutional crisis involving slavery since passage of the Constitution itself—slaveholders had already turned central Missouri into a social replication of Kentucky's Bluegrass.[26] Early settlers in the Boonslick engaged their slaves in commercial production of corn, tobacco, and hemp for sale down the Missouri River to St. Louis and New Orleans. Exemplifying the early "portable planter," Philip Turner, who emigrated from the Kentucky Bluegrass in the 1820s, employed three of his male working-age slaves to tend his Howard County, Missouri, farm in 1830, with two working-age female slaves available for farm and domestic work.[27]

While the movement of people from Virginia to Kentucky, and then to Missouri, was clear among the general population, it was especially apparent among the slaveholding class. Nearly half (48 percent) of the twenty-seven slaveholders from Missouri's Pilot Grove Township in 1860, for example, were born in Kentucky, and nearly a quarter were born in Virginia, even though only 20 percent of the township's population at large was born in Kentucky or Virginia.[28] Although there were some exceptional cases of northern-born slaveholders, the vast majority had been born in the upper South.

As was true in Virginia, most slaveholdings in central Missouri and Kentucky were relatively small. The average slaveholding for Pilot Grove Township in Cooper County, Missouri, was a mere 6.7 slaves per household; in the Deep South slaveholdings averaged 12.7 slaves.[29] The smallholdings indicate farms with a mixed labor force consisting of male household members, hired laborers, and slaves. Included among this small slaveholding class were P. W. Reid, who, without any sons, hired a white man named Israel Cable to work alongside his 7 working-age slaves, and W. M. Taylor, who employed his 21-year-old son as a farm laborer to work alongside 10 slaves. With thirty-six thousand dollars in real estate, Taylor was one of the richest men in Cooper County, underscoring the prevalence of smallholdings in the border South. To put it in national perspective, a labor force of 10 slaves—half the census definition of a "plantation," which required 20 slaves—would signify a modest slaveholding homestead in the Deep South.[30]

The relatively dispersed slave population did not mean that white exposure to the slave system was rare. Nor did it indicate that slaveholders were statistically marginal elements among the white, male, voting population. To the contrary, dispersed smallholdings simply indicated a higher *number* of slaveholders and, more important, white family members living in households headed by slaveholders. Only 27 of the 691 residents of Pilot Grove Township were legal slaveholders (3.9 percent), but 143 white men, women, and children lived in those households. Thus, as many as a fifth of all white residents in Pilot Grove Township lived in households with slaves. This number is not as high as in the Deep South, but it encompasses a considerable portion of the white Pilot Grove population. With slaves constituting a significant portion of the overall property held—in Cooper County, Missouri, slaves represented $1.56 million out of $6.79 million in total property—and with slaveholders as some of the county's wealthiest residents, it is no surprise that protection of slavery would place high on the political agenda of local leaders.[31]

In Kentucky slavery took on similar features: smallholdings and mixed labor arrangements. There were, however, some differences between Kentucky and Missouri. Slaves constituted a larger percentage of the Bluegrass population than they did Little Dixie: 37.7 percent of central Kentuckians were slaves compared to only 28.3 percent of central Missourians. Slaveholding sizes were only marginally higher in Kentucky: 7 slaves per slaveholder in the Bluegrass versus 5.7 slaves per slaveholder in Little Dixie. Not surprisingly, then, a considerably higher percentage of white Kentuckians were exposed to slavery in their households than whites in Missouri. Table 1.3 shows average slaveholding sizes, slaves as a percentage of the entire

population, and the percentage of whites living in houses with slaves for
each of the eight Kentucky counties under study.

TABLE 1.3. Slaveholding in Central Kentucky

County	Number of Slaves per Slaveholder	Slaves as Percentage of Total Population	Percentage of White Population Living with Slaves
Bourbon	7.9	45.5	62.5
Boyle	6.5	35.2	48.2
Fayette	N/A	44.3	N/A
Garrard	6	34.0	49.2
Jessamine	7.5	39.1	48.3
Marion	5.8	27.6	38.3
Mercer	5.7	23.9	31.3
Woodford	9.2	52.0	66.4
Average	7	37.7	47.3

Source: Eighth Census, Population, 1860. Percentage of whites living in households with slaves is calculated by
dividing the number of slaveholders by the total number of white households. A close analysis of some jurisdictions in Kentucky and Missouri reveals that slaveholding household sizes are roughly comparable to overall
household sizes and that nearly all slaveholders are heads of households.

Note: The slave census for Fayette County includes hirers along with owners, making the number of slaveholders
nearly impossible to ascertain. This statistical anomaly comes in handy, however, in assessing the process and
prevalence of slave hiring in the city of Lexington.

As with Missouri, considerable regional variation could be found among
central Kentucky counties. Woodford County was the only majority slave
county in the study. Indeed, Woodford slaveholdings were the largest in
central Kentucky, with the highest percentage of whites living in households with slaves. On the other hand, the slave-to-population percentage in
Marion County on the southwestern edge of the Bluegrass was considerably
lower than in Woodford, as was the average slaveholding size and percentage
of whites exposed to slavery in the household. Overall, however, nearly half
the white population in central Kentucky lived with slaves in the household.
Slaveholdings may have been significantly smaller than in the Deep South,
but the practices, habits, and values of slaveholding stretched into a near
majority of white homes.

Slaveholders in central Kentucky and Missouri employed bondmen and
women to plant, cultivate, and harvest tobacco and hemp as well as corn and
wheat. Slaveholders also directed their slaves to tend the livestock, repair

fences, build barns, and haul supplies from one end of the farm to another. The work required of slaves depended on the particular crop mix and labor supply of each individual farmer, and the evidence suggests that slave owners in both central Kentucky and Missouri operated highly diversified farms. One way to examine crop diversity in the heavily enslaved regions of Little Dixie and the Bluegrass is to compare the ratio of staple and nonstaple production within the region versus the rest of the state, against the ratio of improved land in the region to the rest of the state.[32] The percentage of improved acreage in the central slaveholding belts was considerably higher than in the states as a whole. Table 1.4 illustrates the importance of staple crops—hemp in Kentucky and tobacco and hemp in Missouri—in the farming of these heavily fertile and improved areas. But note also that corn and wheat cultivation roughly correspond to state averages. The only anomaly is the relatively low rate of wheat production in central Missouri; much of this exception can be attributed to the extraordinarily high rate of tobacco cultivation in Chariton County, which effectively squeezed out wheat production. It is notable how rarely this occurred, however, in the rest of the border states. Highly productive, fertile, and slave-tilled Bluegrass and Little Dixie acreage yielded high staple crop production but not at the expense of diversification.[33]

TABLE 1.4. Agricultural Production in Central Kentucky and Missouri, as Percentage of State Total

Region	Improved Acreage	Corn	Wheat	Livestock Value	Tobacco	Hemp
Central Kentucky	12.3	11.8	15.5	14.9	0.2	43.3
Central Missouri	15.8	15.2	9.7	15.4	39.3	43.9

Source: Eighth Census, Population, 1860.

The differing labor demands of each crop meant that farmers required a more flexible workforce than existed in the cotton plantation districts of the Deep South. While tobacco and hemp were highly labor-intensive crops, their time demands differed. Tobacco culture in Missouri necessitated extensive attention throughout the year, whereas hemp needed very little cultivation throughout the year but intense labor during the winter breaking season.[34] Neither tobacco nor hemp cultivation became more efficient with higher volume of production; by contrast, rice, sugar, and cotton could be produced more cheaply with more available lands and a greater labor force. Tobacco culture eroded the soil too thoroughly to permit widespread cultivation at any given time; from the earliest tobacco cultivators in seventeenth-century Virginia to the Chariton County growers of 1860, farmers worked small plots for tobacco while using the remainder of their land for cereal production. This system allowed farmers to exploit the high profits of tobacco production despite the lengthy fallow period necessary to replenish the soils. Hemp, on the other hand, caused little damage to soil minerals. But its cultivation required backbreaking labor that prevented all but the most physically fit slaves to perform. The most taxing part of hemp production was the "breaking" process, whereby laborers would beat the rotted hemp stalks so that the fibers within would fall to the ground. With the intense physical demands of hemp breaking, which was done in winter, slaveholders rarely maintained large slave labor forces or cultivated the product in large quantities.[35]

With land and slave labor available outside of tobacco and hemp production, central Missouri and Kentucky farmers employed their slaves in the production of wheat and corn as well as the raising of livestock. Wheat and corn cultivation required special attention in spring and fall months and much less in summer or winter, but it did entail more skilled work in mills and cooperage. Cattle and hog raising remained immensely profitable for central Missouri farmers throughout the antebellum era, serving a fast-growing meat packing center in St. Louis.[36] And horse breeding, emblematic of the limestone-rich Kentucky Bluegrass from the earliest days, employed slave labor in the stables and saddle shops.

In the cities and towns of central Kentucky and Missouri, factories processed, packed, and rolled tobacco leaf; constructed hemp rope and bagging; produced woolen and coarse textiles, milled corn, and grain; and manufactured myriad other items for local and regional consumption. A tobacco warehouse in Glasgow, Missouri, processed, prized, and packed tobacco produced in Chariton County and sent it down the Missouri River to the St. Louis and New Orleans markets.[37] Rope walks in Lexington, Missouri, turned dew-rotted hemp into cotton bagging for sale to the lower South. And in Lexington, Kentucky, the serendipitously named George Woolley's Woollen Manufactory produced jeans and linsey for the entire Bluegrass region made from locally raised sheep.[38] In each of these facilities a combination of white wage workers, free blacks, and slaves—some, but not all of whom, were hired—worked side by side. George Woolley hired at least six slaves to work in his woolen works alongside his own eleven working-age slaves and a white weaver named Charles Whaler.[39] Factory operators regularly adjusted their workforces in response to changing market demand and labor prices, maintaining both labor flexibility and the social relations of slavery in expanding cities and towns.

Slaveholders in both rural and urban sections of central Kentucky and Missouri employed slave laborers in the home as well as in the fields and factories. Slaves formed a domestic workforce intended to relieve white women of the burdens of household drudgery. Some owners of domestic slaves employed armies of mostly female servants in their homesteads. Lucy Ferguson, for example, who described her occupation as "lady" to the census taker in 1860, owned twenty-six slaves to operate her Lexington, Kentucky, estate.[40] Other domestic slave owners came from considerably more humble circumstances than did Lucy Ferguson. W. Purnell, a carpenter in Millersburg, Kentucky, held six slaves, most likely to help with domestic work; the two adult slaves in the Purnell household were women.[41] Jackson Vanarsdall, a Mercer County, Kentucky, miller, sold a 20-year-old woman named Mary to Bettie Compton, probably for domestic service.[42] Specific mention of domestic service in newspaper advertisements and private letters usually reference a range of domestic activities, including cooking, cleaning, sewing, and general household maintenance. The *Central City and Brunswicker* of Brunswick, Missouri, for example, described the sale of a slave named Kitty, 29 years old, along with her 20-month-old son, John; the note characterized Kitty as a "first-rate house servant, very neat and clearly remarkably pleasant in her disposition, and as a cook, washer or dairy woman is excelled by few."[43] In similar fashion Lexington, Kentucky, attorney James O. Harrison, evinced his desire to purchase a "good cook and washer woman" in a newspaper advertisement.[44]

A diversified economy centered on cereal production, tobacco processing, hempen bagging, and rope manufacturing created a demand for a more flexible workforce than was normally afforded owners of slaves. To exploit the mixed economy efficiently but maintain the slave system as a viable means of labor and social organization, slaveholders turned to slave hiring. The practice of slave hiring took place wherever slavery existed in the American South, but its incidence was higher in the border and upper South than it was elsewhere.[45] And in urban areas, where industrial and domestic demands required seasonal labor to operate the rope walks and grain mills, slave hiring was even more prevalent.

Employers and owners conducted most hiring arrangements privately, with informal receipts spelling out terms of treatment, price, and cause for cessation of contract. On Christmas Day in 1859 Alex Jeffrey of Lexington, Kentucky, hired a female slave named Secly from B. B. Taylor for seventy dollars. The handwritten agreement, typical of most hiring contracts, stated that Jeffrey would "agree to furnish said servant good and suitable clothing appropriate to the seasons; pay her doctor's bills, and treat her with humanity and kindness; this note negotiable and payable in the part of Bank of Kentucky. In case of death the hire to cease."[46] Some contracts spelled out specific articles of clothing to be furnished to slaves, as if to ensure the owner that the hirer had already planned out, in detail, how he or she will care for the owner's property. Jeffrey also hired Mrs. Nancy Warfield's slave named Lavinia; in the promissory note Jeffrey stipulated that he would provide "said girl in the Spring as clothing: two calico dresses, two chemises, two aprons, and a pair of shoes and in the fall one linsey dress, two pair of stockings, one pair of good winter shoes and two aprons, and will pay as hire for said girl on the 25th of Dec. 1860. Sixty five dollars ($65.00). In case of death the hire ceases from that day."[47]

Other personal letters reveal the networks of contact between potential owners and hirers, many of whom shared family or business relationships. Green Clay Smith wrote his cousin Brutus J. Clay: "My wife is very anxious to have a black nurse and I prefer one myself. Have you one about fifteen or eighteen years old that I can hire the year to come? She wants one that is good, neat, and knows something about washing for infants. Please let me know if you have one, the price and if I can get her."[48] Business ties often attracted slave hiring relationships, such as in the case of Richard B. Young, a leather merchant in Lexington, Kentucky, who hired a 22-year-old woman with her two young daughters from an upholsterer named J. McFarland.[49] It is very likely that the business relationship between Young and McFarland facilitated the hiring arrangement. Other hires resulted from administration of estates after the death of an owner. According to a listing in the *Missouri Telegraph,* the administrator of a New Bloomfield, Missouri, estate hired out five male slaves with prices ranging from $156 for a man named John to $50 for a 12-year-old boy named Cupid.[50] As with most hiring contracts, the transaction took place around the beginning of the year and stipulated a year of service.

More detailed information concerning slave hiring is available for Lexington, Kentucky, because the census taker in 1860 accounted for all slaves hired as well as owned, so it is possible to draw some broader conclusions about the prevalence of slave hiring and the effect it had on white business relations, the character of upper South slavery, and slave community life. Table 1.5 shows data on slave hiring for the city of Lexington according to the census, including number, gender, and destination of hires.

TABLE 1.5. Slave Hiring in Lexington, Kentucky, 1860

Total Number of Slaves	2,471
Number of Slaves Hired Out	303
Percentage of Slaves Hired	12
Percentage of Owners Hiring Out	29
Percentage of Hired Slaves Who Were Female	57
Percentage of Hires Sent Outside of Lexington	17
Percentage of "Outside" Hires Who Were Male	52

Sources: Eighth Census, Population, 1860; and 1860 Lexington City Directory.

In a city as large as Lexington, with a wide array of industries ranging from local production of shoes and leather goods to large factories producing hempen bagging and coarse textiles, it is not surprising that slave hiring would play such an important role in the city's economy. A greater proportion of slaveholders, however, hired out at least one of their slaves (29 percent) than the proportion of slaves actually hired (12 percent). Many slaveholders in the city owned more than ten slaves, and of those very few of them hired out more than one or two in a given year. A majority of slaves hired in the city were female (57 percent), thus confirming historian Keith C. Barton's analysis of Bourbon County, Kentucky, that most hires were domestic servants.[51] Yet 17 percent of all hired slaves were sent outside the city of Lexington to work the farms of the surrounding Bluegrass. And of them, a slight majority (52 percent) were males, almost certainly hired out to work the hemp and wheat farms of the countryside, but many were also female domestics sent to the estates of outer Fayette County.

While some slaves were hired out to existing slaveholders looking to expand their labor force for seasonal demand, most hirers were non-slaveholders who needed one or two extra hands to help with domestic work or in small shops run by carpenters, blacksmiths, and other skilled craftsmen. Slave hiring was a vital component of the slave system in Lexington, and it likely was in other parts of central Kentucky and Missouri. Indeed, Henry

Clay Bruce, brother of future United States senator Blanche K. Bruce, recalled in his autobiography toiling as a hired slave in a tobacco warehouse
in Chariton County, Missouri.[52] The incidence of slave hiring may have been
less in more rural areas—it is doubtful as many as 29 percent of all rural
slaveholders hired out their slaves in a given year—but the practice played a
critical role in balancing the social order defined by slavery and the diversified economic demands of the mixed border South economy.

Perhaps most important, slave hiring introduced the habits, values, and
social relationships of slavery into a far larger portion of the population
than would have otherwise been exposed to slavery without the practice of
slave hiring. Thousands of white families in central Missouri and Kentucky
without the wealth to own slaves themselves hired slaves to help around the
house or in the fields. Slave hiring gave non-slaveholders a stake in the protection of slavery and encouraged this larger mass of the white population
to come to slavery's defense in the late antebellum era. The widespread practice of slave hiring thus helped extend the political culture of conservative,
proslavery Unionism to non-slaveholding elements of the white population.

Slavery, Order, and Border State Values

In his 1882 *History of Fayette County, Kentucky* William Henry Perrin wrote,
"To negro slavery we are largely indebted for the chivalric character and
open-handed hospitality of our fathers."[53] James Lane Allen, the great
nineteenth-century raconteur and propagandist of the Bluegrass, echoed
Perrin's assessment. Repeating the typical refrain regarding the "mildness"
of Kentucky slavery—a perspective endorsed by slavery apologists and opponents alike[54]—Allen cited the rolling Bluegrass countryside; the temper-
ate climate; the limitations of hemp, tobacco, wheat, and corn on large-scale
slavery; and the slave anti-importation laws of 1833, which reflected a deep
ambivalence about the peculiar institution, in order to contrast Kentucky's
system of slavery with that of the Deep South.[55] "It is evident that under
such conditions slavery was not stamped with those sadder features which it
wore beneath a devastating sun, amid unhealthy or sterile regions of country, and through the herding together of hundreds of slaves who had the
outward but not the inward discipline of an army."[56] Because of this "mild"
form of slavery, Kentucky's slaveholders attained a "noble character" with
"aristocratic virtues: highest notions of personal liberty and personal honor,
a fine especial scorn of anything that was mean, little, cowardly."[57] Missouri-

ans similarly distinguished the mild slavery of their region from the brutal system existing in the lower South. And like their Kentucky counterparts, Missouri apologists of slavery also connected the supposed mildness of Missouri slavery with a sense of "nobility" and "paternal kindness." Some, such as Governor Robert Stewart, even contrasted slavery favorably with the free-labor "English system of slavery," which "render[s] the laboring classes helpless, dependent and wretched."[58]

But more important than the "chivalric" consequences of the peculiar institution, slavery imposed a distinct racial order that few in the border states dared threaten. Indeed, though some late antebellum Missourians and Kentuckians, such as Henry Clay, offered more tepid defenses of slavery than Stewart and James Lane Allen, nearly all border state whites feared social chaos and the demise of white civilization if the slave population were to be liberated at once.[59] If one ideal characterized late antebellum border state life more than any other, it was the desire for order—social, economic, racial, and ultimately political order. The thirst for order in a region challenged by both abolitionism and secessionism stood as the central pillar to antebellum upper South social thought. It would trump all concerns about sectional honor in the ensuing crisis, revealing a population that embraced slavery and Union, or conservative Unionism.[60]

At the heart of Kentuckian and Missourian values was white supremacy, or more specifically, a belief that Western civilization was a product of characteristics unique to the white race and that all interracial relationships must protect the white race from subjugation or degradation by the black race.[61] Failing to hold the line against attempts at racial equality would yield nothing less than complete reversion to barbarism, which whites believed inevitable wherever blacks lived without white authority. Most white northerners and southerners agreed with this racial order, but each section preserved white supremacy differently. Northerners simply excluded African Americans outright—states such as Indiana and Illinois legally banned black people from entering those states in 1860, and many other states placed onerous taxes on blacks who could not prove employment or property ownership—or failing that, segregated blacks and whites in all facets of social and economic life.[62] White northerners protected white supremacy by monopolizing the property, power, and labor force of the northern states. White southerners, living amid populations that often included large majorities of African Americans, embraced slavery as the natural system of racial and social control. Without slavery, white southerners feared, blacks would

literally overrun and destroy white civilization, re-creating either Haiti or
Africa itself.

Whites in central Kentucky and Missouri embraced a form of white supremacist ideology that fit the culture of border slave life. The slave system
naturally produced excess slaves not needed to work the fields and factories
of the Bluegrass and Little Dixie, and slaveholders sought a means to control
these residual slaves. Kentucky and Missouri slaveholders either manumitted or, more commonly, sold to the Deep South their excess slaves. Where
manumission occurred, it took place very slowly and under the tight control
of former masters. A small free black population emerged in larger towns
such as Columbia, Missouri, and Danville and Lexington, Kentucky, but
never to the size it had attained in the eastern border states of Maryland
and Delaware, where more than half the black population was free by 1860.
Moreover, the free black population in the towns of central Missouri and
Kentucky remained closely tied to white patrons who had posted bond for
former slaves' rights to remain in the state.[63] In Boyle County, Kentucky,
a judge signed ninety-six free black papers, allowing the former slaves to
remain in the community under the watch of their former owners and
other prominent white citizens. The Boyle County court's action undoubtedly helped the white community maintain control over the whereabouts,
means, and "morals" of the community's free black population.[64] Slavery's
apologists and critics in the border states might have differed as to the ef-
ficiency, fairness, or productivity of the slave system, but they agreed in
common that emancipation without complete colonization would result in
total and complete social chaos and very possibly the demise of civilization
as they knew it.[65]

More than just a racial system, however, slavery in Kentucky and Missouri was, as in the lower South, a relationship of production. The diversified
economy of the border relied upon small-scale slavery in ways that some
local emancipationists denied. Of the free labor advocates in Kentucky and
Missouri, especially the Germans of St. Louis, few aspired to grow labor-intensive staple crops like hemp or tobacco.[66] Hemp producers regularly complained that the crop would die out completely without the aid of male slave
labor, especially in the breaking season. In Missouri and Kentucky cereal
production and livestock raising also depended materially on slave labor.[67]
While examples of profitable free labor–based corn and wheat production
abounded across the Ohio and Mississippi rivers in 1860, transition to such
a system would have drastically altered land holdings and labor relations

on the many large farms in Kentucky and Missouri. Free labor would have been possible, as many emancipationists argued, but it would have sown great economic disorder for the foreseeable future; after the Civil War the aspirations and actions of slaves to own their own land, rather than toil for others as wage laborers, would confirm the fears of conservative opponents of general emancipation.

Labor exploitation in the farms and factories of Kentucky and Missouri was certainly a critical way in which the slave system permeated the lives of border state whites. But slavery was a social system every bit as much as it was an economic system. As such, the slave system mediated relationships within and between households.[68] Kentucky and Missouri slaveholders regularly spoke of their chattel using terms such as "my girl" or "our dear servants" and took very seriously the paternalistic prerogatives of the slaveholding class.[69] Perhaps the exception—slave hiring—accentuates the rule here. Even in the many cases in which hiring arrangements intruded market imperatives on an otherwise paternalistic household relationship, masters insisted that slaves be treated with "humanity and kindness."[70] Incorporating such language into hiring contracts meant more than protecting an investment in property. Owners hoped their hiring clients would maintain the owner's paternal obligations vis-à-vis their slaves, thus reinforcing the household ties of slave and owner even when the slave lived outside the master's direct control. Slave hiring, and slave sale for that matter, complicated and at times threatened the paternalistic relationship between slaves and slaveholder, but it rarely undermined it on a systemic level.

In fact, contemporary descriptions of domestic slavery demonstrate how similar the practice was in the upper and lower South. James Lane Allen recounted household relations wherein the mistress played a pivotal role in reinforcing paternalistic social relations between masters and slaves. He emphasized the warm relations between "mammy" and the white children in his appropriately named chapter "Uncle Tom at Home." Allen vividly portrayed the role generous Kentucky masters played in "expounding to him the Scriptures," stressing that the master is "bound to them by live-long associations, hears their communications and complaints."[71] Most interestingly for the border, Allen emphasizes the uniquely humane character of Kentucky slaveholders in his defense of the institution in the Bluegrass. Without a white overseer or an extensive system, or "army," of black slave gangs as found in the Deep South, the Kentucky slaveholder nurtured close and familial relations with his handful of slaves.[72] In fact, the most extensive analysis of slave-slaveholder relations in Deep South yeomen households reminiscent of those predominating in Kentucky and Missouri confirms the presence of the paternalistic impulse among smallholders.[73]

Nevertheless, because of the persistence of slave hiring, the character of household relations implied certain market intrusions largely absent in the great plantation districts of the Deep South. As historian Jonathan Martin suggests, the practice of slave hiring converted both the slave's body and the slave's labor power into a commodity, thus rendering it an item of exchange somewhat more akin to the free wage laborer of the North than the paternalistic subject on the Deep South plantation.[74] Hiring contracts stipulated the precise terms and conditions of the arrangement, thus limiting the absolute authority of the hirer, and the owner, over the slave's body. The triangularity of slave hiring—with the hirer, owner, and slave each playing an integral role in the negotiations over contractual terms—effectively reduced the slave's labor power to a discrete commodity. Nevertheless, slave hiring was not an entirely market-driven transaction wherein hirers and owners traded labor power in perfect market conditions. Family members often consulted one another about the availability of slaves for hire as well as prices, needs, and preferences of slave "clients." Small manufacturers regularly conferred with their own salesmen and warehousemen regarding slaves for hire, including especially domestic slaves. Hired slaves thus did not always contribute materially to the conduct of public business; that is, many slave hires were employed to help the hirer's wife with domestic labor. The process of negotiating slave hiring relationships undoubtedly greased the wheels of business partnerships.

Even more important, slave hiring negotiations underscored the role upper South slavery played in solidifying the social order, including the many non-slaveholders in the white population. After all, the persistent practice of slave hiring directly incorporated non–slave owners into the slave system, with hirers exercising nearly all the racial perquisites that owners possessed. Slave hiring thus dramatically expanded the universe of white Kentucky and Missouri families directly exposed to the slave system. When the time came to defend slavery from its enemies, slaveholders found plenty of allies among the non-slaveholding white population.

CHAPTER 2

IN DEFENSE OF
SLAVERY AND UNION

"What next?" asked the *Glasgow (Mo.) Times* after Abraham Lincoln's November 1860 election to the presidency. Like millions of other Americans, the citizens of central Missouri reacted to Lincoln's victory with a mixture of confusion and trepidation. The lower South states had already pledged to hold secession conventions if Lincoln were elected. And the antislavery forces in New England appeared unwilling to compromise on the grievances of the slave states. The *Times* demanded that a "mass meeting of the whole people" be held to determine an appropriate course of action.[1] In response to the call, a large gathering of men from all political parties assembled at the Fayette Court House on December 3. With apparent unanimity the meeting declared that the election of Abraham Lincoln was a "triumph of sectionalism over nationalism—of fanaticism over patriotism" and that "virtual nullification of [the Fugitive Slave Law] by the legislatures of the States of the North are an actual grievance of which we have a right to complain, as illegal, unconstitutional, and unfriendly to us."[2] But unlike at similar ad hoc meetings across the South, these grievances yielded no call for secession.[3] Instead, the resolutions of the meeting stated, "We believe that the proper remedy is not to dissolve the Union, and fight against the constitution, but to stand by the Union and maintain the constitution and the enforcement of the laws."[4]

If ever there was a manifesto of border state sensibility in the aftermath of Lincoln's election, the Fayette statement was it: stand up to abolitionist demagogues in the North but reject the hotheaded secessionists of the lower South. Be vigilant for slavery and Union. Hold the middle ground against extremists on both sides. Ominously, however, two attendees at the Fayette meeting, Colonel Congreve Jackson and J. H. Robertson, paraded through the town that week with pro-secession cockades.[5] In the end the mass meeting may have given public airing to Unionist sentiment in Fayette. But secessionists lurked in the background and demanded that Missouri consider joining a slaveholders' confederacy.

Despite the presence of secessionists in Fayette, Missouri—and across the border states of Kentucky and Missouri—Unionist sentiment undoubtedly prevailed in the months between Lincoln's election and the firing on Fort Sumter in April 1861 and would retain respectability, if not parity, throughout the war. But the Unionism of the border revealed different ideological currents than existed among Unionists in the free North. As the resolutions at Fayette suggest, Unionists in the border South felt substantially aggrieved by political events and social movements in the North. And although "nullification" of the Fugitive Slave Acts through northern state "personal liberty laws" emerged as the prime object of protest in 1860, political relations between the states on each side of the slave-free line had been tense for decades.[6] The bloody Kansas-Missouri "border wars" of the 1850s and repeated abolitionist forays into Kentucky only exacerbated longstanding friction between the regions.

But the tensions, deadly as they could be, never overwhelmed the larger sense of comity and mutual respect that predominated among the vast majority of whites in the lower North and the border South. Instead, a political culture of conservative Unionism developed that united the slave states of Kentucky and Missouri with the free states of Illinois, Indiana, Iowa, and Ohio and with the federal government as a whole. Followers of this political culture cherished pragmatism, tradition, and stability above all other concerns. To conservative Unionists the "twin heresies" of abolitionism and secession equally threatened the very fabric of border South society by abrogating the tradition of practical decision making and compromise and by threatening to destabilize the slave-based social order.

To be sure, conservative Unionists could be found throughout the South, including in the states that would join the Confederacy. But the brand of conservative Unionism that dominated the border South represented a different social and political phenomenon than the Unionism inside the Confederacy. Before his home state of Georgia cast its lot with the secessionists, the lawmaker Alexander Hamilton Stephens said, "Revolutions are much easier started than controlled, and the men who begin them, even for the best purposes and objects, seldom end them."[7] But once Georgia joined neighboring South Carolina in dissolving its bonds of Union, Stephens cast his conservative doubts about "revolutions" aside and served as the vice president of the Confederacy. Hundreds of thousands of conservatives elsewhere in the South, especially in North Carolina, Tennessee, and Virginia, expressed similar doubts. But they, like Stephens, Virginia's Jubal Early and Tennessee's John Bell, fell in line with their states' secessionist destinies.

Many other Unionists from Confederate states would remain loyal to the federal government even after Fort Sumter. The most famous southern Unionist, senator and future president Andrew Johnson, rejected the Confederate appeal to non-slaveholders in his native East Tennessee: "It is not the free men of the north [the secessionists] are fearing most, but the free men South."[8] Johnson did not reject slavery outright, but he bitterly resented the stranglehold of large slaveholders on southern politics and on the secessionist movement in particular. Johnson contended that the Confederate aim was to create a government "as far removed from the people as they can get it." But few of those who remained loyal to the United States throughout the war lived in the most heavily slave-based regions of their respective Confederate states. Once the hostilities began, in April 1861, most Unionists in the Confederacy were to be found in less-enslaved regions such as the southern Appalachian mountains.[9] In Kentucky and Missouri, by contrast, Unionism remained strong in the central slaveholding belts of the Bluegrass and the central Missouri River Valley of Little Dixie. Unlike in the upland, low-slavery regions of the Confederacy, conservative Unionists in slave-dense central Kentucky and Missouri refused to condemn either slavery or, more important, slaveholders on class or regional terms.

The attitude among most whites in the lower North could also be described as conservative Unionist. Especially prominent in the Democratic Party, many of these Unionists believed strongly in the political compact of federal union but loathed the antislavery "black Republicans" and reaped murderous scorn on outright abolitionists in their midst.[10] The motto of the Democratic Party throughout the war—"the Union as it was, the Constitution as it is"—well reflected the socially conservative spirit of a large minority of the northern populace. But as much as free state Democrats shared a conservative Unionist outlook with their neighbors across the Ohio and Mississippi rivers, they simply did not face the same social reality at home. Slavery fundamentally affected every social relationship in the Kentucky Bluegrass and Missouri's Little Dixie in ways that the most conservative Democrats in places such as southern Indiana could never quite grasp. Labor relations, public order, and gender relations in the household took on an entirely different character, for example, on each side of the Ohio and Mississippi rivers.[11] Thus, conservative Unionism emerged as a national phenomenon and one that would prevail for the entire Civil War. But the nature and intensity of conservative Unionism in the border South not only set that region on a different path than its neighbors to the South but also reflected tensions absent from even the most conservative regions of the lower North.

Support for conservative Unionism was far from unanimous in central Kentucky and Missouri. A small but persistent minority of whites in the border states rejected the conservative Unionist consensus in the decade before the Civil War. Centered mostly in Little Dixie, but with a visible presence in Kentucky's Bluegrass as well, these early secessionists joined with their lower South peers in denouncing the advance of Free-Soil ideology in the North and the much more subversive threat of abolitionism that lurked just above the slave-free line. The Kansas-Missouri border wars of the 1850s, which set proslavery Missourians against abolitionists and Free-Soilers in Kansas, heightened sectional tensions in Little Dixie and helped consolidate Democratic Party control in the hands of Missouri's secessionist zealots such as Benjamin Stringfellow, Senator David R. Atchison, and future Governor Claiborne Fox Jackson. These secessionists employed the honor-laden language of the "fire-eaters" of the lower South and tried to push Missouri and Kentucky out of the Union against the wishes of most of the citizens of these states. Men such as Congreve Jackson supported this small secessionist movement as vital foot soldiers. And when the Civil War began, these white secessionists would serve as the vanguard for a guerrilla insurgency against their own Unionist state governments.

Another more hidden but equally vital element challenged conservative Unionism as well: an increasingly coherent slave politics. Although small slaveholdings and frequent hiring tended to curtail the creation of stable slave communities such as existed in the Deep South, Kentucky and Missouri slaves exploited their relative mobility, proximity to the free North, and the aid of a sizable free black community to strengthen kin ties, broaden communication networks, and attain greater autonomy. As historian Eugene Genovese has observed, the slaveholding system in the South, including the border states, "undermine[d] solidarity among the oppressed by linking them as individuals to their oppressors."[12] But the expanding networks of increasingly autonomous slaves across the border states weakened the individuating process of slave domination that had long defined the institution. Even before the secession crisis reached its breaking point, slaves pressed against the boundaries of conservative Unionist political culture by running away to the free North and by creating alternative communities and economies that fostered black racial solidarity. As a result, the pressure of a broadened slave constituency, increasingly aware of its own potency in national and local politics, positioned the slave population to open the floodgates of emancipation with the coming of civil war.

Political Culture, Ideology and Practice on the Western Border

As political scientists Sidney Verba and Lucian Pye define it, political culture is "the system of empirical beliefs, expressive symbols, and values which defines the situation in which political action takes place."[13] Nowhere was political culture more on display than at a "large and enthusiastic meeting" held in the fall of 1860 in the great Rocheport Tobacco Warehouse on the banks of the Missouri River. At the rally three central Missouri Democrats spoke out on behalf of the one true national party—the Democratic Party—as the only organization with the principles and tradition to preserve sectional peace and the integrity of southern institutions.[14] Claiming the mantle of conservatism and Unionism, these local Democrats praised the honor of the "patriot," Stephen Douglas, a man "who had braved a thousand battles for the South and not one against her." To the Rocheport congregants Douglas was the true representative of the Democratic Party, despite claims from the many supporters of Kentuckian John C. Breckinridge that Douglas was untrustworthy on the great sectional question of the day. It was Douglas, not Breckinridge or the "unprincipled" John Bell of the ad hoc Constitutional Union Party, who fought for Democratic Party values from the age of Andrew Jackson up to, and through, the late antebellum sectional crisis. To the Democrats of Rocheport—and to Democrats across Missouri, the only state in the Union to award all of its electoral votes to Douglas in the 1860 election—Stephen Douglas embodied the values held dear by southerners, westerners, honest northerners, and common men everywhere stretching back to Thomas Jefferson. To many central Missourians Douglas symbolized the political culture of the border West.

The Rocheport meeting contained several key elements of border state political culture. The symbols and slogans of the Democratic Party on display, written upon the party platform and printed in all the party newspapers, including the *Boonville Observer,* venerated the genealogy of local Democrats to the days of Andrew Jackson. The space in which the mass meeting took place—a tobacco warehouse—reflected the material basis of border state political culture. And the ideas that buttressed Democratic political culture supported the values and aspirations of small farmers living in the expanding western frontier. Countless mass meetings held in other Kentucky and Missouri county courthouses, fraternal lodges, and open fairgrounds in the late antebellum era reflected a similar political culture. Nearly all such assemblies witnessed mass white male participation, open embrace of the virtues of the small farmer, and paeans to the "rights" of property holders—especially slaveholders—and of the people at large.

This political culture, based on a common veneration of the yeoman republic and a slaveholders' democracy, refracted into political parties with differing personalities, habits, and visions of the role of the federal government. The Rocheport meeting showcased the Democratic version of this culture, but Whigs and other oppositional parties held equally suggestive, and rhetorically bellicose, rallies. Just as Democratic supporters of Stephen Douglas met in Rocheport, Richard C. Vaughan, attorney in Lexington, Missouri, just upriver from Rocheport, implored the renowned central Missouri orator and Judge Abiel Leonard to speak at a local mass meeting on behalf of the John Bell–Edward Everett ticket. Mixing age-old partisan aspiration with a new sense of sectional crisis on the eve of the November 1860 election, Vaughan asserted, "The prospect of the final overthrow of the Democracy in Missouri as well as everywhere else, is to me a source of infinite and irrepressible pleasure."[15]

The main ideological appeal of the Whigs lay in the party's championing of federal investment in national improvements and a protective tariff. In Kentucky Henry Clay's "American System" advocated the federal construction of the Maysville Road, connecting the Bluegrass to the Ohio River, a high tariff to protect Kentucky hemp, and a federal banking apparatus that would extend credit to Bluegrass businessmen. Within Kentucky itself Whigs chartered the Bank of Kentucky and committed the state to a slack water navigation project to improve river transportation.[16] Whigs dominated Kentucky politics from the 1830s until the early 1850s, electing every governor during this period. Missouri's Whig Party was considerably weaker than Kentucky's but maintained a strong presence within the central Little Dixie region. Especially in Boone County, where the state university served as a center for Missouri Whiggery, businessmen and farmers pressed for improvements on the Missouri River, the establishment of a state bank, and the maintenance of a high hemp tariff. Because of the party's failure to connect culturally with Missouri's fast-growing but still overwhelmingly rural population, the Whig Party would end up contributing its ideas more than its leaders to the state's elective machinery.[17]

The ideology of the Democratic Party of Andrew Jackson also appealed to Kentuckians and Missourians. A distrust of currency manipulation by eastern bankers and federal interference in local governance and an embrace of a small slaveholders' democracy linked whites in the border West to the Democratic Party. The vast majority of Missourians and a sizable minority of Kentuckians supported the party of Andrew Jackson because of the Democrats' cultural hue, not any particular policy position.[18] The Democratic Party celebrated an aggressive "honest white man's" popular democracy removed from the aristocratic pretenses, radical and puritanical heresies, and scheming speculators of "eastern" Whiggery. Thomas Hart Benton of St. Louis and the later leaders of the Howard County–based "Boonslick Democracy" all embodied the western Democratic spirit.[19] Democrats tended to dominate local politics in central Missouri—and state politics in Jefferson City—though a Whig element led by Abiel Leonard and James Rollins maintained a strong presence. In Kentucky, Democrats led by John C. Breckinridge and Beriah Magoffin, acquired power in the Bluegrass after the Whigs faltered nationally in the early 1850s."[20]

At Lexington and Rocheport mass meetings served the immediate purpose of rallying partisans to the polls. But they provided a deeper service in performing, reenacting, and celebrating a political culture held in common by large like-thinking collectivities. The larger social consensus among whites in the rural slaveholding belts of the border states belies the antagonistic, or even apocalyptic, rhetoric of partisan mass meetings. Kentucky and Missouri political culture did, however, place limits upon some outlets of partisan identification. Not only did the handful of Republican supporters of Abraham Lincoln fail to hold any public meeting in central Missouri or Kentucky, but the supporters of the southern Democrat Breckinridge remained remarkably silent as well. Thus, through the proliferation of mass rallies in towns across the border, Missourians and Kentuckians marked the acceptable boundaries of political expression, just as they celebrated their cultural values.

The values of both Democratic and Whiggish whites in the border South stressed the preservation of the existing order: an economic order based on small-scale production among middling farmers and manufacturers, a social order centered on nurturance of familial relationships, and a racial order based on a white numerical advantage and the circumscription of black life. But the conservative value system hardly reflected a static or immobile society with haughty notions of aristocracy. Kentuckians and Missourians were westerners, as they often reminded themselves, and their own journey into the frontier shaped their values concerning slavery, equality, and democracy. Indeed, whites in Missouri and Kentucky valued a conservative order based less on the ancient traditions of the Virginia Tidewater than on social equality among the white masses on the settled frontier.[21] A frontier democracy emerged wherein all economic classes of whites joined in common to subjugate the "wild" West. In this world slavery was no vestige of an earlier quasi-feudal order. Rather, as historian Christopher Phillips suggests, slavery *was* democracy for westerners.[22] With wide availability of open lands across the Alleghenies, only forced labor could render the prairies and forests profitable for agricultural exploitation; of the small Virginia farmers and their wealthier neighbors who trekked into the transmontane, each shared a disdain for laboring for others.[23] Only slave laborers could be expected to toil for others, rendering the mass of white settlers a truly equal yeomanry—a *herrenvolk* democracy—of the sort Thomas Jefferson may have actually witnessed in the Virginia Piedmont; the free-labor haven he legislated into existence north of the Ohio River in the 1780s would not emerge until after central Missouri developed as a slaveholding society.[24]

As a general rule, political leaders in the Bluegrass embraced a moderation that reflected ideological and regional compromise. From the early constitutional debates in 1792, in which Kentucky's founders seriously considered abolishing slavery, to the 1833 Kentucky law banning the importation of slaves, to the presence and relative toleration of outright abolitionists such as Cassius Clay and John Fee well into the 1850s, Kentucky's position on slavery had always listed toward the middle of the political spectrum. Kentucky politicians almost universally defended slavery—though as a "necessary evil" and rarely as a "positive good"—but few among them joined in the national southern rights agitation.[25] Right up through the secession crisis Kentuckians united in favor of moderation and compromise. Even future top Confederates such as John C. Breckinridge and John Hunt Morgan refused to join forces with the new southern nation until September 1861.[26] Morgan, reflecting the moderate politics of Kentucky, went so far as to declare Lincoln's election virtually meaningless. Shortly after the November

1860 election, he wrote to his brother Thomas: "The election is now over and Lincoln is certainly elected. Both Congress and the Senate are Democratic, so he can do nothing even if he wished, but I expect he will make us a good president."[27] Thomas Morgan echoed his brother's moderation when he wrote their mother: "Have any of the Southern States an idea of seceding upon the Election? If there are any I earnestly hope that Kentucky will not figure among them."[28]

Generally speaking, Missouri politicians were somewhat less moderate than their Kentucky counterparts. Indeed, Missouri governor Claiborne Fox Jackson, Judge William Napton, and Senator Davy Atchison assumed positions on the "slavery question" more in line with John Calhoun than Henry Clay. The Missouri-Kansas border wars stoked the flames of proslavery extremism in the mid-1850s, and for some the passions never cooled off. Many border ruffians, including the wealthiest slaveholding sons of central and western Missouri, viewed the local struggle against Kansas Free-Soilism as the first battle in a larger nationwide struggle for the preservation of slavery itself.[29] But for many others the politics of slavery assumed a more moderate and pragmatic course.[30] Especially among former Whigs, moderate defenders of slavery blasted the fire-eaters in their midst and in the Deep South.

A major reason for the general ideological moderation was the social and economic relationship that linked the Bluegrass and Little Dixie to the North. Even more than dependence on the federal government, ties with the free states of the Old Northwest, as well as Pennsylvania, lent caution to political agitation of the slave issue. As E. Merton Coulter correctly termed it, Kentucky was at the "heart of the Union," attached economically to both South and North. Although the Bluegrass trade was more southerly than that out of Louisville, a sizable portion of Lexington's horses as well as its hemp and woolen manufactures made its way into the Cincinnati and greater Ohio market.[31] Missouri's relationships with North and South were just as equally distributed, especially as St. Louis developed into a major tobacco production site of its own.[32] Economic ties between the Bluegrass and Little Dixie to the quasi-free cities of Louisville and St. Louis and to actually free cities such as Cincinnati and Chicago tended to moderate political discourse even in the more heavily slaveholding heartland.

Social and kin ties also linked Kentucky and Missouri with the free North. Perhaps the most famous example was Abraham Lincoln and his Lexington-born wife, Mary Todd. Indeed, the Todd family was one of the oldest and most powerful in Bluegrass society, and the Lincolns regularly visited the

Todd family in the decades before the Civil War.[33] Although Lincoln's association with the "black" Republican Party rendered him a political nonfactor
in Kentucky politics in 1860, his Kentucky provenance undoubtedly helped
soothe the anxieties of ardent defenders of slavery there.[34] Emigrants from
Kentucky to the Northwest were substantial; according to the 1860 census,
60,000 Kentucky-born citizens followed Lincoln's path into Illinois, 68,000
to Indiana, 15,000 to Ohio, 13,000 to Iowa, and 6,000 to Kansas.[35] Senator Garrett Davis, of Bourbon County, remarked in 1861: "Kentucky has almost peopled the northwestern states, especially Indiana and Illinois. I have
no doubt that one-fourth of the people of Indiana are either native-born
Kentuckians or the sons and daughters of native-born Kentuckians. They
are bone of our bone and flesh of our flesh."[36] The political ramifications of
these kin ties across the Ohio River were clear; as one Kentuckian remarked,
"What can she do by secession but make war upon the people of Indiana and
Illinois many of whom Kentucky gave birth to."[37]

Northerly kin ties worked in the reverse direction as well, especially in
Missouri. Some large slaveholders and ardent proslavery activists had family
ties to the North; Judge William P. Napton, the scion of Saline County, advisor to secessionist Claiborne Fox Jackson, and proslavery zealot, came from
New Jersey. Abiel Leonard and his brother Nathaniel Leonard, major slaveholders and prominent Whigs of Howard and Saline counties, respectively,
were born in Vermont. With some other exceptions, such as William Harri-
man of New York, owner of eleven slaves in 1860, few northern immigrants
were slaveholders. In fact, only two of the twenty-seven slaveholders in Pilot
Grove Township were born in the North.[38] Although northerners made up a
tiny percentage of border state slaveholders, a significant share of the non-
slaveholding white population traced its lineage through the northern states,
many of them immigrating to Missouri and Kentucky themselves. Thirteen
percent of all residents of Pilot Grove Township, Cooper County, Missouri,
had emigrated from northern states—7.5 percent from Ohio alone. Moreover, the percentage of Missourians of northern stock had increased pro-
portionally in the 1850s, though most northerners settled in the far northwestern corner of the state or in St. Louis. Thus, the larger ramifications of
social and kin ties between the border South and the North lay in checking
the extremist pro-southern impulse within Kentucky and Missouri politics.

The political culture of conservative Unionism that reflected border state
white values was a result of social and intellectual agitation in a particular
historical setting, with a set of distinct political pressures. In this case it

was the pressure of secession, on one hand, and abolition, on the other, that produced conservative Unionism. Many Kentuckians and Missourians distrusted the secessionist movement in the lower South because the border would bare the brunt of any ensuing military invasion. Others feared that a "Cotton State Confederacy" would subjugate the economic needs of hemp, tobacco, and cereal producers in the border states to the free market, slave-importing demands of the cotton-based lower South. And many more described their bonds of the "Union of our fathers" as too strong to sever for ideological purposes. So long as conservatives in the border believed that northerners would leave slavery alone, they felt the ties of Union were too important to abandon.

The Rhetoric of Conservative Unionism

A month after Lincoln's election and twelve days before South Carolina severed its bonds with the federal union, the Democratic *Boonville (Mo.) Observer* offered a litany of proposals to solve the sectional crisis and concluded, almost glibly, "Let this be done, and all excitement will be allayed, peace will be restored between the different sections of our country, and we will continue to bound onward in our career of greatness and glory as a free, prosperous and powerful nation."[39] The series of compromise measures, including constitutional amendments and concerted action by northern legislatures, reflected the final hopes of conservative Unionism on the cusp of Civil War. Many of these proposals were embraced by conservatives in the future Confederate states of North Carolina, Tennessee, and Virginia and were accepted by Democrats and conservative Republicans in Indiana, Ohio, and Pennsylvania. More interesting than the policy provisions for understanding conservative Unionism was the rhetoric with which whites across central Kentucky and Missouri defended the existing constitutional and social order. After all, policy proposals alone indicate various shades of desperation, horse trading, and provincialism. The proposals incorporated into the Crittenden Compromise, and later the Washington Peace Conference, only superficially reveal the underlying philosophy of conservative Unionism, based on tradition, pragmatism, and stability. The discourse of newspaper editorialists, mass meetings, and private letters reveals more deeply the imprint of conservative Unionism on the larger white political culture.

Conservative Unionism developed in response to dual threats. From the North came radical abolitionists declaring slavery the gravest sin of mankind.

After John Brown's raid on Harper's Ferry in October 1859, southerners of all political stripes reacted with horror to three things: the raid itself; the alleged conspiracy of northerners behind it; and most important, the martyr-like treatment granted Brown after his execution in December. Border state conservatives were especially alarmed, considering the location of Brown's raid, in northern Virginia. A Saline County, Missouri, mass meeting declared, "All persons who give their aid or countenance to that atrocious affair, are traitors to their country, deserving the execration of all good American citizens, and of all good men of every country."[40] The meeting's resolutions then connected the "abolitionist harangues" of northerners to the more pragmatic concern about northern refusal to enforce the Fugitive Slave Act. By putting a stop to this "ceaseless war upon the Southern people," northerners could "give stability and prosperity to the Union." Although the same Saline County meeting would declare that the election of William Seward or "any other member of the Republican Party avowing the same principles, will be a virtual dissolution of the Union," it held out hope that northern suppression of abolitionism and the "circulation of incendiary papers" would clear the air for the return of peaceful sectional relations. Union was possible—even desirable—to this meeting of ardent supporters of southern institutions, but it would require the extermination of abolitionism once and for all.

Less radical but much more powerful than abolitionists were Free-Soilers, who disdained slavery as an institution and viewed it as a patently inferior mode of social and labor organization to the free labor system ascendant across the northern states. But Free-Soilers were pragmatic and recognized that the best way to hedge in the slave system and the ambitions of the "slave power" was to prevent slavery's expansion westward. Codified into the newly formed Republican Party, the Free-Soil doctrine united various streams of antislavery thought into a coherent and powerful political movement.[41] To conservative Unionists, however, the distinction between Free-Soilism and abolitionism was one of tactics, not philosophy. The editor of the *Glasgow Weekly Times* noted, "We are as decidedly and as unalterably opposed to Abolitionism, 'Freesoilism' and all sorts of slavery agitations as any live man on the face of the earth."[42] The *Times* casually lumped together "Free-Soilism" and "abolitionism," even though the two philosophies reflected entirely different visions and attitudes. They were just two birds of the same feather to border conservatives, and neither could be trusted.

From the South, especially the "cotton states," came the fire-eaters, the "Yanceyites," and the "nullifiers," whose excessive zeal to protect the institution of slavery threatened both the federal union and, to conservatives, slavery itself. Slavery-based secession movements proliferated across the lower South, dating from the Calhounite nullification movement in 1832. South Carolina always led the way, but secession drew its strongest adherents from the entire South, including Alabama's William Lowndes Yancey, Tennessee's Isham Harris, and Virginia's Edmund Ruffin. Secessionists failed to convince the southern states to vacate the Union during the compromise crisis of 1850, but they gained considerable momentum throughout the cotton-rich 1850s. Secessionists believed that the emergence of a dominant sectional party based on Free-Soil principles meant that the slaveholding South could no longer coexist in a federal union with its honor intact. Moreover, some secessionists longed for the expansion of slavery not only into the west but into Central America, with Dixie serving as the capital of a hemispheric slave empire.[43] The western territorial issue lay at the heart of southern expansionism, and the blockage of slaveholders' aspirations meant usurpation of their rightful power and the denial of their honor. But if the western territorial issue topped the list of secessionist grievances, Missourians and Kentuckians who actually fought with abolitionists and Free-Soilers in the Kansas wars placed the western status lower down in their list of priorities; nearly every mass meeting, pro-Union or pro-secession, listed enforcement of the Fugitive Slave Act as the prime concern for Kentuckians and Missourians.[44] For secessionists the West signified honor and power—virtually no Alabamian or South Carolinian expressed any intention to carry his slave property into New Mexico or Colorado. For border conservatives such honor-laden language came across as haughty and impolitic in the extreme.

While conservatives in the border states recognized the dangers to slavery and the incendiary effect of abolitionism on northern politics, they viewed the entire crisis pragmatically. Most recognized the imminence of war if the South followed through on secession and feared the consequences for the border states. Richard Hanson, speaking to a Union meeting in Lexington, Kentucky, warned that "slavery could not long exist in a State bordering upon a hostile nation at war with her about the subject of slavery."[45] Indeed, the prospect of "bringing the Canada line to the Ohio River" sobered even the most ardent border supporters of the southern cause.[46] The very act of abandoning Congress to an increased Republican majority struck the members of one Fayette, Missouri, mass meeting as especially unfortunate. They termed the mass resignation of southerners in early 1861 an "injudicious and improper desertion of their friends."[47]

Although advocates of a new southern confederacy regularly referred to themselves as secessionists, their opponents often described them as "nullifiers." This rhetoric clearly referenced the largely unpopular South Carolina nullification crisis in 1832–33. Because many of the secession sympathizers identified with the party of Andrew Jackson, the term *nullifier* carried significant pejorative weight. Thus, when Howard Countian G. W. Miller wrote Judge Abiel Leonard regarding his opposition to secession, he demanded, "Can you do anything to prevent this state from becoming committed to the odious and accursed doctrine of nullification?"[48] Leonard himself agreed that the doctrine of secession was not only odious but doomed to "the most ridiculous failure."[49] Moreover, the locus of nullification, South Carolina, exacerbated border conservative doubts about secession. Border state conservatives repeatedly accused South Carolina secessionists of plotting to exploit the border states as a bloody battleground and buffer zone for the protection of the cotton states. As Richard Hanson of Bourbon County, Kentucky, commented: "There is a great prejudice in this section against South Carolina, and she deserves it all—she has by her rash and unprincipled course forfeited every claim to our sympathy and assistance. She has treated the border states with contemptuous scorn."[50] A Callaway County Missourian acerbically commented that South Carolina "is never without a cause" to secede, "nor has she been for the last thirty years"—a reference to the lingering distaste with which conservatives viewed the nullification controversy. "It was first the Tariff, then the 'Nigger,' then the Territories, and God only knows what its next excuse will be."[51] Because so few Kentuckians and Missourians could trace their lineage to South Carolina, it is not surprising that they could use such vituperative language against a fellow slaveholding state. Kentuckians and Missourians may have shared slaveholding status with the Palmetto State, but they shared little sympathy.

Perhaps the greatest fear of secession was the obvious consequence: civil war. Although many Deep South secessionists yearned to test their mettle on the battlefield, Kentuckians and Missourians viewed the prospect of open warfare with considerably less enthusiasm. After all, Missouri and Kentucky would serve as the front lines in a civil war with the North. To southern rights advocates the fears of the border placed the region's southern credentials in doubt. In response the *Paris Western Citizen* noted, "According

to them no man is a friend of the South who is not willing to risk civil war."
A Fulton, Missouri, Unionist warned of the "boiling, surging whirlpool of
desolation and destruction, the end of which troubles, the youngest child
on earth would never live to behold."[52] He added that secession and the
necessary civil war to follow would "bring upon us one of the most direful
calamities that could possibly befall a happy, free and independent people."
Even if the South were to succeed in its fight for independence, a Bourbon
County man noted, the separation into two republics would inevitably lead
to "continual war" over "a thousand causes which now pass unnoticed," including navigation of the Mississippi River and continual raiding of Confederate slave property by hostile northerners.[53] Inevitably, this perpetual war
would destroy the very thing that secessionists claimed to be defending.
The Bourbon Countian presciently warned: "When it is all over, and civil
and servile war has done its work of desolation, and the bloody drama is
closed—slavery is exterminated or driven to the rice fields of the extreme
South as its last refuge—all prosperity utterly destroyed, and the people are
impoverished and demoralised, by the terrible ordeal through which they
have passed—who then will say that the slight and trivial evils that now
exist justified the destruction of the government? Posterity will proclaim,
with one voice, the ineffable folly and the eternal infamy of the act."[54]

At an ideological level conservatives leveled most of their scorn at the
radicalism of secession, which would thrust a peaceful society into the vortex of the unknown. Conservative Unionists regularly described secessionists as "fanatics" and "revolutionaries," "violent and incendiary," "disorganiz-
ers and disunionists."[55] Ironically, much of the same rhetoric conservatives
used to describe secessionists they also applied to abolitionists, especially
epithets such as *fantastic* and *incendiary*. Whatever the advocates of secession claimed about protecting slave society, they were dangerously uncon-
servative.

Perhaps the worst insult heaped upon secessionists was the term *Yanceyite*.
William Lowndes Yancey was a flamboyant fire-eater from Alabama who advocated secession from his early days as an Alabama legislator in the 1840s.[56]
Yancey provided the public face behind the secessionist movement and led
the anti-Douglas walkout at the Democratic Party convention in 1860, an
event that split the national Democratic Party. During the 1860 campaign
the pro-Bell *Lexington Observer and Reporter* termed a state delegate for
the southern Democratic ticket a "Yancey-Breckinridge elector." Timoleon
Cravens, the elector in question, confirmed the suspicions of the *Observer*

and Reporter when he called Douglas supporters in Lebanon, Kentucky, "the putrid excrescence of the Democratic Party."[57] Advocates for the Douglas ticket also described Breckinridge supporters as Yanceyites. The speaker at a Douglas meeting in Lexington, Kentucky, bemoaned the "disruption in the Democratic Party" that was "caused by those men in the South who are for a dissolution of the Union. The Democratic Party, as it existed prior to the assembling of the Charleston Convention, was an impregnable barrier to the long cherished schemes of such men as Wm. L. Yancey, Robert Barnwell Rhett, Lawrence M. Keitt, and others of that ilk."[58] According to the Democratic *Boonville (Mo.) Observer,* only "the Yanceyites" would fail to commend the speech by the Douglas supporters.

Conservative Unionist rhetoric reflected more than mere rejection of the twin heresies of abolitionism and secession. Although it responded to a particular series of political crises that threatened the slave-based social order, and the constitutional order that protected it, conservative Unionism drew from the great strength of the American Republic and the compromises that had allowed the nation to grow to its prosperous status. Howard County's J. M. Hicky, like many others, celebrated the survival of the Republic through multiple generations. He "intended to fight under the glorious old flag that has for more than 80 years floated triumphantly over the land of the free and the home of the brave."[59] The nation had been established by the "sages of the Revolution and cemented by the purest blood that ever flowed from the veins of man." The resolutions of a mass meeting in Callaway County, Missouri, extolled "this Government, formed out of the privation, the suffering, the patriotism and the sacred blood of our fathers." With the Constitution as the "sheet-anchor of our hopes and the ultimatum of our desires," Unionists pledged to protect the document that was "framed and handed down to us by a brave, a generous and a noble ancestry." To defy the "sacred blood" of the "ancestors" of the Republic was not only impolitic; it was a blasphemous form of patricide rooted in blood libel against the most noble generation in human history. The United States, as Bourbon Countian and future U.S. senator Garrett Davis proclaimed, was "the freest government on earth, one that was devised by the wisest and most virtuous men, and in the full development of a glory and grandeur which the most fertile imagination could not grasp, every citizen prosperous and blessed with the mildest, happiest, and most benignant institutions ever known."[60] The Union was not only wealthy and free; it was powerful. The bonds of union "held us together for eighty years, as one of the noblest, one of the grandest and most potent confederacies upon the foot-stool of God."[61] Unionists at a mass meeting in Paris, Kentucky, asserted that nobody had the right to "weaken or dissolve the relations which bind us to the Government of our Fathers; that we have an inheritance in that symbol of Union and Liberty—that old National Flag, the Star Spangled Banner—and, by the blessing of Heaven, we will not yield up."[62]

Just as Unionists invoked William Lowndes Yancey to discredit the fanaticism of secession, they conjured up their own pantheon of heroes to the great national Union in its defense. Washington and Jefferson naturally played leading parts as soldier and architect of the Revolution, respectively. Interestingly, conservatives hailed the brave and noble men of the Revolutionary generation, yet they denounced secessionists as "revolutionary." Secessionists claimed for themselves the mantle of revolution by insisting that their own struggle was merely a continuation or consecration of the revolution of Washington. But for conservatives the American Revolution of 1776 was the last legitimate revolution, having resulted in the creation of the "wisest government known to history." Indeed, Kentuckians and Missourians referenced the nineteenth century's three greatest conservative Unionists more often than they did Washington and Jefferson. Andrew Jackson, Daniel Webster, and Henry Clay each played integral roles—even in vigorous opposition to one another—in sustaining the Republic through the crises of the early and mid-nineteenth century. Jackson was the great western statesmen and slayer of nullification and hero to most Missouri and Kentucky Democrats through 1860;[63] Webster was the great orator of conservatism during the 1840s and early 1850s.[64] But Henry Clay, above all, had contributed his life toward the preservation of the Union and protection of the social order. A son of the Bluegrass himself, Henry Clay garnered more respect and admiration than any other politician in Kentucky's history. Whigs in Missouri and Kentucky alike cherished the legacy of Henry Clay as the "Great Compromiser" and invoked his wisdom in the secession crisis. B. Gaines of central Kentucky composed a poem entitled "The Union Bell," printed in the *Lexington Observer and Reporter*, that read, "With joy of the good old time, When Clay and Webster stood sublime."[65] The *Paris Western Citizen*, the oldest newspaper west of the Alleghenies, even reprinted an 1850 speech delivered by Henry Clay before the Kentucky legislature in which he declared his eternal support for the Union. In this speech Clay warned of the appearance of future parties favoring disunion and insisted that the Union party, to which he would forever commit, should declare as its platform, "The Union, the Constitution, and the Enforcement of the Laws."[66] The Constitutional Union Party of Bell and Everett adopted Clay's platform in full for the 1860 election.

Pragmatism trumped honor in the conservative Unionist political culture. Border slaveholders had fought, and lost, the battle for Kansas by 1860, and they had no intention to revive that bloody struggle in order to salve their sectional honor. Border conservatives worried about fugitive slaves much more than they did western expansion. Although the number of fugitives who escaped Kentucky across the Ohio River or from Missouri to free Illinois, Iowa, or Kansas was small, slaveholders had reason to be concerned about lackadaisical enforcement of Fugitive Slave Act provisions. Thus, border conservative grievances reflected more practical concerns with protecting a slave-based economy and society in the face of serious, but not unreasonable, threats. Indeed, many border conservatives imagined that secessionists in the lower South were so outrageous that they were bluffing.[67]

CHAPTER 3

REBELS IN BLACK AND WHITE

Rebels against Union

At Big Lick in Cooper County a group of men styling themselves the "Missouri Minute Men" met on January 12, 1861, and passed resolutions in support of a series of drastic compromise measures later to be known as the "Crittenden Compromise," named for longtime Unionist and Whig Kentucky senator John J. Crittenden. Failure to achieve all of the compromise measures, including numerous constitutional amendments, would signify that the "Union ought to be dissolved and the honor and interest of Missouri compel her to join her destiny with her southern sisters."[1] The "Minute Men" organized into a military-style company with Timothy Chandler as "captain," and two lieutenants and an orderly sergeant as his subordinates. Following the pro-South "political" meeting the Minute Men declared their next step unanimously: drilling. Whether the Missouri Minute Men comprised an actual militia or an ad hoc political gathering, the men present at Big Lick clearly envisioned their home state as a future member of the still-forming southern Confederacy. Drawing upon the Revolutionary heritage of Minute Men citizen-soldiers, the men present at the meeting positioned themselves in the vanguard of the coming southern revolution.[2] They held out hope for the Crittenden Compromise and declared fealty to the "sentiments of our forefathers" who established the federal union, but they deemed any refusal to pass all of the compromise measures a sign that the "government has failed to effect the object of its formation." To the Minute Men, northerners and the new Republican administration that failed to curtail abolitionist threats to the integrity of slave property—either in the western territories or as runaways in the free states—betrayed the very ideals of "our forefathers" and rendered the Union moot. It was the Minute Men who stood ready to defend the cause of southern rights from federal depredation at a "minute's" notice.[3]

Despite the conservative Unionist consensus that defined the political culture of antebellum Kentucky and Missouri, a forceful minority pushed the Unionist envelope. Pro-South mass meetings, militias, and pro-southern politicians doubted the sincerity of northern politicians on the slavery question, revealing at the very least the tenuous basis of Unionism on the cusp of civil war. These militant voices, like the Big Lick Minute Men, echoed Deep South secessionists and charged northerners with betrayal of "our forefathers." When Missouri held a convention in February 1861 to determine the state's future "relationship with the Federal Government," Benjamin Tompkins, a Boonville lawyer, declared himself a southern rights candidate on behalf of the Twenty-eighth Senatorial District. His open letter to the constituents of Cooper County revealed a distant longing for the Union of old: "I believe that the Government as framed by our fathers and administered in the true spirit of *that justice and right which are its noblest elements,* is the best Government known in the whole history of man."[4] Like the Missouri Militia Men, Tompkins felt the Crittenden Compromise was the only way to restore the Union of the past. And like his Cooper County paramilitary compatriots, Tompkins declared that if the North refused to pass the amendments, Missouri must immediately consider secession. Tompkins' rhetoric betrayed the appeal—and limitation—of the secessionist argument in the border states. He stated, "I would say to them [northerners], Missouri will no longer remain in a government which forgets the first precepts of christianity, which condemns her rightful appeals, and insults her interests, her feelings and her honor." Tompkins then demanded that Missouri form a union with those who share "her domestic institutions, her interests and her honor." By framing Missouri's future as a question of honor and Christianity, Tompkins crossed the breach of pragmatic discourse and joined his lower South compatriots with the language of uncompromising revolution. Although Unionists in the border states agreed with Tompkins on the importance of the Crittenden Compromise resolutions, they did not share his belief that Missouri's (or Kentucky's) honor dictated that it side with the South.

Pro-secession politicians in Kentucky and especially Missouri drew upon local and national traditions of southern sectionalism. Politicians within central Missouri's "Boonslick Democracy," including future governor Claiborne Fox Jackson and State Supreme Court Judge William B. Napton, laid out a course of militancy throughout the 1850s, beginning shortly after the 1850 national compromise following the Mexican War. At a popular level the Kansas-Missouri "border wars" and the proslavery convention meeting at Lexington, Missouri, in July 1855 served as watershed events in the rise of militant pro-southern extremism in the border states. Proslavery advocates stormed across the border into Kansas Territory, hoping to establish Kansas as a slave territory like Missouri. Like their New England abolitionist foes, these "border ruffians" crossed into Kansas not to settle permanently but to make a political point: Missouri must not be surrounded by free soil on three sides. In the midst of this ongoing struggle in Kansas, James Shannon, president of the State University of Missouri at Columbia, delivered a searing address in defense of slavery. Invoking biblical argumentation the likes of which Reverend Charles Colcock Jones would have been proud,[5] Shannon let it be known that abolition was sacrilege. But more ominous was his willingness to countenance armed force to protect the peculiar institution from "the viper teeth of Abolitionism and the motley crew of his abettors and sympathizers." Shannon declared that he would, "without a moment's hesitation, draw the sword of the Spirit—a *true* Damascus blade as was ever forged in the armory of *Heaven*—and I shall neither ask nor give quarter till the battle is fought and the victory won, or the friends of the Constitution and the rights of the South lie buried in the common grave that entombs the liberties of our country."[6]

Shannon was clearly willing to take up arms against the "abettors and sympathizers" of abolition in defense of the "rights of the South." His martial rhetoric may have reflected the ongoing struggle just thirty miles away in Kansas Territory but it clearly ratcheted up the stakes for southern rights and the Union. Shannon emphasized the consequences of his speech for the deepening national crisis, depicting a government unwilling to protect the rights of slaveholders as a form of "despotism." Shannon declared, "When peaceable modes of redress are exhausted, IS A JUST CAUSE OF WAR BE-TWEEN SEPARATE STATES, AND OF REVOLUTION IN THE SAME STATE . . . And if this be treason let free-soil traitors and abolition negro-thieves, leagued with British tories in an unholy conspiracy to dissolve the Union, make the most of it."[7] Like later secessionists, Shannon blamed antislavery forces for effectively dissolving the Union. And he equated the emerging Republican Party with abolitionism, taking no heed of internal complexities within the northern antislavery movement. Perhaps most telling was Shannon's explication of who exactly constituted "abettors and sympathizers" of abolition:

They must be judged by their acts. If they labor to weaken the South by keeping alive the foul demon of party spirit; if they are ready to palliate the aggressions of the negro-thieves, and the States and parties by which they are
sustained; if they are prompt to exaggerate and denounce the measures of
necessary self-defence that an injured and exasperated community may be
compelled to take in providing new guards for their future security; and, especially, if they denounce by opprobrious epithets those, whose only alleged of-
fence is too great devotion to the constitutional rights of the South—you neither need, nor can get, better evidence of their complicity with our enemies.[8]

By implicating the very party system that helped nurture intersectional
compromise for thirty years and, more important, by condemning both
"negro-thieves" and "the States and parties by which they are sustained"—
a clear reference to northern personal liberty laws—Shannon delivered as
strong a casus belli as any Yanceyite.[9]

In the entire antebellum era few Missourians or Kentuckians employed
such staunchly pro-secession rhetoric as James Shannon, even in the last
months leading up to the Civil War. In fact, the state legislature ordered
his removal from the university shortly after his comments. By signing the
legislation removing Shannon, the conservative governor, Sterling Price of
Chariton County, worked tirelessly to preserve the proslavery cause from
radical proslavery secession extremists such as border ruffian extraordinaire
Benjamin Stringfellow, his Calhounite patron Senator David Rice Atchison,
and, of course, James Shannon.[10] Historian Robert Shalhope captures the
sentiment of Price and other proslavery Unionists in the mid-1850s: "Price
found himself in the anomalous position of being in sympathy with views of
the proslavery radicals but opposed to their methods, which were a possible
threat to the harmony of the Union."[11] The extreme distemper of the Kansas
war era subsided after 1856 as Missourians fixated on preserving slavery
from abolitionists while preserving union from secessionists.

Yet incendiary events such as John Brown's raid in October 1859 encouraged
a resurgence of proslavery militancy, which bubbled over in mass meetings
across Kentucky and Missouri—just as the Kansas wars had buttressed and
stimulated the secessionist bombast of James Shannon in 1855. In December
1859 a public meeting of "the citizens of Saline County" met at Marshall,
Missouri "for the purpose of expressing their views in relation to the present
dangerous condition of our common country."[12] As with other southerners,
the Marshall congregants declared northern sympathy with Brown more

dangerous than Brown's raid itself, going so far as to say that it "placed the Union of these states in imminent peril" and that "all persons who give their aid or countenance to that atrocious affair are traitors to their country." To emphasize the willingness to secede from any union with these "traitors," the meeting affirmed that "the Union will be prized by us only so long as the Constitution in letter and spirit is the supreme law of the land; and that the Southern States have a right to demand of Congress the enactment of such laws as will give them peace and security." Northern states, for their part, must denounce and abrogate all personal liberty laws that harbored fugitive slaves. In the meantime the meeting's resolutions "pledged the state of Missouri to unite with the other Southern States" in defense of their "rights" and, more urgently, demanded the state government revive the state's militia laws. Further resolutions declared, "in the event of the election of a Black Republican President in 1860, that a Convention of the Southern States be called to take such measures as will conduce to the great interests of the South." Alas, the Marshall conclave warned the state to prepare for war and, if war should come, to side with the South.

The Militant South

With the breakup of the Union imminent, or at least likely, in the fall of 1860, supporters of secession in the border states drew upon a long heritage of southern militancy. Perhaps no institution expressed the creed of militancy more visibly than the plethora of militia organizations that dotted the Kentucky and Missouri landscape.[13] As the sectional crisis grew more intense, these militias readied themselves to "defend their homes" and their "rights" should the sectional shouting match become a shooting war. Many of these militia companies would serve in the Kentucky and Missouri state guards, which themselves expanded significantly in 1860. Not all militia activity in the late 1850s explicitly advanced pro-secessionist politics, as did the Missouri Minute Men. In fact, some, such as "Anvil's Artillery" in Danville, Kentucky, and Paris's Bourbon Rangers, launched national salutes and marched in defense of the Union.[14] Elsewhere in the Bluegrass countryside the Woodford Blues, Union Greys, Jessamine Blues, Porter Guards, and Governor's Guards held more "neutral" parades in Versailles and other county seats in central Kentucky, entertaining vast throngs of men and women.[15] Martha McDowell Buford Jones of Versailles reported in her diary the excitement with which her daughter Lizzie had presented the flag to the Woodford Blues at the parade. "All said they had a grand time today," she wrote.[16] They reinforced and performed southern conventions of honor and manhood even if they remained technically aloof from the sectional crisis looming over the country in the summer of 1860. Indeed, most militias at the time declared nominal neutrality, affirming their only obligation to defend Kentucky and their own firesides.

Members of Lexington, Kentucky's three main antebellum militia organizations—the Lexington Old Infantry, the Lexington Chasseurs, and John Hunt Morgan's Lexington Rifles—eventually joined both sides in the Civil War.[17] These militia organizations dated to the early years of Kentucky statehood, all of them playing vital roles in the Mexican War. The Old Infantry, formerly the Lexington Light Infantry, launched numerous campaigns against Indians in the 1790s and served in the War of 1812. The Chasseurs were a more recent creation, appearing in Lexington only in 1860 but very quickly attracting widespread attention. According to nineteenth-century historian William Henry Perrin, "The Chasseurs were the favorites of everybody, and the company rarely had a parade that it was not invited to partake of the hospitality of some private residence."[18] The Chasseurs, like the Old Infantry, sent nearly half its men to each side in the Civil War. Like the Woodford Blues, they served more to train soldiers for future combat and to parade for the entertainment of the masses than they did as sectional organizations. But Morgan's Lexington Rifles stood out for its military spirit and its singular dedication to the southern cause.

John Hunt Morgan—descendant of one of Lexington's wealthiest businessmen and honor-obsessed paragon of Bluegrass society—founded the Lexington Rifles in 1857 and reported the first company of volunteer militia to Governor Beriah Magoffin as part of the reconstituted Kentucky State Guard in 1860.[19] Morgan was a member of Lexington's manufacturing elite, operating a hemp factory in the heart of the city. He was also an interstate slave trader, sending and hiring slave cargoes down the Ohio and Mississippi rivers to Memphis and New Orleans as late as the summer of 1861.[20] Many of Morgan's longtime associates, friends, and neighbors, including Sanders Bruce and William Bodley, remained loyal to the Union. Although the state declared its neutrality in May 1861, some southern sympathizers headed for Camp Boone in Tennessee shortly after Fort Sumter. Morgan, like most eventual Kentucky Confederates, held out until September 1861, when the state officially sided with the Union, and evaded Unionist Home

Guard pickets to reach Confederate lines in occupied Bowling Green. Once in Confederate-held territory, Morgan quickly established himself as an integral component in the Confederate military command. More important than the fate of Morgan himself was his militia; according to Perrin, all but six of Morgan's Rifles joined the Confederacy, most of them in Morgan's own cavalry unit. In the case of the Lexington Rifles loyalty to the captain and loyalty to the southern cause coalesced to form a vital backbone to the Kentucky secessionist movement and to the Confederate army.

Beginning with the Kansas wars of 1855 and accelerating after John Brown's raid in late 1859, these pro-South emergency organizations drew upon an existing martial tradition and embraced the militant rhetoric of honor-driven secessionists from the lower South. Border state militias did not always maintain explicitly partisan and sectarian sentiments, but those that did, like Morgan's Rifles, demonstrated the potency of these organizations in channeling sectional anger into military action. Morgan would later repay his Unionist neighbors more than a few visits, reeking more destruction and terror on Kentucky than any other Confederate commander. The formation of nonpartisan, pro-southern militias such as the Lexington Rifles or separate ad hoc meetings such as those after John Brown's raid did not *cause* Kentuckians and Missourians to abandon the federal union. Unlike their Deep South compatriots, border state secessionists did not relish the thought of independence as a good unto itself.[21] Even militia leaders such as Morgan did not savor the idea of turning their guns against Ohioans or Indianans or fellow Kentuckians in a war for southern independence. Secessionists along the border were nearly all "reluctant," deciding at numerous times between 1860 and 1861 that the once-cherished Union was no longer. Only after war broke out in April 1861—and for many only after Kentucky officially cast its lot with the Union in September 1861—did the vast majority of these former Unionists declare their allegiance to the southern cause. And for these reluctant border Confederates the pro-South militia and caucuses offered organizational support for those Kentuckians and Missourians who rejected the northern war against the southern Confederacy and facilitated the great Confederate assault on conservative Unionism within the border states. Indeed, Missouri and Kentucky secessionists did not wait for external Confederate armies to "liberate" their home states. Rather, they launched a guerrilla-based insurgency against the conservative Unionist regimes that ruled Kentucky and Missouri throughout the war.

Prewar Secessionist Arguments and Rhetoric

In the wake of John Brown's raid the resolutions committee of a mass meeting held in Marshall, Missouri, declared, "The election to the Presidency, in 1860, of William H. Seward or any other member of the Republican party avowing the same principles would be the virtual dissolution of the Union."[22] With Governor Claiborne Fox Jackson present almost exactly a year later, a resolutions committee composed of many of the same citizens from the prior assemblage reaffirmed the earlier militancy by insisting that "the principles upon which a Republican president has been elected, if acted out, will be a just cause for dissolution of the Union."[23] But the December 1860 meeting left room for compromise and the "restoration of fraternal feelings" if, and only if, the North agreed to a "speedy repeal" of personal liberty laws; the noninterference of slavery in the states, the territories, and the District of Columbia; and the punishment of those who violate the Fugitive Slave Act. Knowing that this combination of the Breckinridge presidential platform and the later planks of the Crittenden Compromise would be unacceptable to northerners, the meeting urged the Missouri legislature to call a convention to consider steps necessary to act in concert with the other slave states.[24]

There were few calls for outright secession after Lincoln's election, with most pro-southern militants publicly holding out hope for compromise. Indeed, it is striking to observe the mournful tone of "southern rights" activists concerning the postelection crisis. Whereas pro-secession meetings across the lower South eagerly embraced southern independence, border states' rights and southern rights meetings insisted that they "deeply regret the disruption of the National Confederacy"[25] and that "every dictate of reason, interest and safety should impel Kentucky to use every effort to restore the union of the States."[26] Of course, pro-South zealots held no illusions about the prospects for a sectional settlement. A Bourbon County mass meeting demanded that "the Free States shall reject any agreed ultimatum of the Slave States for the restoration of the Union" if "the best interest, affinities, safety and honor of the Slave States will be advanced by the formation of a union with the Southern Confederacy."[27] Lexington pro-South activists similarly yearned to "bring back our southern brethren and, if possible, reconstruct the Federal Union on a basis of justice and equality" but determined that in the event of a "permanent dissolution," Kentucky will "pledge ourselves to go with the South."[28] Indeed, even the Kentucky statewide convention of the new States' Rights Party expressed an "earnest desire of the people of Kentucky that the Union of all the States should be restored and the Confederacy reconstructed," albeit on the basis of a comprehensive, constitutional adjustment to the slavery question.[29]

Despite these reservations about disunion, prewar secessionists employed rhetoric that reflected a deep sense of cultural identification with the South and a palpable feeling of alienation from and dishonor by the North. Consistent with southern principles of honorable resistance to threats to public standing, border state secessionists found "submission" to the Republicans dishonorable. Thus, members of the States' Rights Party rose in the Kentucky legislature just days before Fort Sumter and resolved "that in the event our cherished hopes for the restoration of the entire Union are blasted, that our affinities, duties and interests unite us with our southern brethren on principles of justice, equality and honor."[30] Defense of southern honor stood astride the remonstrance against federal injustice and sectional inequality in the minds of Kentucky secessionists. Remarking (approvingly) upon the intransigence of southerners in the sectional crisis, Judge William B. Napton of central Missouri noted, "The South regards it as a point of honor not to submit."[31] Indeed, the term *submission* signaled dishonor in the gendered discourse of sectional politics. Secessionists regularly chided Unionists in their midst as "submissionists"; not only were Unionists willing to concede too many principles to the North, but they surrendered the manly vitality of southern honor in the process. Napton's formulation regarding submission and honor would be repeated in almost every secessionist diatribe before, and during, the war.

The honor-bound rhetoric of prewar border state secessionists suggests a supreme militancy in the face of what they saw as an irremediably shattered Union; to them northerners had effectively severed the Union by electing a sectional president and by continually refusing to heed southern demands for the return of fugitive slaves. But border state prewar secessionists employed considerably more cautious rhetoric in defense of their position than did secessionists in the Deep South. Across states such as Alabama, Mississippi, and South Carolina, secessionists drummed up support from the moment of John Brown's raid and never relented. Across the Deep South mass meetings, Minute Men organizations, and militia musters beat the drums of secession across the summer and fall of 1860. The rhetoric of Deep South secessionists betrayed a sense of crisis and paranoia missing from their border state brethren. Conservative suggestions that Lincoln should be "given a chance" or that the North should have an opportunity to answer a unified slate of southern grievances were summarily dismissed by the dominant Breckinridge Democrats and their arch-secessionist allies in the Deep South. In one example of total community repudiation and fear of the Republican Party, a group of Neshoba County, Mississippi, women placed a large banner above the 1860 Election Day polling place that dramatically asserted the stakes at hand for Mississippians: "Death rather than submission to a Black Republican government."[32] Deep South secessionist editors echoed the palpable rage of the Mississippi women. Citing the political threat of delay, the *Charleston Mercury* declared: "If Lincoln's election is submitted for a moment, Southern men will take office under him, then become his partisans. Then an abolition party is formed among us; the South demoralized and all is lost."[33]

In many ways, however, the prewar secessionists in Kentucky and Missouri echoed the sense of effrontery of their Deep South brethren. Like Alabamians, Mississippians, and South Carolinians, they spoke of the evils of "Black Republican rule," the sacred rights of slaveholders, and the indomitable honor of the South. Lincoln's election demanded secession because the northern people had united in order to dishonor the South, and any plan to beg and plead for the new Republican administration to respect long-established rights to slave property would prove futile. Lincoln's own record mattered little as the Sewards and Greeleys surely controlled the "black Republican" party. And like their fellow secessionists in the lower South, they labeled their Unionist opponents "submissionists," suggesting the emasculation of southern manhood and the stripping of southern honor.

But border state secessionists were more willing to wait—either for Lincoln's actions regarding the already seceded states or for northern willingness to compromise on vital principles—than were their crisis-driven brethren in the Deep South. Although many Missourians and Kentuckians also evinced a sense of crisis from the days of John Brown's raid, the vigorously contested 1860 election tended to moderate, rather than exacerbate, "southern rights" rhetoric. In a strong three-party election in which two of the three factions explicitly advocated Unionism, politicians avoided the rush to militancy that characterized electoral politics across the lower South. As a result, even staunch "states' rights" activists such as Missouri governor Jackson publicly yearned for the survival of the Union when he was elected in August 1860. In Kentucky the defenders of Lexingtonian John C. Breckinridge insisted that he was a Unionist, despite the fact that his backers in the

Deep South included the most hotheaded secessionists. The *Kentucky States-man,* a Lexington newspaper committed to the Breckinridge Democrats and to a firmly pro-South policy in general, said of the party's standard-bearer: "He is impregnably fortified by a life of loyalty to the Union and of principles which are the strongest bonds of Union. He is in nowise responsible for or chargeable with the ultra opinions of extremists who may vote for him."[34] There was simply no significant force within Kentucky, especially central Kentucky, that demanded secession in the event of a Lincoln election. The emergence of a rump of border state prewar secessionists would wait until after Lincoln's election became a reality and would not find many new communicants until after the war began.

As the Marshall, Missouri, mass meeting illustrated, postelection pro-South activists hedged their zealotry with reverence for compromise and process. Secessionists hoped the Kentucky and Missouri state legislatures would call sovereignty conventions like those held in the other southern states, and they supported "States' Rights Party" or "Southern Rights Party" tickets in the special elections. But as one Missouri secessionist later recollected, the Unionists, particularly the self-described "Conditional Unionists," simply outflanked the secessionists in the run-up to the February election for the Missouri convention.[35] Affirming that the federal Union, despite its shortcomings, remained the best means to preserve slavery, and committing the state to the Crittenden Compromise as a basis for future adjustment of sectional difficulties, Conditional Unionists dominated the convention canvass. Unionists—Conditional or Unconditional—outnumbered secessionists by eighty thousand votes, and not a single outright secessionist was selected to the convention. In Kentucky secessionists could not even goad the legislature into holding a sovereignty convention, as Unionists under Crittenden's leadership took command of the crisis from the beginning.[36] Yet the abysmal performance of outright secessionist candidates in the Missouri sovereignty convention in February 1861 and the failure of the Kentucky legislature even to call a special state convention did not discourage secessionists. Although on the defensive for much of the period between November 1860 and April 1861, secessionists adjusted their rhetorical strategy in response to multipronged Unionist attacks against secessionist "extremism."

More measured than post–John Brown calls for dissolution of the Union upon a Republican presidency, pro-South arguments after Lincoln's election attempted to rebut Unionist worries and equivocations. Ironically, the camp that once couched its pro-secession argument in terms of unassailable

southern honor and rights now assumed the position of pragmatism and
measured response against Unionist emotional appeals to tradition and
stability. The widely read *Louisville Courier,* along with its fellow secessionist organs, the *Lexington Statesman* and the *Kentucky Yeoman* ridiculed the
unwillingness of local Unionists to appreciate the gravity of the crisis.[37] Continuing a critique that began in the 1860 presidential election, secessionists
challenged the failure of Unionists to take specific, principled stances.[38] The
Courier blasted Unionists for "evading the real issues. They declare for nothing; they commit their advocates to nothing; they leave the whole question
open."[39] In response to the Unionist charge that secession would "bring the
Canada line" to the Ohio River, thus rendering the Fugitive Slave Act null
and void, the *Courier* declared that the Canada line already was in effect
on the Ohio River.[40] Indeed, secessionists concluded that Kentucky Unionists were trying to trick the people into supporting a political settlement
against the real interests of the state, even adopting a new political party
name—the Union Democracy—that belied the staunchly Whiggish past of
its leadership.[41]

The most powerful Kentucky, and Bluegrass, advocate for a southern
rights (though not necessarily secession) position was Governor Beriah
Magoffin of Mercer County. But his response to Alabama secession commissioner S. F. Hale reveals the limitation of secession's pull in Kentucky after
Lincoln's election.[42] On Christmas Day 1860 Governor Magoffin answered
the Alabamian's secessionist entreaty by insisting: "You seek a remedy in secession from the Union. We wish the united action of the slave States, assembled in convention *within* the Union."[43] Magoffin sympathized dearly with
Hale and the southern cause and even proposed that a multistate convention assemble at Nashville to force the North's hand. But ultimately he settled on conservative Unionism as the best guarantor of Kentucky's "rights."
Magoffin's reticence in the wake of Hale's visit reveals the limitations of
prewar secessionism in Kentucky. There was simply no sizable support,
outside some of the far southwestern counties, for immediate secession.

In Missouri open secessionists assumed a more authoritative position
than in Kentucky. The most prominent border state prewar secessionist
of all was Missouri governor Claiborne Fox Jackson.[44] Although Kentucky
governor Magoffin repeatedly declared himself an ally of the South, it was
Governor Jackson who pushed the envelope of border state secessionism.
From Lincoln's election right up through the Camp Jackson affair on May
10, Governor Jackson played a critical role in defining the southern posi-

tion and enticing the federal government into armed conflict, which, as he understood, was necessary to build substantial pro-Confederate support in the state. In January 1861 Jackson declared, "So long as a State continues to maintain slavery within her limits, it is impossible to separate her fate from that of her sister States who have the same social organization."[45] Historian Christopher Phillips describes Jackson's January speech as "completing the cant of Southernness" for Missourians. Indeed, Jackson would identify the slave system uniting the southern states as the deepest ideological tie— much more so than the traditional federal Union. "The identity, rather than the similarity, of their domestic institutions; their political principles and party usages; their common origins, pursuits, tastes, manners, and customs; their territorial contiguity and commercial relations—all contribute to bind them together in one sisterhood."[46] But the strategy employed by Governor Jackson, described by Phillips as a "passive-aggressive policy of secession," cannily exploited the lingering doubts about Union, even after the great repudiation of secession in February. Knowing that mass support for secession would only arise if the federal government attacked the South—or Missouri—Governor Jackson plotted to arm secessionists in St. Louis, establish a secessionist military camp (called Camp Jackson), and seize the federal arsenal. The gambit worked, as a confrontation in St. Louis on May 10 effectively brought the Civil War to Missouri less than one month after the attack on Fort Sumter. The ranks of secessionists multiplied after the Camp Jackson affair as outraged former Unionists rallied to the flag of Missouri against the "black Dutch Republican despots" under the command of antislavery General Nathaniel Lyon and arch-Unionist zealot Frank Blair. Prewar secessionists in Missouri were few in number, but with membership high in the halls of state government, they positioned themselves to entice the federal government into action.

The social and political standing of prewar secessionists reveals a group hailing from both major political parties and all social classes, but they tended to emerge from the Breckinridge Democratic wing and were predominantly slaveholders. Kentucky-born Congreve Jackson, for example, was a wealthy farmer from Chariton Township, Howard County, Missouri, who possessed over ten thousand dollars worth of real estate and held sixteen slaves.[47] Such a holding made Jackson one of the largest slave owners in the township. Major Ben Bailey, member of the Committee of Resolutions at the Woodford County States' Rights meeting, owned thirteen slaves and twenty-two thousand dollars in real estate.[48] Although many attendees at

States' Rights meetings were young attorneys, owning few or no slaves of their own, they envisioned their futures as slaveholders and farmers, in the mold of their elder kinsmen, who owned wealthy hemp, tobacco, and horse breeding estates in the rural regions of central Kentucky and Missouri. Most of these relatively young professionals viewed the slaveholding system, and not the federal Union, as the bulwark of their future prosperity.[49] They saw little to gain from compromise and led the secessionist movement until the war began.[50]

Slave Politics and the Seeds of Rebellion against Conservatism

White secessionist militants would not prove the only threat to conservative Unionism. The slaves developed their own system of secretive communication and organization that would confront border state society at its core. "The negroes would talk among themselves, but never carried tales to the white folks," remembered Bert Mayfield, a former slave from Garrard County, Kentucky.[51] The "tales" Mayfield spoke of may have been religious in nature, about an afterlife free from bondage. "On Sundays we would hold prayer meetings among ourselves," he recalled. Or they may have been the whispers of rumor about life off the Stone farm near Bryantsville, such as slaves passing along the road in shackles to the Deep South. Or about rumors of violence against their master or by other slaves against their masters, though Mayfield insists that "there was no trouble between blacks and whites." Or perhaps the tales related to the latest campaign by John Fee, whose abolitionist settlement at Berea lay a short distance away. Or perhaps the tales referenced free blacks or hired slaves traveling through Lexington, like Harriet Mason, who ran away back to Bryantsville to find her mother.[52] Or even the tales may have been about what lay across the Ohio River, only one hundred miles to the north, and the Underground Railroad of John Parker and Calvin Fairbanks, who carried dozens of slaves from central Kentucky to freedom.

The possibilities are endless, which is precisely why they would have been threatening to Bert Mayfield's master. Indeed, any voluntary assemblage of slaves challenged the authority of the master, whose absolute domination demanded constant oversight. The confluence of small slaveholdings, slave hiring, and a sizable free black population in Garrard County, and elsewhere in the Bluegrass as well as in Missouri's Little Dixie, encouraged the creation and sustenance of extensive social and kin networks. These networks, like the brush arbor meetings where slaves kept their tales to themselves, gave meaning to community life and gave potency to the political aspirations of border state African Americans. As the nation approached a simmering conflict in 1861, these relationships that flourished at the margins of the master's control positioned the black community to exploit the divisions within the white population that ultimately manifested itself in an internal guerrilla war. Thus, as civil war unfolded across Kentucky and Missouri, anti-Unionist whites battled conservative Unionists, while anti-conservative African Americans dismantled the system that enslaved nearly the entire black population. Rebels on the border between slavery and freedom appeared in black and white.

To be sure, the mostly enslaved black population of Kentucky and Missouri in 1860 had virtually no political power, their few legal and customary rights hanging by a thread in the increasingly hostile late antebellum period. In law and in custom chattel slavery in Missouri and Kentucky differed little from the institution thriving deep in the cotton belt.[53] And consonant with the growing antiabolitionist militancy elsewhere in the South, the Kentucky and Missouri legislatures passed increasingly restrictive codes that both strengthened the master's total authority over the slave and pressured free blacks to vacate the region.[54] Much of this pressure arose from the very grassroots mass meetings that sprang up in response to John Brown's raid. A mass meeting held at Marshall, Missouri, in January 1860 that condemned John Brown's "treason" also petitioned the legislature to introduce stricter legislation regarding free blacks and slaves, including: a provision requiring the death penalty for black rapists; a stipulation that masters receive three-quarters of the value of a slave executed; and a demand that whites who buy commodities from slaves be charged as felons.[55] Slaveholders had demanded these provisions for years, but with the increasing panic following John Brown's raid and the imminent admission of Kansas as a free state (thus surrounding Missouri on three sides with free soil), the congregants at Marshall hoped to bolster the institution of slavery from the gathering storm within Missouri itself. The last provision making trading with a slave a felony underscored the sensitivity with which the master class viewed the underground economy; the provision was no cipher, as Robert Ricerby of Callaway County was indicted under the new law in April 1861 for "selling to slaves."[56] Clearly, the leading members of white society recognized the political threat of social and economic networks connecting slaves, hires, free blacks, and poor whites to the overall system of personal domination necessary to sustain slavery. As slaves sought to defy their masters' power of individuation by creating an increasingly autonomous sphere of social, cultural, and economic life, the masters retaliated with renewed fervor.

Perhaps most pernicious about border state slavery was the massive slave trade funneling Kentucky and Missouri slaves downriver to New Orleans or overland to Louisiana, Mississippi, and Texas. The extensive slave trade underscored the relative powerlessness of slaves to dictate their own future or to shape their own communities. Not all slaves sold went to the Deep South; in fact, the majority of private sales and sheriffs' auctions merely circulated the existing slave population within the Bluegrass and Little Dixie region. Glen Hardeman, for example, paid $1,000 for an 18-year-old "negro fellow" named Justin in 1855 in a private transaction with K. Ray Singleton to work on Hardeman's Saline County farm.[57] Countless similar small-scale sales took place between business associates and family friends right up to the Civil War. But long-distance slave traders such as Lexington's Joseph Northcutt and Lewis Robards regularly sought men, women, and children for the Memphis, Natchez, and New Orleans markets and often visited the surrounding Bluegrass to facilitate transactions.[58] Farmers regularly called upon slave traders offering excess slaves whom they had no desire to hire out or unruly slaves whom they had grown tired of disciplining. Either way, slave owners and traders rarely sold entire families together, preferring to reap the maximum gain for prime field hands on the southern market. Sometimes the transaction also included children, who were taken away from parents and other kin. Thomas Jones of Midway, Kentucky, noted that a trader in the area was "buying Boys and Girls," and Jones wished to offer up "his girl" for $350.[59] Jones cared nothing about the fate of the girl's family relationships. Other common occasions for sale were estate auctions, where administrators regularly separated slave families for the lucrative southern trade. W. H. Irwin's slaves in Columbia, Missouri, for example, were sold to various local purchasers and long-distance traders, with children each sold to different buyers.[60]

Slaves did not go without a fight. Some slaves resisted sale to the Deep South by mutilating themselves. One Missouri slave chopped off his fingers when he found out that he was marked for sale.[61] Another slave woman from Boonville, Missouri, threatened from the auction block, "Old Judge Miller don't you bid for me, 'cause if you do, I would not live on your plantation, I will take a knife and cut my own throat from ear to ear before I would be owned by you."[62] More commonly, slaves appealed to their master's sense of paternalism to keep families together. One Kentucky slave pleaded with his master not to be sold away from his wife. The master seriously considered the slave's feelings in the matter and even planned to change the prospects of sale if the slave absolutely refused to go. Writing to Calvin Morgan, John Hunt Morgan's brother, the owner wrote: "Aleck promised to think about it today and let me know this evening. He will try and make up his mind to go with Bryant in which event I think I can get 1900 for him, not more. Don't know positively yet."[63] Hoping his master's paternalistic sympathies would trump market imperatives, the slave's protest forestalled an otherwise cold business decision.

All told, approximately seventy-seven thousand slaves were sold to the Deep South from Kentucky during the entire antebellum era, thirty-four hundred per year in the 1850s.[64] For Missouri the net exportation numbers are harder to gauge because the state continued to import slaves from the East well into the 1850s, even as it sent excess slaves to the Deep South. Historian Michael Tadman concludes that during that decade 11.6 percent of all male Missouri slaves in their 20s were sold to the lower South; no other Missouri slave population segment experienced such a net loss.[65] Kentucky exported considerably more slaves to the lower South than Missouri. More-over, nearly a quarter of all Kentucky slave women in their 20s were sold away, thus permanently severing kinship bonds between women of child-bearing age and their children.[66] Contrary to the pervasive and erroneous myth about border state slavery, it was no "milder" than bondage in the Deep South, and the wanton destruction of slave families is the strongest evidence of slavery's unique brutality along the border.[67] Even without the slave trade itself, the small size of slaveholdings, and the frequent long-term hires of prime age slaves served the effect of damaging family and commu-nity life. Moreover, the proximity to freedom across the Ohio River or over Missouri's borders only exacerbated the cruelty of the border slave's fate.

Yet like their compatriots in the Deep South, border state African Ameri-cans employed a familiar array of tools to resist slavery's total domination. At no point did slaves actually foment—or openly threaten—a large-scale insurrection against the master class and their white non-slaveholding allies who roamed the countryside as patrollers.[68] But as elsewhere in the South, slaves whispered rumors of plots and rumors of rumors—enough to petrify the master class. One large slave "conspiracy" in the western border states occurred not in the Bluegrass but in western Kentucky's Hopkinsville, where a foiled Christmas insurrection in 1856 spurred panic and "excitement" throughout the entire state.[69] The largest plot in the Bluegrass occurred in the summer of 1848 and involved seventy-five slaves who had escaped Fayette and Bourbon counties with the help of a white abolitionist at Danville's Centre College and numerous free blacks. The slaves were all caught in Cynthiana, most likely on their way to the Ohio River; many had pistols and rifles with them. Lexingtonians were especially shocked because most of the participating slaves were "trusted house servants of Lexington's most socially prominent families."[70] Relationships connecting the white elites of Bluegrass society facilitated the creation of networks among their own servants. Meanwhile, slaveholders blamed white emancipationists who had been demanding the gradual elimination of slavery and had agitated the subject in advance of a constitutional convention in the following year.[71] Whatever effect the white Danville abolitionist had, the plot would never have taken hold without well-established social and kinship bonds extending throughout the city.

Few actual runaway plots resembled the mass Fayette attempt of 1848. When group runaways took place, they typically involved entire families. Thus, when eight Bourbon County slaves headed for Maysville on the Ohio River, five men and three women were among them.[72] A Lafayette County, Missouri, family, including a "negro man, woman and a lot of children bound for 'sweet Illinois,'" garnered the attention of the *Randolph Citizen*.[73] Two recent studies of slave runaways in Kentucky and Missouri show that while the slave populations of these states were concentrated in the Bluegrass and Little Dixie, the vast majority of runaways headed out from large cities such as Louisville and St. Louis or the areas along the Ohio and Mississippi rivers.[74] This is not too surprising considering the extensive patrolling system in the central regions of the states. Moreover, masters offered extensive awards to slaves who betrayed runaway plots. A slave informant foiled a forty-person runaway scheme in Bourbon County in November 1848; as with the August 1848 Fayette case, a white abolitionist had offered assistance to the fugitives.[75] Numerous Howard County, Missouri, slaves who were offered twenty-five dollars each if they helped apprehend runaways chased John Anderson, a Saline County slave trying to escape across the Missouri River.[76]

Runaways were a persistent form of slave resistance, made more available because of the geographic location of the Bluegrass and Little Dixie, never more than 150 miles from free soil. Thus, George Henderson, a former slave of the Cleveland family in Woodford County, Kentucky, recalled, "I have seen old covered wagons pulled by oxen travelling on the road going to Indianny and us children was whipped to keep us away from the road for fear they would steal us."[77] Children and other kin regularly faced the reality of sudden sale to the Deep South. But "theft" for the sake of emancipation was entirely different. Henderson was unclear in later life about who might have threatened to steal the Cleveland slave children, as he certainly was unclear as a slave child. But the knowledge that some force outside the plantation—whether a white abolitionist or a free black—just might carry away the Cleveland family slaves to freedom nurtured the aspirations for emancipation among the general slave population along the western border. With Madison, Indiana, and its well-known Anti-Slavery League only eighty miles away and wagon traffic regularly traversing the Bluegrass roads on their way to the Ohio River, "Marse Cleveland" understood the threat to his absolute domination over his slaves.[78] Severe whippings may have discouraged the slaves from gazing on the local highway to freedom, but the prospect that an alternative to bondage lay such a short distance away undoubtedly tarnished the slaves' conception of the master as absolute patriarch.

Historian J. Blaine Hudson estimates that overall twelve hundred Kentucky slaves ran away each year in the 1850s, though only a fraction came from the Bluegrass.[79] Although no reliable estimate exists for Missouri runaways, the *Glasgow Times* estimated in 1859 that Missouri lost $100,000 in slave property every year.[80] The limited scale of runaways from Kentucky to Indiana and Ohio or from Missouri to "sweet Illinois" belies the extensive, informal set of relationships between fellow slaves, free blacks, and white abolitionists upon which slaves could rely for their escape to freedom. Other than outright insurrection, running away was the slave's gravest political act of resistance. It directly usurped the master's authority and severed the vital master-slave relationship that lay at the heart of any slave-based society. To make this "quiet insurrection" possible, slaves had to rely on their "courage, patience, and above all, incisive intelligence" as they "waged a continual war against slavery."[81] Without a subterranean network aware of the routes to freedom and the intimate details of patrol activities, the deeply political act of running away would have been even less common.

Adding to slaveholders' anxiety, small-scale rumors of runaway and rebellion schemes simmered across the Bluegrass and Little Dixie. In Frankfort senior officers at the Kentucky Military Institute ordered the cadets to stand ready and armed in the event of a planned slave rebellion in April 1861.[82] No plot was discovered, but several blacks were arrested with "loaded guns and pistols." Undoubtedly, the nation's state of emergency that month accentu-

ated the anxieties about slave intentions across central Kentucky. A rumored
insurrection plot at Cynthiana, Kentucky, involving blacks and whites along
the Lexington and Covington Railroad was "uncovered" shortly after John
Brown's raid.[83] As usual, no actual plot existed, but the networks of slaves,
free blacks, and white abolitionists meeting in "secret societies," as the local
newspaper stated—most likely just for the purpose of absconding a handful
of slaves to Ohio—did little to calm the nerves of an excited white population in the wake of Harper's Ferry. The appearance of slave conspiracies
during seminal events—such as John Brown's raid, the Christmas season,
or the attack on Fort Sumter—underscores the latent political power vested
in the "apolitical" slave population. Although the insurrectionary fears may
have been imagined, slaveholders ironically imputed to their slaves the political savvy to exploit white moments of panic for their own ends.

In some cases slaves did openly threaten violence when they felt that
their masters usurped the prerogatives that the slaves had attained. In one
case slaves on a Woodford County, Kentucky, farm insinuated that they
would destroy their master's home if he continued to interfere with their
separate religious services. One of the former slaves there recalled: "We
had our churches too. Sometimes the white folks would try to cause trouble
when the negroes were holding their meetings, then at night the men of the
church would place chunks and matches on the white folks gate post. In the
morning the white folks would find them and know that it was a warning
if they didn't quit causing trouble their buildings would be burned."[84] Slave
autonomy was the only sliver of political power the slaves had achieved,
and the nightly church meetings served as the parliament halls of rural
slave power. In the end fear of insurrection was usually overblown; even the
Woodford County case may have been more bark than bite. But the slaves
knew that by harnessing their collective power outside the purview of the
master, especially in the tense late antebellum days, in which rumors of Hai-
tian style uprisings abounded, the slaves dealt a serious psychological blow
to the absolute political dominance of the master class.

Individual acts of violence and theft against the master provoked panic
and outrage across the white community as well. When Susan Barnes, a Callaway County slave, murdered her mistress in late 1860, a mob of forty or
fifty men lynched her.[85] The *Fulton Vox Populi* declared that "some of our
best and most respectable citizens," unembarrassed by the display of mob
law in dispensing "justice" to a slave, had "engaged in the mob. It seems to
have met the approbation of the owners of the negro."[86] In Bourbon County,

Kentucky, a slave thief wrestled and ultimately killed an old white man who had apprehended the slave.[87] The appearance of white authority did little in this case to prevent the thief from fighting back.

But a more serious social—and political—threat to the master class was the development of an underground economy through which slaves, hires, free blacks, and poor whites traded goods at the margins of the master's domain. One of the most lucrative trades was the "hemp tow." Slaves gathered the broken fibers of hemp throughout the Bluegrass and Little Dixie and sold them to paper and rope makers.[88] In other cases hired slaves convinced hirers and owners to allot them some of the wages earned for service. As Henry Clay Bruce remembered, "We usually made some little money every week, which we could spend for whatever suited our fancy."[89] The underground economy "problem" was widespread enough to encourage whites to petition for new laws banning any white person from trading with slaves without the master's permission, as evidenced at Marshall, Missouri, in January 1860. Because free black communities developed in close proximity to slaves, especially in the towns such as Boonville, Danville, and Lebanon and the larger cities such as Columbia and Lexington, it was nearly impossible for masters to prevent the development of social and economic networks across status lines.

Considering the individuating effect of personal domination that the master held over slaves, the fields of resistance were broad.[90] Even acts not calibrated to resist the master's yoke, such as marriage or the construction of black religious groups, had the effect of limiting the master's total dominance. Indeed, as historian Diane Mutti Burke has uncovered, Missouri slaves relied on long-distance, or "abroad," marriages more than did slaves on large Deep South plantations; as many as 57 percent of all Missouri slave marriages joined slaves living on separate farms.[91] These abroad marriages helped to extend kinship networks across a large geographic space, thus facilitating the transfer of news from "farm to farm." As acts of resistance, these seemingly mundane moves to create social relationships outside the master's immediate purview actually served as "the most basic and the most profound of political acts in which they engaged."[92] In addition to the bonds of marriage, the act of performing weddings enhanced the autonomy of the slave community as slave ministers regularly performed wedding ceremonies both under and outside the purview of the master. Sandy Bruce, brother of Henry Clay Bruce, performed numerous marriage ceremonies for slaves and continued to do so after emancipation.[93]

Indeed, the most powerful institutions of slave autonomy in Kentucky and Missouri were the churches—both formal structures and informal "hush arbor" meetings. Black churches thrived in both urban and rural settings along the border. Many of these churches, filled with free and enslaved African Americans, began as adjuncts to the white church and then split off. The First Colored Baptist Church of Danville, Kentucky, broke away from the white First Baptist Church in 1846.[94] In rural Jessamine County, Kentucky, three separate black congregations—the African Methodist Episcopal Church, Colored Christian Church, and Colored Baptist Church, all in Nicholasville—were founded in the mid-1840s. All three churches primarily served the free black population of Jessamine County, but each catered to slaves in Nicholasville as well.[95] One of the largest church buildings in antebellum Kentucky was the First African Church of Lexington. With the aid of small donations, the congregation built a two thousand–person capacity meeting house that cost eight thousand dollars in total.[96] By drawing small contributions from the slave and free community of Lexington, the First African Church, whose roots dated back to 1786, established a bulwark of political power in a hostile environment.[97] Unlike the myriad hush arbor meetings on rural farms, these large, permanent structures established within the public space the black community's demand for humanity, respect, and autonomy.

Border state slave families persevered despite isolated settings and smallholdings that limited contacts with fellow African Americans. If the greatest bane of upper South slavery was its isolation and circumscription of black social and family life, mobility—whether sanctioned through weekend familial visit passes or not sanctioned through running away—was the only tonic. In fact, most runaways in the border states aimed to find family, not free soil.[98] Harriet Mason escaped bondage in Lexington as a little girl and headed for rural Bryantsville in Garrard County to find her mother.[99] When Betsy, a 40-year-old Lexington slave, ran away, her owner guessed that she would be hiding out in a farm on Richmond Road where her husband lived.[100] Mobility was more often a curse than a blessing, however, as slave hiring tended to separate families for a year at a time, with visitation rights determined by the lessee and the owner.[101] Thus, when Alex Jeffrey of Lexington, Kentucky, hired Mrs. Nancy Warfield's "girl" Lavinia for a year, he stipulated numerous obligations in support of Lavinia's material comfort.[102] But nowhere did Jeffrey promise Lavinia time to visit her family. Her material comfort bolstered her economic value to hirer and owner alike, but her emotional welfare was of little concern to the hirer.

Proximity to freedom, then, was a two-edged sword. On the one hand, it underscored the cruelty of the slave's present circumstances. That freedom was so near almost certainly made slavery even harder to bear. Stories of the free North trickled into Kentucky and Missouri, making freedom a tantalizing—though unlikely—possibility for border slaves. Even a quick glance upon the teamsters headed for "Indianny" could result in a severe whipping. But the chance to steal away to free soil was in fact greater in the border than anywhere else, and an active Underground Railroad, staffed almost entirely by free blacks, ensured that slaves who decided to make the trek had a fighting chance of success. And because of the relatively high level of black mobility in the border states, along the carriageways, railroads, and rivers where hired slaves and free blacks routinely traveled between employers, the ability of the white population to prevent runaways was always in question. Slaveholders were acutely aware of the risk of losing their slaves to free soil. In response, owners upped the reward payments if their slaves were caught outside the county, especially if it was in the free North. Mrs. Thomas Reed of Danville, Kentucky, offered $25 for the return of her male slave Isaiah if he was found within Boyle County, $40 if he was found in another county, and $100 if he was found outside the state.[103] The notice did not specify the state to which Isaiah was likely to run, but clearly Indiana and Ohio were real possibilities. Other slave notices specifically referenced the Ohio River. One broadside appearing in Lexington, Kentucky, in late 1859 described the runaway slave named Tom and offered $20 if he was caught in Fayette, $50 if he was caught elsewhere in the Bluegrass, $100 if he was caught in a county bordering the Ohio River, and $150 if he was captured outside the state.[104] Laws within Missouri increased the pay of slave catchers, and local ordinances in both cases intensified patrol responsibilities.[105] Running away to freedom was rare in the antebellum era, but it was not unheard of. Slaves undoubtedly knew of the various schemes and organizations that could facilitate such a brave gambit and would eventually exploit them when the surrounding white population was distracted by civil war.

What differentiates the border state story from that occurring in the Deep South, then, was the structure of the African American community, which encouraged networks of resistance across the free-slave divide and across vast stretches of territory and which carried powerful—though different—political possibilities. As Steven Hahn points out, the black politics of emancipation and Reconstruction emerged directly out of existing networks of slave politics.[106] This was true in the border as well as in the lower

South. And the networks relied upon the movement of hired slaves, free blacks, and non–hired slaves living on small farms scattered throughout the central Missouri and Kentucky countryside. Various black community actions in defense of social autonomy, familial solidarity, and economic self-determination formed the backdrop of later political agitation. Although no specific evidence of Kentucky or Missouri slaves actually commenting on the vicissitudes of electoral politics or even the coming sectional conflict is available, it is likely that the mobile black population carried political news and rumors across the border countryside. Indeed, the transfer of news and information, whether rumored or confirmed, from one community to another in the antebellum era helped establish a larger black polity that transformed into an explicit and open emancipation force at the first sign of civil war. With the outbreak of war, the African American population in Missouri and Kentucky knew exactly what to do, whom to trust, whom to avoid, and perhaps most important, what the stakes entailed.

CHAPTER 4

HOLDING KENTUCKY AND MISSOURI FOR THE UNION

As Abraham Lincoln assumed the presidency over a fractured republic in March 1861, Kentucky and Missouri conservative Unionists remained confident that Lincoln's triumphant Republican Party posed no threat to their way of life. The *Nicholasville Democrat* in Jessamine County, Kentucky, declared: "We do boldly assert that the Union party in Kentucky is as sound on the slavery question as the States Rights party can be. We believe that four-fifths of the slaves of the State are owned by Union men. Would it not be strange that the owners of this species of property should decide to deprive themselves of it to their own loss? There is no sort of affiliation whatever between Lincolnites and Unionists." To emphasize the distance between Lincolnian Republicanism and conservative Unionism, the editorial remarked, "The Union men love the Union for the sake of the Union and not for the man who may chance to be President at the time."[1] Conservative Unionists never adored President Lincoln, but they doubted secessionist claims that support for Union was really support for an abolitionist regime. They remained loyal to the federal government because they "love the Union for the sake of the Union" and nothing else. The Union they knew and loved was one in which the Constitution, southern representatives in Washington, and the great mass of antiabolitionist northerners had protected the citadel of slavery for seventy years.

Conservative Unionists confronted the reality of war in 1861 in different ways. Some, such as Chariton County, Missouri's General Sterling Price, declared his allegiance to the Confederacy and led the state's Confederate forces under the auspices of the Missouri State Guard. But this was only after militant General Nathaniel Lyon allegedly threatened Price and Governor Claiborne Fox Jackson that he would "see . . . every man, woman, and child in the State, dead and buried," if they refused to submit to federal authority.[2] Others remained steadfast and loyal, preferring to fight for the Union because they "love the Union," and no armed rebellion of fellow southerners would sway them. Richard Hanson of Bourbon County, Kentucky, joined other local Unionists in November 1861 in insisting, "We are devoted to the Government under which we have lived, so happily and prosperously and we deem it the duty of every good and loyal citizen to resist by all the means within his power every effort to destroy it."[3]

The majority of white Kentuckians and Missourians, however, initially chose a third course: neutrality. The Kentucky legislature ratified the state's neutral spirit by declaring itself a nonparticipant on May 20, 1861.[4] Many Missourians hoped that their state would follow the same course. James Rollins, a prominent Boone Countian, implored at the same time: "I hope peace may be restored, but if our land is to be desolated, disgraced and ruined, with civil war, let its theatre be upon the Atlantic coast and upon the Potomac, and not upon the rivers and prairies of the west. Let us especially, by remaining where we are, and by a position of strict neutrality say to all that *our soil* shall not be desecrated by shedding upon it, of one drop of fraternal blood; and in order to prevent it, let Missouri be placed at once, in a complete state of preparation for any emergency."[5] Unfortunately, the course of events within and outside the border states rendered neutrality increasingly untenable, as both states entered the vortex of a chaotic guerrilla war by the end of 1861.

The central question for Kentuckians and Missourians in the summer and fall of 1861, then, was a matter of loyalty. Whose side did one support? But an even greater question superseded the sectional one: what did loyalty mean, and what did it require? Loyalty depended on how one defined the existing Union. Conservative Unionists agreed that the Union was worth protecting only insofar as it could protect the slave-based social order. And all border state Unionists paid homage to the value of the Union of the past, as a provider of strength, prosperity, and liberty. But the long-standing differences regarding the voluntary nature of the federal Union and the long held reverence for coequal federal-state sovereignty reached a breaking point in April 1861, when President Lincoln ordered the forcible suppression of the Confederate rebellion. For many conservatives a "coerced" Union was unacceptable under any circumstance; it was despotism, tyranny, empire, even slavery, for white men. For others it was the only honorable course in light of an illegal, rash, and revolutionary rebellion led by demagogues and schemers. The mass of white conservative Unionists favored the status quo, but that was no longer an option. The war against the Confederacy irreparably changed the nature of Union, even before the social revolution of emancipation.[6]

The moment of decision arose at different times for different people, and the motivations and justifications for loyalty—to the Union or the South— were as varied as the people who held them. But once the war took hold, it was increasingly difficult to switch sides, unless under duress. The cause, whether for the Union or the South, transformed into a struggle to defend comrades, kin, and community. Hundreds of thousands of white Missouri and Kentucky men and women moved from neutrality to Unionism or secessionism and support for the Confederacy at some point in 1861. And they did so in myriad ways: by enlisting in the official army; joining a local militia; taking to a guerrilla band in the bush; sewing uniforms and flags for soldiers; harboring insurgents and counterinsurgents; holding mass meetings, flag raisings, and marches; or feeding—or poisoning—occupying soldiers. But rarely did the conservative mass of whites in central Missouri and Kentucky voluntarily abandon whatever course they chose, even if they despised the increasingly radical direction of their cause.

The Secession Crisis and Reaction to War

The *Paris Western Citizen* informed its readers on April 12, 1861, "The telegraph has been furnishing for several days warlike and startling dispatches, which are well calculated to inflame the public mind."[7] The editor of the *Western Citizen* noted that many of these dispatches from far-off Charleston Harbor, Washington, and the Brooklyn Navy Yard were "sensational" but that something serious was undoubtedly afoot. "A few days will be sufficient . . . to remove all suspense in relation to these rumors of war."[8] With the advent of the telegraph and the instantaneous dissemination of news to small towns such as Paris, Kentucky, public reaction to faraway events exploded in real time. Without the major time lags of the past the mass public could, theoretically, wait for corrections to rumors. Yet the expectation of immediate news rendered the public even less patient to hear out all the details of war. At some point between April 12 and 13, 1861, the rural, widely scattered population of central Kentucky and Missouri heard of the events unfolding in South Carolina. Whatever the truthfulness of individual stories circulating through the countryside in this tense hour, Kentuckians and Missourians responded to the various "rumors of war" with shock and "excitement." Indeed, for decades conservative Unionists had successfully stewarded the nation through sectional crises, and many held out hope that the secession crisis of 1860–61 would also end peacefully. Although some in the border states clearly welcomed the imminent civil war, most viewed the prospect with terror. The reality of war and the death of peaceful compromise was a shock, unlike any the border state political landscape had ever experienced. Speaking for most conservative Unionists, the *Louisville Journal* remarked just days after Fort Sumter, "The tenor of despatches, we are sorry to say, hardly justifies the hopeful opinion of the future we have expressed elsewhere in our paper."[9]

Up to that point most Kentuckians and Missourians had already cast their lot with the Union in the months following Lincoln's election. In Missouri the pro-secession governor Claiborne Fox Jackson successfully convinced the state legislature to call a sovereignty convention in February 1861 to determine the "future relationship with the Federal government." Despite the hopes that voters in Little Dixie would help nominate a convention filled with delegates in support of immediate secession, Unionism won out almost universally. Of 140,000 votes cast in the convention 111,000 of those, or 80 percent, went to pro-Union candidates. Even in the more pro-secessionist Lafayette and Saline counties, the delegates to the state convention were staunch Unionists at the time—Vincent Marmaduke from Saline and Samuel L. Sawyer from Lafayette.[10] Although Kentucky's governor Beriah Magoffin pleaded for a sovereignty convention there, the state's legislature refused to hold one. It did send delegates to a border state convention in Frankfort in May, hoping to unite with the border slaveholding states on a future course. Sensing certain defeat and the futility of continued compromise, the secessionists withdrew their support for the border state convention, resulting in a near unanimous pro-Union presence.[11] Like in Missouri, Kentucky's delegates affirmed the state's commitment to the Union.

Events in April 1861, however, drastically altered public sentiment in the border states, as elsewhere in the South. If the Confederate attack at Fort Sumter shocked the sensibilities of Kentuckians and Missourians and forced the people to reassess the sectional crisis, President Lincoln's subsequent plan to raise 75,000 troops to put down the rebellion shook the border states like an earthquake. Within days—even hours—the conservative Unionist cause literally evaporated in much of Arkansas, North Carolina, Tennessee,

and Virginia. In those cases an existing plantation-belt secessionist movement captured new supporters from the smaller slaveholding sections to
overpower the remaining Unionists within their respective states.[12] Although Kentucky and Missouri never possessed the sort of politically powerful plantation district like Tidewater Virginia or southwest Tennessee,
outrage at Lincoln's troop call-up was still quite strong in the Bluegrass and
Little Dixie. Indeed, with very few exceptions central Kentuckians and Missourians viewed Lincoln's troop call-up as an outrageous violation of the
federal compact. The governors of Kentucky and Missouri reacted immediately. Governor Magoffin, a longtime sympathizer with the secessionist
cause, declared, "I say, emphatically, Kentucky will furnish no troops for the
wicked purpose of subduing her sister Southern States."[13] Governor Jackson,
a considerably more vehement advocate of secession than Magoffin, went
even farther: "Sir:—Your requisition is illegal, unconstitutional and revolutionary; in its object inhuman and diabolical. Not one man will Missouri
furnish to carry on any such unholy crusade against her Southern sisters."[14]

Editorials and mass meetings held in the two weeks following Lincoln's
"infamous" troop call-up echoed the governors' outrage, with many calling
for action. For many whites in Little Dixie and the Bluegrass, Lincoln's actions meant immediate secession was necessary. In one mass meeting assembled at Fayette in Howard County, Missouri, on April 29, the congregants echoed Governor Jackson's refusal to "furnish the Black Republican
Administration *one man* to slaughter our friends and kindred of the Southern States and to destroy their property and institutions."[15] Unlike the meeting held in the same place four months earlier, the citizens present on April
29 declared that the time for Union had passed: "The citizens of Howard will
never consent to take a position of armed neutrality between the Administration of Lincoln and the Confederate States, but like freemen will take
part in the perils of the conflict and share alike with them the misfortune of
defeat or the fruits of victory." Not surprisingly, Congreve Jackson, the man
who stalked the Union meeting in December 1860 with a southern cockade,
was now a committee member representing Chariton Township at this April
pro-secession gathering. More telling were the eight other men named as
officers and committee members at the April meeting who had previously
declared that Lincoln's election was "no cause for disunion."[16]

Although they had never explicitly declared their Unionism to be "conditional" upon a no-coercion policy, the pro-secession congregants clearly felt
that the threshold of Unionism had been breached as a result of Lincoln's

war policy. As former conservative Unionists who once praised the patriotism of millions of "patriotic freemen" in the North willing to stand up to
abolitionist fanaticism[17]—an obvious reference to the Douglas voters and
conservative Republicans—they now declared themselves ready to do battle
with their former Union allies.

The meeting at Fayette typified the palpable sense of outrage that over-
took conservative Unionists across central Kentucky and Missouri at Lincoln's troop call-up. Yet Lincoln's actions alone did not necessarily tip the
balance in much of central Missouri and central Kentucky toward secession.
Subsequent events in St. Louis quickly shortened the "telegraph distance"
of faraway war and brought armed conflict to the border states. Immediately
following Lincoln's troop declaration, Governor Jackson plotted with state
militia commander Daniel Frost in St. Louis to seize the Federal arsenal
there and to procure arms for the Confederacy. St. Louis's ardently Free-Soil
congressman Frank Blair and his militantly abolitionist ally General Nathaniel Lyon spirited away all of the arms from St. Louis to Illinois before state
forces could seize them (as they had already done at the much smaller post in
Liberty in western Missouri). Unbowed by Lyon's demands, Frost established
a militia camp just west of the city, known as Camp Jackson in honor of the
governor. Frost planned to funnel arms received on the St. Louis levee to the
camp to await further orders. Meanwhile, Lyon and approximately ten thousand mostly German Unionists marched into Camp Jackson on May 10 and
promptly arrested Frost and the seven hundred militia members stationed
there. As Lyon marched the prisoners through the city, secessionist mobs
pelted the soldiers with rocks and shouted insults. One protester fired a shot,
killing one of Lyon's soldiers. The troops responded by firing into the crowd,
killing twenty-eight people. St. Louis erupted in riot, with mobs stamped-
ing all pro-Union newspaper offices and the homes of prominent Unionists.

In the tense days leading up to the Camp Jackson confrontation, the Missouri legislature stalled on a bill granting total authority over the state's militia to Governor Jackson. Unionists in the legislature rightly worried that
he would use his authority to turn the state militia into a Confederate military force. But when Jackson shared the news from St. Louis with the legislature, the militia bill passed, and the governor took command of the newly
created Missouri State Guard (MSG). Significantly, many former Unionists,
shocked by Federal actions at St. Louis, offered their services to Jackson,
including, most prominently, Chariton County's Sterling Price.[18] Southern
sympathizers joined the Missouri State Guard in droves across Little Dixie.

Although a more conservative commander named William Harney took control of Union troops in St. Louis, somewhat calming passions across the state, the war had already begun. A truce of sorts between newly appointed MSG head Sterling Price and William Harney temporarily stalled all-out war in Missouri; Governor Jackson pledged official neutrality within Jefferson City in return for Federal commitments not to interfere with state affairs. The truce collapsed, however, due to rumors of maltreatment of Unionists by Missouri Guardsmen and the reemergence of Nathaniel Lyon in command of Union troops. The truce finally broke on June 11 as Lyon cut off all negotiations with the Missouri State Guard and supposedly vowed to "kill every man, woman and child," if necessary, to reestablish Federal rule in the state. Lyon immediately followed up his edict by sailing for Jefferson City and occupying the city, chasing the Jackson administration to the far southwest and eventually into exile. If the shock of Lincoln's troop declaration on April 15 did not drive these former Unionists into the secessionist camp, the actual employment of Federal power on Missouri soil nudged them to the Confederacy. After Camp Jackson and Lyon's declaration of war against Price and Jackson, the war began in Missouri in earnest. Governor Jackson called up fifty thousand troops for the Missouri State Guard to defend the state from the hostile Federal invader. With Lyon's subsequent occupation of Jefferson City and Jackson's flight from the state, the war enveloped all of central Missouri by the summer of 1861.

In Kentucky the careful actions of President Lincoln and the Kentucky legislature ensured that the Bluegrass State would not repeat the calamity of Missouri. Although central Kentuckians expressed similar outrage to President Lincoln's troop call-up, they evinced fewer calls for immediate secession.[19] Unionists in the state and a pliant though pro-Confederate governor ensured neutrality as official state policy on May 20, thus keeping the war off Kentucky soil for several months. Thousands of Kentuckians left the state to join the Union or Confederate armies, but the vast majority embraced neutrality and remained aloof from the conflict until the fall.

In theory, then, white Missourians and Kentuckians had three options at their disposal once the war commenced: support the Union (and the state government, especially after September 1861), fight for the Confederacy and against the Unionist state government, or declare neutrality. But the reality was far muddier, with a spectrum of possibilities inviting white men and women across the border states. Out of these choices emerged a vexing question of loyalty. What were the demands of loyalty? What did loyalty—

to the South or the Union—entail? Through what cultural means did Kentuckians and Missourians express their loyalty? An examination of these umbrella positions—South or Union—reveals the complexities of civilian engagement in an increasingly guerrilla-oriented civil war.

Loyalty to the Union

With secessionists plotting "lawless, violent and revolutionary" means to goad Kentucky out of the Union, a Bourbon Countian declared on May 10, 1861, that the people of Kentucky will "never submit to it. They love order, peace and freedom, and these priceless blessings can be secured only by sustaining the Union, the Constitution and the laws."[20] The engulfing civil war swallowed Arkansas, North Carolina, Tennessee, and Virginia into the Confederacy and threatened Kentucky and Missouri as well. To keep "order, peace and freedom" within the Union a border state convention composed entirely of Unionists met at Frankfort in June 1861. With representatives from the Democratic and Opposition/Constitutional Union (ex-Whig) parties from across the Bluegrass and Little Dixie, the assemblage declared the principles of Union in terms of ancestral fidelity. "It is no longer a question of party politics, no longer a question about the right to hold slaves in territories, or to retake them when they escape," the convention's official address insisted. Rather, with war now raging and all but four slave states in rebellion against the United States, "the question now to be settled is whether we shall live in the same Union as formerly, or whether our fathers formed a government upon such principles that any one State may, at her own pleasure, without the consent of the others, and without responsibility to any human power, withdraw her connection with the government and claim to be sovereign as a nation."[21] Like border state Confederates, Unionists employed a language of faith, fidelity, and honor. But unlike Confederates, border state Unionists in their own eyes obeyed the wise counsel of the sage forefathers of the Revolution. The founders had formed a more perfect *Union*, and it was the duty to country and to the blood of the Revolutionary generation that Kentuckians and Missourians must rally. Just days after Lincoln's troop call-up, the very conservative Unionist *Missouri Telegraph*, an influential organ in the heart of Confederate-leaning Callaway County, insisted, "We love the government in which we live—we are not yet prepared to desert it and to say that the Stars and Stripes, under which our fathers fought, are not to be protected and defended."[22] And the conservative vision of a voluntary compact of states did not mean that states could voluntarily withdraw from the Union once they joined. With rebellion now open across the nation and neutrality utterly abandoned by an intemperate, scheming secessionist governor in Missouri and threatened by menacing troops along Kentucky's southern border, Unionists faithfully issued calls for arms.

The shock of Fort Sumter and Lincoln's troop call-up initially placed conservative Unionists on the defensive across central Kentucky and Missouri. All conservatives expressed outrage at Lincoln's veritable declaration of war against the seceded states. The Unionist *Louisville Journal*, speaking for most border state Unionists, protested Lincoln's troop proclamation: "The policy announced in the Proclamation deserves the unqualified condemnation of every American citizen. It is unworthy not merely of a statesman but of a man. It is a policy utterly hair-brained and ruinous."[23] The *Missouri Telegraph* insisted, "We will, under no circumstances, when a war of extermination against any particular institution of our country is inaugurated, give aid or comfort to any invading force."[24] Unlike in the free northern states, Kentucky and Missouri Unionists did not rally to Lincoln's call or join up en masse to put down the "treasonous rebellion." But unlike those who jumped to the Confederate camp, Unionists did not equate Lincoln's rash reversal of his earlier conciliatory policy as indicative of a desire to abrogate the entire conservative basis of Union. Coercion was disastrous, but it did not necessarily mean Lincoln had become an abolitionist or that he would break his promise to protect southern institutions. Disappointed Unionists did accuse Lincoln of treachery; the *Journal* noted: "If Mr. Lincoln contemplated this policy in the inaugural address, he is a guilty dissembler; if he has conceived it under the excitement raised by the seizure of Fort Sumpter, he is a guilty hotspurt. In either case, he is miserably unfit for the exalted position in which the enemies of the country have placed him."[25] But Lincoln's utter failure of leadership, in conservative Unionist eyes, did not necessarily signify the failure of Union itself.

Because of the panic across the border countryside following Lincoln's troop call-up and Virginia's immediate secession from the Union, Unionists placed their hopes in neutrality. Nobody wanted war, Unionists proclaimed, and only armed neutrality could effectively keep both armies at bay. The *Paris Western Citizen* appealed: "Let Kentucky go neither north or south, but stand firmly where she has always stood. Let her enter into no fratricidal war."[26] James Rollins of Columbia, Missouri, begged his fellow statesmen to adopt a course of neutrality so that not "one drop of fraternal blood" would be spilled on "our soil." Neutrality served as a defensive measure for Unionists given the early momentum in favor of secession; Unionists would eventually abandon neutrality in the summer of 1861 once they regained the initiative in Kentucky and encountered open warfare in Missouri.

As Unionists regrouped in the last days of April 1861, their rhetoric reaffirmed their prewar condemnation of the principle of secession. In a May assembly in Columbia, Missouri, Odon Guitar responded indignantly to a provision to recognize the seceded states by declaring secession to be "the most damnable political heresy ever invented by the brain of the vilest demagogue."[27] Others echoed Guitar's Unionist militancy. In some counties Unionist Home Guards formed immediately after Fort Sumter. In Brunswick, Missouri, the largest town in Sterling Price's native Chariton County, the major newspaper carried an advertisement proclaiming: "Attention Home Guards: YOU are notified to meet at the City Hall on Monday night at 7 o'clock, to attend to business of importance. By order of the Captain. J. M. Staples, O.S."[28] Another writer, using the pseudonym "H," boasted that there were "at least Seventy thousand Rifles, in the possession of private citizens in Missouri."[29] A Bourbon Countian insisted that "the mass of the people will meet them in deadly strife at the threshold, before they are installed in their places as pieces of a bloody Moloch. We will never submit to the anarchy and horrors of their rule, and if fall we must, we will fall in defense of the great principles of constitutional liberty and social order."[30] Although the white Missouri and Kentucky population as a whole embraced the Union cause with much less unanimity than before Fort Sumter, the Unionists remaining showed no decline in militancy.

As the propaganda war between Unionists and Confederates intensified, partisans traded barbs challenging the very authenticity of their opponents' position. After listening to Confederate paeans to southern honor and loyalty to southern institutions, Unionists defrayed the charge by doubting the honesty of secessionist leaders and charging them with deceiving citizens into fomenting rebellion. In October 1861, after Kentucky officially adopted the Union cause, General William "Bull" Nelson wrote an open letter to the "People of North Eastern Kentucky now in Arms against their National and State Governments," offering them amnesty in return for loyalty to the Union: "I sincerely believe that many of you have been deceived and led into rebellion, who this moment regret the step they have taken, and would return to their families and homes if they could do so in safety."[31] There was no honor in fighting "against your Government, against your State, your neighbors, and in some instances, your nearest relatives, without any cause, or any object that is worthy of brave and good men." To Unionists such as Nelson, Confederates not only betrayed the United States government but also betrayed the social fabric of Kentucky and Missouri life. Unionists held that border Confederate leaders served the interests of the cotton states and their extremist demagogues and not the people, values, and interests of Kentucky and Missouri. By linking the Confederate cause with unpopular fire-eaters of the Deep South, Unionists cast the Confederate cause as a distinctly foreign and, consequently, inauthentic and illegitimate mode of protest against the federal government.

One important similarity between Unionist and Confederate rhetoric was the appeal to home protection. In some ways the peculiarities of war in Kentucky and Missouri dictated this rhetorical strategy. Because Federal troops from St. Louis had forced the elected, secession-sympathizing government out of Jefferson City, many Missourians could claim, in good conscience, that the federal government had acted as the aggressor. In Kentucky, on the other hand, Confederate general Leonidas Polk's invasion of Columbus on September 2, 1861, dramatically violated the terms of neutrality that had prevailed in the state since May.[32] Unionists in Kentucky chided the Confederate aggressor for threatening ruin upon the inhabitants of the state. In Lancaster, Kentucky, in October 1861 a group of former political opponents once arrayed against one another as "Unionists" and "States' Rightists" jointly proclaimed that "so long as there is a vestige of an invading foe on our soil, we will forget all former political difference of opinions and unite as one man in defence of each other, our families, and our homes." Casting aside any doubt about whom these Garrard Countians considered the "invading foe," they continued, "We regard the invasion of Kentucky by Tennessee and the Confederate States as wanton and wicked, and without pretext or palliation; and we pledge our property, lives and sacred honor that we will wage an exterminating war on the invaders of our soil, and all who may aid them in their wicked and treasonable purposes, until the last invader shall have left our sacred soil."[33] John Harlan then proceeded to enlist Garrard County men into a Unionist regiment. At Paris a rally organized to "raise volunteers for the defense of Kentucky" proclaimed, "Ye true men of Bourbon come to your country's call, and hurl the audacious invaders from the soil of Kentucky." [34] Unlike in Missouri, Kentucky Unionists could legitimately claim defense of state as a pillar of the Unionist cause.[35] With the exception of Pennsylvania in the summer of 1863 and Maryland in the fall of 1862, no other Union state experienced such a significant Confederate invasion. As such, Kentucky Unionist rhetoric betrayed a uniquely defensive quality to it, ironically mirroring the gendered discourse of protection of hearth, home, and womanhood uttered by many non-slaveholding southerners within the Confederate states.[36]

Border state Unionists also employed more traditional rhetoric concerning the inviolability of the Republic and the revolutionary—if not treasonous—implications of secession. For those in the free North such statements were a matter of course and were widely shared across the political spectrum. With the exception of arch Copperheads, nearly all northerners, including conservative Democrats, viewed secession as an act of treason and certainly as an unprovoked, unjustified attempt at a destructive revolution.[37] As a result, many ardent secessionists in the border and Confederate states embraced the doctrine of "revolution"—comparing their own cause to that of George Washington—rather than "secession." To discredit this assumption of the Revolutionary tradition, Unionists blasted secessionists as illegitimate and fanatical revolutionaries, mimicking not the sage patriots of 1776 but the French Reign of Terror. A Bourbon Countian exposed the "Marats, Dantons and Robespierres" within Kentucky, "who have planned their reign of proscription and blood."[38] Some identified the only legitimate course of revolution as laid out in the Declaration of Independence; any revolution not meeting the specific criteria of that document was, by definition, illegitimate. At a mass meeting in Paris, Kentucky, a speaker drove the point home, claiming that "secession is another name for revolution, and that no cause for revolution has existed or now exists, most of which causes are enunciated in the preamble to the Declaration of Independence."[39] The *Paris Western Citizen*, a staunchly Unionist journal, rejected the "right of revolution" as a matter of course: "The people of the State have positively said in the most emphatic manner that they are for the preservation of the Union and opposed to the doctrine of secession in all its forms, whether it be a constitutional right or only the right of revolution. They wish to remain in the Union and intend to do so."[40] Trying to preserve peace in secessionist-heavy Callaway County, the Fulton *Missouri Telegraph* noted Unionists' continual reference to secession as an "uncalled for revolution"; the same author then referred to the ensuing conflict as a "revolution such as has never before been witnessed. In extent of territory comprised, numbers engaged and bitterness of feeling excited the history of civilized nations can furnish no parallel."[41] The revolution may have been unwanted, but it was definitely at hand.

The social background of Unionists revealed less of a dependence upon slavery than those who tended to favor the Confederacy. And not surprisingly, those in Missouri who immigrated from northern states or from Germany—central Missouri welcomed a massive influx of such immigrants in the 1850s—also tended to side overwhelmingly with the Union. But the social basis of loyalty rarely followed any absolute pattern. Although Unionists tended to possess less wealth—and slaves—than their Confederate counterparts, there were certainly many wealthy Unionists, especially in the larger towns. In Fulton, the county seat of pro-secessionist Callaway County, the overwhelming majority of merchants whose loyalty could be ascertained sided with the Union.[42] Upon reaching Lexington, Kentucky, from nearby Georgetown in late October 1862, one Union soldier wrote his wife: "This is the only place we have been in since we came into Kentucky where the folks act as if they were glad to see us. When we came through the city they had flags strung across the street and they cheered us and hurrahed for the Yankees the biggest kind and when we were on picket they fetched in all kinds of provisions for us to eat and of the best kind."[43] The section of Lexington that hosted the Union troops during this tense period was among the most prosperous in the Bluegrass. "The farmers are very wealthy. They own large plantations and lots of niggers. They have the finest buildings that I ever saw, have nice horses and carriages and nigger drivers."[44] The enthusiastic support for these Union troops may have been a reflection of relief at liberation from recent Confederate occupation as much as it did genuine, long-standing Unionist sympathy. Nevertheless, the fact that exuberant Unionists could be found in the heart of the slaveholding Bluegrass testifies to the complex social basis of loyalty.[45]

By the fall of 1861 Kentucky and Missouri Unionists regained the upper hand they had held before Fort Sumter. Both state governments pledged full support to the Federal cause—Kentucky's legislature officially embraced the Unionist position on September 18, and Missouri's provisional government under Governor Hamilton Gamble assumed full control under Unionist auspices in July.[46] Both states enrolled soldiers in either the Union army or Unionist militia. Federal and local authorities cracked down on secessionists, arresting and banishing hundreds, while shuttering pro-Confederate newspapers. Many decades-old newspapers that had come to support the Confederacy simply disappeared without a trace in the summer of 1861, including the *Lexington Statesman* in Kentucky and the *Boonville Observer* in Missouri; a combination of official state policy banning "treasonable" public

statements and unofficial harassment by Union soldiers and militia effectively shut down the pro-southern press for the remainder of the war.[47]

The Union army established posts at urban centers such as Danville, Lebanon, and Lexington in Kentucky and at Boonville, Columbia, and Lexington
in Missouri. With the greater reliance on state militias in Missouri, smaller
posts guarded the countryside around hamlets such as Glasgow, Keytesville,
and Miami. With a greater number of Unionists already in urban areas, Federal troops and militias generally received warm support from a community
demanding protection. As the Missouri war deteriorated into guerrilla conflict by late 1861, Federal troops turned towns such as Boonville, Columbia,
and Fayette into garrisons.

Kentucky Unionists feared an organized Confederate invasion and occasional large-scale raids from Lexingtonian John Hunt Morgan more than
chaotic raids from bands of bushwhackers. Thus, traditional Federal troops,
including many from Indiana and Ohio, protected the larger towns such
as Danville, Lexington, and Paris from an organized foe. Although Home
Guards, drawing from within the Unionist community throughout the Bluegrass, aided the Federal troops, they were less critical in the overall defense
of community than were the Unionist Missouri State Militia (MSM) in Little
Dixie. Even more than mere protection of Unionists, the Federal and MSM
troop presence gave Unionism the imprimatur of legitimacy that its advocates had long sought.

While a sizable Union troop presence helped secure the towns of central
Kentucky and Missouri, the use of loyalty oaths legitimized Federal military
and political authority. In both states governments required public officials
to take loyalty oaths in order to maintain their official positions and to vote
in elections. Because of the viable threat from Confederates, the Missouri
convention that established the provisional government on July 31, 1861,
stipulated that all state officials must take a loyalty oath within sixty days
or vacate their offices.[48] With Jackson and the official state government now
in exile, the convention arrogated to itself the right to establish a new state
government. All new state officials, no matter how minor, were required
to sign a test oath in which they vowed to support the constitutions of the
United States and Missouri, never take up arms against either government,
and never give "aid or comfort" to the government's enemies.[49] As the war
progressed and the Unionists solidified their hold on state government,
many Confederates abandoned the cause and sought amnesty. The Gamble
administration and Union military command under Henry Halleck agreed

that the test oath would provide the most efficient and honorable means for readmitting former Confederates into Union-dominated society; violation of the test oath by former Confederates was punishable by exile, imprisonment, or death. By late 1862 the test oath was applied to all prospective voters in state and federal elections, thus ensuring that Confederate sympathizers would never dictate state government policy as long as the war continued.

For most Kentuckians and Missourians loyalty oaths treaded heavily upon honor-bound conventions of public performance. For a known secessionist sympathizer to take an oath to uphold the federal government and the Unionist state government was deeply humiliating and caused considerable consternation, even among many neutrals. Some government officials, such as Judge William B. Napton of Saline County, Missouri, resigned their commissions rather than take an oath under "bad faith."[50] It was precisely because of the seriousness with which Kentuckians and Missourians took loyalty oaths that the state government administered them. Even if expediency demanded that many pro-Confederates take the oath, most refused out of a deep sense of honor. Yet the administration of loyalty oaths effectively cast Confederate sympathizers as noncitizens, even if a majority of whites in central Missouri and Kentucky supported the South.

Kentucky's state government passed a similar set of loyalty oath proscriptions in late 1861. Even ministers and teachers were required to take the loyalty oath. The provost marshal in Kentucky enforced the strict loyalty oath, which, as in Missouri, disfranchised Confederate sympathizers and marginalized pro-Confederate voices in the public sphere. By 1863 Kentucky effectively disfranchised as many as one-third of the voters statewide—and a much higher level in the Bluegrass—with Union soldiers ensuring that Confederate sympathizers not affect the vote. As in Missouri, Unionists maintained full authority in the state, even if many of those Unionists were committed and consistent conservatives opposed to the increasingly radical course of the Lincoln administration.[51]

With firm control of state and local government in Kentucky and Missouri in 1862, Unionists could respond to the threat of Confederate invasion or large-scale guerrilla insurgency with vigor. When Confederate generals Braxton Bragg and E. Kirby Smith launched a major invasion of Kentucky in the late spring of 1862, Unionists rallied well-organized Home Guards and supported Federal troops to protect towns across the Bluegrass. Confederates earnestly hoped that their invasion would cause the "slumbering majority" of Confederates to rise up and join their southern liberators. Yet

Confederate failure was palpable as new recruits numbered in the hundreds, not the tens of thousands, as Confederates had hoped. Despite the highly symbolic occupation of Frankfort—for a few hours—the evacuation of Louisville, a short-lived occupation of Lexington, and panic in Cincinnati, the Confederate invasion failed to attract large-scale support, even in the heavily enslaved Bluegrass region. A well-established Unionist regime based on the conservative defense of slavery and protection of hearth and home held off Confederate entreaties to rise up and rebel against the Union. After a military stalemate at the Battle of Perryville in October 1862 in Boyle County, Kentucky, Confederates abandoned their Kentucky dream forever. Only periodic raids from John Hunt Morgan—most of which aimed at capturing supplies and disrupting communication and transportation networks—threatened Kentucky from the South after Perryville. The timing of the Confederate invasion could not have been better for Unionists: it came after Unionists had consolidated support in the Bluegrass but before the Federal conversion of Unionism into an abolitionist project soured many Kentuckians on the whole Union cause.

In Missouri the provisional Gamble administration relied upon heavier tactics to ensure loyalty than did the Unionists in Kentucky. This reflected the nature of warfare in Missouri. An intense guerrilla insurgency erupted across central Missouri after the pro-Confederate Missouri State Guard abandoned Lexington in September 1861.[52] With Confederate troops in far southwestern Missouri or outside the state altogether, pro-Confederates in Little Dixie had little opportunity to reach Confederate recruiters. Trapped behind Union lines, pro-Confederates in central Missouri resorted to guerrilla war. Unconventional tactics involving large-scale robbery and intimidation of the civilian populace only encouraged a heavy-handed Unionist response. The Unionists created two separate major militias to deal with the guerrilla threat.[53] The first, the Missouri State Militia, was created in February 1862 and answered to the provisional government, though it received funding from the federal government. These full-time soldiers served as the primary Unionist military force in the state for much of the war, although they only included ten thousand men. As the guerrilla campaign spread in the summer of 1862, the Gamble administration created a second militia in July 1862 that drafted all able-bodied men into service. This second militia, known as the Enrolled Missouri Militia (EMM), incorporated only part-time soldiers but established a much more extensive presence across the state, numbering over fifty thousand men. Whereas the MSM drew its resources from committed Unionists in the early phase of the war, the EMM was composed of men who had once hoped to sit out the conflict and even included many captured Confederates now under the Unionist loyalty oath. Despite the questionable loyalty of some EMM soldiers, the breadth of service across the state—especially in the bushwhacker-infested central and western part of the state—made it a formidable counter-guerrilla force. As table 4.1 illustrates, hundreds of EMM members served regiments across central Missouri as early as the end of 1862.

TABLE 4.1. Enrolled Missouri Militia by County in Late 1862

County	Colonel in Command	Number of Men
Chariton	William Moberly	706
Howard	Thomas Bartholow	759
Cooper	William Pope	598
Boone	J. B. Douglass	587
Lafayette and Saline	Henry Neill	527
Howard	B. Reeves	445

Source: Report of the Adjutant General of the State of Missouri, December 15, 1862 (St. Louis: Adjutant General's Office, 1862), 11–12.

Missouri militiamen brought the war home to each and every household in Little Dixie. White men across central Missouri were required to choose service in the EMM, flee the state and join the Confederacy, or take to the bush as guerrillas. As counterinsurgent strategy grew more desperate with each month, larger numbers of Missourians joined—or harbored—the Confederate bushwhackers. Militiamen assumed greater authority over political and civil life in central Missouri, including monitoring polls, guarding courthouses and bridges, and pursuing secessionist sympathizers across the countryside. Neutrality, already difficult to maintain before 1862, was now an impossibility in Missouri.

As the Civil War reached into homes across the Bluegrass and Little Dixie countryside, Unionist women assumed an increasingly public role in the cause. At a Union meeting in Fayette, Missouri, in February 1861, the resolutions committee spelled out the nature and significance of women's participation in the Union effort.[54] They declared "that the one hundred ladies whose names are here enrolled do still love our Country, our whole Country, and our Country's Constitution; and we feel that it is perfectly consistent with the character of refined, intelligent and patriotic ladies to make a public demonstration of our feelings in this time of peril to our country and our liberties." These "refined" women deemed it appropriate to make a "public" demonstration because of the unique nature of the sectional crisis; by implication refined women would normally not make such a public gesture. The women then dedicated themselves to sew an American flag and established a committee for "purchasing materials for the Flag," with the members' names printed in the newspaper account of the meeting. Especially significant about this occasion was that other women performed the identical service for the opposite cause, only a few miles away. With civil war approaching, women not only assumed public roles in support of a cause but brought to public light the animosity existing between women in the community. Many of these women's husbands, sons, and fathers would fight in area battlefields against one another. And many of these women would harbor and feed troops from opposing armies.

As the war spread, women volunteered to sew uniforms for Union soldiers; Confederate women did the same, but because of official repression of public Confederate sympathy, local newspapers could not trumpet their activities.[55] At first public meetings dominated by men appealed to women to lend their support. In Paris the resolutions committee of a Union meeting implored, "Let no lady absent herself, who can knit a pair of socks, or even speak a good word for the cause."[56] Shortly afterward permanent committees, including the Bourbon County Volunteer Aid's Society and the Ladies' Soldiers Relief Association, met regularly to sew uniforms and obtain supplies for Union soldiers and lend moral support to the Union cause.[57] Many of these committees were led by wives of prominent Unionist politicians and soldiers.[58] As military action encroached upon Bluegrass and Little Dixie soil, Unionist women opened makeshift hospitals and assisted local relief efforts. After the epic battle of Perryville in Boyle County, women in nearby Danville helped turn the entire town into a vast Union hospital.[59] Women also advertised and performed in concerts to benefit the "suffering soldiers." Frances Dallem Peter, for example, a Unionist in Lexington, Kentucky, sang a duet with Lieutenant Burgen at the Odd Fellows Hall in Lexington in late November 1862 to support Union soldiers recovering in Lexington hospitals.[60]

In at least one case women forcibly intervened to protect the symbols of the Union from Confederate desecration. When Confederate troops occupied the Bluegrass in September 1862, they regularly replaced the Stars and Stripes with the Confederate flag, attempting to erase all symbolic attachments of the region to the Union. Physical desecration of the Union flag symbolized Unionist impotence in the face of Confederate occupation. But as Kentucky Unionist army officer Green Clay Goodloe heralded, Ella Bishop, "a bold and patriotic, yet beautiful and modest lady, and scarcely eighteen years of age, one of Kentucky's proudest daughters rushed forth, with wounded spirit, yet undaunted courage, wrested it from the traitors grasp, defied their threats, waved it above their heads, and dared them touch it with their polluted hands."[61] In honor of her defiance of Confederate "pollution," Goodloe renamed the local army post "Camp Ella Bishop." In this case womanhood stood both symbolically for the purity of the Union cause and bravery in the face of Confederate treachery. Although Ella Bishop was a "beautiful and modest lady," she was hardly the private, fragile, and apolitical woman of the Victorian imagination. By publicly recognizing her actions in defense of the Union flag, the army celebrated the new "bold and patriotic" woman standing on the ramparts of Unionism as the last line of defense against Confederate treason. Goodloe's public celebration of Bishop's heroism straddled Victorian gender norms by revering Bishop's "beauty" and "modesty" while testifying to her untraditional female virtues of "defiance," "courage," and "daring." As with supporters of the Confederacy, Unionists identified their cause with the defense of womanhood. And as in the Confederacy, Unionist women were quite willing to play an active and public role in defending their own honor. Thus, for Unionists women such as Ella Bishop performed a double service to the cause by being a "modest lady" worthy of armed protection and "bold and patriotic" enough to contribute to the cause herself.

By late 1861 a combination of local politicians, local civilians, state militias, the Union army, and the careful actions of the federal government had secured Missouri and Kentucky for the Union. In 1862 a large-scale Confederate invasion of Kentucky failed to pull the Bluegrass State out of the Union. In the Missouri theater Confederate troops under General Earl Van Dorn suffered a major defeat in northwestern Arkansas, effectively ending the Confederate military threat against Missouri. Moreover, Kentucky and Missouri Unionists effectively held off the tide of emancipation in 1862, making a true conservative Unionist victory still a possibility by the time General Bragg retreated to Tennessee in October of that year. But internal pressure from Confederate guerrillas in the bush and from slaves pressing for Union military lines, especially in 1863, brought the conservative Unionist order to its knees.

CHAPTER 5

DUAL REBELLION AND THE DEATH OF CONSERVATIVE UNIONISM

Two distinct but mutually dependent rebellions arose against the conservative Unionist state governments in Frankfort and Jefferson City. On one hand were Confederates who distrusted the intentions of President Lincoln and viewed their states' honor and interests as imperiled by a northern-dominated federal government. With the lower South already removed from the Union, the uppermost slave states would surely possess even less leverage in the halls of Washington than they did when eleven other states could come to the defense of slavery. It mattered little how conservative Kentucky and Missouri's Unionists leaders were; the federal government would ultimately force well-intentioned conservative Unionists to give up the slave-based social system at home and without a real fight. On the other hand stood the slaves themselves, poised for rebellion against conservative Unionism for its defense of an unjust social system. To them the Union was only worth defending if it was to be radically remade into one based on universal freedom and racial equality, a proposition that nearly all white Unionists in Kentucky and Missouri found abhorrent. By late 1863 conservative Unionism, a political culture that had come to define the upper South for decades, would lie in ruins.

The timing of these twin rebellions reveals the instability and complexity of political matters in the border states during the early part of the Civil War. While some Kentucky and Missouri Confederates declared their opposition to the Union following Lincoln's election in November 1860, these "original secessionists" would prove to be a distinct minority. Instead, most Kentucky and Missouri Confederates rejected the Union only after Lincoln's April 1861 troop call-up and, in many cases, only when the war actually reached Missouri soil in May and Kentucky in September. That said, few actively switched allegiance to the Confederate cause after mid-1862, despite the disenchantment among border state Unionists with a cause that would eventually be identified with emancipation.

Reluctant Confederates

As Missouri's secession convention and Kentucky's legislature revealed in the spring of 1861, relatively few Kentuckians and Missourians pledged themselves to secession and the Confederacy as a result of Lincoln's election. Yet a significant portion of the population transferred its allegiance to the South as a result of war. Over the course of a five-month period—from Fort Sumter in April 1861 to Grant's invasion of Paducah, Kentucky, in September 1861—tens of thousands of Kentuckians and Missourians determined that they would fight against their state, and national, governments. These "reluctant Confederates," as historian Daniel Crofts terms them, had once supported the Union, only switching allegiances after Lincoln declared war upon the Confederacy by calling up seventy-five thousand troops, including men from Kentucky and Missouri. As former Unionists, they had once hoped that a peaceable solution could be reached after Lincoln's election but pledged their loyalty to the Confederacy once hostilities began. For them Lincoln's proclamation of war signaled the death knell of the conservative and voluntary basis of Unionism. A "coerced" Union was no Union at all to these reluctant rebels, even if the lower South states were a bit brash in seceding following Lincoln's election.

Before the war some of these reluctant Confederates made specific demands and conditions stipulating the bounds of their loyalty to the Union. In a particularly revealing mass meeting held in Lexington, Kentucky, in January 1861, delegates from all major political factions articulated the principles of conditional Unionism. Resolutions adopted at the meeting praised the Union in unambiguous terms: "That unalterably attached to the Federal Union under which for more than three quarters of a century we have progressed in prosperity and power as no other nation upon earth has ever done, we pledge ourselves in our determined conservatism of this Union to exert all our favorable and patriotic efforts to preserve it inviolate as bequeathed to us by our fathers."[1] As a practical matter, the success of a sectional, and "avowedly hostile," party to the presidency was not a "just cause for revolution, or any ground to obstruct the inauguration of the president elected by that party." As a proposed solution to the sectional crisis, the Lexingtonians advanced the Crittenden Compromise "as the very best which can secure peace and permanence to the existing Union." The references to "our fathers," the "prosperity and power" of the United States, and length of the Union's survival for "three quarters of a century" were stock phrases in the Unionist lexicon across the border states. And like other Unionists—and unlike nearly all white Deep Southerners—the Lexingtonians considered Lincoln's election insufficient grounds for secession. Indeed, few Unionist meetings eschewed these vital points in bestowing praise upon the federal Union. But this meeting differed from other Unionist meetings by incorporating a conditional phrase: "Unless this ultimatum or such equivalent as will remove the question of slavery forever from the arena of national politics be accepted by [the northern states], its rejection will be considered as such a settled determination by the North to make war upon the institutions of the South as will lead to a separation of these States." Kentucky would then reserve the right to act in concert with "her interests and her honor," even if that meant secession. To follow up, the meeting warned against "coercion" as "unwise, impolitic and inexpedient." Terming the Crittenden Compromise an "ultimatum" sent an unmistakable signal that the Unionism of those present was truly conditional. Interestingly, rejection of this ultimatum triggered Kentucky's rightful secession more than Federal coercion itself; most conditional Unionists elsewhere in the South placed nonaggression as the fundamental condition upon which their Unionism relied. As for the future course of the attendees present, some ended up supporting the Confederacy once the war began. Robert J. Breckinridge Jr. (whose father's Unionism remained unconditional and absolute throughout the war), Colonel Roger W. Hanson, and James B. Clay (son of Henry Clay) assumed significant military leadership roles in the Confederate cause. But others present, including A. Vanmeter, remained loyal, if very conservative, adherents to the Union cause. The positions advanced at the meeting articulated negotiating signposts for loyalty, but they left considerable room for interpretation by members present and by the community at large.

Most reluctant Confederates in the Bluegrass and Little Dixie gave little public indication that their Unionism was "conditioned" on a set of circumstances, whatever those may have been. The men appearing at the two Fayette, Missouri, meetings showed no inclination toward secession in November 1860, even as they served leadership positions in the pro-Confederate gathering in late April 1861. The Unionism of these now-reluctant Confederates was always conservative, drawing from a wide array of principles, including respect for state sovereignty in social matters (i.e., slavery), intersectional comity, a willingness to compromise, and the voluntary compact of federal union. Lincoln's troop call-up openly violated the last principle, which regarded the Union as a voluntary agreement between states. But this violation of the voluntary nature of Union offended many conservatives more because it suggested that Lincoln was willing to violate *any* conservative principle when he and his Republican allies deemed it suitable. If the Republicans would go to war against the South, what was to stop them from forcibly emancipating the slaves? How could conservatives ever trust the administration when it had just reneged on its supposed unwillingness to "coerce" the South?[2] Lincoln's decision to coerce the South back into the Union did not merely offend the sensibilities of those who sympathized with the South. It meant that the entire relationship between the federal government and the states and the tradition of respect for southern institutions had been nullified. The coercive Union resembled a dictatorship, with Lincoln playing the role of absolute tyrant. Before Fort Sumter reluctant Confederates had rejected prewar secessionist contentions that Lincoln's election alone signified the death of slavery and the rights of the South. Lincoln should be afforded a chance, they insisted. But his "reckless" and "illegal" actions on April 15 demonstrated to reluctant Confederates that Lincoln simply could not be trusted on any matter of importance. With the die cast, the only acceptable means to protect the slave system was to rebel against Lincolnian tyranny.

Given the relative paucity of explicitly conditional statements of Unionism—unlike in North Carolina, Tennessee, and Virginia, where politicians regularly established explicit conditions for loyalty before Fort Sumter[3]—the most plausible explanation for these reluctant Confederates was not that they were acting on well-established conditions but that they were truly shocked by the rapidly unfolding events of April 1861. Their belief in compromise and peaceful reconciliation held out until the bitter end because they never imagined that the abyss of civil war would be broached. Unlike prewar secessionists, who had embraced the inevitability of war from the beginning, the much larger mass of reluctant Confederates employed every possible means to avoid a calamitous war. Although they abhorred the notion of fighting against fellow southerners, they viewed a prolonged struggle against their Illinois, Indiana, and Ohio neighbors with trepidation. They were reluctant morally to fight their social and kin ties over the Mississippi

and Ohio rivers, and they feared the consequences of social destruction at
home. But in the end, as the congregants at Fayette, Missouri, insisted in
May 1861, southern conventions of public honor, cultural attachment to the
South and its institutions, and repugnance toward "Black Republican" aggression trumped long-standing Union ties.

Indeed, it was defense of "hearth and home" from Federal aggression
that animated reluctant Confederates in Missouri and, to a lesser extent,
Kentucky. In typically gendered language one Saline County military unit
declared to the women of the county, "It is for you that we fight."[4] Connecting the Confederate defense of the household with the sovereign territorial
boundaries of the state, Saline County Sergeant Gaines insisted, "It is to
avenge the slaughter of women and children that we take up arms, and our
grasps shall not be relaxed, nor our energy abated until the barbarian emis-
saries of a ruthless tyrant shall be driven beyond our borders." Manly honor
demanded that Missourians and Kentuckians prevent the "barbarian emis-
saries" from attacking the symbolic hearthstone of the state.[5]

The Saline County example demonstrates, however, that women played
an equal role in employing the language of militancy. The occasion of Sergeant Gaines's commentary was the presentation of a large Missouri state
flag to the unit then on its ill-fated journey to Jefferson City to defend the
capital from Union general Lyon in June 1861. Mrs. John Davis, wife of the
editor of the *Marshall Democrat,* designed the flag, which flew over the state
troops in the capital. "Miss Isaacs" presented the flag to the Saline Jackson
Guards—named in honor of secessionist Governor Claiborne Fox Jackson—
and solemnly declared, "We hope that it may be to you in the hour of trial
and of battle an evidence of the interest that will ever be manifested by the
ladies of your county in the glorious cause you have so nobly espoused."
This gendered language helped mobilize Confederate support throughout
the community and across class lines. In a sign of the increasingly public
posture of women in the now open rebellion, Davis and her fellow embroi-
derers stitched their names onto the flag. While these women willingly employed a gendered defense of the county's manhood, they would not serve
as private, anonymous partners in the struggle. Formerly private women of
the household in slaveholding Saline County had now permanently declared
their public stance in a civil war in which their own neighbors and acquain-
tances would be their enemies.

Kentuckians employed a similarly gendered language to describe the
threat of war and Federal invasion. But the peculiarities of neutrality in

the Bluegrass State, in effect until September 1861, altered the posture of Confederate sympathizers. As momentum in the state swung to the Unionists—with Unionists sweeping into the legislature in August statewide elections—secessionists adopted an overall antiwar tone akin to the Copperhead Democrats in the North. Thousands of Kentuckians fled to Tennessee in the spring and summer of 1861 in order to enlist with the Confederacy. But it was Confederate general Leonidas Polk's invasion of Columbus, Kentucky, followed immediately by Ulysses Grant's invasion of Paducah, that broke the state's neutral position and launched it firmly into the Unionist camp. As the state legislature officially declared Kentucky's loyalty to the Union, thousands more prominent men from the Bluegrass fled to the southwestern part of the state in order to form Confederate units. The most prominent Kentucky Confederates, including John C. Breckinridge, Simon Bolivar Buckner, and John Hunt Morgan waited until September 1861 to abandon their support for the Union. The now openly Unionist state government and an assertive Federal military presence staffed by men from Illinois, Indiana, and Ohio harassed pro-Confederates, thereby adding to their ranks. Indeed, the statements of those who joined the Confederacy in September 1861 reflect a deep reluctance, more so than those who pledged their loyalty to the South after Lincoln's troop call-up. Many of these men, though deeply entrenched in the southern military tradition and vested with the prerogatives of southern manliness and honor, had cleaved desperately to neutrality and peace throughout the summer of 1861. Faced with Federal harassment and the collapse of peace within Kentucky, they now embraced the Confederate cause with zeal.

Some joined the Confederate cause in response to Federal activity on the ground as the war spread across the region in 1862 and 1863. Martha McDowell Buford Jones recalls in her diary that her husband, Willis Jones, did not leave for the Confederate army until General Braxton Bragg's invasion of Kentucky in the summer of 1862.[6] Many Missourians took to the bush and fought as Confederate guerrillas only after their families suffered depredations at the hands of the Federals and the Union-backed Missouri State Militia and Enrolled Missouri Militia. But these actions served little military purpose in the overall Confederate war effort. They were even more defensive in nature than those joining Price's or Buckner's forces in 1861, and more often than not, they were disorganized. For all intents and purposes September 1861 would be the last real moment for Confederate recruitment in the war.[7]

Although both Kentucky and Missouri never really seceded and would remain loyal throughout the war, prewar pro-southern proclivities in the Jackson and Magoffin administrations ensured that military backing for the Confederate cause would receive official imprimatur. In both states the government had revived and strengthened militia laws in the summer of 1860 in anticipation of possible civil strife, though not until 1861 did the military organizations mobilize for war. In fact, both legislatures refused to endorse a comprehensive militia law until war was inevitable. After Camp Jackson the Missouri legislature granted authority over the militia to Governor Jackson and dubbed the new outfit the Missouri State Guard (MSG). Chariton Countian Sterling Price commanded the MSG, which officially defended the state against Federal transgressions. After Union general Nathaniel Lyon's veritable declaration of war against Jackson and his supporters on June 11, Governor Jackson called for fifty thousand men to repel the Federal invaders. Although the MSG would eventually merge with the Confederate Army of the West in March 1862, the MSG was the primary military recruiting tool for Confederate sympathizers in the state.

The Kentucky State Guard (KSG), made up of militia units from individual counties across the state, was created in March 1860. Some of the state's oldest militia organizations, including the 1812-era Lexington Old Infantry, readily accepted commissions in the new unit. Before Lincoln's election most militia organizations that received KSG commissions offered no overt political allegiance.[8] But with the sectional crisis reaching fever pitch after the election, KSG units from counties across the state began to assume more outward political postures. The top leadership of the Kentucky State Guard, including Simon Bolivar Buckner, increasingly revealed pro-South proclivities. While some militias, including the Woodford Blues, readily accepted the pro-Confederate stance, others, such as the Lexington Chasseurs, were torn asunder. Nevertheless, the KSG was the primary enlistment tool for those interesting in serving the southern cause. Part of the attraction of the KSG was its state-centered mission. Opposing all transgressors of state sovereignty, the KSG appealed to those who anticipated a Federal invasion as well as those who embraced the more popular vision of armed neutrality. But across the summer of 1861 secessionist units gradually abandoned Kentucky and enrolled in official Confederate army centers in Tennessee. Divided units simply dissolved or reformulated under united pro-Confederate leadership; Unionists, such as Chasseurs leader Sanders D. Bruce, formed Unionist Home Guard units after abandoning the KSG.

The social background of Confederate soldiers reveals more than the class position of local political leaders. Every county in the Bluegrass and Little Dixie produced large numbers of soldiers for each side in the war. Certain subregions, however, tended to favor one side over the other. In Missouri, for example, rural Callaway and Saline counties and Davis Township in Lafayette County were overwhelmingly pro-Confederate. Woodford, Mercer, and outer Fayette counties in Kentucky tended to favor the Confederacy as well. Some towns, such as Danville, Kentucky, and Columbia, Missouri, tended to support the Union. In mixed regions, such as the city of Lexington, Kentucky, many militia units sent half their members to each warring camp.[9] An analysis of the Lexington Chasseurs reveals some telling patterns regarding Civil War loyalty.

Of the seventy-four members of the antebellum Lexington Chasseurs who fought in the Civil War, forty-two sided with the Union and thirty-two with the Confederacy.[10] Most members of the Chasseurs were young men between the ages of 17 and 23; there was no significant age difference between those who fought for the Union or the Confederacy. There was, however, a sizable difference in real estate wealth. The median real estate wealth for Lexington Chasseurs who fought for the Union was ten thousand dollars; the median real estate wealth for Chasseurs who fought for the Confederacy was eighteen thousand dollars.[11] The sample size is small, so due caution is necessary when extrapolating from this one unit.[12] But considering that the militia unit sent approximately half its members to each side and drew its members almost entirely from inside the city of Lexington, the wealth divide likely reflects a larger class-influenced loyalty pattern. Wealthier Lexingtonians tended to side with the Confederacy, though with some very important exceptions. The head of the Chasseurs, Sanders D. Bruce, occupied one of the finest mansions in Lexington near Gratz Park, alongside his neighbor John Hunt Morgan.

Perhaps more telling than real estate wealth was slave ownership. Unionists and Confederates both embraced the slave system as integral to their sense of loyalty. But the size of slaveholdings differed significantly between Unionist and Confederate members of the Chasseurs. The median holding for Confederate Chasseurs was seven slaves; for Unionist Chasseurs the median slaveholding was a mere two.[13] A sizable number of Unionist Chasseurs owned no slaves, and only three Unionist members of the unit owned more than ten.[14] Among Confederate Chasseurs seven members came from families with more than ten slaves; only one Confederate Chasseur held no slaves in his family.[15]

Loyalty patterns in heavily pro-Confederate Callaway County, Missouri, reflect a similar class divide though one that underscores the somewhat lighter presence of slavery in Missouri vis-à-vis the Bluegrass. The average real estate wealth for a sample of Callaway Countians who fought for the Confederacy was $3,686, with personal wealth at $3,857.[16] For those in Callaway County who fought for the Union army or in pro-Union militias, the average real estate wealth was $1,276; average personal wealth for Callaway Unionists was $1,224. Slave ownership patterns also differed considerably between Callaway Confederates and Unionists. Although roughly half of Callaway Confederates came from non-slaveholding families, the overall average measured 2.96 slaves per soldier's household. Of the Unionists in Callaway County only 2 soldiers owned any slaves at all, with one holding an unusually high 14 slaves and the other with 2. The average for Callaway Unionists was 0.76 slaves per soldier's household. Although non-slaveholders supported both sides in Callaway County, slaveholders overwhelmingly favored the South. Thus, the social basis of Civil War loyalty in one major Kentucky unit and one Missouri county indicates that those with a greater stake in the slave system tended to support the Confederacy. Those who longed to protect slavery but whose wealth relied comparably less upon slave labor tended to privilege loyalty to the Union over the South.[17]

Once white Missourians and Kentuckians pledged their fealty to the South, they confronted a challenge not borne by those in the Confederacy: oppose both their home state and the nation to which their state belonged.[18] Those who joined the southern cause bristled at Unionist suggestions of "disloyalty" or "treason." They insisted that it was Confederates who remained true and loyal to constitutional principles and to the institutions and ties of the South. Martha Jones, wife of Woodford County Confederate Willis Jones, insisted in a letter to her father, "My husband is not a refugee from justice, and not a traitor, a rebel I admit he is from the whole abolition faction."[19] The Unionists, according to Confederates, had betrayed their society, their cousins in the South, and their honor in order to submit to a committed antislavery aggressor. In a desperate appeal for volunteers for the pro-Confederate Missouri State Guard in December 1861, Chariton Countian General Sterling Price decried the Federal government's "most causeless and cruel despotism known among civilized men," as exhibited at Camp Jackson and afterward.[20] The Unionists failed to recognize that a coerced Union meant a violation of the "equality of the states" under the voluntary compact of union and so was no union at all.

An intriguing difference between border state Confederates and those in the Confederacy proper was the refusal of most in the border states to identify with southern independence and the new Confederate government. Although large numbers in the actual Confederacy disputed the policies and directions of the Davis administration, few questioned the whole concept of southern independence. To them the war was a positive one: to create a new nation and defend it in its infancy from the Federal aggressor. But for Kentuckians and Missourians the southern cause assumed a more negative posture. Defiance of the Federal government and Federal action subsumed the larger quest for an independent Confederacy. Federal despotism—"the causeless despotism" that, as Price insisted, resulted in the destruction of property at the hands of the "Hessian and the Jay-Hawker," who have "murdered" more men "at home than I have lost in five successful battles!" demanded resistance for the political salvation of Missouri. Tellingly, however, nowhere in Price's proclamation did he mention the Confederacy or the creation of a new nation in the South. Price's appeal illustrated the perceived treachery of Unionist state governments in Frankfort and Jefferson City and the Federal government, now run by Germans (Hessians) and abolitionists (Jay-Hawkers).[21] Confederates in Jo Shelby's Missouri cavalry or John Hunt Morgan's raiders or John C. Breckinridge's Orphan Brigade dreamed as much about returning home as they did heralding in a new nation. Indeed, as the war dragged on into 1862 and 1863, Confederates continued to define their loyalty in regional terms. Historian Richard Franklin Bensel notes that Confederates arrested and forced to take the oath of loyalty to the Union almost never defined their loyalty as to the Confederacy. Universally, they said they were for "the South."[22] Martha Jones described her husband as "trusting his fortune with the Southern people," with the hope of "bring[ing] the blessing of civil liberty once more to our bleeding country."[23] Nowhere did she cite her husband as fighting for a *new* country. Indeed, the new Confederate nation was an afterthought for many Kentucky and Missouri Confederates.

The cultural and social production of Confederate loyalty in the border states reflected the defensive nature of rebellion against both state and Federal authority. Conventions of honor demanded that southern white men defend their firesides from Federal attack, and their vicarious hearthstones—state government—from Federal usurpation and deceit. Not surprisingly, those Kentuckians and Missourians most steeped in the South's slave-based code of honor disproportionately sided with the Confederacy once hostilities began. With the failure of Braxton Bragg's 1862 invasion of Kentucky and the strengthening hold over state authority by the provisional administration of Governor Hamilton Gamble in Missouri, the border state Confederate cause was effectively lost by the fall of 1862. But as a mode of protest against perceived Federal excess and especially as a testament of the last bastion of social conservatism in an abolitionizing war, the Confederacy endured as a symbol of resistance long after the reality of southern independence had been defeated.

Rebels against Slavery

The *Central City and Brunswicker* of Chariton County, Missouri, declared on September 4, 1862: "The other day one of our shrewdest businessmen near Brunswick wanted to sell a negro carpenter for whose services he has heretofore got three hundred dollars a year. He was only offered two hundred and fifty dollars for a life-time sale! Comment is unnecessary, except to inquire who is the practical abolitionist? Clearly, Jeff. Davis." Unionists across Missouri and Kentucky complained after late 1862 that the actions of secessionists had effectively destroyed slavery. The reference to declining slave prices accurately reflects the status of slavery in the border states in the second and third year of the Civil War. Even before the war began, fear of emancipation drove the price of slaves down as much as 25 percent in central Missouri.[24] But the spread of guerrilla insurgency in the border countryside, accompanied by mass slave escapes, drove slave prices down dramatically by the end of 1863. In one estate sale in Columbia, Missouri, on January 1, 1864, dozens of slaves were sold to the highest bidder, with none yielding more than $312.[25] Most slaves, including prime age male slaves, sold for less than $200. Before the war these slaves would have sold for at least $1,300.[26] What is noteworthy about these observations and complaints is not that the war had somehow destroyed the slave system or even that Unionists termed Confederates "practical abolitionists" for launching the war that dismantled the institution. Most intriguing about such comments is their timing: long before the Union army considered raising black troops in the border states. Not until December 1863 did the Union army begin to recruit African American soldiers in Missouri, with black Kentuckians only joining the military in large numbers in June 1864.[27]

Scholars of the border states generally agree that black enlistment effectively destroyed the slave system in Kentucky and Missouri. As Ira Berlin has argued, "Slavery did not give way in the border states until black men began entering the Union army in large numbers."[28] Undoubtedly, black enlistment accelerated the destruction of slavery, with farm discipline impossible to maintain as army recruiters openly traveled the Little Dixie and Bluegrass countryside. But the comments of contemporaries, including slaves and slaveholders, and the precipitous drop in slave prices in the middle of 1863 suggest that slavery had effectively deteriorated in Missouri and Kentucky as a viable labor and social system several months before black enlistment.

Long before direct black military participation finished off the slave system in Missouri and Kentucky, African Americans employed existing social and kin networks in myriad other ways to spread news and plot escape plans. In doing so, slaves exploited weaknesses that developed in a countryside increasingly beset with guerrilla war. Henry Clay Bruce, a former slave in Chariton County, detailed the network of communication through which slaves living on small, scattered farms passed news of Federal troop activity and the changing politics of war to fellow slaves throughout central Missouri: "The Colored people could meet and talk over what they had heard about the latest battle, and what Mr. Lincoln had said, and the chances of their freedom . . . When the news came that a battle was fought and won by Union troops, they rejoiced, and were correspondingly depressed when they saw their masters rejoicing . . . slaves who could read and could buy newspapers, thereby obtained the latest news and kept their friends posted, and from mouth to ear the news was carried from farm to farm, without the knowledge of masters."[29] Evidently, these communication networks relied upon social and kin relations stretching back through years of slavery. Bruce found the level of trust across the vast slave community of central Missouri to be remarkable: "There were no Judases among them during those exciting times."[30] Racial and status alliance undoubtedly encouraged slaves to share information across a wide swath of land, but the extensive system of abroad marriages and affective relationships, which linked African American social and kin relations from one end of Little Dixie to the other, likely played an even greater role in establishing lines of trust from "farm to farm."[31] Relationships across dispersed slaveholdings, long circumscribed through years of restrictive pass systems and slave patrols, received new sustenance with the war-induced breakdown of the white social order.

Indeed, the guardian of public order holding the slave system intact throughout the antebellum era was the slave patrol system. And the slave patrol became one of the Civil War's first casualties, as longtime patrollers left for competing militias and armies. More often than not, slave patrollers sided with the Confederacy and consequently became public enemies of the Unionist state regime. As Bruce remembers, "After the war commenced . . . it was not safe for patrols to be out hunting Negroes, and the system came to an end, never to be revived."[32] As Unionist militia officers often deemed slave patrollers to be secessionist sympathizers, patrollers felt the wrath of well-armed troops chasing these erstwhile protectors of the public order. With patrollers themselves harassed by militia and Federal troops, slave runaways increased.

For those slaves remaining on the farms, the war effectively undermined slave discipline enough to render slave labor unmanageable. As elsewhere across the South, slaveholders abandoned their farms for the military, leaving the care and discipline of the slave force in increasingly dubious hands. As Bruce notes, "The regular confederate troops raised in [Chariton] and adjoining counties went South so fast as recruited, so that only bushwhackers remained."[33] Although bushwhackers, many of them sons of slaveholders in Little Dixie, tried to enforce slave discipline both on and off the farms, their higher priority was to fight the Union army. Women and younger sons assumed more control over farm affairs. Inexperience and constant raids by guerrillas and militias made an already formidable task nearly impossible. Slaves took notice of the new executors of farm discipline and immediately exploited the transition.

Concomitant with the breakdown in the patrol system was the rapid rise in the number of fugitive slaves. Given the politically sensitive nature of the fugitive issue in the antebellum border states and the suspicion in which border slaveholders held Union troops hailing from such ultra-Free-Soil states as Michigan, Minnesota, and Wisconsin, Federal policy played an integral role in shaping the extent of fugitive slave activity in Missouri and Kentucky. And as elsewhere in the South, Federal policy affected, and was influenced by, slave activity.[34] In the early part of the war Federal policy discouraged slaves from running into Union lines, including those owned by rebel masters. With one major exception early Federal commanders in Kentucky and Missouri yielded to the conservative Unionist demands of state government in Jefferson City and Frankfort. Gamble's provisional administration in Missouri and Kentucky governor Magoffin's—and later James F. Robinson's—insistence that neither the Federal government nor Union soldiers interfere in any way with slavery met general approval by Federal commanders Henry Halleck and John Schofield in Missouri and Don Carlos Buell in Kentucky.[35] Indeed, the sole Federal act governing slaves in the first year of war—the First Confiscation Act—only allowed for interference and confiscation of slave "contraband" in cases in which slaves were directly aiding the rebel military cause. Yet, applying the strict policy of noninterference proved much more difficult, especially in Missouri, as slaves continually escaped their masters and visited military posts or Union military columns across Little Dixie. Low-level Union officers, some of them abolitionists from Iowa, Minnesota, and Wisconsin, offered protection to these runaways despite their masters' profession of loyalty and official Federal policy prohibiting the harboring of fugitives. Federal policy from mid-1861 on responded haphazardly to the conflicting demands and desires of border slaves and slaveholders.

In a high-profile break with existing Union policy, newly appointed Federal commander for the district covering the state of Missouri, John C. Fremont, gave voice to abolitionist officers and declared that all slaves held by disloyal masters would be immediately freed. This August 1861 decree, part of a declaration of martial law and foreshadowing the later Federal Second Confiscation Act passed in July 1862, represented an open affront to conservative Unionism in all of the border states—not just Missouri—and provoked a crisis within Missouri political circles. Missouri's provisional governor and nearly all central Missouri newspapers responded with indignation. Not since President Lincoln's proclamation of war against the Confederacy in April had conservative Unionists been placed in such an awkward position. Fortunately for conservatives, President Lincoln summarily countermanded Fremont's order on September 11, 1861, thus ending an embarrassing episode that threatened to undermine Unionist momentum and even the Unionist cause. Fremont's insistence upon a more radical antislavery posture led to his dismissal in October 1861 and replacement with the more conservative Halleck. To prevent any future discrepancies between lower-level officers and top commanders regarding the fate of fugitives in Federal lines, General Halleck ordered that all future fugitive slaves be summarily expelled from all Federal encampments. Halleck apparently felt that prohibiting slaves from reaching Federal sanctuary would prevent conflicts between Federal officers over fugitive policy, assuage the concerns of conservative Unionists regarding the epidemic of runaways, and dissuade slaves from escaping their masters. Halleck's measure ultimately did little to stanch the flow of fugitive slaves bent on attaining their own freedom.

Evidence of Halleck's failure to hold back the tide of fugitives appeared early in 1862, as Missouri Unionists regularly wrote to commanders and published letters in area newspapers complaining of the massive loss of slave property. On the well-traveled road from Fulton to St. Louis, slave men regularly abandoned their Callaway County farms to join the Federal columns. In March 1862 the *Missouri Telegraph* wrote a letter of complaint to Union general Henry Halleck regarding the "several negro men [who] had joined [the Federal troops] on the march through the county."[36] In April 1862 a Marshall, Saline County, MSM commander wrote to his superior regarding the presence of large numbers of slave men who had absconded from their masters. Because of strict loyalty oaths and the threat of arrest of secessionist sympathizers, many Little Dixie slaveholders refused to recover their own fugitive slaves, thereby putting the planting season in jeopardy. A Missouri provost marshal officer commented: "Their masters will not come and take them away, but object to anyone hiring them. Our county needs all the labor this year she can possibly get."[37] Slaves clearly understood the predicament created for their masters by their fugitive status. In a guerrilla war in which loyalty proved increasingly difficult to ascertain, masters could not confidently appeal to state authorities to return fugitive property. Farmers looking to hire slaves faced a similar conundrum as the available pool of slave labor migrated to MSM or Federal lines. As the Marshall MSM commander complained, "The farmers about here are anxious to procure all the labor they can possibly get but are deterred from hiring their negroes for fear of being Indicted by the Grand Jury."[38]

Because of the different nature of war in Kentucky, fugitive slave activity followed a slightly different course than it did in Missouri. Whereas in Missouri the countryside erupted in guerrilla war as early as 1861, Kentucky slaveholders generally experienced the first summer of war peacefully. A small-scale Confederate invasion of the fringes of the Bluegrass in the fall of 1861 and a massive Confederate invasion of central Kentucky by the armies of generals Braxton Bragg and E. Kirby Smith in the summer of 1862 provided the sort of social disruption that had initially facilitated fugitive slave activity in Missouri. Before Bragg and Smith's great Kentucky invasion of 1862, the slave system in Kentucky remained largely undisturbed.

Because of the prominence of conservatives in the Union cause in Kentucky and Missouri, it is possible that many slaves in the border states may have imagined that both sides in the Civil War were equally opposed to the freedom of the slave. Indeed, public pronouncements of both sides made

abundantly clear the hatred both Unionists and Confederates felt for abolitionists. In December 1862 a friend of Danville, Kentucky's Susan Grigsby
wrote to her regarding the source of slavery's decline: "My honest convic-
tions are the South has set more negros free and depreciated those who
are not yet free in 18 months . . . than the *Abominable* Abolitionist[s] have
done in 18 years or could have done in 18 years to come."[39] Regardless of
these ironic charges against the rash, destructive course of the Confederates,
slaves understood early on that the preponderance of large slaveholders and
their most zealous advocates tended to side with the South, not the Union.
And slaves understood that despite the conservative rhetoric to the contrary, a Union victory over the slaveholder's rebellion was the best chance
for emancipation. Henry Clay Bruce wrote that "slaves believed, deep down
in their souls, that the government was fighting for their freedom, and it
was useless for masters to tell them differently."[40] Bruce recalled many slaves
who fled their masters and sought work "with pay, for some Union man."[41]
Slaves who long overheard the political arguments surrounding the tables of
their masters understood quite clearly who were their greatest enemy. Bruce
remembered slaves "would listen carefully to what they heard their owners
say while talking to each other on political matters, or about the fault of another slave, and as soon as opportunity would admit, go to the quarters and
warn the slave of his danger, and tell what they had heard the master say
about the politics of the country."[42] And with the explosion of conflict within
the master class and between the master class and its erstwhile white allies,
slaves knew exactly which direction to turn. Slaves' knowledge of formal
politics and the vicissitudes of war formed the backdrop to their own emerging political consciousness and to the development of a distinct black polity.

The number of fugitive slaves lagged in Kentucky, compared to Missouri.
Yet early military activity in the far southern portion of the state from September 1861 to March 1862 placed an immediate strain upon slaveholders
and Unionist commanders. Highly sensitive to any Federal interference with
slave property, the Army of the Ohio, in command in the southern part of
Kentucky, replaced all midwestern troops—some of whom held strong Free-
Soil views—with native Kentuckians schooled in the state's social traditions
and practices. Like their Missouri counterparts, Kentucky Union troops ex-
pressly forbade slaves to enter Union lines, posts, or camps and promptly
turned back fugitives to their owners. But with the major invasion of the
Bluegrass in the summer of 1862, Kentucky troops could no longer stem the
Confederate tide. Union troops from the Northwest entered Kentucky and

helped fight back the Confederate invasion, which threatened the states north of the Ohio River. These new recruits from Indiana, Ohio, and elsewhere in the Midwest reinserted antislavery attitudes on Kentucky soil and complicated conservative Unionist policy regarding fugitives. The presence of midwestern troops on Kentucky soil in the summer of 1862 marked the turning point for slavery's demise in the state and in the Bluegrass region in particular.[43]

To assess army attitudes toward slavery, historian Victor Howard analyzed letters and regimental histories from each of the 108 Union regiments operating in Kentucky from August 1861 to March 1863. Despite repeated protestations from Kentucky state civilian officials, Kentucky military officers, and statements from private citizens and newspapers of all political persuasions, these Union regiments continually failed to heed the official conservative policy regarding fugitive slaves. Although they were obligated by official policy to return all fugitives to their masters, 93 percent of these units refused. Only the regiments drawn from Kentucky itself followed the noninterference course throughout. In many instances Union regiments from Kentucky and the Midwest nearly came to blows. One midwestern Union soldier named Markham stationed at Lebanon, Kentucky, in April 1863 bristled at the local Kentucky regiment's insistence upon turning fugitive slaves out of Union lines: "There is a Kentucky regiment stationed here to keep the darkies from going out of the State with other regiments and there being a number in ours and the 22nd [sic] the General commanding here wanted Colonel Doolittle to give them up but he told them he was not doing that kind of business."[44] When the Kentucky regimental leader threatened to arrest the midwestern commander for refusing to turn away fugitives, the commander demurred. Markham approved of the commander's intransigence: "We were not to be frightened in that way." While awaiting further instructions from General Burnside, the soldier dismissed the Kentuckians' concerns regarding the ongoing destruction of slavery. "I guess they will find out before long that we did not come here to catch niggers for them." Considering the sentiments of soldiers such as Markham and the increasingly radical posture of his superiors, it is hardly surprising that slaves found the soldiers in Union camps scattered across the Bluegrass to be trustworthy allies in their struggle for emancipation.

By late 1862 a confluence of events solidified the emancipationist course of the Union army in Kentucky. First, the defeat of Bragg's army at Perryville in October ended the Confederate threat against Kentucky. No longer did Union troops need to worry that every misstep would lead to a massive defection to the Confederate cause. If the populace would not rise up in support of Bragg in the summer of 1862, many Unionists quipped, then they would never support the Confederacy.[45] Emboldened by the victory of Unionism on the battlefield, ardent Free-Soilers among the Union regiments opened up their lines to fugitives in defiance of slaveholders' threats. As midwesterners increasingly associated all Kentucky slaveholders with secession sympathizers, Union regiments aggressively rebuffed conservative protests.

The second factor energizing Free-Soilers among the Union troops was the changing national policy in Washington. The more restrictive standard set out in the First Confiscation Act gave way in 1862 to the Second Confiscation Act in July, the Preliminary Emancipation Proclamation in September, and the full Emancipation Proclamation in January 1863. With radical antislavery sentiment ascendant in Washington—and increasingly among the top general corps of the Union army—local midwestern officers felt themselves on more solid legal ground in harboring fugitives. The Emancipation Proclamation did not apply in Kentucky or Missouri, but it sent an unmistakable signal to Union soldiers and officers that in order for the Union to prevail, slavery had to be everywhere eradicated.

It is difficult to assess the extent to which Kentucky slaves abandoned their masters in 1862 and early 1863, but the desperate rhetoric of Kentucky conservatives suggests a widespread "epidemic" of fugitive slave activity—enough to undermine the institution in the state. Indeed, Ira Berlin's thesis regarding the demise of slavery rests on stronger footing in Kentucky than in Missouri. Despite massive fugitive slave activity in the Bluegrass from the summer of 1862 through 1863, slavery remained intact. Slave prices fell drastically but did not collapse the way they did in Missouri. Martha Jones of Woodford County was still able to get five hundred dollars for a young female adult slave in August 1863.[46] Before the war Jones would have received considerably more than that, but there was probably no other state in which a slaveholder could receive as much for a slave in August 1863.[47] With the state still under civilian rule and the slave patrol system intact, capture and return were real possibilities for potential fugitives in the Bluegrass. And with conservatives maintaining control over state government, Bluegrass slaveholders had little reason to panic in the spirit of their Missouri cousins, who were increasingly squeezed by radicals on one side and Confederate guerrillas on the other. Nevertheless, despite the persistence of a unified political conservatism in Kentucky in 1863 and the exemption of the state from the Emancipation Proclamation, the slave system buckled under the combined pressure of rebellious slaves determined to reach Union lines and the free soil of Indiana and Ohio and the antislavery midwestern troops intent on destroying the social system they intimately connected with the Confederacy itself.

1863: Guerrillas and the Death of Conservative Unionism

By the end of 1863 conservative enthusiasm for the Union cause in the border states had faltered as emancipation emerged as a major war-making policy. Benjamin Jones, a Kentucky soldier serving the Union army in Chattanooga, reflected the larger conservative disappointment in Lincoln's course in a letter to his brother: "I saw a guard of negroes, that is something that you never saw . . . That is [something] that I don't want to see anymore if I can help myself but I understand that the negroes will be freed before this war is ended and then old abe Lincoln will be satisfied. I wish that he had to sleep with a negro every night as long as he lives and kiss one's ass."[48] The presence of liberated slaves serving in the Union army in late 1863 underscored the changing nature of the Civil War. The enemy of conservative Union soldiers such as Jones was no longer simply the gray uniformed men in General Braxton Bragg's Confederate army then laying siege to Union-held Chattanooga. Instead, conservative Unionism faced two full-on rebellions: one from secessionists bent on an increasingly destructive guerrilla insurgency across the border states; and the other from slaves, abolitionists, opportunistic Union military commanders, and an increasingly radical administration. It would survive neither.

For the first year of the Civil War the defense of slavery survived as the driving force behind border state Unionism. Official Union policy protecting slavery and the need of Unionists to defend their homes against guerrillas and Confederate invaders helped buttress these conservative war aims. But the exigencies of an extended war weakened the policing apparatus that kept slavery intact, and the increasingly desperate character of guerrilla insurgency destroyed the existing social order in the countryside. By the end of 1863 the conservative foundation of Union in Kentucky and Missouri no longer existed. Although no major military offensive seriously threatened the Union status of Kentucky and Missouri after 1862, partisan insurgency continually destabilized political and social life. In 1863 uncertainty, racial revolution, general emancipation, and total guerrilla warfare snapped the last thread of conservative Unionism in the border states.

Guerrilla war infected every facet of life in central Missouri, and to a lesser extent in Kentucky, in 1863. The first targets of guerrillas were public thoroughfares, including the public roads, railroads, bridges, and boats passing along the rivers. After bushwhackers attacked a steamboat on the Missouri River at Rocheport, the *Howard County Advertiser* begged, "Such men as these are bringing unnecessary trouble upon the State, and it is to be hoped that they will be caught and punished."[49] As early as August 1861, Confederate guerrillas under the command of "Captain" Cason fired on military boats traveling down the Missouri, luring the Federals into a vicious firefight that left sixty-two Union soldiers dead.[50] Guerrillas early on discovered how their knowledge of terrain could devastate a better-armed foe.

In Kentucky during the early portion of the war most irregular military activity centered on the units under John Hunt Morgan's command. A scion of the Bluegrass himself, Morgan led numerous high-profile raids into central Kentucky and even into Ohio and Indiana. Unlike the Missouri bushwhackers, Morgan operated under official Confederate auspices, thus maintaining the pretense of following modern codes of war.[51] It was precisely this affectation of gentlemanly soldiery that drew the ire of Kentucky Unionists during his many raids. Missouri Unionists wasted little time referring to area guerrillas as "outlaws" and "bandits," but Kentucky Unionists initially assumed that Morgan would follow the conventional tactics of large infantry units like Braxton Bragg and E. Kirby Smith. In July 1862, in the midst of the Confederate invasion of the Bluegrass, the *Paris Western Citizen* asked, rhetorically: "Did Morgan keep his word to protect private property? Pshaw, not he! Four thousand dollars would not pay the amount of his stealing, in horses, buggies, etc. Not a Union man within his reach escaped him."[52] The *Western Citizen* then detailed some high-profile thefts: "He took from C. O. Smither, who has a livery stable, six horses, two buggies, and three sets of harness, and that, too, after stabling and feeding a large number of horses, free of charge, and to rob him of his property was a deed of the deepest perfidy and rascally swindling; a fine horse from Hon. J. K. Goodloe, six horses from Captain Wm. Garrett and from numerous other persons; from Zeb Ward six horses, besides occupying his spacious and luxurious grass lots, and mutilating his elegant garden by destroying vegetables, shrubbery, and flowers, which adorned and beautified his premises."[53] Only a common horse thief would behave in such a fashion, the Unionist newspaper believed. With such tactics Morgan had become a mere brigand, thus demeaning the political significance of his "cause."

Unionists and neutrals repeatedly referred to guerrillas as "outlaws," not simply because they regularly violated the law but because, in the Unionist estimation, the Confederate cause, by relying so heavily upon irregular warfare, had itself become criminal. Guerrillas regularly robbed banks and other major public institutions in order to survive in the bush, thus reinforcing the image of lawlessness. In late October 1862 C. Bodley of Lexington, Kentucky, referenced John Hunt Morgan's "thieves" who stole horses from the city and "paid" in Confederate scrip.[54] By coupling Morgan's theft of valuable war-related property with the use of illegitimate currency, Bodley delegitimized the Confederate cause itself. Not only had Confederate currency become illegal in Lexington by late October 1862—after a brief Confederate occupation of the city—it represented an illegal and fraudulent cause. Even under Confederate occupation Lexingtonians refused to use the southern currency, prompting the ire of General Bragg.[55] And once rebel troops vacated Kentucky, there was neither a moral nor practical reason to continue trading in Confederate money.

Unionist counterinsurgent strategy vacillated between attempting to coax rebels into Union service and collective punishment of Confederate sympathizers. General John Schofield, responsible for all of Missouri in the summer of 1862, issued General Order No. 3, which stipulated severe punishments for any Confederate activity, including utterance of "treasonable language." It also assessed southern sympathizers five thousand dollars for every Union soldier or citizen killed, with a slightly lesser assessment for Unionists wounded.[56] Finally, the general order declared, "The full value of all property destroyed or stolen, by guerrillas, will be assessed and collected from the rebels and rebel sympathizers residing in the vicinity of the place where the act is committed."[57] As Michael Fellman, noted historian of Missouri's guerrilla war, points out, the differing counterinsurgent strategies reflected a fundamental division "not about their shared goal of preservation of the Union, but about the means by which it might be accomplished."[58]

Inevitably, Missouri's guerrilla conflict devolved into a struggle for vengeance, wherein victims of bushwhacker violence vowed to eradicate the guerrilla threat, while those subject to punitive Unionist militias responded by taking to the bush.[59] One MSM soldier stationed in Fayette pleaded to General Odon Guitar for revenge against the guerrillas who had killed his brother. After his brother was "shot all to pieces," his body dumped in the Missouri River, and one thousand dollars in cash stolen from him, "leaving his mother and two sisters to live upon the charity of the public," Sanford

Bullock first demanded his right to steal a horse from the burgeoning population of bushwhackers in Howard County.[60] But Bullock sought more than remuneration for his brother's loss: "I Pray for a more vigorous prosecution of the war for the utter extermination of all Bushwhackers." Only total and complete vengeance would suffice: "I dare say you would avenge the death of that Bro. with the blood of at least one hundred Rebels, and all Sympathizers who are engaged in it, if not directly they are indirectly . . . I long to see the day [that] all who are guilty of treason will share the fate of old John Brown." Thousands of other Missourians shared Bullock's outrage over the "lawless" guerrilla bands infesting the countryside, and many shared his genocidal fantasies of "exterminating" all the rebels "and all sympathizers." Considering Bullock's own admission that "there are many in this County who are daily joining the Bushwhackers," Bullock's humble demands would have resulted in the deaths of perhaps a majority of the white population of Howard and Chariton counties.[61] By 1863, then, many desperate Missouri Unionists sought more radical means to eliminate their intransigent enemy, even if it meant jettisoning their formerly conservative war aims.

Both sides employed eliminationist rhetoric to describe their enemies. Union general Benjamin Loan noted that guerrillas in central Missouri had waged, what they term, a "war of extermination."[62] The growing practice of guerrillas wearing Federal uniforms particularly galled Loan. This tactic violated all accepted modes of warfare and signaled early on that the Civil War in Missouri and Kentucky would play by a different set of rules than existed elsewhere in the country. As guerrillas became increasingly expert at waging irregular warfare, they turned to more brutal methods. The greatest massacre during the Civil War, and one of the largest mass killings ever of white American civilians by other white Americans, occurred in the raid on Lawrence, Kansas, in August 1863. Notorious guerrilla leaders William Clarke Quantrell, "Bloody" Bill Anderson, and their band of 150 Missouri guerrillas invaded that abolitionist stronghold and murdered over 150 men and boys in cold blood. The ostensible justification for the raid was the collapse of the Kansas City jail, which resulted in the death of Anderson's sister and several other siblings and wives of guerrillas.[63] In response Union general Ewing issued Order No. 11, clearing out four counties on Missouri's western border. While none of this activity affected any of the Little Dixie counties under study, it reflected the increasingly vicious character of insurgent warfare across the central portion of the state. Both sides dreamed of "exterminating" the foe, and at times both sides acted accordingly.

Guerrilla sympathizers became targets for Unionist vengeance as much as guerrillas themselves. The consequences of this broadening of counter-insurgent strategy pressured family members to turn against their own. Daniel Hord of Boone County was arrested for "Feeding and Harboring Bushwhackers."[64] As the major in the MSM cavalry unit noted, however, the only people Hord harbored and fed were his own sons, who had joined John Poindexter's guerrilla raid a year earlier.[65] Hord's neighbors insisted that he was and had always been a Union man and that he was being punished for his son's transgressions. The MSM commander proposed that Hord's sons be allowed to come home so long as they actively supported, or even joined, the Unionist militia. "Hord's sons could be made of great use to us," the commander predicted, considering the sons' earlier refusal to join up with another guerrilla band in recent weeks. The Union solution to such cases of divided families was to force the rebel son to reconcile with the Unionist father and serve the Union cause.

Property used by Confederates was also targeted by Unionists, including the burning of the Mt. Zion Church in Boone County. In October 1862 the Unionist *Columbia Statesman* still believed that Unionists should operate at a more civilized level than the guerrillas and expressed disappointment at the Mt. Zion arson: "It gives us pain to announce a series of outrageous acts committed by Federal troops . . . Whilst we have weekly recorded the crimes and robberies of the guerrillas, we have hoped that it would not become our duty to record any act of violence or outrage committed by Federal troops in our county. We greatly regret that we have been disappointed in that hope."[66]

Unionist reprisals against guerrillas were no less brutal than the acts of the guerrillas themselves. In many cases Union aggression preceded any considerable guerrilla activity. Callaway County established a reputation early in the war as a Confederate stronghold when an elderly man and a young boy convinced Federal forces that the county was guarded by hundreds of pro-Confederate soldiers. The two were bluffing, but the Federals avoided entering Callaway County for months, leaving the county outside the authority of the state or the Union army. It had become, in local parlance, the "Kingdom of Callaway," a quasi-independent territory that drew the ire of Federal officers until the end of the war.[67] After Unionist complaints of maltreatment, Union troops entered the county and promptly arrested dozens of leading Confederate sympathizers. A memorandum from a Fulton citizen to Governor Gamble described wanton confiscation of property and arrest. Most troublesome to the author of the memo was that many of those targeted were Unionists.[68] Such indiscriminate treatment of Callaway citizens reflected the desperation of counterinsurgency. Callaway's reputation alone was enough to convince Union soldiers that the entire population was of dubious loyalty, even though at least a third of white Callaway citizens were Unionists.[69]

By late 1863 guerrilla warfare engulfed every corner of Little Dixie. Mass evacuations, shuttering of businesses, burning of entire towns, and increasingly bloody public confrontations between guerrillas and militiamen destroyed the conservative social order in central Missouri. In Kentucky only John Hunt Morgan's periodic raids incurred the same sort of wrath from Unionists as did guerrilla depredations in Missouri. After 1863 Kentucky would witness more Missouri-style bushwhacking, with many Missouri guerrillas importing their style of war to the Bluegrass State themselves.

Moreover, the entire white population of central Missouri and Kentucky, including women, endured the guerrilla struggle either as victims or in some cases as belligerents. Indeed, the Civil War shattered many existing gender conventions for both Unionist and Confederate women. Women across the North and South played unprecedented public roles on both sides of the conflict. But the increasingly bitter guerrilla struggle in the border states added a special burden on women. Especially in Missouri, but also in Kentucky during John Hunt Morgan's various raids, Unionist women played a balancing act between performing the apolitical private lady for the invader and secretly assisting, harboring, and feeding Union militia and soldiers. Confederate women faced an even more precarious struggle as Unionists increasingly targeted sympathizers for arrest, confiscation of food and property, and banishment. Some Confederate women waved flags and sent secret signals to Morgan's men passing through the Bluegrass on his many raids.[70] They especially vexed Union authorities, who hoped to avoid violating codes of white womanhood while engaging in a ruthless campaign of counterinsurgency. Although white women rarely suffered direct acts of violence at the hands of Confederate guerrillas or Unionist militias, they endured severe privations as marauders regularly stole their provisions necessary for survival and burned their dwellings and barns. Many women responded in the only way possible: evacuation. Women and small children, left unprotected by men fighting in the countryside against one another, escaped to small towns across central Kentucky and Missouri, while many left the states altogether.

But the spreading guerrilla war that ripped apart the white community in Missouri and threatened the fabric of Kentucky society by late 1863 did not in itself destroy the social order. The thousands of slaves living on farms in central Missouri and Kentucky, who witnessed their masters and the remaining white ruling class murder each other in cold blood, fled in droves for Union camps. Guerrillas tried in vain to keep slaves on the farms, and Union military policy still wavered between turning slaves away and harboring and freeing them. The year 1863 proved to be the tipping point for emancipation, however, as Union military authorities increasingly concluded that the slave population was too valuable to reject for military service and the desperate measures of Confederates—many of them from the slaveholding class—demanded more radical measures.

In some cases the spreading guerrilla war in Missouri encouraged once-conservative Unionists to abandon conservatism outright. Brigadier General Benjamin Loan wrote Missouri commanding general Samuel Curtis in 1862 that a Unionist counter-guerrilla band "stole some 50 or 60 slaves" of rebel masters. One counter-guerrilla declared to General Loan, "I will emancipate every slave of the disloyalists."[71] Henry Clay Bruce also recollected some radical Chariton County Unionists who "advised the slaves who belonged to those called disloyal, not to work for men who had gone or sent their sons South, to fight against their government."[72] Even formerly conservative Unionist newspapers such as the *Central City and Brunswicker* began to embrace emancipation as a proper war measure by 1863, laying the blame for the loss of slavery on the Confederates: "The secessionists are indebted to no other party than themselves for the destruction of slavery in Missouri. Emancipation is inevitable and no plan that we have seen proposed suits our views so well as immediate emancipation with compensation to the loyal owners. Then the bone of contention will be forever removed and peace restored to our State."[73]

As the *Central City and Brunswicker* statement suggests, there were several emancipation proposals afoot in Missouri by 1863. Conservatives, who had summarily rejected President Lincoln's offer of gradual, compensated emancipation in the spring of 1862, now pushed for just such a course in the summer of 1863. The Gamble provisional government, solidified in office in 1862 after an election heavily monitored by Unionist militiamen, confronted emancipation on the state level in late 1862 and 1863. The state convention eventually decided upon a gradual scheme of emancipation with compensa-

tion for slaveholders; their major opponents were those who sought immediate emancipation, not those who wanted to keep slavery indefinitely. Radicals under Charles Drake quickly assumed the initiative and called for a new
constitutional convention that would effect immediate and general emancipation. In the midst of a war that brought conservative Unionists to their
knees, Missouri's growing base of white radicals, emboldened by their aggres-
siveness in fighting the guerrillas, drove home the stake of emancipation.[74]

But the Missouri radicals would never have been able to wrest control of
the emancipation debate if not for the concerted acts of slaves themselves.
Slaves had already forced the Union army to alter long-standing policy regarding fugitives by continually fleeing to Union camps. General Samuel
Curtis issued General Order No. 35 in December 1862, which effectively applied the Second Confiscation Act to Missouri, freeing rebel-owned slaves
who reached Union lines.[75] Alas, John Fremont's outrageous proposal of a
year earlier had now become standard policy. Meanwhile, Missouri radicals
gained a statewide hearing for immediate abolition but only because the
slaves had effectively dismantled the system by mid-1863. Conservatives and
radicals debated the best means to finish the job of emancipation, but it was
the slaves—who carried news "from farm to farm," fled to Kansas in droves,
joined military units on their way to St. Louis, provided critical intelligence
for Unionist counter-guerrillas, and laid down their tools—who began the
process. When General John Schofield issued General Order No. 135 in November 1863, enlisting into the Union army any able-bodied African American male—free or slave, owned by a loyal or disloyal master—slavery had
already effectively been destroyed.[76]

As expected, the light load of guerrilla warfare in Kentucky in the early
years of the war placed less strain on the slave system. But by the middle
of 1863 Kentucky's slaves upended even the last slaveholders' redoubt.
Although the Emancipation Proclamation did not apply in Kentucky, the
slaves in the Bluegrass read into it a fundamental change in the course of
the war. In November 1862 the *Lexington Observer and Reporter* asserted
that nearly all slaves in Kentucky believed that they would be freed by the
proclamation on January 1, 1863.[77] The Kentucky legislature responded to
the Emancipation Proclamation with grave alarm, with all members rejecting the proclamation as unconstitutional, unwise, and unjust. Conservative
Unionists such as Robert J. Breckinridge of Danville believed the proclamation "a folly, if not a sin, to attempt to frustrate the course of Providence—

whether by hastening or by retarding it."[78] In typical conservative Unionist fashion Breckinridge pledged his continued loyalty to the Union and to the defeat of the rebellion, but he rejected any radical means of social change.

By the end of 1863 central Missouri and Kentucky stood on the cusp of a complete social revolution. The social order based on slavery, community, and kin ties shattered amid a burgeoning guerrilla insurgency and the complete rejection of slaveholders' authority by the slave population. The two phenomena constituted a dual rebellion against the conservative Unionist order, with emancipation and guerrilla war feeding off one another. Before most black Kentucky or Missouri soldiers fired their guns for the Union army, the system of slavery had collapsed in many parts of the slave-rich Little Dixie and Bluegrass regions. Guerrilla rebels against Unionism colluded, ironically, with black rebels against conservatism to usher out the social and political order that had prevailed for decades in the border states. Only through complete social revolution and a veritable race war between 1864 and 1866 would the border states confront and create a new social and political order.

CHAPTER 6

BLACK SOLDIERS AND REGULATOR VIOLENCE

African Americans in Kentucky and Missouri faced an unprecedented wave of violence between 1864 and 1866. By and large violence targeting African Americans in late–Civil War and postwar Kentucky and Missouri was not random. Many of the black victims were either soldiers in the Union army or members of their families. The prevalence of violence aimed at this subset of the African American population seemed to reflect underlying tensions regarding the contours of citizenship and white supremacy within conservative border state society during the Civil War. The wartime realignment of white conservative men from the Whig Party to the self-described "White Man's Democracy" and the identification of white conservative women with their struggling sisters in the postwar South emerged out of these tensions as much as did the racial violence.

In 1861 large numbers of conservative whites in the western border states fought for the Union precisely because they thought it would best preserve slavery. The abolitionist turn of the Civil War demoralized such border conservatives, caught between vicious and desperate guerrillas on one side and, by 1864, an armed African American population on the other. African Americans who took up arms and used them to target local white Confederates dramatically altered the balance of power in border state society as white conservatives saw it. When African Americans joined the Union army, they not only contributed vital manpower to the Union cause. They also recast the Union cause as a struggle for liberation, even though many fought on the same side as their own masters. As historian Linda Kerber points out, white Americans in the nineteenth century equated the prerogatives of citizenship with the obligations of military service: "Citizenship and civic relations in a republic were tightly linked to race and manhood; it was white men who offered military service, white men who sought honor, white men who dueled in its defense."[1] Black slaves who took up arms for the Union cause both challenged and sought to animate this bedrock social principle of the American Republic. For white Unionists in Kentucky and Missouri a black soldiery mocked the conservative social basis of the Union. For outraged white conservatives the violent suppression of these aspiring black citizens, rejection of radicalism at the ballot box, and the formation of women's southern aid societies throughout the border countryside resuscitated long-standing social relations and restored honor to themselves and to the Republic.

Historians have long identified the post–Civil War era in the South with an epidemic of racial violence. The rise of the Ku Klux Klan and like-minded groups in 1866 threatened African Americans across the South with summary violence. In looking for explanations for this outbreak of racial violence, historians have for the most part pointed to Democratic efforts at "redemption" and the economic demands of former slaveholders to reestablish plantation discipline.[2] But the violence that engulfed the border state countryside in the years following Appomattox only partly resembled the partisan paramilitary warfare or violent labor struggle that afflicted the lower South.

In the former slaveholding Union border states of Kentucky and Missouri, African Americans did not attain the right to vote until passage of the Fifteenth Amendment in 1870. Although Missouri fell under Radical Republican rule between 1865 and 1870, the basis for the party's power lay with the state's German population, whites long subject to brutal guerrilla violence in the southwest, and the more northern-born community centered in St. Louis.[3] Instead of expanding the franchise to the African American population, Missouri radicals sought to build a party base by disfranchising any and all Missourians who had ever participated in or sympathized with the rebellion. The political alliance of former Free-Soil whites and Ozark Unionists, on the one hand, and the massive disfranchisement of rebel sympathizers, on the other, made formal black political participation superfluous to the Radical regime. Although African Americans actively campaigned for the franchise as early as 1865, they never achieved full political rights until the Radical government's dying days in 1870.[4] Kentucky similarly barred African Americans from the political process until 1870, offering even fewer legal and civil safeguards than in Missouri. Indeed, the Kentucky state government passed seamlessly from conservative Unionists to Democrats in the postwar era, offering Radicals and their beneficiaries no chance to establish hegemony. If Missouri blacks posed little threat to the white political order in that state in the late 1860s, Kentucky blacks provided even less.[5] Thus, unlike in the lower South, black votes never threatened the white political order in the immediate postwar border states.

The traditional economic interpretation of postwar racial violence also fails to account for the persistence and virulence of racial attacks in the border states. Many so-called Regulators indeed attacked black families because of black demands for social and economic autonomy. At a rudimentary level much of the violence reflected the chaotic politics of land and labor all over the post-emancipation South. But the context of border state agricultural life differed significantly from the lower South. Slave labor was never as integral a part of Kentucky or Missouri economic life as it was in, say, Mississippi or South Carolina. Although slaves tilled the hemp and tobacco farms of Little Dixie and the Bluegrass right through the early years of the Civil War, neither of those regions relied upon slave labor on the scale of plantation owners in the Deep South. Slaveholdings in the Bluegrass averaged 7 slaves per holding, and in Little Dixie the number was even smaller.[6] Many of these relatively small border state farms employed a combination of white family members, hired skilled laborers, hired slaves, and resident slaves. Although slaves performed critical work, especially the laborious task of hemp breaking, their labor was hardly indispensable to the degree it was in the cotton, rice, and sugar plantations of the lower South. Moreover, the decline of the American hemp industry and the rise of white burley tobacco, which could be profitably raised by small family farmers, made slave-based labor even more redundant.[7] Whereas lower South planters desperately sought African American labor to grow cotton, Kentucky and Missouri farmers adjusted more easily to free labor. Indeed, the flexible work relations in antebellum Kentucky and Missouri eased white landowners' transition to free labor, at least in comparison to the lower South. With black labor now less critical to landowners, border state whites had less need for violence to force former slaves back to work.[8]

The origins of postwar racial terror in the Union border states thus lay elsewhere. In fact, the lynchings of Al McRoberts in Danville and the elderly African American outside Columbia suggested a more convincing explanation for racial violence. With roots in the Civil War and particularly with the rise of black enlistment into the Union army, whites in the border states no longer viewed the war as a struggle over union or disunion but as a struggle for white dominance in all facets of social, cultural, and political life. As African American men joined the Union army in large numbers beginning in early 1864, they made an unprecedented bid for citizenship in a republic that had long treated them as nothing but mere property. In doing so, they also asserted the masculine rights of martial self-defense that had long been restricted to white men.

Federal emancipation edicts and abolitionist harangues may have annoyed and angered conservatives in the border states, but the arming of former slaves transformed social relations on the ground in ways that threatened the basic social and racial order. To conservatives—whether Unionist or Confederate—race relations resembled a zero-sum game; every gain for African Americans signified a loss in honor and power for whites. For decades white Kentuckians and Missourians of all political stripes expected slaves to exercise deference to white authority, both within slave households and in public spaces. Slavery was a means of labor exploitation for border slaveholders, but it was also a means of racial control; with a miniscule free black population in Kentucky and Missouri, whites found the slave system sufficient to manage the black population.[9] With the utter breakdown in slave-based social relations during the Civil War, however, and the loss of trust in the newly radicalized Union, border state whites turned increasingly to mob violence to reestablish white supremacy. And because the surrender of Confederate forces in April 1865 only reified the new social order characterized by general emancipation, white violence against newly freed slaves did not diminish with the Civil War's end. The war over Union and Confederacy had devolved into a veritable race war, wherein former white foes settled old accounts and turned their guns toward the newly emancipated populace.

Slaves, Soldiers, and Citizens

Peter Bruner, a slave in central Kentucky's Bluegrass region, appeared at the Union army enlistment center at Camp Nelson with "plenty of company." "I came there to fight the rebels and . . . I wanted a gun," Bruner recalled.[10] Joining thousands of other slaves across central Kentucky in the summer of 1864, Bruner fused his own liberation with the war effort against the Confederacy. And his tool of emancipation, the gun, bore revolutionary consequences for black liberation in the border states. This was not the first time Bruner had sought his freedom at the Kentucky River encampment. Before

Camp Nelson became a major black soldier recruitment center, it was an army camp for the Union's Department of the Ohio. In August 1863 Bruner attempted to escape his brutal master for the safety of Camp Nelson, only to be captured and jailed by a Unionist proslavery judge in nearby Nicholas-ville. "Oh, how hard some of us poor slaves labored for our freedom," Bruner explained.[11] In the summer of 1863 the Union army still rejected African American soldiers in Kentucky. "When I had run off before and wanted to go in the army and fight they said that they did not want any darkies, that this was a white man's war."[12] But in his successful 1864 venture Bruner found a radically altered Camp Nelson awaiting him. Unlike the all-white unit that guarded central Kentucky for the Union in 1863, the new army welcomed, initiated, trained, and commanded thousands of African American soldiers willing to "fight the rebels" and, more immediately, to "gain our freedom."[13] Elijah Marrs, another African American soldier at Camp Nelson, heralded the revolution at hand: "I can stand this, said I. This is better than slavery, though I do march in line at the tap of a drum. I felt freedom in my bones, and when I saw the American eagle with outspread wings, upon the Ameri-can flag, with the motto E Pluribus Unum, the thought came to me, 'Give me liberty or give me death.' Then all fear banished."[14] Although this statement certainly exhibited a bit of rhetorical flair and hyperbole, there is little doubt that for African Americans at Camp Nelson such as Peter Bruner and Elijah Marrs, the transformation from slave to soldier suggested a potent assertion of manhood and signified the first great step toward American citizenship.

When the first slaves enrolled in the army at Camp Nelson, they followed tens of thousands of their brethren throughout the Confederacy who had enlisted as early as 1862.[15] Indeed, with enrollment delayed until Febru-ary 1864, Kentucky slaves were the last to join en masse, with the similarly late-enrolling Missouri slaves waiting as late as December 1863. Thus, the prospect of black enlistees surprised neither black nor white in early 1864. Nevertheless, with the Lincoln administration handling the border states with great caution—exempting the states from the Emancipation Proclama-tion in January 1863 and generally yielding to conservative Unionist civilian officials in Kentucky and Missouri on all significant political matters—the reality of black enlistments in the border states brought home to white Unionists the radical turn of the Civil War.

Throughout the South black enlistment played an integral part in usher-ing in the social revolution of general emancipation and, soon afterward, the transformation of former slaves into citizens. But in the border states of

Kentucky and Missouri black enlistment played a particularly acute role in bringing this social revolution to fruition for four important reasons. First, the number of slaves who joined the army from Kentucky and Missouri far exceeded in proportion and number enlistees in virtually every Confederate state. Out of 41,935 military-age African Americans in Kentucky, 57 percent joined the Union army; in Missouri 39 percent joined the military.[16] Even these numbers somewhat downplay the total of black recruits in the western border states, as many joined in neighboring free states.[17] It is very likely that a significant percentage of the 2,080 African Americans credited to Kansas actually came from Missouri.[18] Similarly, a sizable portion of the recruits credited to Indiana (1,537) and Ohio (5,092) were black Kentuckians who had crossed the Ohio River earlier in the war to enlist. And in the heavily enslaved Little Dixie region of central Missouri and Kentucky's Bluegrass, the proportion of slaves joining the army was even higher. In Howard County, Missouri, for example, nearly two thirds of all military-age male slaves entered the army; Howard County possessed the largest percentage of slaves of any county in Missouri.[19] In both Kentucky and Missouri nearly all black enlistees were slaves, as both states possessed minuscule free black populations.[20] The sheer volume of black—and particularly slave—enlistment in Kentucky and Missouri transformed much of the labor force into a vital weapon in the Federal government's counterinsurgency campaign against rebels, led in many cases by their former masters.

The second reason black enlistments in Kentucky and Missouri proved so significant lay in the speed with which slaves joined the military. The slaves of Kentucky and Missouri flooded recruitment centers, with more than half of Kentucky's entire military-age male slave population joining within the span of ten months—and most of them in the three summer months of 1864. A local provost marshal officer wrote to commanding general John Schofield in December 1863 that a "stampede of negroes" enlisting in the army had thrown conservative white Unionists into a "state of desperation."[21] By January 15, 1864, dozens of slaves had enlisted in central Missouri's slave-rich Howard County alone. By the end of February more than 3,700 African Americans had enlisted in Missouri, with central Missouri's Little Dixie producing a significant portion of the total. Many slaves traveled to recruitment sites on their own, while others joined as a group. Seven of John R. White's slaves—William, Adam, Alfred, Sam, Andy, Preston, and Jacob—all enlisted together at the Fayette provost marshal post in the first weeks of January 1864.[22] White was one of Missouri's largest slaveholders; the 7 who joined represented a mere tenth of White's total holdings, though it signified collective action on the part of a portion of his slaves.[23] At Fayette, where John White's slaves enlisted, 174 African Americans joined the service in the first two months of the year. In Brunswick, just up the Missouri River from Fayette, another 128 slaves joined in the same period. Perhaps the most impressive recruitment site in central Missouri was Boonville, where Lieutenant C. S. Swamp presided over the enrollment of 436 African Americans—nearly all of them slaves—into the Union army.[24] By the end of 1864 slaves rushing into the Union army across central Missouri destroyed the last vestiges of the peculiar institution, thereby making the state's constitutional abolition of slavery in January 1865 a mere acknowledgment of reality.

In Kentucky slave enlistment began later than it did in Missouri, but once state officials removed restrictions to recruitment in June 1864, enlistment proceeded at an even more fevered pace. A February 1864 circular issued by James B. Fry, provost marshal general of the United States, to all assistant provost marshals in Kentucky directed the enrollment of free blacks in accordance with the new congressional Enrollment Act.[25] Despite conservatives' vehement opposition to black enlistment in March 1864, General Stephen Burbridge, commander of the District of Kentucky, began recruitment in earnest in April with the release of General Order No. 34. But the new circular restricted recruitment to free blacks and slaves "whose owners may request the enlistment."[26] Clearly, the new enlistment procedures exempted the vast majority of potential black soldiers, giving the Union cause the political grief of conservative alienation without the benefit of increased manpower. Rumors that the army would remove all remaining barriers to enlistment reached the slaves of the Bluegrass in the next few months. In late May 1864 a provost marshal in Boyle County, Kentucky, reported to his superior officer, "It became known to these negroes that they could enlist without the consent of their masters, whereupon they thronged the office of the Dep[uty] Pro[vost] Mar[shal] clamoring to be enlisted."[27] In response, whites in nearby Danville "commenced abusing and threatening them," trying to prevent the slaves from enlisting at all. The provost marshal was surprised at the "stampede" of blacks to Camp Nelson and imagined, erroneously, that enlistment would continue "singly and in squads" as it had up to that time. But the rumors reflected reality as the army removed all remaining obstacles to enlistment two weeks after the "stampede."[28]

Full black enlistment finally arrived in Kentucky on June 13, 1864, when Lorenzo Thomas, adjutant-general for the United States Army, issued

General Order No. 20, accepting "any slave who may present himself for enlistment" at one of eight recruitment centers located throughout Kentucky.[29]
Camp Nelson in southern Jessamine County and a recruitment center in
Lebanon served the heavily enslaved Bluegrass area. With the final barrier
to enlistment removed, slaves poured into Camp Nelson, with most coming
from the Bluegrass region. Nearly 2,500 black soldiers entered the Union
army by the end of August 1864 at Camp Nelson.[30] By the end of July 1864
Boyle County alone had contributed 275 black enlistees to Camp Nelson[31]—a
number that represented 42 percent of Boyle County's entire military-age
black male population.[32] The flood of enlistees continued throughout the
summer of 1864, roiling the Kentucky countryside and shaking the peculiar
institution to its core. The enrollment of more than half the military-age
black population of Kentucky—nearly all of whom were enslaved—in less
than a year suggests a revolutionary war under way in the region.[33]

The pace of enlistment shocked both Union officials and white conservatives of Unionist and Confederate loyalty. At the very least the deluge of
enlistment threatened a calamitous breakdown in social order as thousands
of slaves immediately abandoned decades-old relationships with their former masters. More ominously yet, in the white imagination the sudden-
ness of the black enlistment stampede heralded the sort of disorderly racial
catastrophe befitting the onset of a slave uprising.[34] African Americans in
their midst had become a powerful political force, and unbeknownst to the
master class, the newly militarized black population drew energy and organization from decades of kin and social networks built during slavery.

Henry Clay Bruce, a slave in Missouri's Chariton County, recalled in his
autobiography that border state slaves were intimately aware of the politics
of war and emancipation. He outlined the vast networks of communication across the scattered, small slaveholdings in Little Dixie through which
slaves could pass news "from mouth to ear" and "from farm to farm."[35] By
1864 one of the most important pieces of news to arrive was the possibility
for enlistment in the Union army. Given the underground network through
which slaves passed information, it is hardly surprising that hundreds of
slaves would rise up "in a stampede" at the first chance to enlist in Danville,
Kentucky, or Fayette, Missouri. If the sheer magnitude of black enlistment
in the border states heralded the emergence of a broader black political consciousness, the speed with which slaves answered the enlistment call suggests the political and organizational sophistication of a population previously underestimated by white society.

The location of blacks under arms reveals the third reason slave enlistment proved so revolutionary. After slaves entered the service, their primary duty was to guard the towns across the border from guerrilla raids and Confederate attack. Black soldiers were rarely sent to some far-off battlefield; they were stationed at home, squaring off with their own outraged former masters. Given that Kentucky remained under martial law for several months after the war's completion, many of these black soldiers continued to stand as armed guards in towns and posts across the Bluegrass. Despite white protest—including from solidly Unionist sources (many of whom were now migrating to symbolic, belatedly Confederate positions)—former slaves would serve at public guard posts well into the fall of 1865. The staunchly Unionist *Paris Western Citizen* in Bourbon County, Kentucky, wrote with relief in June 1865 that "efforts would be made by the Administration to conciliate the people of Kentucky, and that all negro troops would accordingly be soon removed from among us."[36] The editor remarked that "this is pleasing intelligence, and we sincerely hope it may be true." Unfortunately for the *Western Citizen,* ten thousand black troops would remain stationed on Kentucky soil as late as October 1865.[37]

In Missouri black troops played an integral role in enforcing civil law, especially after passage of the new radical constitution in 1865. In Lafayette County, Missouri, black troops arrested two pro-Confederate judges for refusing to abdicate their offices in accordance with the new constitution.[38] For whites outraged at the presence of black troops, then, the continued presence of these soldiers threatened a permanent, direct, and official rejection of white supremacy. For African Americans, on the other hand, possessing the power and obligation to keep the peace in a place where they had legally served as slaves as late as 1865 signified a dramatic reversal of the social and political order. Moreover, as new guardians of the public order, uniformed and armed blacks stationed in towns across the border states made an unprecedented bid for the equal rights and responsibilities of citizenship.

The fourth, and perhaps most important, consequence of slave enlistment was the opportunity it gave African Americans to recast the Union cause as a struggle for liberation. Since the outbreak of war in 1861, white conservative Unionists vowed to preserve the federal government precisely because it was the best way to preserve the slave-based social order. Indeed, the governors of Kentucky and Missouri encapsulated the conservative Unionist spirit throughout the war, rejecting immediate emancipation and black soldier enlistment but supporting an otherwise vigorous prosecution of the war against both external Confederate invaders and internal Confederate guerrillas.[39] Slaves joining the Union war effort threatened to overturn the conservatives' original rationale for Union in the border states. While tens of thousands of whites fought for the Union to protect slavery, tens of thousands of their own slaves fought for the Union to destroy slavery.[40]

For slaves in Missouri and Kentucky the vast black army also signified a critical moment in the development of a highly politicized racial consciousness. Upon witnessing thousands of other slave enlistees in army camps from central Kentucky to central Missouri—slaves who once toiled on isolated farms throughout the border countryside—African American men developed a critical understanding of their own potential for political expression and power. Indeed, the very act of joining the military proved the most vital political statement most of these slaves had ever made, as it yielded the only viable path to emancipation; with both states exempt from the Emancipation Proclamation, Kentucky and Missouri slaveholders were under no federal pressure to free their slaves.

But what made black enlistment in the border states so troubling was the fact that slaves ostensibly fought on the same side as their masters, even if their reasons for doing so were completely contrary. There are other examples in the nineteenth century of slaves and masters fighting as allies; in Cuba, for example, slaves formed the backbone of the slaveholder-led insurrection against Spanish rule.[41] Nevertheless, the border state picture markedly contrasts with the traditional narrative of Civil War slave enlistment, which portrays slaves taking up arms against their own masters.[42] To be sure, a significant proportion of owners of black enlistees in Kentucky and Missouri supported the rebel cause. Federal Walker, for example, a well-known Confederate in Howard County, witnessed his three slaves—Shelby, Daniel, and St. Andrew—join the Union forces.[43] For these slaves the process of enlisting in the Federal forces resembled the experience of black soldiers in the Confederate states. But for other enlistees, such as those owned by conservative Unionists like Columbia's William Switzler, the social consequences of enrollment differed from those who took up arms against their own masters. Slaves understood that, despite the conservative basis of Unionism in Kentucky and Missouri, a Union victory would result in the destruction of slavery. As Henry Clay Bruce recalled, slaves believed the government was "fighting for their freedom," regardless of what their masters had to say.[44] Considering the communication network among blacks accustomed to abroad marriages, slave hiring, and small-scale slavery, it is hardly surprising that Kentucky and Missouri slaves would offer a coherent picture of the Union war effort that so differed from that of their own masters. Border state slaves such as Peter Bruner, Henry Clay Bruce, and Elijah Marrs never accepted the conservative reading of the Union cause offered by their own masters. Regardless of their masters' loyalty, border state slaves joined the Union army because it provided their own freedom and the opportunity to liberate their people. This recasting of the Union cause by ex-slave soldiers as a war for emancipation constituted the first great step in the social revolution of the border states.

White Conservatives and Black Soldiers

White Kentucky and Missouri Unionists viewed the prospect of black enlistment with anger from the moment the army and the Lincoln administration first broached the subject. Like leaders in the Confederate states, whites in Kentucky and Missouri vigorously opposed arming their own bondsmen. The Confederate government introduced the concept of arming slaves as its prospects for southern independence dwindled in late 1864 and early 1865. Historians assessing the rancor within Confederate military circles over black soldier enlistment at the conclusion of the war have accurately disposed of the plan as a desperate last stand that ultimately went for naught.[45] Historians have also examined the debate over black enlistments in the free North and the effects of such a revolutionary move on long-held doctrines of white supremacy and an all-white citizenry.[46] Only in passing, however, have these historians discussed the impact of black enlistment on the white Unionist cause in the border states. And it was in the heart of black enlistment—Kentucky and Missouri—where the social effects of black soldier enlistment yielded some of its most vitriolic reaction.

Perhaps no better exemplar of conservative Unionist protest against black enlistment exists than Kentuckian Colonel Frank Wolford. A longtime inhabitant of Casey County on the southern edge of the Bluegrass, Wolford was a dedicated Union commander of the First Kentucky Cavalry. As the oldest cavalry unit in the state and the most successful opponent of John Hunt Morgan's Confederate raiders, the First Kentucky Cavalry had achieved legendary status across the Bluegrass by the middle of 1863. Its commander regularly received applause and accolades from grateful Unionists in towns such as Lebanon that faced Morgan's assaults and in cities such as Lexington, where his presence ensured protection against guerrilla depredations.

But Colonel Wolford drew the most attention to himself when he delivered a series of speeches in March 1864 denouncing the enlistment of black soldiers into the Union army.

With Governor Bramlette standing by his side, Colonel Wolford declared in a Lexington speech that President Lincoln was a "traitor, tyrant and usurper" for daring to enlist African Americans into the army from Kentucky.[47] It is the "duty of the people of Kentucky to resist it as a violation of their guaranteed rights," he insisted.[48] Wolford's grievances extended beyond black soldier enlistment to the entire abolitionist course of the war. According to a Lexington newspaper's paraphrase of Wolford's comments, "The purposes of the war were the same today that they were when Mr. Lincoln in his inaugural and Congress by resolution declared that they were not for conquest or subjugation, nor for interference with the domestic institutions of the States, but simply to preserve the honor and maintain the supremacy of the Constitution—The effort to pervert the war from this legitimate purpose, and to make it a war upon slavery, was an issue which the dominant party had no right to make—it was a startling usurpation of power."[49] Soon after Wolford's incendiary speech he was arrested and sent to Nashville to meet with General Ulysses S. Grant. Governor Bramlette immediately sought to defuse the crisis by insisting that the highest priority at the time was to employ Kentucky's "gallant soldiers" to defeat the rebellion, after which Kentuckians could redress their grievances over enlistment of slaves through constitutional means at the ballot box and the courts.[50]

Bramlette's attempt to quell the anger did little to prevent an outbreak of violence.[51] Just days after Wolford's speech, one hundred Kentucky Union troops fired on members of the Eleventh Michigan Cavalry, declaring that they would "clean out the town of Michiganders and Yankees."[52] The reason for the disturbance was the presence of a mulatto soldier standing guard near the Eleventh Michigan Cavalry regiment. A Kentucky colonel warned the Michigan regimental commander, "If [the mulatto guard] was not immediately removed there would be trouble, as his men would not suffer a nigger soldier to be on duty in their presence." A Union officer stationed in Lexington wrote to the war department, "The excitement about the enrollment of negroes is intense, and many professed friends of the Govt say that it shall be resisted and they rely upon their own (KY) officers and troops to do it."[53]

Open attacks against fellow Union troops initially threatened to destroy the entire Union war effort in the state. Consequently, conservative Union officials, from Bramlette on down, preached restraint and acquiescence to the law. While outbreaks of violence between units disappeared after the Eleventh Michigan incident, white Kentuckians—and Missourians—merely redirected their anger at the slaves who sought entry into the Union army. Although many of these attacks came from rebel guerrillas, not all can be traced to supporters of the Confederacy. And even when conservative white Unionists did not openly attack African Americans, they expressed virtually no disapproval of these increasingly common acts of racial violence. Their acceptance of racial violence encouraged further depredations and made Union military prosecution of assailants more difficult.

In some cases military authorities had to alter recruitment procedures for fear of violent interference. James Fidler, provost marshal in Lebanon, Kentucky, began sending black recruits by train to Louisville to protect them from guerrilla attacks. "There is no possible chance," he wrote, "to disguise the fact that there is great opposition, amounting almost to an outbreak, to these enlistments, all through the centre of the state."[54] Fidler, like other Union army officials, implied that vehement opposition came from all quarters of the white population, Unionist and Confederate. Opposition grew so intense that the provost marshal worried that transporting the recruits to Louisville would not sufficiently protect them: "Information came to me yesterday that a band of guerrillas were on the RR ten miles from Lebanon, there leaving to burn the train." Fidler also witnessed local citizens catching and whipping potential slave recruits. As the whip represented the crudest tool of control over the slave, employment of it to prevent slaves' enlistment in the army served as a visible reassertion of the traditional prerogatives of slaveholders' power.

Because the slave code remained in full effect in Kentucky until passage of the Thirteenth Amendment in December 1865, slaves seeking the safety of enlistment camps were considered runaways under Kentucky law, regardless of the presence of Union troops or the state's official standing within the Union. As a result, slave enlistees were treated by law and by custom as runaways. Violence against them reflected the slave patrol system that governed the movement of slaves in the antebellum era. Near Lebanon in June 1864, for example, two "boys" named James and Jasper Edwards walking on the road to the enlistment center in town encountered an Irish immigrant named Michael McMann, who accosted them and cut off their ears.[55] An officer at the Lebanon post immediately arrested McMann and an accomplice named William Burns, though only McMann was positively identified by the boys as the assailant. Mutilation of the recruits undoubtedly served to intimidate others who considered joining the military. It hardly went unnoticed that cutting off ears was an occasional punishment of slave runaways by slave patrols.[56] McMann, who likely served on a slave patrol in the community around Lebanon, maintained full civil authority to inflict whatever punishment upon slave runaways he deemed appropriate, including bodily mutilation.[57]

Whites angry at black soldier enlistment also directed their violence at the families of recruits. The wife of a black recruit appeared before the office of Hiram Cornell, an assistant provost marshal in Fulton, Missouri, and reported that she and her child had been severely beaten and driven from her home by her master. She asked to follow her husband into the army, offering to work at the camp if necessary.[58] The black recruit, unable to protect his wife and children from the master's assault—either at home or in the army camp—faced a dilemma that would survive the war. Violence against the families of recruits continued as long as blacks served in the army, and in many cases these kinds of attacks lasted until late 1866. Masters also attacked slave families because the labor value of the remaining women and children did not warrant further support for them. In the Fulton case the slave owner was an "aged man" and had already complained to the army that he could not afford to feed and clothe the remaining slaves. Ironically, earlier in the war masters despised the Union army for luring their slaves away. Yet once they decided to rid themselves of their remaining slave property, the army proved an inviting destination.

Whites in central Missouri and Kentucky regularly harassed, intimidated, and attacked black recruits en route to enlistment camps to prevent them from entering the army. They also attacked black soldiers already in uniform carrying out their duties, especially when on guard or traveling through the border countryside. In Woodford County, Kentucky, which held the largest percentage of slaves of any Kentucky county in 1860, a black soldier transporting official army dispatches was stopped by a man who stole his bridles, led him for two miles into the woods, and shot him.[59] The murderer, identified by witnesses as Maddox, told the toll keeper guarding the road that he intended to kill the black soldier.[60] According to the toll keeper, the only reason Maddox killed the soldier was that he was black and wearing a Federal uniform. Blacks in uniform, like the Woodford County soldier, represented an affront to prevailing white conceptions of citizenship; for many whites racial violence against blacks was a way to enforce this restrictive understanding of citizenship.

With Missouri formally abolishing slavery in the war's final months,[61] bushwhackers and other rebel sympathizers transformed their existing practice of threatening African Americans who joined the military into a generalized terror campaign. The purpose of this campaign was the expulsion of blacks from the border states. Near Columbia, Missouri, and just days after Captain Cook found the elderly black man hanged by Jim Jackson's gang, Union troops discovered another black man murdered by Jackson. According to the Union officer present, Jackson's men had threatened "that all blacks were to leave in 10 days or be killed by them."[62] The officer noted that most black men from the vicinity were already serving in the army, leaving behind the "unarmed and helpless" in a state of "terrible alarm." With the abolition of slavery in Missouri, bushwhackers who had once threatened violence against slaves escaping their masters now used terror and violence to remove all remaining African Americans from the region. Although Kentucky did not formally abolish slavery of its own volition—only ratification of the Thirteenth Amendment in December 1865 brought the institution to an end—slaveholders in the Bluegrass also recognized the demise of the peculiar institution. Like their Missouri compatriots, they viewed freedmen and women with complete disdain. Not only had their former slaves forcibly severed their bonds of slavery, but they had the audacity to claim the prerogatives of equal citizenship commensurate with a Union soldier. As the Civil War came to a conclusion and the Union army destroyed the last redoubts of Confederatism in April 1865, the battle over the place of African Americans in Kentucky and Missouri society merely entered a new phase. Patterns of violence committed by white rebels against black soldiers, and especially by white conservatives of both loyalties against all African Americans, would change after Appomattox—but they would not diminish.

Black Citizenship and Racial Violence

The Danville Fair held in Boyle County in the fall of 1865 brought to the surface simmering tensions over emancipation, guerrilla war, and the use of black soldiers, forces that continued to roil the community months after Lee's surrender at Appomattox. The Danville Fair provided one of the first public recreational spaces in which central Kentuckians, regardless of race or previous loyalty, congregated openly after the close of the war. At county fairs in nineteenth-century America farmers and townsfolk gathered to discuss business matters such as crop prices and conditions, show off livestock, and participate in a rare moment of social revelry. The county fair also offered an arena for rural men and women to discuss current political matters, hear politicians speak, and resolve local disputes. The racial makeup of the Danville Fair added a novel dimension to social relations in the region. Never before had African Americans legally assembled in public in Boyle County without direct white supervision; slavery was still legal in Kentucky for a few more months, but most slaves in central Kentucky had been freed by that point. Whites long feared that an all-black meeting would lead to general insurrection, regardless of whether or not the congregants were enslaved. At the same time, whites insisted that blacks refrain from interaction across the color line for fear of miscegenation. As a result, the fair's organizers divided the crowd, establishing a separate zone for black fairgoers, enforcing the segregation rule with force. The volatile mix of black soldiers, returning rebels, and conservative whites who prowled the fairgrounds exploded into violence when newly freed African Americans challenged the segregated boundaries.

According to U.S. Army major A. H. Bowen, charged with investigating the incident, several blacks had attempted to "pass out of the ring allotted to the blacks."[63] Two white men, one a conservative Unionist parade marshal named Thomas Moore and the other a "returned rebel soldier" named Thomas Tadlock, tried to force the blacks back into their specified section. Bowen reported that Moore "fancied" that he saw a black soldier pull out a gun, and Moore promptly shot the would-be assailant. Immediately afterward, other black soldiers fired back at Moore and Tadlock, causing a general riot. Thirty white "citizens" with pistols and bowie knives chased the entire population of African Americans out of the fairgrounds, firing at them along the way. Moore caught a black sergeant and began kicking him, threatening to "blow his brains out" if he did not give up his pistol. As the blacks— soldiers and civilians alike—regrouped outside the fairgrounds, many demanded that they return to the fairgrounds with reinforcements and guns.

The *Lexington Observer and Reporter*, the largest conservative Unionist newspaper in central Kentucky, described the incident differently than Major Bowen. According to the newspaper, "Four negro soldiers were promenading in a careless manner among the gentlemen and ladies when the Marshal, named Moore, told them to go around and occupy a place amongst other negroes. Three of the four started willingly but the fourth grew somewhat stubborn and was being pushed along by Moore and another gentleman, when he drew his pistol and fired, shooting Mr. Thomas Tadlock of Perryville."[64] After shooting Tadlock, the "negroes ran into Danville and being re-inforced by their entire company declared their intention to go to the Fair Ground and shoot every white person they saw." Inexplicably, according to the newspaper, the blacks did not attack the fairgrounds, instead shooting "promiscuously" at people coming from the fair and shooting a black woman in the streets of Danville.

The two explanations of the "Danville Shooting Affray," as it came to be known, reveal competing narratives of racial violence in post–Civil War Kentucky. They also uncover, in their contradictions, the tensions within a border state society undergoing a revolutionary challenge to the existing social order. Union officer Bowen presented the fair marshal and his rebel compatriot as primarily culpable for the incident. The officer made sure to describe Tadlock as a rebel, thus identifying his Civil War loyalty with his propensity to commit violence against African Americans, especially black soldiers. While conservative Unionists shared local Confederate disdain for black soldiers, most Union officers—particularly those from the North— had long accepted African Americans, including those from Kentucky and Missouri, as courageous and effective soldiers.[65] Although conservative white Unionists often participated in, and even led, episodes of violence against African Americans, white rebels clearly took the lead in inciting at-tacks.[66] Thus, by describing Tadlock as a "rebel soldier," the officer placed blame for the incident on the whites. Moreover, the officer's account claims that Moore "fancied" he saw a black soldier pull out a gun, raising doubt in the officer's mind about whether or not Moore was telling the truth. This statement is especially significant because Kentucky forbade the right of African Americans to testify in court, based on old prejudices regarding the inability of blacks to speak truthfully and the belief that blacks had no claim to the same civil rights accorded whites. By doubting the word of a white man in a case involving violence between blacks and whites, the officer re-vealed the difference between the values of white Kentuckians and himself, at least in this instance.[67] Most important, the officer concluded, after tak-ing evidence from numerous witnesses at the fair, "I can see nothing in the conduct of the negroes that is deserving of censure." And while the officer mildly chastised the black soldiers for returning to the fair with guns and re-inforcements, he remarked, "This is little more than could be expected even from men supposed to possess cooler judgment than the colored soldier." As respectable soldiers, they held the right to use violence for self-protection. To him, then, the black soldiers had behaved honorably—especially when they sought revenge against those who had attacked them. Perhaps more significantly, a white man believed that African Americans even had honor to defend.

The contrasting account offered by the *Lexington Observer and Reporter* placed in sharp relief conservatives' attitude concerning race and the right to commit violence. In the newspaper account primary responsibility for the violence lay with the black soldiers, not with Mr. Moore. In addition, the newspaper represents the black soldiers' conduct as both dishonorable and dangerous. First, the newspaper claimed that of the four black soldiers "promenading in a careless manner," only one chose to fight back against the marshal when told to return to the black section of the fairground. Like the prototypical "bad slave" who negatively influences or "demoralizes" his fellow slaves, the instigator, out of "stubbornness," set the bad example, and the remaining blacks followed along. Second, without any reference to the white attacks against African Americans at the fairgrounds, the article plays up the decision of blacks to return with arms and reinforcements. It claims that the black soldiers and their compatriots planned to "shoot every white person they saw." The utter incompetence and timidity of the blacks, however, convinced them to halt their offensive and shoot "promiscuously" at random targets, killing only a black woman. The newspaper account thus portrayed the black soldiers as cowards who illegitimately claimed access to the right of organized violence. To conservatives, then, blacks were not respectable soldiers capable of keeping order. Rather, they formed a degraded mob hell-bent on race war and anarchy.

Not all white violence against newly freed African Americans in central Missouri and Kentucky targeted black soldiers or their families. As the Union army mustered black troops out of the service by late 1865, the immediate threat of a black military to white sensibilities died down. The general level of violence against blacks continued apace, however, and in some parts of the Bluegrass and Little Dixie increased in ferocity. New white paramilitary organizations, known as the "Regulators," emerged in late 1865 and committed hundreds of acts of violence, from arson to lynching. The stated purpose of the Regulator campaign was to restore order where former slaves had resorted to acts of theft and murder. The superintendent of the Lexington subdistrict of the Freedman's Bureau reported a "regular organized mob known as Negro Regulators who go about through these counties at night in disguises, beating and abusing these people in a most shocking manner."[68] In 1866 in Lebanon, Kentucky, site of the earlier mutilation of the black recruits, a gang of thirty Regulators, under the leadership of Captain Skaggs, attacked a black grocer named Edward Tucker and a black restaurant owner named Allen Drake. They also ransacked the homes of Tucker, Drake, and seven other black families in the area, and they "broke down doors, tore down chimneys, unroofed houses, shot at men and women, and scattered in every direction the papers and books of the Rev. Wm. Miles, a Methodist colored minister, who was absent from home."[69] A radical newspaper in central Kentucky noted that Skaggs's Men had targeted Drake and Tucker before this incident as well and that all of the victims were "the most quiet and industrious colored men in our county."[70] It is likely that men like Drake and Tucker were targeted precisely because they were relatively successful and served as an inspiration for African Americans seeking autonomy and the right to own land.

Some violence appeared to target blacks who refused to acknowledge the demands of racial segregation and restriction from white public spaces. In Versailles, Kentucky, Captain Campbell of the Shelton House violently ejected a black man who had "cooly sat at the table and ordered supper."[71] For this action, the conservative newspaper reported, "Cuffee receive[d] a pretty severe drubbing, and afterward [was] lodged in the jail for disorderly conduct." Before 1865 white Kentuckians had long restricted free blacks' access to public spaces. In the years after the war white businessmen maintained the right to exclude any patron whom they deemed "offensive"; violation of segregationist custom met swift violence in response.

Foreshadowing the major lynching epidemic in the late nineteenth century, many whites justified racial violence by appealing to the protection of white womanhood.[72] In Paris, Kentucky, a mob lynched a black man named Burt for raping and murdering an Irishwoman named Millie Dolan.[73] The staunchly conservative *True Kentuckian* mocked a visiting "abolitionist" who dared to question the propriety of lynching in an argument with an Irish waitress named Maggie Short. After the visitor claimed Short should be tarred and feathered for defending lynching, Short rounded up a collection of "ladies and gentlemen" and threatened the man with a stick. Short accused the visitor of being "no better than the negro" and chased him out of the town. Here an Irishwoman rose in defense of the honor of her countrywoman allegedly "outraged" by a black man. Indeed, community violence in defense of white womanhood was not restricted to men.

In some cases whites killed black people for no apparent reason. After consuming several bottles of liquor, three brothers named Elson entered

Miami, Missouri, and announced to all present that they planned to "kill a nigger."[74] Shortly afterward, they shot a black man randomly. After the black man ran into a hotel for protection, the brothers shot at the white hotelkeeper. Perhaps because of the second transgression—attempting to murder a prominent white businessman—a white mob retaliated and shot the Elson brothers. Even though they were drunk, the Elsons apparently felt they could murder at will any African American they chose. The random nature of the attacks undoubtedly contributed to a generalized fear among the black community in central Missouri. But neither of the two published accounts of the incident suggest any community outrage at the attempted murder of the black man.[75]

The conservative press that emerged after the war, including the *Lexington Gazette,* offered insight regarding the epidemic of racial violence. These newspapers characterized the great political struggle of postwar Kentucky and Missouri as a struggle over the survival of white supremacy in an age of emancipation. Editors from longtime Unionist papers such as the *Missouri Telegraph, Paris Western Citizen,* and the *Lexington Observer and Reporter* made common cause with former rebel sympathizers (and formal rebel soldiers in some cases) who produced such popular Democratic Party papers as the *Danville Advocate, Paris True Kentuckian,* and perhaps the most virulently white supremacist newspaper of all, the *Lexington (Mo.) Caucasian,* formed in late 1865. Former Whigs and supporters of the Constitutional Union Party of John Bell joined forces with stalwart Democrats to defend President Andrew Johnson's conservative vision of Reconstruction, including his rejection of the Civil Rights Bill, the Freedmen's Bureau Bill, and the congressional Reconstruction bills advanced by Radical Republicans. All of these newspaper editors vehemently opposed black soldier enlistment during the war and continued their rejection of the radical course of the Union cause long after the war's conclusion.[76]

Establishing itself as the preeminent white supremacist newspaper in the West, the *Lexington Caucasian* unified political protest against radical claims of racial equality. Billing itself as the largest newspaper west of St. Louis, the *Caucasian* affirmed, "We are Caucasian in blood, in birth, and in prejudice, and do not expect to labor to place above us in the scale of civilization, in morality, in usefulness, in religion, in the arts and sciences, in mechanics either the Mongolian, the Indian or the Negro."[77] The *Caucasian* consistently argued for the rights of former rebels within Missouri who were disfranchised by the new radical regime. But as the *Caucasian* duly noted, the more pressing concern for conservatives of all prior loyalties was the status of African Americans in border state society. "Today the question is whether these liberated slaves shall be enfranchised—made the equals of the Caucasian. Radicals say they shall. Conservative Union men say they shall not."[78] For former rebels such as the editor of the *Caucasian,* the threat of racial—or "social"—equality united all white conservatives, regardless of past loyalties. Although the *Caucasian* never explicitly advocated violence against African Americans, its harsh editorials in opposition to the rights of former slaves gave voice to conservatives who, up to that point, had expressed their opinions under the cover of night, in disguise, and with arms.[79]

The *Caucasian* did, however, routinely describe black soldiers in dishonorable terms. Citing a story in Hermann, Missouri, in which an anti-Radical school board voted to eject all black students from the town's schools, the *Caucasian* sarcastically titled the article, "And the Colored Troops Fought Nobly."[80] Hermann, the heart of central Missouri's burgeoning German immigrant population, proved to be one of Missouri's most steadfast Unionist strongholds, and it continued to support the Radical Republican Party for the first few years after the war. Citing, approvingly, the conservative drift in Radical Hermann, the *Caucasian* mocked the "myth" of noble black soldiers often employed by radicals to justify black education and other civil rights for former slaves.[81] The *Caucasian's* disparagement of black troops' honor was especially important because, as elsewhere in the South, Missourians associated honor with the right to self-defense and the ability to wield that right to protect one's social standing. Under the slave system white men "defended" their honor in myriad ways, including duels, militia participation, and the public demonstration of authority over slaves.[82] As black men entered the military service during the Civil War, they, too, associated military prowess and fearlessness with public honor. For most border state whites only those willing to defend their honor with violence deserved the rights of citizenship. By mocking black military service, the *Caucasian* did more than express disapproval for racially integrated schooling in Hermann or elsewhere. It directly attacked African Americans' claims to equal citizenship in a biracial republic.

In many ways the Regulator campaigns of the late 1860s that afflicted black men and women across central Kentucky and Missouri resembled the lynch mobs that terrorized communities across the South in the 1890s and early 1900s. But the social and political context for Regulator violence differed from the great lynching wave of the turn of the twentieth century.

Whereas latter-day lynching apologists such as South Carolina's Ben Tillman and Mississippi's James Vardaman cited the generation growing up after slavery as insufficiently respectful of white authority, white border state supporters of racial violence in the 1860s viewed the revolutionary changes *within* the last generation of slaves as particularly threatening. In particular, white conservatives identified the disturbing potential of armed former slaves for upending social relations. Even as former slaves mustered out of the army, whites feared that freedmen and women would summarily reject the long-standing social mores and customs that held central Kentucky and Missouri together. Although the threat of political "negro domination" was a needless and chimerical fear in the border states, as it was not in the Deep South, where blacks outnumbered whites, the critical role that African Americans played in emancipating themselves revealed uncomfortable possibilities for whites accustomed to unchallenged rule.[83] The use of extralegal violence, employed with "solemnity" by organized white mobs, helped fend off the revolutionary challenge of an armed, assertive black citizenry.[84]

The epidemic of racial violence afflicted the central Kentucky countryside more than in central Missouri for a number of reasons. First, the Radical Republican state government in Jefferson City effectively deployed militia throughout the Little Dixie region, preventing the growth of large, organized white supremacist groups such as the Regulators. Second, what violent response there was targeted the officers of the Radical government and the symbols of the new Radical-driven economy; the infamous James-Younger gang of former rebels that prowled the towns of central and western Missouri attacked white employees of the armored express companies and the Radical county government officials much more often than they did freed African Americans. Third, the violence against African Americans *during* Missouri's guerrilla war forced a significant portion of the black population to flee to St. Louis or Kansas even before the war's end. And fourth, because of the existence of a large white Unionist militia in Missouri, black soldiers formed a small minority of the overall Union army there. In Kentucky, by contrast, where no special white Union militia (beyond ad hoc "Home Guards") patrolled the towns and countryside, black soldiers staffed the Union army in greater proportion.[85] Correspondingly, the fears—and violence—associated with a black soldiery ran higher in Kentucky than in its western neighbor.

A cumulative effect of this ongoing racial violence was the permanent emigration of African Americans from the border countryside. The black population in Little Dixie and the Bluegrass dropped considerably between 1860 and 1870. Overall Kentucky and Missouri were the only states—Confederate or Union—to witness a decline in their black populations during this ten-year period.[86] By 1870 the black population of Kentucky had dropped by 6 percent from its 1860 total, while Missouri's black population dropped by a smaller margin. Within the Bluegrass and Little Dixie the black population declined even more. In eight Bluegrass counties the black population fell from 42,033 to 40,190, or by 7 percent.[87] Yet if Fayette County, home of the burgeoning city of Lexington, is removed, the black population dropped by 10 percent. Thus, many African Americans in the surrounding Bluegrass countryside emigrated either to the urban safety of Lexington or to a different region altogether. In Missouri the story is even more dramatic. Of seven Little Dixie counties along the Missouri River, where the black population traditionally clustered, the number of African Americans dropped by 19 percent. Lafayette County, home of the *Weekly Caucasian*, witnessed the greatest decline, at 37 percent. As in Kentucky, however, not all African Americans left the state altogether. The two largest cities in the state—St. Louis and the newly developing Kansas City—experienced a significant growth in black population between 1860 and 1870 (325 and 30 percent, respectively).[88] Black populations in states and counties immediately outside Kentucky and Missouri grew exponentially as well, with Kansas growing from 625 African Americans in 1860 to 17,108 in 1870. Ohio River counties, from Cincinnati's Hamilton County to sparsely populated Switzerland County, Indiana, likewise experienced major increases in black population between 1860 and 1870.

Not all black migration from the border countryside was driven by racial violence. Indeed, a significant number of black migrants escaped bondage during the war in order to enlist in Union army regiments in Indiana, Kansas, and Ohio. Nevertheless, it is significant that so few of these migrants moved back to their homes in the border countryside after the war ended; African Americans across the North returned to states in the former Confederacy in order to reconnect families and communities torn apart by slavery, especially as the immediate prospects of Radical Reconstruction portended a better life.[89] But somehow life in postwar central Kentucky and Missouri proved uninviting for African Americans. The epidemic of racial violence played a central part in keeping blacks away, and the benefits of Radical Reconstruction became more elusive or even unobtainable for most African Americans.

The enlistment of African Americans into the Union army shook the social and political world of the border states like no other event before it.

Although white radicals, both within and outside Kentucky and Missouri, played a critical role in reshaping the Union cause into a war for emancipation, it was the slaves themselves who most dramatically altered the conflict within the border states. From the beginning of hostilities in 1861 the Lincoln administration yielded to the social and political demands of conservative whites in Kentucky and Missouri. The Emancipation Proclamation never applied to the border states, and the enrollment of African Americans into the Union army was postponed there until manpower requirements rendered further delay impossible. But once the Union army lifted final restrictions against black enlistments, the rush of slaves off the farms of Little Dixie and the Bluegrass stunned white conservatives and Union military officials alike. Sporadic violence against enlistees hardly stemmed the tide of black men—and often black women as well—who "stampeded" into the army of liberation. Liberated slaves with guns now manned posts in communities where slavery still legally existed. The new social order patrolled by armed African Americans rested upon a revolutionary biracial conception of the body politic. Blacks declared themselves equal citizens of the biracial republic, having served with honor on the battlefield.

By directly asserting martial rights of citizenship, African Americans in Kentucky and Missouri undermined the hegemonic conservative Unionist order once and for all. No longer could white conservatives argue that the Union cause was merely a struggle to preserve the antebellum status quo. More important, conservatives could no longer maintain the illusion that whites possessed a monopoly on political power at the grassroots level. The effects of black enlistment were immediate and multidimensional. A flood of violence targeting black soldiers and their families revealed the gravity of the former slave population's challenge to the white conception of citizenship. For border state whites the revolution brought on by emancipation and especially by the enlistment of former slaves in the Union army signaled a coming reign of terror. If not the great race war of Saint-Domingue, the newly armed black citizenry would at least usher in the rule of what the *Caucasian* termed "the Jacobin Party."[90] In a war hijacked by radicals bent on social revolution, the use of violence could help conservatives restore the long-held prerogatives of white supremacy. Whether bushwhackers in the late-war central Missouri countryside vowing to return slave runaways to their "rightful" owners or Regulators prowling the black districts of Danville, Lebanon, and Lexington in postwar central Kentucky, extralegal mobs asserted the right to maintain a racial order based on black deference and subservience to whites in all facets of social, cultural, and economic life.[91] Regulators even established a mock "court" of "Judge Lynch" wherein they published their "official proceedings" in the Kentucky newspapers.[92] With the civil law weakened under the yoke of the Freedmen's Bureau, Regulators arrogated to themselves the legitimate right to exact community vengeance upon social, and especially racial, transgressors.[93]

The Union cause that many border state whites had long espoused had by the end of the war fulfilled Confederate prophecy. Whites across Kentucky and Missouri who had once rallied to the Union standard in 1861 precisely because it promised to respect slavery now found their cause usurped by their own slaves. The rumblings of discontent threatened to sever the Union cause in the latter years of the Civil War, as popular officers such as Colonel Wolford demanded the right of Kentuckians to resist black enlistment by any means necessary. After April 1865 many conservative Unionists joined their former Confederate foes and attacked the most salient symbols of the Civil War's social revolution—black soldiers and their families. In doing so, the conservative white masses of central Kentucky and central Missouri found redemption in their new capacity as the conscience, arbiter, and ambassadors of the South. By the end of 1866 conservative whites in the border states had completed their own transformation from staunch Unionists to belated Confederates.

CHAPTER 7

THE PERILS AND PROMISE OF
SELF-RECONSTRUCTION

Gibeon Doram wrote to General Clinton Fisk just months after Lee's surrender at Appomattox, "I deem it my dewty to inform you the undertakings of the coloured people of danville Ky we have a school of about fifty pupils supported by our Selves the same is progressing finely."[1] Doram proudly refused aid from the government, offering not only to educate the former slave population of Boyle County but also to provide "aid in secureing for such persons as are thrown out employment homes . . . will and do look after children and wifes whose husbands are dead and in the army &c"[2] With private aid and assistance from the likes of white Kentucky abolitionist John Fee, Doram hoped to build more schools in the community and even establish a "boyle co. aid society," run by whites and "especially colored." With Fee's help Doram expected that blacks and sympathetic whites could build schools for African Americans throughout Kentucky at "little expence to the government."[3] More important, Doram imagined that construction of black schools—by African Americans—would play an early and integral role in the development of a powerful black political culture in the Bluegrass.

The Politics of Black Education

Doram's dream became a reality two years later, as schools for African Americans proliferated across the Bluegrass region of Kentucky. In Danville and nearby Harrodsburg the local Freedmen's Bureau agent reported, "Freedmens' Schools as at present organized are as good as they can be made. All the children are enabled to attend school and appear to improve rapidly in their studies."[4] In most cases funding for black schools came entirely from the black community. In Danville a Freedmen's Bureau agent guessed that the black population could contribute as much as one thousand dollars toward the construction of schools in 1868; the agent determined this amount after attending a meeting of the town's black elite.[5] At Nicholasville, Paris, and Versailles new schools opened to serve African American children in the towns and the surrounding countryside.[6] Regular Freedmen's Bureau reports suggest that the schools thrived, even though most whites vehemently disapproved of them.

As Doram's letter suggests, schools for African Americans appeared shortly after emancipation in Kentucky and, in many cases, before final emancipation. By October 1865 five black schools were built in Lexington, all paid for entirely by the black community.[7] As early as May 1865, a white woman just outside of Lexington noted: "Negro schools are already in operation here. I don't know who teaches it nor where it is at but I see the negroes going to and fro with their spelling books in their hands. I heard of one negro *lady* who spoke of sending her children to Louisville thinking that the schools there were better than here."[8] Some radical whites helped with the overall school construction effort. Even before the war ended, for example, white abolitionist John Fee established schools for black soldiers and eventually other black families at Camp Nelson in Jessamine County.[9] The Camp Nelson School for Colored Soldiers, established in July 1864, eventually taught seven hundred students. What was remarkable about these early Kentucky schools was that slavery remained legal and in force until December 1865. Thus, freedmen and women had begun to construct schools and prepare their children for lives as educated citizens even as white Kentuckians continued to enforce the slave code.

After final emancipation in December 1865, the Kentucky legislature passed a law that ostensibly provided for black schooling. The February 1866 law created a separate "Negro fund," half of which was to be used for black paupers and the remainder for black schools.[10] In reality, however, the law provided virtually no funding for black schools and was eventually replaced by an 1867 law that decentralized black schooling to the counties, all of the white leaders of which had expressed no interest in black education.[11] By the late 1860s Kentucky's African American population remained subject to various forms of special taxation, including a two-dollar-per-head "capitation tax." Yet whites refused to expend any of the state's black tax dollars on black education. After 1867 black Kentuckians placed equal education and fair taxation at the center of their political agenda. But with the state dragging its feet and counties refusing even modest spending on black schools, African Americans turned to the Freedmen's Bureau for assistance in constructing and operating schools.

In the fall of 1866 the Freedmen's Bureau conducted a survey of the Bluegrass region to determine "where it is practicable and desirable to establish schools."[12] Although African Americans took the lead role in financing, constructing, and teaching the new schools, the Freedmen's Bureau played an important part in organizing them, especially in more rural settings or in places where the black population had recently migrated. The bureau issued a directive stipulating the sort of information needed before supporting construction of a school, including the number of likely pupils, the availability and condition of schoolrooms, the prospects for finding teachers, and the attitudes of the white community toward black schooling.[13] In the years following this directive, schools multiplied across the Bluegrass, in many cases following the guidelines laid out by the bureau. In large towns such as Danville, smaller villages such as Hustonville and Crab Orchard, and rural sections where a still-scattered black population toiled on small farms, African Americans and the Freedmen's Bureau constructed schools.[14] By the end of 1868, 577 pupils attended schools throughout the Lexington Sub-District of the Freedmen's Bureau, including a new night school in Lexington that served 69 students.[15] Students unable to pay for admission received free "tickets" from the bureau to attend school.[16]

The bureau sought placement of local African Americans in normal schools or at the biracial college at Berea in order to create a corps of black teachers. In March 1868 Danville's "leading colored citizens" convened a meeting to encourage local black parents to send their children to schools and to urge black men and women to attend Oberlin College or any other normal school so they could become teachers in the community.[17] Danville's bureau agent, H. G. Thomas, underscored the importance of a normal school–educated black teaching force: "Twenty really well-educated colored people will do more for the cause of education than two hundred" limited by the training in "ordinary colored schools."[18] The black citizens at the meeting also hoped that freedmen would dedicate physical labor toward the construction of schools; they cited a carpenter who had agreed to build a school in Lebanon and assumed others would soon follow.[19] At an April meeting of the "colored men of Danville" the congregants agreed to raise one thousand dollars for the construction of a new schoolhouse and requested information regarding bureau policy on the title to the new school. In a sign that grassroots black organizations planned to assume the initiative in school construction in the future, the meeting's leaders offered to raise money for schools and school lots and sought clarification of bureau protocol *after* local people had raised the money.[20]

The Freedmen's Bureau never intended to establish a permanent presence in Kentucky, and few African Americans or white radicals had any illusion that the bureau would remain indefinitely. Nevertheless, when the Freedmen's Bureau hinted that it would vacate central Kentucky in the late 1860s, local African Americans and bureau agents feared the worst. In July 1868 bureau agent H. G. Thomas predicted, "If the Bureau ceases to exist in Ky July 15 by August 1st one half my schools will have ceased to exist."[21] The most vulnerable schools were those in the smaller hamlets and in the countryside; Thomas believed that the schools in Danville and Lexington would be the only ones to survive without bureau financial support and military protection.

To make up for the loss of institutional support, some black educators and supporters of the schools directly appealed to the local white population. In a letter written to the deeply conservative *Kentucky Gazette*, trustees of black schools in Lexington noted that there was only one schoolhouse in the city for thirteen hundred schoolchildren. The trustees hoped to construct or procure another building but admitted, "We are very poor and not able to do it ourselves."[22] The trustees hoped "our white friends" would provide some of the four thousand dollars necessary to build the school. And following the advice of the "white friends" of the schools, the trustees then hoped that "our white citizens" would assist with purchasing a lot and building through further small contributions.[23] This appeal is especially noteworthy considering the *Gazette*'s dubious opinion of black education. Indeed, later that year the newspaper blasted a plan for large-scale black school construction in Lexington: "It is nonsense to be teaching this class the accomplishments of scholastic education when their utmost need is food and raiment. We should like to know what an educated darkey would find to do, be his attainments in that line never so remarkable, while all who know how to work are greatly in demand . . . Teach the negroes to work and keep them at it, and this is the best education they can have."[24] Most likely, the *Gazette*'s readers shared the editor's disdain for black scholarship. Yet the trustees of the city's black school insisted on appealing to this readership regardless, which may be a sign of desperation or a belief that the readers held more enlightened opinions than the editor. By 1870 Kentucky's black schools remained vastly underfunded, though they survived thanks to the

tireless efforts of black laborers and professionals who raised their own
money to build and teach in the new schools.

In Missouri black education received more institutional support than
in Kentucky. Although the Freedmen's Bureau established only a marginal
presence in Missouri, the state's government provided the legal framework
for black education in 1865. Like Kentucky, Missouri barely maintained a
semblance of a public school system in the antebellum era, and it forbade
African Americans from attending school. The new 1865 Constitution,
however, encouraged counties and townships to create schools for African
Americans and, at least in law, equalized funding for these schools.[25] The
first General Assembly meeting under the 1865 Constitution required townships to provide schools for African Americans and placed black schools under the same school boards that controlled white schools.[26] The new school
law made exceptions for districts with fewer than twenty black children. In
those cases local school boards were required to reserve the school fund and
determine an appropriate means of educating the district's black children.[27]

Yet local school boards and townships, especially in Little Dixie, refused
to apply the new black school law and left the black population bereft of
its legally mandated public education. To get around the law, many local
school boards failed to enumerate black children in the school census.[28] So
effective was this act of subterfuge that of the thirty-four black schools in
existence in 1866, only two were in the more heavily African American Little
Dixie region, where "the southern element predominated."[29] The state law
provided no enforcement mechanism for the school law or for the enumera-
tion statute.[30] Nevertheless, as table 7.1 illustrates, the number of African
American children attending public schools in Missouri, and the number of
schools available, grew considerably in the years following the Civil War.

TABLE 7.1. Black School Attendance in Missouri, 1866–1871

Year	Black Children Enumerated in Census	Black Students Attending School	Number of Black Schools
1866	19,910	N/A	34
1867	33,619	N/A	56
1869	34,000	6,240	59
1870	N/A	9,080	114
1871	37,173	N/A	212

Source: Henry Sullivan Williams, "The Development of the Negro Public School System in Missouri," *Journal of
Negro History* 5, no. 2 (April 1920): 142.

Clearly, then, African Americans in Missouri placed a special emphasis on educating their children in the post–Civil War years. With the radical state government doing little to follow through on its commitment to black education, outside organizations such as the Freedmen's Bureau and the American Missionary Association (AMA) pressured local school boards into building black schools and in some cases constructing schools themselves.[31] The bureau's disbursement officer in Missouri hired a black Missourian named James Milton Turner to investigate the districts and townships that had neglected their legal obligations. Turner immediately headed for the hornet's nest of antiblack education sentiment—Little Dixie—and personally stewarded the creation of black schools in the region.

James Milton Turner grew up a slave in St. Louis and received a clandestine education from a local black minister. Turner's father successfully manumitted the entire family, and James attended school at Oberlin College before the war. Following the Civil War, James Milton Turner worked as a teacher in Kansas City before settling in Boonville in Cooper County. As historian Gary Kremer suggests, Turner's work as a teacher in the immediate postwar years, his tireless support of black education, and his service in the pro-suffrage Missouri Equal Rights League made him a perfect advocate for black school construction in the more hostile portions of the state, especially Little Dixie.[32] After visiting the new Lincoln Institute in Jefferson City, funded by soldiers of the Sixty-second and Sixty-fifth Colored infantries, Turner consulted state superintendent and Radical Republican Thomas A. Parker about investigating school conditions in Little Dixie.

Traveling from town to town in central Missouri, Turner discovered the intensity of white opposition to black education. As an agent of the state superintendent, he sought to enforce compliance with the state education law and in several cases successfully convinced hostile local school board officials to provide adequate schools for African Americans. In Fulton, for example, Turner confronted the county superintendent regarding the poor quality of teachers assigned to black schools. To rectify this problem, Turner insisted that the superintendent, Thomas Russell, hire more black teachers who were motivated to teach black students. Russell demurred, refusing to consider hiring any "colored person as teacher."[33] It is unclear if Russell ever changed his hiring policy, but the presence of a black Missourian at his office undoubtedly shocked the sensibilities of other white conservatives.[34] Turner found more success in Cooper County, where he accused a board member in Otterville of refusing to build a school for black children even though the population of eligible students exceeded twenty and the money for such a school was available. The board member, A. M. Gibbs, relented and offered to build a school as long as Turner could provide a teacher. To this end Turner enlisted the support of Charles H. Howard, American Missionary Association western district secretary and brother of Freedmen's Bureau head, Oliver O. Howard, to provide teachers for black students in Missouri.[35] Turner continued to travel to small towns throughout Little Dixie, pressuring school board members and superintendents into complying with the state's black school law. In some cases, such as at Arrow Rock in Saline County, Turner solicited the direct support of the black community, whom he encouraged to "tease" the board spokesmen "until he gives them a school that he may be rid of them."[36] Sensing the need for more black teachers, Turner pressured the state government into providing funds for a normal school at Lincoln Institute in Jefferson City. In 1870 the state government passed a law providing five thousand dollars annually to the Lincoln Institute, stipulating that the school apply the money toward training black teachers.[37]

In many ways the grassroots struggle to obtain equal access to education generated as much political value for African Americans in Kentucky and Missouri as the schools themselves. The education movement also revealed disagreements within the black community regarding the goals of the post-emancipation black population, the tone of political engagement, and the extent of activism necessary to secure basic rights. Even as Turner served as a chief advocate for civil and political rights for Missouri's African Americans, many blacks resented Turner's eagerness to bring in white AMA teachers.[38] Although Turner and his wife lived in Boonville for over a year, the local radical newspaper, the *Boonville Eagle,* commented, "In this community, where he is well-known, the colored people have no use for him."[39] Gary Kremer cites Turner's "paternalism," distrust of blacks' ability to "take care of themselves," and Turner's "middle class values of white Christian America" as the cause of black distrust in him, even though Turner himself served as a teacher in Little Dixie, and he generally advocated the hiring of black teachers.[40] Undoubtedly, these factors help explain the disconnect between James Milton Turner and the grassroots black community of central Missouri. But this division should hardly be surprising given Turner's prewar experience both as an educated, manumitted slave and a resident of relatively cosmopolitan St. Louis. Perhaps more telling were the competing conceptions of citizenship and freedom between Turner, the outsider accustomed to hobnobbing with the state's Radical elite, and the rank-and-file black population, whose members saw little meaningful benefit to white Radical rule. For the state's black population white Radicalism delivered no economic gains, demonstrated bad faith toward black education, and continually refused to provide suffrage rights for African Americans. White Radical rule may have prevented some of the worst abuses of the sort that ensued in postwar Kentucky, but that comparison was of little consolation when black Missourians could look to the Deep South and see African Americans assuming real leadership positions in government and society.

In Kentucky the divisions within black political circles revealed themselves only months after final emancipation. In March 1866 African Americans met in a convention in Lexington, among other things, to pressure the state into providing more funding for black schools. The preamble to the resolutions passed at the convention stated, "Education, wealth and character are essential to the elevation of any people." The convention resolved to "labor to the utmost of our poor ability to infuse into the minds of our Colored Fellow Citizens, the desire to educate themselves and their children."[41] But more interesting than the resolutions themselves were the deliberations over one of the clauses. The final draft declared: "Resolved, That while we claim each and every right and power guaranteed to any and all other American Citizens, including even that of suffrage, as naturally and legally belonging to us, to day, *waiving for the time being, the ballot box and the doctrine of equality before the law,* we ask the opportunity, we demand the privilege of achieving for ourselves and our children, under the regulation of impartial State and Federal law, the blessings which pertain to a well ordered and dignified life."[42]

Others at the convention offered an amended version, striking out the italicized portion and the word *while* from the resolution. In a "considerable discussion" over the proposed amendment, all of the delegates from the Bluegrass region opposed the change to the resolution, preferring the more conservative original version.[43] Dennis Doram of Danville denounced the amendment, claiming "it was calculated to incense the people amongst whom we live, and will be productive of ill feeling."[44] Horace Morris of Louisville castigated the amendment as "mischievous and calculated to do harm; we live amongst the southern people and it will not do for us to put anything on paper that will have a bad effect." Morris continued: "Gentlemen be practical. This may not hurt you or me individually living in great cities, but it will do incalculable harm in the back counties. We must act for the public good."[45] Those living in the "back counties" of the outer Bluegrass—such as Garrard, Boyle, Jessamine, and Mercer—understood the risks to which Morris referred.

The Thirteenth Amendment had abolished slavery only three months earlier, and in many of those back counties former slaves still toiled on their former masters' farms in a state of virtual bondage.

Nevertheless, the proponents of the amendment insisted that black Kentuckians should demand the rights to the ballot box and equality under the law at that juncture. J. H. Campbell of Covington in northern Kentucky remarked, "This Convention could not have been treated better in any part of the country than it has been here in Lexington, by the whites; this is the first Colored Convention ever held in the State; if they act so well are we not induced to demand our rights?"[46] Interestingly, Campbell's pro-amendment position—the only such quote listed at length in the *Proceedings* of the convention—did not tie the more radical position to necessity or honor. Rather, Campbell and other proponents of the amendment felt that the conservatives had overestimated the hostility of white Kentuckians to the cause of racial equality. Because white Kentuckians had been gracious enough to allow the first black convention to meet, unharassed, within the confines of Lexington, Campbell assumed that white community sentiment approved of the longer-term objectives of the delegates to the convention. But Campbell was completely wrong in his assessment of white Bluegrass attitudes, and it begs the question of how a black resident of the state could be so naive. The only explanation for Campbell's statement is that he accepted the age-old dogma of border South moderation and assumed that the conservative Unionist mentality would continue into the postwar era.[47] Those living far away from heavily Republican Cincinnati—and especially within the Bluegrass—had few illusions about the attitudes of whites toward black claims to equal citizenship.

The amendment was defeated by a vote of twenty-three to sixteen, suggesting that a sizable percentage of the delegates supported the more radical position. Considering that most of the pro-amendment advocates identified in the *Proceedings* lived in places such as Kenton County, just across the Ohio River from Cincinnati, it is likely that the other amendment supporters also lived in regions with smaller black populations where they felt their presence proved less menacing to whites.

The Politics of Black Testimony

Access to education was a critical component in the construction of a black citizenry, both in the border states and in the nation as a whole. As the 1866 convention in Lexington demonstrated, education was an early goal of the state's black elite. And with the victory of conservatives within Lexington's convention, Kentucky's African American leadership refused to press for full civil or suffrage rights so soon after emancipation. But Kentucky's denial of African Americans the right to testify in court did more than remind blacks that they were far from equal citizens. It rendered them legally powerless against the gangs of white mobs terrorizing black communities throughout central Kentucky. Although the Lexington convention did not specifically cite the testimony issue, subsequent meetings made it the highest priority within the state.

Kentucky's refusal to allow black testimony played a central role in the Freedmen's Bureau's presence in the state. Just after ratification of the Thirteenth Amendment in December 1865, Clinton B. Fisk, commissioner for the District of Tennessee, issued a circular declaring the bureau in force in Kentucky. The bureau established courts in the state to adjudicate all cases involving blacks and whites. Governor Bramlette responded to the bureau's circular by calling on the state legislature to repeal Kentucky's slave code and allow blacks to testify against whites in court. But the legislature balked at Bramlette's request, passing instead a more conservative "Civil Rights" act that allowed blacks to bring charges for prosecution against whites but prohibited them from serving as witnesses, even when a white person had committed a crime against them.[48] Only the Freedmen's Bureau, empowered by the Federal Civil Rights Act and a new bureau authorization act passed over President Johnson's veto, could provide any semblance of justice for African Americans left completely helpless by Kentucky's state law. Kentucky state courts curtailed the authority of the new bureau courts whenever possible.

Lawsuits challenging the constitutionality of bureau courts when civil courts were otherwise present succeeded in driving the bureau courts out of the state.[49] In one such case in Lexington a white man beat a black man with a gun while returning to town. According to the victim, William Roberts, the white perpetrator, named Thomas Outten, told Roberts: "I have got to shoot a parcel of you God damned niggers running about all night. They have shot old Lincoln and I am going to kill about half of you damned niggers."[50] Based on Roberts's testimony, Outten was convicted by the federal judge advocate general (JAG) and fined ten dollars. Outten's attorney appealed, declaring that the JAG had no jurisdiction in Kentucky because the civil courts still functioned; an 1866 United States Supreme Court ruling in the *Ex Parte Milligan* case declared all military tribunals unconstitutional so long as a functioning civil court system existed. In accordance with this ruling, the federal district court in Kentucky declared that *Milligan* prohibited the use of bureau courts in the state and that state courts remained in effect. After Outten's successful appeal under the *Milligan* ruling, blacks could only testify in federal district court subject to the federal Civil Rights Act and in the state court of Fayette County under Republican judge William C. Goodloe.[51]

With Freedmen's Bureau military tribunals outlawed, the bureau helped remove cases from the state courts to the federal courts but only after state courts had refused to hear black testimony. Bureau commissioner Fisk initiated this policy after a highly publicized case involving a white man named James Poore, who had shot and killed a black man named Peter Branford in Boyle County in 1866. While awaiting civil trial, Judge Goodloe ordered Poore to be arrested and placed in Camp Nelson for military trial.[52] After widespread outrage and near unanimous passage of a resolution in the Kentucky legislature condemning Fisk and Goodloe, Fisk ordered that Poore be released to civil authorities and rearrested if the black witness's testimony was refused.[53] "Let this be the rule in similar cases," Fisk informed the local bureau agent in Danville.[54] Knowing that the only witness available was an African American, Governor Bramlette pardoned Poore without a civil trial.[55] The whole affair completely soured Fisk and the bureau on the willingness of the state to budge on the testimony question. After 1867 Fisk instructed bureau agents to help hundreds of African Americans try cases against whites in federal courts and to initiate indictments against state judges for refusing to adhere to the Civil Rights Act. The continued presence of federal authority in a "loyal" state applied pressure on Kentucky's ruling Democrats to give in. Although some Democrats—including former Confederates such as W.C.P. Breckinridge of Fayette County and J. Warren Grigsby of Boyle County—and many Democratic newspapers supported allowing black testimony, conservatives prevailed. The state legislature refused to alter its law in 1867 and then again in 1869. The federal-state crisis empowered the more hawkish conservative Democrats for the time being.

African Americans, locked out of the electoral process, under constant assault from violent bands of Regulators and denied basic rights under state law and an overburdened federal judiciary, took action to change public opinion and eventually state law. Once the federal courts reaffirmed the constitutionality of the Civil Rights Act of 1866, African Americans in Kentucky orchestrated a mass movement to pressure the state's legislators into allowing black testimony. One component of this mass movement was the proliferation of secret societies devoted to equal civil and political rights. Without direct evidence from the societies themselves, commentary from antagonists reveals the real depth of these organizations in black Kentucky. A writer from Clark County, just east of Lexington, complained, "In our own community the Sons of Ham are most numerous, we learn, and have frequent and regular meetings for the transaction of business, whose nature we cannot find out."[56] The agenda of this society was to "consult about the best means of obtaining the right to testify and vote in Kentucky, and to look to the interests of the race in general." The same writer also identified an organization he called the "Benevolence Society," "which is said to be a charitable association, with politics mixed in to give it interest and zest." Almost certainly, the Benevolence Society to which this Clark County writer refers is the Kentucky Benevolence Society established at the Lexington convention in March 1866; there is little indication to suggest, however, that the Benevolence Society conducted its business in secret. Nevertheless, the writer clearly feared the effect of these societies as he compared them to Union Leagues in East Tennessee and elsewhere in the South. And it is likely that all of these societies made black testimony a central issue in their campaigns for civil rights.

Secret societies ultimately played a minor role in the equal testimony movement, yet they made a significant impact on grassroots social relations simply by virtue of their secrecy. In the antebellum border states slaveholdings were typically much smaller than in the Deep South, with no more than two or three slaves in many households. Social relations between whites and blacks were closer, but black solidarity was harder to maintain. Thus, it was comparably easier for whites to keep tabs on the nightly activities of their slaves; in the lower South, where dozens or even hundreds of slaves lived on dense plantations, large black communities created complex internal relationships with which overseers, slave patrollers, and masters had little insight or interaction. When black Kentuckians, once scattered on small farms throughout the countryside, started to meet in secret, whites had little reference point to make sense of these conclaves. Instead, they could only blast these secret meetings for encouraging blacks not to "teach their children all the virtue and morality that they can, be honest, observe their contracts, and manifest a disposition to take an interest in the affairs of their employers."[57] Whites could only ascribe the most nefarious motives to these secret societies because they represented, at a basic social level, a repudiation of interracial rural relationships that had once defined the border South.

Nevertheless, with secret societies largely ineffectual in securing equal testimony and other civil rights, black Kentuckians turned to more public activities such as ad hoc mass meetings, politicized emancipation celebrations, and formal civil rights organizations. Following the March 1866 convention, the Benevolence Society convened regularly, the politics added "for zest" undoubtedly including references to the testimony question. A Colored Methodist Conference met in April 1867 in Lexington in which the speaker urged the audience to push for equal testimony rights.[58] Blacks held mass meetings at Nicholasville, Paris, and other small towns around the Bluegrass calling for equal testimony in the summer of 1867.[59] White bureau officials and judges openly encouraged black efforts to demand equal testimony at events in Lebanon and Lexington.[60] Judge Goodloe spoke to a "large audience" at Lexington in July 1867, informing them: "The law must be changed by your Legislature, and your testimony admitted; otherwise you may be beaten and robbed nightly, nay, to use the language of one of the most prominent members of the Fayette bar not of my political views, your ministers may be shot down every Sabbath in your pulpits, with impunity. I take pleasure in saying to you that every respectable member of the Fayette bar favors this change of the law."[61]

In the fall of 1867 a Colored State Central Committee called a major convention in late November to discuss the testimony question and sought delegates from throughout the state.[62] One group from Clark County in the eastern Bluegrass insisted that the convention "consult about the best means of obtaining the right to testify and vote in Kentucky."[63] Delegates from more than fifty counties met at Lexington, declaring their manifold grievances for a state and nationwide audience.[64] Of the protests against discrimination in public spaces, taxation without representation, and denial of equal testimony rights, it was the final issue that headed the convention's list of grievances. "The want of testimony in the courts leaves our families exposed to the wiles of the dissolute and unprincipled who may approach them with insulting and degrading propositions."[65] The gendered language regarding the exposure of "our families" to the "dissolute" who use "degrading propositions" reflected a conflation of testimonial rights with the dictates of manhood. Black men unable to testify against whites in courts of law were legally incapable of protecting their wives and children from assault by white men. The convention's delegates assumed that a white national—and conservative state—audience steeped in Victorian conceptions of manly honor would gravitate toward the cause of equal testimonial rights if presented in this gendered manner. Also, by casting the testimony question as a moral issue, blacks hoped to convince white Christians that equal testimony would prevent immoral sexual advances against black women.

The protests and petitions from Kentucky's African American population added momentum to a movement among the state's leading Democratic party to grant equal testimonial rights. Some prominent Democratic newspapers such as the *Danville Advocate,* the *Frankfort Yeomen,* the *Lexington Observer and Reporter,* and the *Louisville Courier* came around to the support of equal testimony rights by 1869. Even some key Democratic politicians, including Robert Breckinridge Jr. of Boyle County, supported changing Kentucky's law. Ultimately, threats of federal indictment against state judges who continued to refuse black testimony and the continued presence of the highly unpopular Freedmen's Bureau in the state encouraged the state legislature to grant equal testimony rights in 1872. But it was the statewide black-led movement devoted to the law's alteration from 1865 on that helped consolidate disparate political forces in the state in favor of change.

By the late 1860s African Americans in both Kentucky and Missouri turned toward the struggle for suffrage rights. Although the March 1866 convention in Kentucky asserted the right to vote in the abstract, it was not until the November 1867 Kentucky convention that African Americans statewide mobilized for suffrage. Here the example of black voting in the former Confederacy both inspired and agitated border state blacks, who saw no reason why they should still be restricted from the ballot box. The 1867 convention resolutions drew upon Revolutionary War rhetoric condemning taxation without representation. The initial meeting at the First Colored Methodist Episcopal Church in Lexington that had called for the March 1866 convention noted the "anomalous political condition" of blacks in Kentucky, who would receive no congressional Reconstruction support as in the former Confederate states.[66] Nevertheless, assuming the Kentucky state legislature to be a lost cause, the March convention delegates appealed directly to the United States Congress, "praying the honorable members to secure us the right of suffrage."[67] Meanwhile, during the August 1866 election rumors of impending suffrage rights encouraged the appearance of "flocks of negroes" in Lexington, who "hung like a cloud around the polls, eager and solicitous" for a Republican victory.[68] In 1867 African Americans across Kentucky signed suffrage petitions so the Freedmen's Bureau could deliver them to Congress.[69]

The statewide struggle on behalf of black suffrage as well as equal testimony rights helped organize African Americans in the Bluegrass for the day when the vote finally arrived. But as with the equal testimony movement, black protests for suffrage rights in Kentucky faced long odds. Several obstacles stood in the way, not the least of which was a dominant Democratic Party that viewed black suffrage as nothing short of treason against the white race. The state's Republican Party also rejected black suffrage until 1868, basing its political support among the white Unionists of the eastern mountain counties and along the Ohio River.[70] And the minority status of the state's black population convinced the state's Republican Party that black voters would add little electoral clout in the end; if anything, white Republicans calculated that black suffrage would only alienate potential white Republican voters without a sufficient offset in new black voters. Only the Fifteenth Amendment, ratified in March 1870 against the wishes of the Kentucky legislature, extended voting rights to African Americans in Kentucky.

The Politics of Land and Labor

The struggle for equal testimony rights in Kentucky and educational and suffrage rights in both Kentucky and Missouri involved the entire black population, including numerous mass meetings and Emancipation Day celebrations. Yet the movements on behalf of these projects drew heavily from a select group of elite African Americans. In many ways, then, the battle for civil and political rights was led by the "grasstops" rather than the grassroots.[71] But the economic struggle for autonomy, good wages, and freedom from exploitation was a truly grassroots effort. Ordinary freedpeople altered labor relations on the ground level in ways that grasstop leaders could neither steward nor influence. Yet the political significance of labor struggle was every bit as far-reaching as the fight for civil and political rights.

The politics of labor relations on the small farms in the Bluegrass and Little Dixie underwent a radical shift in the postwar years as freedmen and women sought land of their own or, barring that, the right to work the land without regular interference from a white owner or overseer. Black Kentuckians and Missourians, like their counterparts in the former Confederacy, sought land ownership in the years after the Civil War. A former slave from Mercer County, Kentucky, named Will Oats reported to his Works Progress Administration (WPA) interviewer in the 1930s that his grandmother had "bought a little land and they all lived there" shortly after the war.[72] Another former slave from Bourbon County told her WPA interviewer that her master "gave" her mother a house and 160-acre farm; after the former master died, his son drove the family off the farm.[73] But these cases were unusual, as white intimidation prevented most African Americans from obtaining their land. As a Freedmen's Bureau agent in Lebanon, Kentucky, summarized, "Blacks . . . would love to own farms in the countryside but cannot because of mob violence."[74]

With few opportunities to own land, freedmen and women turned to other labor and land relationships that maximized autonomy, especially renting and sharecropping. A white Fayette County farmer named "Simeon" wrote a lengthy series of articles to the *Kentucky Gazette* that gauged the contours of this new struggle over labor relations. In the first years after slavery freedmen and women refused to work under the direct guidance of their former masters, seeking to rent land instead and farm it without white oversight. As Simeon described: "Some farmers in the bluegrass region have set up cottages on their farms, more remote from their family residence than in the former servants' quarters. The object is to rent them to negroes for the ensuing year, and thus secure the services of the tenants as laborers."[75] In some cases landowners established elaborate sharecropping arrangements in which landowners "rented their farming stock and implements to negroes on the shares; that is, dividing the crop in an agreed proportion between the owner and cultivator." Although black landownership may have been the ultimate goal for freedmen and women, tenantry and sharecropping sufficed as the most acceptable alternative. "Negroes are very desirous to obtain the creation of such tenements as we have above referred to, for the accumulation of themselves and families and for that purpose are willing to make boundless promises of faithfulness, etc. They are even more anxious to rent farms on the shares."

Simeon warned against these sharecropping "partnerships" and counseled Bluegrass farmers to formulate farmers' committees to help dissuade fellow farmers from engaging in the practice.[76] For whites the dangers of sharecropping were threefold: first, blacks could abuse the contract, and whites would "have no adequate remedy" if their black tenants were to "destroy . . . farm implements" or "neglect and abuse . . . stock." Freedmen and women would feel no compunction about stealing the white man's property because "the negroes have been taught by their Radical confreres and now thoroughly believe that all the wealth of this entire section is the result of their labor, and justly belongs to them, and consequently it is neither stealing or dishonest to take anything they can lay their hands on belonging to the whites, and that like the Israelites of old, they are merely spoiling the

Gyptians."[77] Moreover, blacks would open their cottages to "all worthless vagrant, unemployed, and criminal negroes," and whites would be powerless to protect themselves.

Second, the economic partnerships with blacks would only lead to political equality. "If they are worthy thus to become your business partners, it gives them a strong claim to be heard in the witness-box, to sit as jurours, and to vote at the polls." Sharecropping and tenant farming thus opened a Pandora's box in which blacks would use their economic rights earned on the ground as leverage to seek civil and political rights.

And third, the economic partnership would ultimately lead to claims of social equality. Already, Simeon complained, former slaves asserted in their daily habits and speech a level of dignity unbecoming their actual condition: "That they deem themselves better than any white person is evident from their conversation. In speaking of negro men, though possessing neither wealth, education, intelligence, or honesty, they always dignify him with the title of Mister, and a negro woman *with* children, though *without* a husband, education, refinement, honesty or virtue as a lady, or at least Mrs. So-and-So, while no matter what may be the social position or personal attainments with them when among themselves, is 'Old Dick,' or 'Old Sal.'"[78] In the future these haughty former slaves would transgress all sexual boundaries. "Where Dinah is making a call upon your wife, or Sambo is requesting the pleasure of escorting your daughter to a meeting or some public assemblage, you will be reaping the natural results of these initial measures."[79]

Despite Simeon's warnings, sharecropping spread rapidly across the Bluegrass. A bureau agent in the southern Bluegrass counties of Garrard and Madison reported in July 1867 that former slaves were "working lands on the shares, getting one third of the crops for their labor."[80] But many white landowners did follow the advice of Simeon and colluded against farmers who rented lands to blacks or established sharecropping arrangements. Sometimes whites used violence against those who refused to comply. As a result of these white actions, former slaves found it increasingly difficult to secure equitable terms with landowners. White landowners insisted on paying wages and locking in wage contracts at terms favorable to the owner. But black men and women resisted these moves and refused to sign long-term wage agreements with landowners. R. E. Johnston, chief superintendent for the Freedmen's Bureau's Lexington subdistrict, complained that "there is a disposition on their part to only engage in short contracts, and as most of them are verbal, and hence not recorded, in many cases they violate them

and leave the employer just at the time their Services are most needed."[81]
Daily wages often exceeded long-term wages established in annual contracts, and freedpeople used their monopoly on labor power to negotiate
favorable wages. In 1867 Johnston elaborated, "Many freedmen refuse to
enter contracts because they want to work daily during the harvest. Farmers
pay $150 per year but $2 per day so daily wages are worth more."[82]

In Kentucky the Freedmen's Bureau entered the fray as a third party interested in securing contracts between former slaves and employers and
keeping the laboring population on the farms. Although the bureau scoffed
at sharecropping in favor of straight wage contracts, it insisted that existing contracts be honored by all parties involved. In some cases the bureau
threatened to take landowners to federal court in Louisville for defrauding
sharecroppers. Johnston threatened a white Bluegrass farmer: "James Coleman states that he has been farming your place this past year and that you
agreed to give him a certain portion of the crop and that as the crop is now
raised and harvested you have refused to allow him to take his portion away
threatening to kill him etc. if he comes on your place. You are respectfully informed that steps will at once be taken to bring a suit against you in the US
Court at Louisville for damages to the full amount of his portion of the crop
unless you at once report to this office in person or by letter your reason for
treating this man as he claims you have done."[83]

As this case illustrates, Kentucky's refusal to grant testimony rights to
African Americans forced the bureau to remove such cases to the federal
courts. The Coleman case was hardly an isolated incident, and as a consequence many freedmen and women refused any sort of long-term contract
whatsoever—even for crop shares—because of distrust in the landowner's
willingness to honor the contract. In March 1868 Johnston remarked to
Runkle, "I notice in many instances an aversion on the part of the Freedmen to making Contracts and am led to believe it arises from the ill wages
they have received since their emancipation from their employers in various
ways—chiefly by being cheated out of their portion of crops (when farming
on shares) and oftentimes being driven off and not receiving remuneration
of any kind for their labor."[84]

Occasionally, whites used a cultural pretext to justify the violent expulsion
of freedmen before they could receive their crop shares.[85] In Raywick, Marion
County, a black man named Harry Lewis contracted with a white man named
Heely to work 125 acres on shares, with Heely providing half the necessary farm implements and the crop to be divided equally between Lewis

and Heely. But after breaking only 80 acres of corn and oats, white men in the town of Raywick accused Lewis of "insulting a lady in town."[86] The men broke into Lewis's house, beat him severely, and drove him off the farm, threatening to shoot him if he returned. The gang of white men thus relieved Heely of his contractual obligations by accusing Lewis of violating the gender and racial conventions of Kentucky society. Heely and other white men in the community employed gendered language in order to amplify their own class-based objections to the wage demands of Harry Lewis.[87]

In Missouri the story was substantively similar. Freedmen and women aspired to own land, as in Kentucky, and many took advantage of the Southern Homestead Act, which made land available to blacks in Missouri. According to Freedmen's Bureau head Oliver O. Howard, as many as four thousand black Missouri families took advantage of this program.[88] But blacks seeking their own property found numerous barriers in the way. Those with property faced summary violence from white ex-guerrillas and often immediate loss of property; in one celebrated case a widow was violently driven from her property by her neighbor as soon as her husband died.[89] With landownership a mirage for most black Missourians, former slaves sought sharecropping arrangements whenever possible.[90] Barring that, they weaseled out of long-term deals in favor of daily contracts that paid higher wages, especially around the harvest. A white man named Montague, who lived near Glasgow in Howard County, Missouri, tried to kill a black employee who had the temerity to argue with him over wages.[91] General John Sprague, assistant commissioner for the Freedmen's Bureau's Arkansas-Missouri district, found most African Americans in the Missouri River counties of Little Dixie "disinclined to labor except for a short time and then they remain idle until they have expended their earnings."[92] With no permanent agent in Little Dixie, Sprague had no ability to place black demands for short labor contracts in any sort of context. As in Kentucky, blacks sought short contracts because they paid better, and they offered flexibility to test the market for better employers. Sprague interpreted this as simple spendthrift behavior on the part of former slaves unaccustomed to the rigors of a wage economy.

Because of white violence, white collusion against black land and labor demands, and the dearth of schools in the countryside, among other reasons, many African Americans in the Bluegrass and Little Dixie moved to the towns and cities or left for Indiana, Kansas, or Ohio. Vulnerable to roving gangs of Regulators, former bushwhackers, and similar paramilitary outfits, African Americans sought refuge in the towns and cities of the

Bluegrass and Little Dixie. The black populations of Danville, Lexington, and Versailles in Kentucky grew significantly in the first five years after the war, as did Columbia, Fulton, and Lexington in Missouri. Relations between newly arrived freedmen from the countryside and town dwellers, white and black, were tense. Both the Freedmen's Bureau and the conservative press denounced the urban migration of blacks, often with similar language. A bureau circular written in January 1867 noted that blacks were "refusing to contract for the present year where their services are required, congregate in towns and villages without any visible means of support, which action tends to create additional destitution and vagrancy."[93] The mayor of Paris, Kentucky, complained in the year after emancipation, "The great desideratum is to rid ourselves of a population that will not labor but simply exist as a nuisance—Where they go or to whom they are sent is a matter of little moment to us, so that they be constrained to active honest labor and we relieved of a burden."[94] The exodus of blacks from the border countryside dated to the war and continued apace in the war's aftermath. But the rationale for this large-scale migration shifted from escape from bondage during the war to escape from white terror and exploitation after the war.

Ironically, blacks remaining on the small farms of central Kentucky and central Missouri found themselves in a favorable negotiating position with their landlords. To the dismay of landowners like Simeon, blacks held a monopoly over the labor necessary to grow corn, oats, hemp, and tobacco; despite numerous desperate appeals for Chinese immigrant labor, whites understood that blacks were the only viable labor supply.[95] Although bureau agents and white radicals regularly complained that former slaves did not understand the obligations and machinations of the free market, the freedmen and women understood perfectly well how to secure optimal wages by holding out for day wages during the harvest. And when white landowners refused any terms acceptable to black laborers, they simply abandoned the countryside for the burgeoning towns and cities of the Bluegrass and Little Dixie or for the former free states of Indiana, Kansas, and Ohio.

Particularly intriguing about this struggle for favorable land and labor terms was that it produced no noticeable leadership cadre.[96] In fact, not only did this movement produce no noteworthy black labor leaders in Kentucky and Missouri; it drew little attention from the black elites, who spent their energies fighting for suffrage and civil rights.[97] Yet this grassroots labor movement followed an undeniable pattern that repeated itself across the border countryside. Black men and women who roamed from farm to farm

in the postwar period traded news about the best wage rates and stratagems
to secure them. Blacks exploited social and kin ties going back to slavery but
reenergized after emancipation in order to develop a cohesive labor movement. In many ways the struggle for land, crop shares, and good wages reflected a more substantive grassroots political struggle than the elite-led
fight for suffrage, equal testimony rights, and other civil rights. African
Americans thus developed a political culture strong at the grassroots but
less so at the grasstops.

At a deeper level the black movements for economic and social autonomy
and civil and political rights revealed the aspirations and priorities of black
citizenship in a biracial republic. The myriad black movements between
emancipation and passage of the Fifteenth Amendment revealed complexities and tensions within the border state black community. As urban-based
black leaders sought acceptance in white society as equals, including the witness and jury box, the polling booth, and public accommodations, members
of the black grassroots aspired to autonomy from the long reach of their
former masters. Both the masses and the elites cherished equal rights under
the law; ordinary blacks wanted the vote and access to the courts in large
part because it would help to achieve a level of autonomy and protection
from white harassment. But the differing priorities of citizenship reflected
class and geographic divisions within the black population that lasted well
beyond the 1860s. And together they gave voice to the emerging black political culture of post-emancipation Kentucky and Missouri.

Black Missourians and Kentuckians acutely experienced their anomalous
position in the postwar period. They held little or none of the rights that African Americans in many northern states had earned, and they enjoyed none
of the radical congressional support that blacks in the former Confederacy
received. They were truly caught in between, in a new, raw kind of middle
ground both north and south of freedom and equality. When African Americans challenged the testimony law in Kentucky or the suffrage restrictions
in white radical Missouri, they drew almost entirely from internal resources
nurtured through decades of small-scale slavery. Although blacks elsewhere
also built their postwar politics on the foundation of antebellum practices
and structures, they exploited congressional tools and white abolitionist
cultural impulses to assist them in asserting their power. For African Americans caught within the unfortunate interstice between North and South,
internal grassroots resources and traditions played a comparatively crucial
role. The Freedmen's Bureau and the federal courts eyed the machinations of

white conservatives in Kentucky and Missouri, but they did little to ensure justice at the ground level. Between the end of the war and passage of the Fifteenth Amendment in 1870, border state blacks experienced the perils and promise of self-reconstruction.

In this effort border state blacks built schools, churches, and benevolent organizations that catered to the specific needs of newly freed people once scattered across small farms and villages in Little Dixie and the Bluegrass. They also held regular political meetings that agitated the state and federal governments for the same rights granted to blacks in the former Confederacy. And on anniversaries of particularly notable events, such as the Emancipation Proclamation (which, ironically, did not apply to them) or the Fourth of July, black Kentuckians and Missourians promoted a biracial vision of the Republic consecrated during the Civil War. Although they fought alongside many of their former masters for the maintenance of the Union, they recast the Union cause as a radical project for a "new birth of freedom."[98] Their relatively critical role in staffing the military ranks—in no slave state did a higher percentage of blacks join the Union army than in Kentucky or Missouri—added blood and sweat to this radical challenge to both conservative Unionism and Confederatism. Border state blacks used this revolutionary military service to the Republic as a mere stepping-stone to the more peaceful, but equally important, postwar task of securing political power and rights granted by neither state nor federal governments.

Yet white Kentuckians and Missourians from all classes and political backgrounds reassessed their own notion of the post–Civil War Republic. As blacks advanced their own conception of a biracial republic, white former conservative Unionists and Confederates responded with ideological vigor, advancing a politically unified "White Man's Democracy" designed to keep the aspirations of former slaves in check. The struggle between these rival conceptions of citizenship, class, race, and region would influence both the substantive political system in the border states and the symbolic framework through which white Kentuckians and Missourians remembered the past.

CHAPTER 8

REMAKING THE WHITE MAN'S DEMOCRACY

With the presidential campaign heating up in the summer of 1868, the *Weekly Brunswicker* invited its Democratic readers to attend a "grand rally" to hear Union Civil War general James Shields give a speech on "the great questions which agitate this country."[1] The *Brunswicker* extended a "special invitation" to the women of Chariton County, Missouri, who the newspaper "beseech[ed] . . . to lend us their influence, by their presence and their smiles, in this great struggle for White Supremacy and Constitutional Government."[2] The *Brunswicker*'s call mirrored those of hundreds of editors, partisans, and activists across the nation. Indeed, the 1868 presidential election witnessed some of the most explicitly white supremacist discourse of any election in the history of the United States, as the Democratic Party made opposition to the congressional Reconstruction program a central plank in the campaign of presidential nominee Horatio Seymour and vice presidential nominee Frank Blair of Missouri. At similar rallies in cities across the North and in the states in the South already readmitted to the Union, white men and women paraded with banners proclaiming: "This is a White Man's Republic" and "We Oppose Negro Rule."[3] The Chariton County rally brought home to central Missouri a national campaign already characterized by racist rhetoric.

But the rally in Chariton County took place in the context of local transformations that challenged the cultural and regional identity of border state whites. Although Missouri had operated under a Radical Republican constitution from 1865 on, the state did not allow African Americans to vote. Nevertheless, African Americans in central Missouri and in central Kentucky were far from politically dormant. Beginning with service in the Union army as soldiers and continuing with the construction of independent schools, churches, and other community institutions, border state blacks used their Civil War service as a starting point for further claims to citizenship in the Republic. Black Missourians and Kentuckians did not merely seek access to the outer limits of the "White Republic"; rather, they aimed to transform the Republic itself into a biracial compact based on universal rights and, eventually, equal suffrage. And as they undoubtedly understood, African Americans in the former Confederate states had already exercised the rights of suffrage in congressionally mandated constitutional and legislative elections.[4] Why, they wondered, should Missouri or Kentucky be any different simply because their respective states never seceded from the Union? Although punishment of former rebels lay at the heart of congressional Radical Reconstruction, and especially Radical Reconstruction within Missouri, African Americans refused to stand idly by and wait for their erstwhile friends to secure them the same blessings of citizenship conferred on the vast former slave population of the lower South.

White conservatives in Kentucky and Missouri also sensed the unique nature of the all-white political arrangement in the border. They felt blessed—even those in radical Missouri—to live in a White Republic, but they understood that the radical experiment in racial equality threatened to take root in Kentucky and Missouri. They also realized that white radicals, both within and outside the border states, were only partially to blame for this grave threat to the White Republic. African Americans in the border states had usurped the Union cause once embraced by border conservatives and now planned to use their experience to push for legal, civil, and political equality within Missouri and Kentucky. White conservatives feared that blacks would never relent until they achieved "social equality."[5] Thus, when the Democrats of Chariton County invited women to lend their "smiles for White Supremacy," they had in mind more than moral support for the Seymour-Blair ticket. As conservative newspapers across central Missouri reminded their readers, white civilization itself lay in the balance.

The "betrayal" felt by many conservative Unionists in Kentucky and Missouri over emancipation and Radical Reconstruction only exacerbated the sense of crisis over the postwar order. After all, local elites could not blame their misfortunes on military defeat. As one Lexington, Kentucky, writer under the pseudonym "Fairness" put it in a letter to the conservative, Democratic *Kentucky Gazette*, critiquing Kentucky's small Radical Republican Party, "[Conservative Unionists] fought their own kith and kin to save the

Union and uphold the Constitution," and while they were away from their homes, Union soldiers and officers were "stealing their slaves and robbing and plundering their houses and farms, and insulting their wives and children."[6] Because conservative Unionists refused to "sing hosannas" to these "robbers and plunderers," they were "denounced as traitors." Alas, despite the conservative war aims of these Unionists to "save the Union and uphold the Constitution," and, more important, "not to deprive the people of any State of any of their rights," even their right to their slaves, the radicals "violate their pledges . . . with a perfidy that would have disgraced a band of savages."[7] This was the betrayed conservative Unionist charge par excellence.

Conservative Unionists responded to the "perfidy" of white and black radicals by generating new ideologies and discourses of citizenship and by recasting power and authority at the local level in the wake of a dubious Union victory. With neither Kentucky nor Missouri subject to the congressional Reconstruction Acts of 1867, state political parties continued to limit the basic rights of citizenship—including suffrage and office holding—to whites. Radicals and conservatives alike rejected black suffrage, though with differing levels of intensity. Despite conservative hostility and white Radical indifference to their demands, border state blacks persisted in their efforts to gain civil equality and the right to vote. They fully understood that they had no serious allies either in Congress or among leaders of either political party in Kentucky and Missouri and that their efforts would yield vicious white reaction. The resulting formation of a solid white Democratic political order, the outbreak of violence against African Americans and white radicals, and the cultural reorientation of regional identity toward southern solidarity reflected, to a considerable extent, a coherent conservative protest against black radical assertions of equal citizenship in a biracial republic.

New Parties, New Alliances

Just one month before Abraham Lincoln's November 1860 election as president, Richard C. Vaughan implored Missouri Whig leader Abiel Leonard to give a boost to the Constitutional Union ticket at a meeting in Lexington, Missouri. The stakes for the nation could not have been higher. But for Vaughan the partisan prospects of defeating the long-dominant Missouri Democratic Party outweighed the larger sectional question to be decided at the polls. In a fit of partisan militancy Vaughan exclaimed, "The prospect of the final overthrow of the Democracy in Missouri as well as everywhere else, is to me a source of infinite and irrepressible pleasure in which I know you participate fully."[8] After Lincoln's victory, Vaughan reaffirmed his partisan glee in another letter to Leonard. "No matter what sad disaster may follow . . . I shall regard it as a less grievous affliction than the continuance of that party in power."[9]

Five years later, after contributing to the Union cause with dignity as a general in the Enrolled Missouri Militia, Richard C. Vaughan served as circuit clerk in Lafayette County. Under the new radical constitution of Missouri, all existing county judges were to be removed from office and replaced by men selected by Radical governor Thomas Fletcher. When a group of black militiamen appeared to arrest the current county judges and remove them from office, Vaughan and Sheriff J. A. Price forcibly resisted the militiamen.[10] The appearance of black militiamen to enforce the new radical constitution was the last of many indignities and radical "usurpations" of power that drove Vaughan into the party he had once mocked with unmasked glee. Alas, Richard C. Vaughan found no greater friend in 1865 than the Democratic Party he once wanted to destroy.

In Kentucky the peregrinations of conservative former Whigs such as Bourbon County's Brutus Clay and Richard Hanson to the Democratic Party had more immediate impact than in Missouri. Historian E. Merton Coulter commented that the peace in postwar Kentucky was that which existed "between the frog and the snake which had swallowed it."[11] Indeed, the strange ascendance of the "vanquished over the victor" in postwar Kentucky found expression in myriad cultural forms, including the appearance of Southern Ladies' Aid Societies and the rise of Regulators, who violently attacked the former slave population with impunity. But it was in the realm of formal partisan politics that the emergence of belated Confederatism had its most obvious impact in Kentucky.

On the surface the political story in Missouri appears to be the polar opposite of that of Kentucky. In Missouri a Radical Republican Party took control of the state's provisional government by 1864 and wrote a punitive new constitution in 1865 that effectively disfranchised all Missourians who had ever sympathized with the Confederacy. The Radical Party dominated the state for five years and extended its tentacles into every county. Yet underneath the Radical cover, especially in Little Dixie, lay a vibrant Democratic Party plotting its return to power. And among its leaders were former staunch Unionists and recalcitrant Whigs such as Richard C. Vaughan. The social revolution engendered by the Civil War permanently altered the partisan landscape in Little Dixie and the Bluegrass.

Before the Civil War white Missourians and Kentuckians had contributed to a vibrant two-party system that survived the many schisms and alterations of the 1850s. Although the national Whig Party effectively disappeared after 1853, adherents to Whig doctrine on matters of federal-state relations and the role of the government in the economy carried the flame right through the 1860 election season. These former Whigs coalesced around the newly created Constitutional Union Party and its nominee, John Bell of Tennessee. In the Little Dixie region of Missouri and the Bluegrass of Kentucky, former Whigs carried special strength in local elections until the outbreak of Civil War. Central Missouri former Whig political leaders such as Abiel, Nathaniel, and Reeves Leonard of Howard and Cooper counties, William Switzler and James Rollins of Boone County, and Richard C. Vaughan of Lafayette County all earned the support of a majority or a near majority in every election they contested. In Kentucky former Whigs were even more prominent as the legacy of Henry Clay cast a strong afterglow on the tradition of Kentucky Whiggery. John J. Crittenden, Brutus Clay, and Robert J. Breckinridge were but a few of the former Whigs to dominate Bluegrass politics right up through the early Civil War. Unlike in many lower South states, then, Kentucky and Missouri maintained a viable ex-Whig political organization that continued to oppose Democrats through the November 1860 election. Because of the long-standing two-party tradition in Kentucky and Missouri, the massive jump of former Whigs into the Democratic Party after the war is particularly noteworthy. As Richard C. Vaughan revealed in 1860, partisan rivalry animated politics more than national crisis or sectional militancy. Indeed, had the ex-Whig organization disappeared long before 1860, as it had in much of the lower South, the sojourn of these white conservatives to the Democratic Party would have been more seamless. The near complete transition of former Whigs into postwar Democrats in Kentucky and Missouri requires further explanation, and its sources lay in the events of the Civil War.

The Democratic Party had faced a set of crises of its own in 1860, both in the border states and in the nation as a whole. Missouri Democrats had dominated state government from the earliest days of statehood until the early 1850s. But a split in the party developed between a Free-Soil faction led by aging stalwart Thomas Hart Benton and a well-organized core of southern rights militants under the stewardship of Claiborne Fox Jackson, Judge William Napton, and the Little Dixie–based "Central Clique." Although Missouri Whigs exploited divisions within the Democratic Party briefly, it was the pro-southern bloc with its base in Little Dixie that emerged victorious by the late 1850s. Claiborne Fox Jackson triumphed as the state's gubernatorial standard-bearer in 1860, and he proclaimed himself the chief defender of slaveholders' rights. Nevertheless, Jackson's position both within the Democratic Party and in Missouri politics as a whole reveal some intriguing complexities. First, when the presidential election approached, Jackson bucked the trend of most pro-southern fire-eaters by endorsing the candidacy of "northern" Democrat Stephen Douglas over "southern" Democrat John C. Breckinridge. Jackson's endorsement of Douglas helped the Little Giant secure his only electoral victory in Missouri.[12] Second, though the militant Jackson wing dominated the Democratic Party in the state and in the legislature, the very region that spawned the Central Clique divided its support in half between the Jackson Democrats and the former Whigs. It is easy to read into Jackson's ascendancy a widely held pro-southern militancy in Little Dixie. Yet the near parity of the Bell faction in the 1860 election and the continued success of former Whigs in congressional and state elections in Little Dixie suggest that the region embraced conservative Unionism more than militant secessionism. In fact, the conservative Unionists prominent among the ex-Whig element helped secure near unanimous support for the Union in a February 1861 sovereignty convention—a convention that Governor Jackson called because he thought it would lead to disunion.

Although the ex-Whig element remained strong in Kentucky through the secession winter of 1860–61, the Democratic Party of Kentucky had achieved unprecedented power in the state and in the Bluegrass by that point. The famous Ashland congressional district long held by Whig standard-bearer Henry Clay fell into the hands of Democrat John C. Breckinridge in the early 1850s, signaling an opening for Democrats in the epicenter of Kentucky Whiggery. By 1859 a Democrat from Mercer County, Beriah Magoffin, attained the governorship and sympathized with more militantly pro-secession Democratic governors in the lower South.[13] It seemed, in early 1860, that Kentucky, like Missouri, would follow its pro-secession Democratic governor into a solid alliance with the Deep South in the event of a Republican victory in the 1860 election. But as in Missouri, Kentucky's brief prewar Democratic hegemony masked serious differences both within the Democratic Party and across the state's political spectrum. In early 1861 the Kentucky legislature repeatedly refused Magoffin's call for a sovereignty convention and eventually, in late May, pledged the state to neutrality. Meanwhile, as Kentucky's political leaders kept the state out of the Civil War, ardent pro-southern Democrats fled to Tennessee to enlist in Confederate units. By the summer of 1861 the hardest core of secessionist Democrats had already vacated the state, leaving behind an electorate dominated by conservative Unionists. When Confederate general Leonidas Polk invaded Columbus, Kentucky, in early September 1861, the legislature and the electorate rallied to the Union standard. Kentucky's Democrats had split, and the ex-Whigs rode back into power as leaders of the new conservative Union majority.

The first major partisan transition in wartime was the consolidation of Union forces in both Kentucky and Missouri. In Kentucky the Douglas Democrats and ex-Whig Constitutional Unionists even formed a new political party called the Union Democrats. In opposition stood the Breckinridge Democrats of secessionist proclivities who remained in the state. This new States' Rights Party, as it called itself, never stood a chance against the governing coalition as long as the Union itself remained popular. Nevertheless, as Coulter acutely observed, the States' Rights Party "was an ever ready refuge for those Unionists who could no longer endure the Lincoln administration and the military regime."[14] After Lincoln issued the Emancipation Proclamation, the administration's favor expired with much of white Kentucky. Seizing the moment, the States' Rights Party renamed itself the Democratic Party and immediately began organizing for the state's gubernatorial election that year. Although chastised as a gang of rebels by the ruling Union Democracy and forbidden from meeting by the military authorities in the state, the newly minted party insisted it was not a secessionist outfit, declaring: "We hold this rebellion utterly unjustifiable in its inception, and the dissolution of the Union the greatest of calamities. We would see all just and constitutional means adopted to the suppression of the one and the restoration of the other."[15] Its position on the war called for an immediate armistice, the complete restoration of habeas corpus rights, and reversal of the Emancipation Proclamation. The reborn and "pure" Democratic Party—aligned nationally with the "Peace" Democrats under Ohioan Clement Vallandigham—nominated Charles Wickliffe for governor and continued to maintain the conservative flank in the Union coalition.

In fact, Kentucky's Unionists split into three factions over the course of the war, each of which would become a distinct political party in the war's aftermath. Although the Union Democrats and the Peace Democrats were both ostensibly conservative Unionists, the latter group was more consistently critical of the Lincoln administration. The Peace Democrats blasted the Union Democrats for acquiescing to heavy-handed military interference in the state's affairs and especially for failing to object strongly to the Emancipation Proclamation. The Union Democrats occupied a more moderate position, generally yielding—though with some verbal protests—to the Lincoln administration's demands, until the moment of black soldier enlistment. The radical wing of the Unionist coalition supported Lincoln unequivocally and called itself the Unconditional Union Party. Although its leader, Danville's Presbyterian minister Robert J. Breckinridge, had a national following and a core of support in the eastern mountains and among some Union soldiers in the Bluegrass, the radical Unconditional Unionists never approached a majority in the state.[16] The moderate Union Democrats dominated the state legislature and took the governorship in the August 1863 election, thanks in large part to military interference at the polls and intimidation of potential Peace Democrat voters.

In the war's latter years Union Democratic governor Thomas Bramlette moved sharply to the right in response to black soldier enlistment. Although once accused of being a Lincoln lackey, Bramlette stood aside Frank Wolford in 1864 when he called for armed resistance to black recruitment. From that moment to the end of the war Bramlette and the Union Democrats joined forces with the conservative wing of the national Democratic Party and opposed Lincoln in every possible way, including endorsing George McClellan in the 1864 presidential election. Bramlette's protest against black soldier enlistment represented the first rumbling in the eventual reunion of Union Democrats with the Peace Democrats in the postwar period. For former Whigs such as Bourbon County's Brutus Clay to migrate to the Democratic Party, the Union Democracy served as a vital way station.

In Missouri the pro-Confederate Jackson administration fled the capital in June 1861 only to be replaced by a provisional government led by conservative ex-Whig Hamilton Gamble and Douglas Democrat Willard Hall. Like the wartime Kentucky government, the Missouri provisional government stoutly defended the state's right to be free from federal interference in "social matters," and it jealously guarded the civil powers of the state. But Missouri's wartime political alignment differed from Kentucky's in one key respect: a viable Republican Party based in St. Louis contributed to, and eventually dominated, the provisional government in Missouri, while the Republican Party remained virtually dormant in Kentucky throughout the war. Helping to push the provisional government into the hands of the radicals was a ruthless Confederate guerrilla insurgency that threatened the livelihood of all Union supporters in the interior of the state.

By mid-1863 the provisional government debated the fate of slavery and concluded that the institution's days were numbered. Moderates in the provisional government, including Hamilton Gamble, sought a gradual plan of emancipation. Conservatives such as Boone County's James Rollins opposed any emancipation plan whatsoever, especially under the unusual circumstances of a civil war. But as the war destroyed slavery one farm at a time, the facts on the ground dictated the solution favored by the radicals: immediate emancipation. Radicals argued insistently—and erroneously—that most of the state's remaining slaveholders were rebels and deserved to have their slave property freed. More persuasive was their argument that emancipation was a fait accompli and that it was foolish to pretend otherwise. Radicals successfully scuttled the moderates' gradual plan and called for a new constitutional convention with the full power to abolish slavery immediately. When the new constitutional convention met in January 1865, it immediately abolished slavery, on January 11, and set about the long-term business of reconstructing the state according to radical plans.

Thus, the logic of events on the ground—particularly guerrilla war and the destruction of slavery—pushed Missouri's wartime government to the left. Ironically, by contrast, Kentucky's relative lack of guerrilla insurgency and slave unrest encouraged that state's wartime government to shift to the right, as federal interference in state affairs appeared unnecessary and burdensome to the state's Union population. With slavery still mostly intact until early 1864, black soldier enlistment and the resultant destruction of slavery that enlistment effected played a much greater role in souring white Kentuckians on the Union cause than it did in Missouri. The conservative government that emerged in Kentucky at the end of the war belatedly recognized the Confederate argument that Lincoln could not be trusted to protect slavery. Although many white Missouri conservative Unionists felt the same way, especially in Little Dixie, they had little power to control the state's course, now in the hands of St. Louis–based radicals.

In the central portions of Kentucky and Missouri conservative Unionists maintained control over national and state civilian offices throughout the war. With the helping heavy hand of military interference, Union Democrats won election to the state legislature in all Bluegrass counties in 1861 and later in 1863; supporters of Robert Breckinridge's Unconditional Union

Party fared miserably in the Bluegrass despite running popular men for office. Like Unionists elsewhere in Kentucky, Bluegrass politicians moved sharply to the right in the war's latter years. Some of the region's staunchest wartime Unionists—such as United States Senator Garrett Davis and state representatives Brutus Clay and Richard Hanson of Bourbon County, Joshua Fry Bell of Boyle County, and George Shanklin of Jessamine County—vehemently rejected ratification of the Thirteenth Amendment and the recognition of slavery's demise after the war's completion. On the stump congressional candidate George Shanklin reminded Bluegrass voters that the Thirteenth Amendment was the culmination of the work of abolitionists such as Wendell Phillips and would result in the theft from Kentucky of $150 million in property.[17] Senator Davis warned voters in Paris that the Thirteenth Amendment's passage would "elevate the negro to all the social and civil rights of a citizen."[18] Indeed, a plank in the new Conservative Union Party's 1865 platform stated, "No power has been delegated by the constitution to the government of the United States to emancipate the slaves of any State," thereby declaring the Thirteenth Amendment unconstitutional.[19] Although some prominent Kentuckians supported the Thirteenth Amendment, including Governor Thomas Bramlette and former governor Beriah Magoffin, the anti-amendment men accurately gauged the intensity of Bluegrass Unionist alienation from Lincoln's emancipation policies.[20]

Confederates returned home in droves in the summer of 1865, with many conservative Unionists welcoming them with open arms. Although many of these conservatives balked at allowing ex-Confederates to take over the state's political leadership—they formed a Conservative Union third party to stand between the Confederate-dominated Democratic Party and the Radical Republican Party—their substantive positions on Reconstruction matters matched the revived Democrats. As early as 1866, Bluegrass counties would begin voting former Confederate leaders to state office, with the assistance of former conservative Unionists.[21]

In Missouri's Little Dixie the political picture is harder to assess because the guerrilla disruptions and the extreme disfranchisement law passed in 1865 rendered a majority of the prewar population unable to participate in elections. In some counties Radicals managed to secure victories in elections for state and national offices, though often with meager vote totals. But conservatives did not give up power easily. Viewing the strict loyalty oath provisions of the new constitution as nothing short of a Radical power play, conservative Unionists responded by encouraging ex-Confederates to defy

Radical election judges. In Callaway County, a former hotbed of Confederate support, former Confederates terrified the election judge into allowing hundreds of obviously disqualified men to vote.[22] In June 1866 the *Lexington (Mo.) Caucasian* encouraged former rebels to vote and proffered specific instructions for how to do so:

1. Be registered; demand it as a fight; and let registrars reject you if they will. But if rejected sue registrar, commissioner and whoever else gets between you and your right of suffrage.
2. Offer your vote at the polls. If rejected, keep the proof of the fact and sue every mother's son of the judges.
3. Take the oath, as you would take anything else forced upon you—a man's life in self-defence.
4. If you are still refused, establish polls of your own, outside of the radical graveyard, appoint judges, take the votes in regular order, and according to law, and let the poll books be held in judgment against the party in power. They will not always be in power.[23]

Missouri conservatives in the postwar period set out to cast the new radical voting system as illegitimate and undemocratic. One critical component to what nearly all border state whites considered legitimate democracy was the restriction of suffrage rights to white men. Not surprisingly, conservative Democrats portrayed their radical opponents as supporters of Negro suffrage and, consequently, defilers of the American democratic tradition. But white Missouri Radicals rejected black suffrage as well and often for the same reasons as conservatives. The 1865 radical constitution, unlike every Reconstruction-era radical constitution in the former Confederate states, refused to give African Americans the right to vote. As historian William Parrish points out, some Radical leaders believed in universal manhood suffrage, but they feared that many rank-and-file Unionists—especially those in the Ozark region of southwestern Missouri—would reject any constitution that provided voting rights to African Americans.[24] More important, white Radicals did not need the votes of blacks, as they could count on strong support in St. Louis, among the German population scattered throughout the state, and Ozark Unionists, who suffered grievously from bushwhacker violence.

Although Missouri Radicals refused to grant voting rights to African Americans, they found it necessary to offer a sort of negative franchise in the form of the right to testify against whites in contested election cases.[25]

In one particularly interesting case in Chariton County the depositions of African Americans led to the reversal of a state legislative election. In November 1866 conservative Unionist Judge Lucius Salisbury won election to the state legislature but found his majority thrown into question by his opponent, Alfred Griffin. In order to prove that Salisbury's voters were former rebels, Griffin deposed many former slaves, including a 16-year-old named Ann Wheeler, in order to ascertain the disloyalty of Salisbury's voters. Wheeler recalled the suspicions of her rebel former master that she would tell Union authorities of the presence of guerrillas on his property. She testified that her former master "threatened to hang me if I told anyone of their being there . . . and whipped me because he thought I had told some one."[26] Other former slaves, including Smallwood Starks, also revealed the hospitality their former masters showed to bushwhackers. These black men and women never received the right to vote under Missouri's radical regime; however, in the zero-sum game of Missouri's radical constitution, they exploited a negative franchise to remove the voting rights of their former masters. Perhaps more important, the depositions of African Americans in this contested election case demonstrated the limits of white Radical rule, even after disfranchisement of former rebels.

African Americans were not the only ones locked out of the formal electoral system to engage in formal—if not "partisan"—politics in some fashion. Many conservatives who could not take the loyalty oath participated in a series of Andrew Johnson Clubs that met in nearly every township in central Missouri. As backers of the Johnson Clubs claimed, they formed "so that an approximation of the strength of the President may be known, and the programme of the operations of the party shaped accordingly and that the President might be still further strengthened in his war upon the enemies of the white man and the white man's government."[27] A Washington Township Johnson Club leader blasted the Freedmen's Bureau and averred, "This is a white man's country and a white man's Government and belongs to him and his posterity forever; taxpaying white men are legal votes."[28] The Johnson Clubs sought not only to protect white supremacy but to form a distinct political party program based around defense of President Johnson's conservative Reconstruction policy. Although the Freedmen's Bureau had virtually no authority within radical Missouri, the new federal bureau served as a nationally resonant symbol in the propaganda war against local radicals. Moreover, with many Johnson Club participants disfranchised under the 1865 Missouri constitution, the movement provided an opportunity to plan and develop a strategy for the return of the Democratic Party and its ideals to prominence in Missouri. Linking their own struggle for voting rights against Radical Missourians, with the beleaguered president fighting desperately against congressional Radicals, Missouri conservatives (including former Confederates) gave national significance to a local movement.

The strict disfranchisement provisions in the 1865 Missouri constitution helped unite Little Dixie conservative Unionists such as Richard C. Vaughan and James Rollins with their former enemies who had once fought for the Confederacy. In some ways it was just a marriage of convenience; conservatives needed ex-Confederate votes to defeat the Radicals. But the reunification of Missouri conservatives under the umbrella of a revived Democratic Party represented much more than a simple Faustian bargain between power-hungry Conservative Unionists and ex-Confederates looking for a ticket back into the electoral process. It served the purpose of expressing the sentiments of conservatives of both loyalties who had lost everything in the war—slaves, farms, money, and social standing—and who stood to lose even more in the radical peace.[29] By 1866, with the ex-rebel *Lexington Caucasian* as the organ of the united conservative forces in Little Dixie, a new Democratic Party found a voice in opposition to what it deemed an illegitimate usurpation of power.

Consolidating the White Man's Democracy

Border state Democratic ideology drew from many sources, some of them national and others distinctly local. The campaign for "white supremacy" promoted by Democratic newspapers and politicians across Kentucky and Missouri in the late 1860s mirrored the Democratic campaigns of the North. Just as often as the cry for white supremacy was the call for "Constitutional Government," a refrain that reflected national Democratic anger at the excesses of Lincoln's wartime government and the postwar radicals' predilection for amending and ignoring the Constitution at will.[30] *Constitutional Government* meant a return to the sort of small federal government and local control over social affairs that characterized the antebellum era. Some Kentucky Democrats consciously proclaimed their state a sanctuary for white conservatives abused in the Reconstructed ex-Confederacy. Conservative Kentuckians proclaimed, "This State will become the refuge of the oppressed from the Southern States, who will flee from the horrors of negro supremacy to find political and social security."[31] But with both of these ideological impulses, local dynamics shaped the course and strategy of the border state Democratic parties.

Although white conservative ex-Unionists united with their former wartime foes in the newly invigorated "White Man's" Democratic Party, many of the strongest Democrats in postwar Kentucky and Missouri had despised the old party of Jackson before the war. Lafayette County's Richard C. Vaughan exemplified this shift from arch-Whig and conservative Unionist to militant Democrat. Vaughan, who in 1860 heralded the "sad calamity" of civil war as better than Democratic victory,[32] migrated toward the conservative position during the war and buried the hatchet with the postwar Democracy. Like Unionist General James Shields, who spoke of "white supremacy and constitutional government" to "smiling ladies" in Brunswick, and other prominent wartime Unionists such as Democratic vice presidential candidate and Missourian Frank Blair, Vaughan epitomized the betrayed conservative Unionist after the war. As a convert to the Democratic Party with unassailable Unionist credentials, Vaughan received regular praise from the rabidly white supremacist and Democratic *Lexington Caucasian* newspaper. At one point the *Caucasian* referred to Vaughan as "the most abused man in the state," especially for the ways in which Missouri's Radicals prevented him from claiming his rightful office of circuit court clerk and later U.S. assessor for the district. His regular protests against Radical Governor Fletcher's policies represented a "masterly production in defense of the people of the state . . . and for which the people of the State owe him a debt of gratitude that, it seems to us, can only be paid by placing him in the executive chair."[33]

Democrats in Kentucky also took great effort in declaring their party the voice for conservatives, regardless of wartime loyalties. Confederate general W.C.P. Breckinridge wrote a resolution at a Fayette County Democratic meeting laying out the postwar olive branch across the Civil War divide. "We protest against any effort to keep alive the antipathies of the past, and pledge a cordial support to the nominees of the Democratic Convention, without stopping to inquire as to the flag under which any one of them may have served during the late unhappy war."[34] Another local Democratic Party meeting proclaimed, "The main issue now is the Africanization of the late slaveholding States, and their consequent control by the Federal government, and up on that simple issue we invite union."[35]

Although the Democratic Party embraced all conservatives in the postwar era, the dynamics of ex-Unionist and ex-Confederate reconciliation differed somewhat in Missouri and Kentucky. In Kentucky the Democratic Party,

dominated by returning Confederates, took power in the state as early as
August 1865.[36] A third party, calling itself the Conservative Union Party,
served as a way station for former Whigs and supporters of Governor Bramlette's Union Democracy who felt uncomfortable with Confederate ascendancy in the revived Democratic Party. W. B. Kinkead headed the Conservative Union Party and declared the principles to be identical to those of the
Democrats, the only point of difference being the makeup of the Democratic
leadership. The third party never seriously caught on among the Kentucky
electorate or within the Bluegrass elite.[37]

The Democratic Party, with its roots in the wartime States' Rights Party,
established hegemony in nearly every corner of the Bluegrass by mid-1867.
In the Lexington city elections in March 1867 Democrats defeated Republicans for every single office. In the elections for mayor, city attorney, city trea-
surer, captain's night watch, keeper of the poor and work house, and coun-
cilman for wards 2, 3, and 4, Democrats won with nearly two-thirds of the
total vote; in Ward 1 the Democratic victory was narrower. This total repudiation of radicalism pleased the Democratic *Gazette*. "An obnoxious heresy
which finds no place within our borders, and the little that has been trans-
planted here will soon become extinct unless kept alive by Federal pap."[38]
In statewide elections held in May 1867, the radical *Central Kentucky Gazette*
bemoaned, "Rebel Democracy Carry the State," the Democrat having defeated
the Conservative Unionist and Republican for Congress in Boyle County with
79 percent of the total vote.[39] The Democrat, James Beck, swept every other
Bluegrass county as well, as did Democrats running for lesser offices. Democrats also dominated outside the Bluegrass, securing victory in every part of
the state with the exception of the heavily Unionist southeastern mountain
region. "Thank Heaven Kentucky is not the world, nor the United States,"
the radical Danville paper sighed.[40] Democrats rolled on to victory in 1868 as
well, sweeping city and county elections in August and Kentucky's presidential vote in November. With the Democrats in solid control of the Kentucky
legislature and most local offices in the Bluegrass, the "rebel Democracy"
could magnanimously open its doors to ex-Unionists seeking new ideological
compatriots. In January 1868 Kinkead himself declared total and complete
unity with the Democratic Party, thus ending the third party movement and
solidifying the conservative phalanx under the auspices of the Democracy.[41]

Ex-Confederate domination stretched to all corners of the Bluegrass Democracy. One prominent former Confederate colonel in Woodford County
named Hart Gibson hosted a "beautiful picnic" for all of the leading Demo-

crats in the county and the surrounding area. Gibson was the first elected former Confederate to the state legislature from the Bluegrass when he won office in 1866.[42] Some of the more renowned ex-Confederates in the Bluegrass, including W.C.P. Breckinridge, who also assumed editorship of the *Lexington Observer and Reporter,* won elected office in 1867. Former Confederate general William Preston won state legislative office in Fayette County in 1868.[43] Beriah Magoffin, the former governor and Confederate sympathizer, won election to the state legislature in 1867 from Mercer County, with his support for "states' rights" during the war a major part of his appeal. As historian E. Merton Coulter points out, former Confederates simply dominated the Democratic Party in Kentucky as soon as their voting disabilities were removed by the state legislature in December 1865.[44] With their support from the "stay at home" rebels who populated the wartime States' Rights Party of Charles Wickliffe and actual returning Confederates who drifted back into the state in the spring of 1865, the Democratic Party helped lend post-facto legitimacy to the Confederate cause. And with the region's "best men" serving in the party's ranks, the Democratic Party quickly established itself as the natural ruling faction in Kentucky state politics.

In Missouri, however, the state's postwar Constitution disfranchised any man ever associated with the Confederate cause. Conservative Unionists such as Vaughan, who pledged to remove the disfranchisement provisions from the Constitution, served as the conduits for ex-rebels to return to power. James Shields, Union general and conservative advocate for "White Supremacy and Constitutional Government," won election to Congress in 1868—no small feat considering the disfranchisement of such a sizable portion of the western Missouri electorate.[45] Lucius Salisbury, whose victory over Alfred Griffin in the 1866 state legislature race from Chariton County was overturned thanks to the testimony of many African Americans in the district, won election comfortably in 1868. Salisbury had been a conservative Unionist judge during the Civil War and had advocated on behalf of Chariton County citizens jailed by the Unionist militia. Like Vaughan and Shields, he was the appropriate sort of principled, conservative ex-Unionist to lead the Democratic Party still smarting under Radical domination. By 1870 these Democrats, aided by a split in Republican ranks between Radicals and Liberals, successfully submitted a constitutional amendment to the voters removing the rebel disfranchisement provisions. The re-enfranchisement referendum passed easily in 1870, and former rebels rejoined the political field as staunch Democrats.

Although the fortunes of the Democratic Party in Kentucky and Missouri differed significantly in the late 1860s, there were some important common threads that united their experiences and set them apart from the former Confederacy. The most important mutually shared grievance was the threat—though not yet reality—of black suffrage. As in the lower South, the transformation of border state conservative Unionists—and in many cases vitriolic Whigs—into Democrats had as much to do with African American claims to the mantle of equality as it did with the actions of white radicals. But the external political context shaping border conservative fusion under the Democratic umbrella hardly resembled the political earthquake shaking the states of the former Confederacy. After March 1867 congressional Radicals established a series of electoral procedures that allowed the black population to share formal political power with white Radicals in the former Confederate states. The Reconstruction Acts led to the creation of a dominant, biracial Republican Party across the South, with white southerners, northerners, and African Americans sharing local and state offices in every former Confederate state. Because neither state rebelled against the Union, Kentucky and Missouri were both exempted from the 1867 Reconstruction Acts. Missouri's anomalous form of white radicalism, wherein blacks never received the right to vote, meant that conservatives had nothing to fear from actual black voters.

Although African Americans never threatened white Democrats as actual voters, their potential electoral strength and, more significantly, their ideological challenge to the white monopoly on political power led Kentucky and Missouri Democrats to assume a viciously white supremacist posture in the late 1860s. The *Kentucky Gazette* encapsulated conservative fear of potential black suffrage in an 1867 editorial: "Negro suffrage would be a calamity justifying almost any measure to protect society from it." The editorial than compared the "treacherous banner" of black suffrage to a "plague," which would result in "social dissolution." Blacks were a "loathsome, fetid and abhorrent race," and black suffrage would inexorably yield "social equality." Moreover, enfranchised blacks would be "controlled" by "negro bureaus" and "Radical demagogues" and would lead to "agrarianism" and every other sort of "social abomination."[46] Fear of black political power thus included two elements. First, black suffrage was a crime against "birthright" and "race . . . as offensive in the sight of God and man as that unpardonable sin for which scripture saith there is no forgiveness in this world nor the world to come." Political equality would inevitably lead to social equality, which would endanger

the white race and white civilization through miscegenation. But black suffrage engendered a second fear as powerful as the first. If enfranchised,
blacks might advocate "agrarianism," or the redistribution of property to
the laboring classes. To whites black claims for land signaled not a desire to
form an independent yeomanry but, rather, a plot to steal the white man's
land and drive the white man from the region. White conservatives looked
to the wartime experience of planters in South Carolina's Low Country,
where slaves appropriated their masters' property and divided it among
themselves.[47] More important, however, white Democrats observed black
Kentuckians and Missourians negotiating for better wage rates, sharecropping arrangements, and even land ownership. Although virtually no white
radicals supported "agrarianism," white Democrats had reason to fear that
an increasingly class-conscious black population would threaten white economic hegemony, especially if granted formal political power.

The fear of black suffrage thus incorporated a host of social, economic,
and cultural grievances cited by Democrats. In addition to the labor question, Democrats cited an outbreak in crime and violence among the black
population, with some of it targeting whites. These charges of rampant black
criminality helped bolster the Democrats' political strategy of rallying public
opposition to civil or political equality. The Democratic press delighted in
informing its readers of the feckless criminals who lurked amid the newly
freed population. One *Kentucky Gazette* article mocked a potential hog thief
found stabbed to death in Nicholasville: "It appears from the inquest that
the negro had stumbled and falled upon [his] knife, and that it had pene-
trated his heart. Fresh pork is a good thing, but if every darkey who endeav-
ors to get a little of it in a quiet way is to be disposed of in this way, they will
have to give it up."[48] In 1868 the paper complained that the Lexington jails
were filled with black criminals, some from the lower South but most from
Kentucky. The editor considered hanging all of them but realized that such
a method contravened the "delicate sensibilities of the age." Rather, the editor proposed deporting the entire black population and making them "live
among the abolitionists."[49] The *Caucasian* of Lexington, Missouri, claimed
that criminality and dishonesty were literally marked upon the skin of black
people: "The original nigger was the traditional man who lied—not only till
he was black in the face, but till he was black all over."[50] The Democratic *Kentucky Gazette* placed daily stories of crime within the context of the larger
political struggle facing white conservatives: "Negro Outrages—The daily
papers are filled with accounts of murders, robberies, rapes, and other out-

rages by negroes in this and other States. This is the necessary consequence of their emancipation and the attempted elevation of the negro to an equality with the white race . . . One thing is certain, that the people of Kentucky will not suffer their civilization to be overwhelmed by the black cloud of negro barbarism."[51]

White conservatives also feared that political equality necessarily led to a much greater evil—social equality, miscegenation, and the destruction of white civilization.[52] The conservative Fulton *Missouri Telegraph* explained how these "evils" emerged from the relatively benign result of black political equality: "No people or nation on the globe ever received the negro on terms of political equality that did not speedily receive him on terms of social and moral equality, marrying with him, and multiplying human mongrels."[53] The timing of this comment is important, as the Missouri legislature had recently submitted a black suffrage bill to the electorate for ratification, and the *Telegraph* had played a leading role in opposing its passage. Regarding connections between black suffrage and white sexual fears during Reconstruction, historian Martha Hodes has observed, "The idea of manhood, which had long implied the rights and responsibilities of citizenship in American political thought, now assumed connotations in white minds of black men engaging in sex with white women."[54] To drive home the exigency of this gendered threat to political white supremacy, the newspaper cited a white woman "of acknowledged beauty and refinement" in Chicago who took her black coach driver as her lover. After her plan to elope with the "buck nigger" was "frustrated," the man was arrested, and the woman's father came to Chicago from Iowa to "rescue" her. The man was a "radical philosopher and moralist of the practical school."[55] It would only be a matter of time, the *Telegraph* warned, that such incidents became commonplace in Missouri. And the only way to prevent this "degraded" form of social equality was to prevent political equality.

African American demands for political and civil equality played an integral role in transforming the white conservative Unionist political culture into a militantly white supremacist Democratic order. In some cases conservatives who directly and physically opposed the efforts of African Americans were rewarded by the Democratic press and the Democratic electorate. Richard C. Vaughan, for example, played an important role in staving off the local black militia that had come to arrest a conservative court officer. Vaughan literally stood up for white supremacy in the minds of Lafayette County conservatives. Although the full "horrors" of black suffrage lay beyond the borders of Missouri and Kentucky, the actions of blacks at the grassroots and grasstop level were enough to scare white conservatives into political unity under the Democratic umbrella. To be sure, white radicals, both within and outside the border states, also facilitated conservative Democratic angst. But African Americans, with their heretical conception of biracial citizenship and their willingness to act on behalf of their own interests, pushed white conservatives into the Democratic camp for good. And white conservatives did much more than turn to the "White Man's Democracy" to thwart black political aspirations. They also turned to violence.

Judge Lynch and the Persistence of Border Violence

The wave of violent attacks against African Americans that began during the latter years of the Civil War continued to spread in the years after Appomattox. The spectacular Christmas Eve lynching of Al McRoberts in Danville epitomized the trend, and others would follow a similar script—even if the specific issues and "provocations" at hand differed. In 1869, for example, a mob lynched a black man accused of raping the wife of Dr. Scott of Fulton, Missouri. While awaiting completion of his trial, Daniel Baker, a "negro of bad reputation," was taken from the jail by a large group of "citizens" and hanged a half-mile outside of town.[56] This case fit the gendered narrative of racial violence that afflicted the entire South. Daniel Baker had transgressed racial, class, and gender lines by allegedly raping the white wife of a doctor. The white community, unwilling to let the judicial process run its course, hanged Baker in public.

Despite the sensational case of Daniel Baker, racial violence was less common in Missouri than it was in Kentucky. To be sure, "outlaws" and other violent actors prowled the central Missouri countryside in the postwar years, and on occasion targeted African Americans. Some of these outlaws, such as Jesse James, became nationally notorious, carrying on Missouri's bitter guerrilla war well into the postwar era and targeting symbols of radicalism as far away as Minnesota.[57] But the racial component of Missouri's postwar violence was less stark than in Kentucky. As historian T. J. Stiles remarks, Missouri "was not the Deep South . . . it was heavily white," and the "white majority was bitterly divided."[58] As a result, most of these former guerrillas turned their guns toward the white Unionist population—and especially adherents of the Radical Republican Party—who had secured control over the state in 1865. Surely the former guerrillas and their conservative Unionist allies despised African Americans as strongly as did their compatriots in Kentucky. The viciously racist rhetoric of the *Lexington (Mo.) Caucasian* revealed antiblack hatreds in starker terms than did any major newspaper in Kentucky. But an effective radical Missouri militia tasked with enforcing the ordinances of the new Radical regime kept ex-guerrillas on the run and limited violent incidents to shootouts between the two white factions of postwar Missouri. Moreover, the ability of black people to testify in court gave black Missourians a tool of protection that they never possessed in Kentucky.

In Kentucky the greatest threat to African Americans came from shadowy paramilitary organizations known generally as "Regulators." Danville's Radical organ, the *Central Kentucky Gazette,* regularly apprised readers of the nightly outrages committed on the black population of Boyle County and the surrounding area.[59] When a chief among the Regulators submitted a "Proclamation from Judge Lynch" to the state's largest newspapers in 1867, the *Gazette* took the opportunity to catalog the activities of this band of night riders and terrorists.[60] On October 19, 1866, a group calling itself "Skaggs's Men" ransacked the black community of Lebanon, Kentucky, "tearing down several cabins, gutting one or two negro stores, shooting at the fleeing inmates, yelling and creating general terror." Skaggs's Men targeted other symbols of black autonomy in Marion County through the fall of 1866.[61] According to the *Gazette,* they were a "preliminary to the operations of the party terming themselves Regulators, whose commander was, and is, Judge Lynch." In the early months of 1867 the Regulators "posted sentinels" and raided jails in Danville, Harrodsburg, Lebanon, and Perryville, seizing black and white inmates charged with violent crimes and hanging them in the woods.

The Regulators established regular rendezvous points throughout central Kentucky, with the Freedmen's Bureau always a step behind. A bureau agent reported that Parksville in southern Boyle County was the "Head Quarters of the Regulators," with several men named in a federal affidavit living in the vicinity. To the dismay of the bureau agent, the Regulators were very well organized and had near universal support in the white community: "There is no question as to the strength of these outlaw bands, the rich and the poor are combined together and money is spent profusely when needed to accomplish their villainous ends."[62] Prominent men in the area, including Louisville and Nashville (L&N) Railroad agent George Proctor and the deputy sheriff for Boyle County, David Prewitt, were leaders in the Regulator bands. Federal forces arrested Prewitt and other well-respected Boyle County residents and sent them to Louisville, where they were released on bond.[63] The bureau agent encountered great difficulty in executing their arrest warrants: "I am surrounded by spies who watch my every action, the whole country is banded together with a very few exceptions, and to achieve success, it is necessary to resort to all kinds of subterfuges, and where we do move, to move with great rapidity, and before anything can be done it is necessary to find the exact location of the house in which they reside so that when the place is surrounded you do it with certainty, and when you get the men, you must be off just as quickly as you came."[64]

The Parksville Regulator gang was not the only mob to terrorize blacks and whites in the area. Another Regulator band based in Crab Orchard, just south of Garrard County, also operated with relative impunity. The L&N Railroad connected Crab Orchard to Parksville, and it is likely that Regulator mobs exploited this transit mode, with the assistance of L&N agent George Proctor, to escape federal pursuit and plot further depredations against blacks as well as teachers at black schools.[65] In one example a group of thirty Regulators in disguise kidnapped four African Americans from a house, shooting one man in the leg and hanging and whipping the other three.[66] A black man named Henry Dawes was forcibly kicked out of his home because his employer, James Ferris, refused to pay him wages. The bureau identified Ferris as a leader in the Crab Orchard Regulators. One victim of the Crab Orchard gang, Monroe Simpson, was a black preacher who had once informed the Union provost marshal of false Unionists who claimed lost slave property for compensation. Simpson also regularly addressed a black school in southern Garrard County and attended a black convention in Frankfort to press for equal testimony rights. For his service to the black community of the southern Bluegrass, white Regulators whipped him one hundred times.[67]

The Regulators attacked both whites and blacks. In an analysis of the victims of Regulator activity, the *Gazette* uncovered the political pattern of the violence. Ironically, the newspaper earnestly believed that the Regulators were once an honest crime-fighting vigilante group who merely stepped into the breach left after years of civil war. Judge Lynch's proclamation had declared that they were "honorable and honest" and that they made "war only on bad men."[68] But the resultant pattern of violence revealed an unmistakable trend. Of twenty-six white victims of Regulators' violence, twenty-one were Unionists. Only three were known to be Confederates during the Civil War, with two others unknown to the *Gazette*. Bureau Chief Superintendent Ben Runkle added: "The prime object of these organizations is . . . intended to settle old war grudges and is directed principally against men who were active in the cause of the Union during the war. It is true, some bad men who were in the Union Army have been punished, but it is noticeable that no bad rebels have met the same fate, though they have shot down men in open day."[69] This sort of violence against white Unionists mirrored the campaign of violence and intimidation by former guerrillas in postwar Missouri.

The *Central Kentucky Gazette* conducted its analysis in July 1867 at the height of a wave of Regulator activity. Later that month the Regulators murdered their most important target among the white population—United States Major James Bridgewater. During the Civil War Bridgewater had earned a reputation as a fierce Unionist, which he carried over into the postwar period. From 1865 on, Bridgewater worked with the Freedmen's Bureau to track down and arrest Regulators, especially those around Crab Orchard. In the summer of 1867 fifteen young white men found Bridgewater at a saloon and murdered him on the spot. The conservative *Kentucky Gazette* hoped that Bridgewater's murder would signify the end of a terrible "feud" with roots in the Civil War.[70] The *Danville Advocate,* also staunchly conservative and Democratic, believed Bridgewater's murder resulted from a series of apolitical threats and counterthreats between himself and a few Regulator leaders named Sanders and Burch. The Radical press disputed these accounts, noting that Bridgewater was a "superb Union man" murdered by "stay-at-home rebels and guerrillas" for his politics. The murderers were "composed of young men of high social respectability" and were not a band of desperadoes and thieves.[71] Bridgewater was, in fact, an agent of the bureau and had actively pursued the Crab Orchard Regulators for months. Surely, Bridgewater and Sanders issued threats against one another and probably continued a feud dating to the Civil War. But that hardly suggests the murder was apolitical. Subsequent generations would recall the Bridgewater murder as a feud between a few bad men, but the reality is that Bridgewater was murdered because he was a staunch and unrepentant Unionist.[72]

In addition to the Regulator mobs, the Ku Klux Klan operated in both Kentucky and Missouri. Like the Regulators, the Klan wore disguises and intimidated and attacked both white Unionists and blacks. A white teacher named Close who taught black children in Arrow Rock, Missouri, received an intimidating note in 1869 from a self-described Klansman: "Mr. Close, Sir. Having received information that you are teaching a negro school; now sir I give you to understand that if you don't stop it and abstain from it in future I as captain of the Klu [*sic*] Klux Klan will pay you in a midnight visit, and you will be either hung or shot so you can judge what is best for you to do.

By the Eternal God if you don't stop I will make you a spectacle to behold, as no such damned nuisance or imposition on the community will be allowed. Take this as a timely warning, you damned Carpet-bagger. KLU [*sic*] KLUX KLAN, Capt. Bill Anderson, Carry Boy."[73] The name attached to the end of the letter is quite noteworthy, as Bill Anderson, the notorious Confederate guerrilla butcher, was killed in 1864. It is possible that another man with the same name assumed a leadership position within the central Missouri Klan, but more likely the group's leader adopted the old bushwhacker's moniker out of respect for the terror that he had struck in the hearts of Missouri Unionists during the war.

The Klan occasionally used the favorable Democratic press to organize meetings. The *Lexington Caucasian* printed a small advertisement that read, "X—KKK—X Attention, I. O. V., Subdivision No. 10, Snag Den No. 2 of the Bleeding Heart, and Mangled Frame. Special Orders No. 3. You are hereby commanded to meet in secret conclave next Saturday night, at 11 o'clock, at our place of rendez-vous. Blood! Vengeance!! Death!!! By order of Sub-Royal Turk and Bearer of the Crown."[74] In many cases white Unionists termed all white terror activities the work of the Klan without evidence that the organization actually participated in the violence. The editor of the *Boonville Weekly Eagle* exclaimed, "The Ku Klux Klan at Work in Saline!" after he was attacked by a man described as a "mean, bad man, who is an habitual drunkard and a notorious rebel."[75] The editor offered no evidence that the assailant was in fact a member of the Klan.

To an extent the Ku Klux Klan was indistinguishable from the Regulators. Both served the same ends in Kentucky and Missouri: to intimidate African Americans and white Unionists, whether they happened to occupy positions of political power (as in Missouri) or not (as in Kentucky). But as Steven Hahn points out, the Ku Klux Klan carried deeper symbolic import that connected its activities to others across the postwar South. "The Klan was less a formal organization than a rubric embracing a variety of secret vigilante and paramilitary outfits showing the marks of their local settings."[76] The Regulators may have simply been a local Kentucky variation of the Ku Klux Klan, occasionally swapping the identities of the two "organizations" as local needs demanded.[77] Because of its notorious reputation across the South, the Klan's identity came to symbolize for all Kentuckians and Missourians any paramilitary organization that targeted white Unionists and African Americans.

Although white Unionists suffered at the hands of the Regulators and the Ku Klux Klan, African Americans—and particularly men—endured a disproportionate share of the attacks. Perhaps no group of African Americans came under fire more than those who transgressed gendered and sexual norms of border state society.[78] The black man accused of raping a prominent physician's wife in Fulton violated race, class, and gender boundaries and met his death at the hands of a public mob. For so-called sexual offenders violence often took the form of open community action rather than disguised night riders.[79] The act of lynching a black man accused of sexual assault against white women helped reinforce class hierarchy and white community norms that proscribed interracial sexual contact.[80] For black men who simply carried on peaceable—though scandalous—relations with white women, smaller or secretive parties executed the violence. In Garrard County a white woman named Nancy Ridge lived with a "full-blooded negro" blacksmith named George White.[81] The bureau agent investigating the case noted that Ridge was a prostitute, living in a "little hovel" in Shelby City and "begging food from the blacks."[82] Ridge's brother-in-law, John Proctor, felt that George White's relationship with Ridge was an affront to his honor so he shot at White. This sort of "social equality" represented the "final stage" of racial equality in the white mind, a necessary outgrowth of the movement toward civil and political equality. Relations between poor white women such as Nancy Ridge and African Americans such as George White provoked less outrage among white elites than did liaisons that crossed class lines. As Victoria Bynum remarks, "Poverty defeminized white women much as race defeminized black women."[83] Still, even poor whites felt compelled to police these racial boundaries with violence.

More common than attacks against "miscegenation" were assaults on blacks accused of seeking economic autonomy. Runkle commented, "If a negro does anything that offends these 'Regulators' as for instance, ceases to work, differs with his employer, gives a social party, or does any acts considered wrong in negroes, he is waited upon by an armed and disguised mob and shot, hung or unmercifully whipped and so great is the terror inspired by these mobs that the Freedmen do not report these acts to the Bureau Agents for fear that vengeance will be visited upon them."[84] Regulators targeted black institutions that symbolized autonomy, such as schools and churches, often killing occupants inside. Explicitly political meetings were especially vulnerable to attack. John Fee, the white former abolitionist, wrote from Camp Nelson in Jessamine County, "Lawless men have recently seized several colored men who were formerly soldiers and abused them most brutally. The occasion being that the Freedmen were engaged in holding Union League Meetings."[85] Many of these political activists targeted by the Regulators were former soldiers in the Union army, thus continuing a trend that began shortly after the war ended. One of the victims cited by Fee was Monroe Simpson, who had served in the army in addition to his other activities in Garrard County. The other men mercilessly beaten by Regulators along with Simpson were also former soldiers in the Union army.

White landowners were less interested in securing a pliable and profitable farm labor force per se than they were in reinforcing white supremacy in all facets of social, economic, and political life. And here the patterns of racial struggle after emancipation mirrored the sort of conflict that once enveloped masters and slaves. Considering that slavery had once suppressed social autonomy as much as practicable, any black effort to create space outside the purview of whites signaled a major threat to white supremacy.[86] This threat was political in the most rudimentary sense, underscored by African Americans' determination to remove themselves from the economic and social sphere of their former masters immediately after emancipation. White violence against blacks exercising autonomy was a direct political response, then, to the most basic political aspirations of freedpeople. When, for example, a white mob shot into a black church in Woodford County filled with schoolchildren, it hoped to intimidate blacks into avoiding any form of collectivity outside the purview and supervision of the white population.[87] In this case it was black women, as schoolteachers, who proved to be the agents of black autonomy. Thus, both black men and women served as community leaders in the struggle for social autonomy, and correspondingly both black men and women (and in this case children too) faced violence. Indeed, this sort of violence targeted a wide array of men and women in the black community, from those living in towns away from their former masters, to schoolteachers and students, to property holders and professionals, to sharecroppers and other laborers who negotiated terms on an "equal" basis with whites.

The cause of this epidemic of murder, arson, and general terrorism had more to do with grassroots social and political activities than it did with formal partisan politics.[88] Even the rabidly white supremacist and Democratic *Kentucky Gazette* sought to distance itself from the Regulators: "The idea goes abroad that these lawless acts have their origin in the spirit of the Democratic Party, and especially of the late Confederate soldiers, and that they are done in the interests of that party. In the name of the Democratic Party, and especially of the Confederate soldiers, we repudiate all responsibility for, or sympathy with, such acts or the parties who perpetrate them . . . We hope the Democrats, and especially the Confederate soldiers, will zealously support and aid the civil authorities in punishing the guilty parties."[89]

After a group of men referring to themselves as "Ku Klux" attacked any and all African Americans they saw on the road between Versailles and Lexington, the *Gazette* castigated the perpetrators as frauds. The *Gazette* imagined that the "real" Regulators would actually arrest and hang these impostor Klansmen for attacking such "unoffending negroes."[90] By late 1868, with the national elections on the horizon, Democrats nervously distanced themselves from paramilitary mobs that lent easy propaganda to northern Republicans. They may have been more interested in staving off a potential federal investigation into conditions in Kentucky than they were in abjuring the Klan. Nevertheless, the protests of the *Gazette* reflect at the very least discomfort with the conflation of extralegal violence and the Democratic Party.

Despite the protests of the conservative *Kentucky Gazette,* the Regulators were explicitly political actors, even if their aim was not to establish Democratic hegemony, as was the case in the lower South. The political purpose of this epidemic of violence in postwar Kentucky, and to a lesser extent in Missouri, was to disrupt, intimidate, and stifle black aspirations for equal citizenship in a biracial republic. This claim reminded white conservatives of what they had lost during the Civil War and, more important, the ongoing threat to white Kentuckians and Missourians' ascriptive conception of citizenship based on race and white supremacy. Just as white conservatives of all prior partisan loyalties coalesced around the "White Man's" Democratic Party, they sought more direct means to preserve white supremacy at the ground level. Democratic Party membership and Regulator violence against African Americans and unapologetic white Unionists served the same political purpose: defense of the white republic. A third element—the cultural reorientation of border state memory toward the Confederate Lost Cause—would reinforce the shift away from moderate prewar conservative Unionism to virulently white supremacist belated Confederatism.

Belated Confederates

At a Lexington "Confederate Reunion" in 1871, some of Missouri's most distinguished generals and officers addressed the enthusiastic crowd. Some speakers adopted a vindictive pose toward the Unionist victors. Captain Knisely of Columbia raged, "The last flame of Constitutional liberty died with the Confederacy, and the Confederates would have won in Missouri if it weren't for the Dutch and the niggers."[91] But most speakers conveyed a conciliatory and moderate tone toward the Unionists victors. General Vincent Marmaduke expressed admiration for those who "fought against me. I say to them today, we are your friends."[92] But one general present at the reunion, James Shields, offered a different perspective. He was a Union general, though his remarks did not offer a symbolic response to Marmaduke's magnanimity. Rather, Shields assumed the posture of advocate for Missouri's postwar Confederates, and he thanked the "liberality" of those Liberal Republicans who helped return voting rights to ex-Confederates. Why was a Union general even present at a Confederate reunion? And more important, who was General Shields to offer "thanks" to the Liberals on behalf of actual Confederate veterans? Had Union general James Shields become a Confederate after the war ended?

The story of people such as General Shields repeated itself throughout Missouri and Kentucky. Conservative Unionists who had fought against the Confederacy during the Civil War morally identified with their former Confederate foes in the war's aftermath. They became, in essence, belated Confederates, and they shared with the genuine rebels a celebration of the Confederate cause, sacrifice, and narrative of the Civil War. They yielded public space to former Confederates and made little or no effort to present a pro-Union narrative in response. Union colonel Frank Wolford, the commander of the First Kentucky Regiment and outspoken opponent of black suffrage, explained the deep sense of betrayal at the heart of belated Confederatism in a speech delivered to a Democratic Party meeting filled with actual ex-Confederates: "No party here can ever erase from the tables of stone and the pages of history the record of [the ex-Confederate soldiers'] sincerity, sustained, as it is, by a heroism almost if not quite unparalleled in the annals of the world."[93] Although Wolford reinforced his own Unionism in this speech, he found little of postwar Unionism to admire. "If history shall show, in the end, that the war was for the overrunning and subjugation of the Southern States, for the purpose of elevating the negro to political power at the expense of white men, born freemen, descendants of our revolutionary sires, then I shall turn from that sword with sorrow, if not with shame." Coming on the very day that the Congress passed the Reconstruction Acts, which placed the South under direct military occupation and granted suffrage to African Americans, Wolford's speech bore a tone of immediacy and crisis. Unlike Union veterans across the North who waved the bloody shirt to intimidate Democratic opponents and sow the seeds of Radical Reconstruction, these Missouri and Kentucky former Unionists figuratively switched sides and attacked their former comrades-in-arms.

Just as revealing of the culture of belated Confederatism was the proliferation of Confederate memorialization movements and the advertisement of Confederate hagiographies in the conservative ex-Unionist press. When Confederate general Sterling Price passed away in St. Louis, the formerly conservative Unionist *Weekly Brunswicker* claimed, "Few men have lived and left behind them a brighter or fairer record of great deeds."[94] The *Caucasian,* perhaps reflecting actual ex-Confederate sentiment more than the opinion of a belated Confederate, noted: "This noble old Roman departed this life . . . No man in Missouri, be he a political friend, or a political enemy (for Gen. P. had no personal enemies) enjoyed more of the respect of the people than he; and the loss of no one will be more sincerely felt and regretted."[95] Newspapers and citizens commemorated the lives of ordinary Confederate soldiers in conspicuous fashion as well. The "Ladies Memorial and Monumental Association," including relatives of John C. Breckinridge and John Hunt Morgan, met regularly in 1868 to decorate graves in the main cemetery in Lexington, Kentucky. After a Confederate Memorial Day ceremony at the cemetery, the *Kentucky Gazette* remarked, "No other observance is necessary to testify the grief which is felt for lost brothers and their lost cause than to strew flowers upon their graves."[96] As elsewhere in the South, women played a leading role in the decoration of Confederate soldiers' graves.[97] In Missouri the Fulton *Telegraph,* a once-conservative Unionist newspaper, celebrated the efforts of a man who built a memorial at the Battle of Lone Jack for the Confederate commander Jo Shelby.[98] The *Telegraph* also heartily approved of efforts to reinter the Confederate dead at Wilson's Creek, site of one of Missouri's most bloody battles. Nowhere in the formerly conservative Unionist press did editors describe or advocate similar commemorative efforts for Union soldiers.

The border state press also apprised readers of new historical works that celebrated the trials and tribulations of prominent Confederate officers or border state Confederate regiments. Alongside an advertisement for Basil Duke's "History of Morgan's Cavalry," the *Gazette* asserted that Unionists would find "much to like" in the book as it "corrects many false impressions."[99] Duke's history of Morgan's cavalry and the *Gazette*'s presentation of the work did more than ease the consciences of potential Unionist readers. The Unionists to which the *Gazette* referred were undoubtedly conservatives who longed for an excuse to jettison their wartime hatreds of the feared Morgan. Other histories, including a 930-page account of the Confederate First Kentucky Brigade, also known as the Orphan Brigade, received unqualified praise in conservative Unionists' papers. The *Paris True Kentuckian* methodically printed the names of Bourbon County men who had served in the famed Confederate unit.[100] After Robert E. Lee's death in 1870, newspapers rushed to express their condolences for the great "Christian patriot." When James McCabe published *Life of General Stonewall Jackson* and *The Life and Campaigns of General Robert E. Lee,* the *Danville Advocate* referred readers to the local agent of the new books. And when Colonel Charles Marshall, aide-de-camp of Lee, planned to publish an "authorized biography" of the former Confederate commander, the *Advocate* bragged that it had been appointed the "official agent" for the books in Boyle, Mercer, and Garrard counties.[101] The *Advocate* also ran a series of miniature biographies of Confederate leaders such as Stonewall Jackson by John Imboden, titling the series "Heroes of the War."[102] The *Missouri Telegraph* also dutifully printed portions of Imboden's Confederate hagiographies.[103]

Former Confederates reunited in social gatherings to proclaim their own devotion to the Lost Cause and celebrate the glory and bravery of fellow soldiers who could not make it. Conservative former Unionist newspapers dutifully heralded the honor and gallantry of Confederate officers and soldiers who gathered at these reunions. The *Caucasian* offered a description of the Confederate reunion at Lexington, Missouri, in 1871: "The Great Re-Union. A Legion of Old Rebels Hobnobbing Together. A Splendid Crowd—A Beautiful Day—A Bountiful Dinner—Music—Cider—Eloquence—And a Huge Time Generally."[104] Even the *Lexington (Mo.) Register,* arch rival to the *Caucasian,* offered a detailed, and generally positive, portrayal of the reunion.[105] Physically and figuratively, conservative ex-Unionists yielded public space to Confederate celebration without a word of protest.

Former Unionist George Caleb Bingham offered one of the starkest examples of belated Confederatism in the form of a single painting, titled simply *General Order Number 11.* Bingham's portrait, created between 1868 and 1870, visually reproduced the Missouri Confederate narrative of Federal despotism to powerful effect. The painting, which Bingham carried with him as he campaigned for Democratic candidates across the Midwest, depicts a western Missouri town on fire, with furniture and personal possessions strewn about. In the foreground is a white woman kneeling, with hands clasped, at the feet of an imperious Union officer. The officer clutches a pistol in his holster while staring down what appears to be the woman's elderly father, standing behind her. To one side an elderly black man in a hat covers his face to conceal his sadness at the sight of destruction. On the other side of the painting a black woman is sitting down, holding a white woman who has just fainted or died. And in front of the kneeling woman is a white man lying dead, shot in the head, with a pool of blood next to his head. Presumably, the dead man is the kneeling woman's husband.

Union general Thomas Ewing issued General Order Number 11 in September 1863, which expelled all residents from four western Missouri counties in retaliation for William Quantrell's murderous raid on Lawrence, Kansas. Historian Albert Castel has emphasized, however, that the order had its roots in Ewing's continued frustration at the persistence of bushwhacker violence on Missouri's western border.[106] Castel deconstructed the propagandistic elements of the portrait, including inaccurate portrayals of Union officers present and the supposed use of wanton terror against innocent civilians. One item that Castel ignores is the role of the slaves in the portrait who, like Mammy in *Gone with the Wind,* desperately appealed on behalf of their masters against nefarious Yankee intruders. But coming only a year after the Civil War, long before the maturation of the well-established canon of Lost Cause literature, Bingham's portrayal accomplished a different sort of political work.

Bingham's painting unleashed a firestorm of criticism among Radicals. The *St. Louis Democrat,* the banner Radical organ in Missouri, denounced the work upon its appearance in 1869. Bingham himself responded to the criticism by defending the truthfulness of the painting's representation and, more important, carrying a reproduction of it on the campaign trail wherever Democrats ran for office.[107] Regardless of the merits, both sides recognized that Bingham's portrayal painted Kansas supporters of the Union as the more culpable agents in the state's guerrilla war. As such, Bingham's work fit within an emerging body of Missouri neo-Confederate propaganda that reinforced the wartime Confederates' resentment of federal authority while adding postwar "usurpations" to the overall narrative. Missouri Democrats, including ex-Confederates and former conservative Unionists, pointed to Bingham's painting for propaganda effect.

Most striking about the construction of Civil War memory in the Reconstruction border states was the near total absence of white Unionist commemoration. In Boonville, Missouri, Union soldiers held a celebration of the Battle of Boonville, the pivotal battle early in the war that led to Governor

Claiborne Fox Jackson's evacuation from the state. The radical *Boonville Weekly Eagle* proclaimed, in strictly partisan tone: "Turn out in your strength and let the enemies of liberty and equality know that you are still in earnest . . . No Radical should stay away . . . If you feel any interest in the welfare of your country, if you feel any interest in the success of the Radical party, come. If you desire the election of Grant and Colfax, if you want peace restored through all the land, come. If you want the last remnants of rebellion extinguished, if you desire the defeat of Seymour and Blair, come."[108] In the only other instance of border state public commemoration or celebration of the Union, a group of citizens met on Decoration Day in 1872 in Centralia, Missouri, at the site where the unarmed soldiers of the Thirty-ninth Volunteer Infantry were butchered to death by Bloody Bill Anderson. But for true reconciliationism to make sense in a border context there would have to have been an equal number of Unionist reunions, memorials, and celebrations as there were Confederate—perhaps more so considering that a sizable majority of white Kentuckians and Missourians had supported the Union. Yet white border state Unionists held virtually no major public commemorative acts after the Civil War.[109] Every county seat in the Bluegrass built a Confederate memorial in the years following the Civil War; only Marion County's Lebanon built a Union statue in the national cemetery that housed the graves of Union soldiers killed at the Battle of Perryville.[110] In essence former Unionists completely yielded public space to pro-Confederate propagandists. Their silence in the face of Confederate Lost Cause hagiography underscored their bitter rejection of the Unionist cause every bit as poignantly as Wolford's proclamation to the same effect.

African Americans' open identification of the Union cause with their own liberation undoubtedly contributed to the damaged white ex-Unionist spirit. At an 1867 Fourth of July picnic in Paris, Kentucky, for example, African American historian George Washington Williams addressed a crowd of more than five thousand African Americans on the gallantry of black soldiers in the Union army and the fruits of emancipation.[111] In January 1870 blacks in Fulton, Missouri, held an Emancipation Day celebration, with public speakers reminding the audience that "the Colored Troops Fought Nobly."[112] Indeed, the emancipationist narrative of the war advanced by black Kentuckians and Missourians reinforced white ex-Unionist humiliation and conversion to belated Confederatism.[113] As historian Anne Marshall has discovered, even modest efforts by white border Unionists to hold picnics and reunions in the latter decades of the nineteenth century failed, in large part because white Unionists refused to associate themselves with African Americans, who had so identified the Union cause with their own emancipation.[114]

As returning Confederates assumed formal political authority in Kentucky and regained moral authority in radical-controlled Missouri, the large repository of former conservative Unionists began to view their former battlefield enemies as genuine allies. Most former Unionists completely yielded the public commemorative spirit to former Confederates and in some cases even joined them. A smaller core of whites did support the Radical Party, and shared with African Americans the emancipationist narrative of Civil War memory. But far more common were conservatives who felt little more than shame and betrayal at their own participation in the Union cause. For them the architects of the Union cause and their black minions had betrayed them and the cause of conservatism for which they had fought. If they were to think of the war at all, it would be to share in the celebration of Confederates—living and dead—who truly labored for the honorable cause of "Constitutional liberty." Belated Confederates dominated the political culture of Kentucky and Missouri and uniformly defined the memorial narrative of Little Dixie and the Bluegrass for over a century following the Civil War. Not until the Second Reconstruction of the Civil Rights movement in the 1960s, and even afterward, would Kentuckians and Missourians acknowledge the sacrifices and achievements of border state Unionists.[115]

The process by which conservative Unionists became belated Confederates manifested itself in various ways. There were individual Union veterans, such as James Shields, who literally adopted Confederate memory as their own, participating with ex-Confederates as if they had worn the gray and not the blue. More common—though less poignant—were former conservative Unionists such as Wolford who made a concerted effort to reconcile with their former Confederate foes and fight the greater menace of "negro equality" and "subjugation" of the South. To some extent Wolford's critique anticipated what historian David Blight referred to as the reconciliationist school of Civil War memory.[116] But the context within which these border state reconciliationists reestablished ties with their former enemies differed significantly from the magnanimous hand of solidarity offered by latter-day Yankees. Unlike northerners who waited decades before making the same symbolic trek to the old battlefields to relive wartime memories with Confederate foes and reinscribe a united nation on the keystone of white supremacy, the Kentuckians and Missourians looked to their own comrades right after the war ended as the greater evil in the larger struggle.

They might refer to the Confederate cause as "mistaken," as Wolford did elsewhere in his speech, but they would view the Union cause as "shameful." And in a former slave society beholden to codes of honor, the admission of public shame was among the most egregious signs of capitulation.

As belated Confederates, these ex-Unionists did not seek to create a new southern republic. Considering that border state Confederate ideology lacked the sort of nationalism that defined the cause in the lower South—secessionism in Kentucky and Missouri reflected a far more defensive spirit against the aggressions of Yankeedom than it did the earnest desire to create a new republic—it follows that Confederate memory itself would emphasize the defense of Constitutional liberty. Rather, they joined with their former Confederate foes to remake the white supremacist nation they had unwittingly undermined with their own guns. Alas, Frank Wolford's diatribe against the radicals who dismantled the old republic on the very day that he spoke echoed the "bitter" charges of Captain Knisely. To belated Confederates such as Wolford and actual ex-Confederates such as Knisely, "the last flame of Constitutional liberty died with the Confederacy."

Ladies' Aid and the Southern Conscience

In a notice appearing in the *Lexington (Mo.) Caucasian* in June 1866, a writer identified as "Southerner" addressed the "Ladies of Lafayette County, in behalf of the poor and destitute women in the South who have staked all upon the altars of their principles and what they considered the good of their country."[117] The writer exhorted the women of Lafayette County to organize fairs and other forms of entertainment in order to raise money for their suffering southern sisters in the former Confederacy: "Organize a society and go to work in earnest and let it not be said that Lafayette is behind other parts of the State." The writer referenced common objects of maternal sacrifice that women North and South encountered: "dependent little ones deprived not only of the necessary means of subsistance [sic] but bereft of fathers, sons, brothers, husbands, and friends, who like Trojans fell." But the author's appeal to southern women's dedication to principle and country betrayed a confidence in Missouri women's orientation toward the unique plight—if not the cause—of the South. White southerners in the former Confederacy knew they could count on genuine support in postwar Missouri. More important, white Missouri women positioned themselves at the vanguard of the belated Confederate movement in the border states.

Across the Bluegrass and Little Dixie in the spring and summer of 1866, women held fairs and meetings to raise money for assistance to the starving white people of the South. Just one day after "Southerner" appealed to the women of Lafayette County, a "large number of ladies" met at the Baptist Church in Lexington Township and formed a Southern Ladies' Aid Society.[118] The new organization then appealed to women in the other townships in Lafayette County to form similar associations and work in conjunction with the Lexington Township society.

The relationship between black enlistment and the overall transformation toward a pro-Confederate regional identification followed several jagged paths. Although violence committed by former Confederates and conservative Unionists against black soldiers and their families revealed an immediate connection between a black soldiery and conservative anger, the appearance of pro-southern aid societies—particularly those organized and operated by women—suggests a more complex relationship. But when the southern aid associations are placed in context with the national postwar aid movement across the Union states—nearly all of it directed toward the former slave population—the border state women's political goals stand out with special clarity.[119] They both reflected and energized a budding sympathetic movement toward the now "lost cause" of the ex-Confederate white South.

Appeals for aid before the letter in the *Caucasian* focused solely on the Christian charity of border state women, leaving aside any mention of principles or even common southern solidarity. In March 1866, for instance, a group of women in Boone County, Missouri, appealed to women throughout Little Dixie to "relieve the suffering ones in less favored parts."[120] An advertisement for the group appeared in the Fayette, Missouri, newspaper and proposed the creation of a relief organization both within Fayette and in "each neighborhood" in the surrounding countryside to establish a week-long relief fair. The group asked women to "beg money, to make and collect articles for sale, anything that will sell, no matter what—take cattle or corn, linsey or cotton, pin-cushions or door-mats, flowers or fruit, wood or woodlands, in fine anything that will bring money."[121] The group also proposed the establishment of an orphans' home in "some part of the South" to go along with whatever aid the women could deliver. The advertisement couched its appeal "in the name of humanity and christian charity" but not in the name of "principle" or southern solidarity. Even the accompanying editorial in the newspaper restricted its praise to "the example of Christian benevolence" offered by "the ladies of Boone County" who so selflessly volunteered their time and energy to the "people of the Southern States . . . made so poor by the operations and events of the war."[122] Both the advertisement and editorial promoted aid to the war-torn South as if the region had merely suffered a natural disaster or an epidemic. The Boone County appeal revealed little in the way of southern regional solidarity.

But when "Southerner" appealed to the women of Lafayette County in June 1866, she joined her mission of Christian benevolence with the burgeoning pro-southern patriotism that flowered in the months and years after Appomattox. These Southern Ladies' Aid Associations formed in early 1866 and expressed the conscience of white conservatives of both loyalties. Border state women's support for the cause of southern postwar aid followed a long trajectory of public activity by border state women on behalf of both sides in the Civil War. In the early years of the war women in Kentucky and Missouri formed Union Ladies' Aid Associations and similar organizations, with full moral and financial support from Union men. Like the postwar Southern Aid Societies, these Union associations served a very practical purpose. Upon Kentucky's entrance in the war on the Union side in the fall of 1861, Bourbon County women held a meeting to support the Union soldiers. "Let no lady absent herself, who can knit a pair of socks, or even speak a good word for the cause," implored the *Paris Western Citizen*.[123] Various women's organizations dedicated to sewing uniforms and providing other material and moral support for Union soldiers proliferated across the border states with names such as the Patriot Ladies of Paris, Ladies' Union Aid Society, the Ladies Soldiers' Relief Association, and the Bourbon County Volunteer Aid Society.[124] Like the southern associations, the Union groups offered invaluable moral authority to the cause by linking the Victorian conception of benevolent Christian womanhood with the principles of one of the belligerents in the Civil War.[125]

It is not surprising that pro-Confederate women's organizations failed to materialize in Kentucky and Missouri during the war because they would have been immediately suppressed by state and military authorities. Countless pro-Confederate women supported guerrillas by feeding and harboring them or by acting as spies on the lookout for Union militiamen. Privately, pro-Confederate women met to sew clothing for guerrillas or provide support for fellow women missing their husbands and sons in far-off battlefields. A friend of Danville's Susan Grigsby, wife of Confederate colonel John Grigsby, wrote upon hearing rumors of a Confederate invasion of Kentucky in early 1863, "I hope so you will then get to see your husband."[126] It would be a mistake, then, to read into the lack of public pro-Confederate women's activity during the war as a sign that the Confederate cause lacked moral support in the border states. Indeed, some of the women who emerged as leaders in the postwar Southern Aid Society movement began their public activism in the early part of the Civil War. Sue McCausland of Lexington, Missouri, was harassed by Union troops in the Federal siege of the town in September 1861 for refusing to take down her Confederate flag.[127] She defied the Federal soldiers by daring them to take the flag down themselves. With the war's completion in April 1865, women such as McCausland seized upon the border states' peaking sympathy for the southern cause and converted her militant support for the Confederacy into a wider humanitarian mission to aid whites suffering in the South.

It is noteworthy that all postwar women's aid societies in Little Dixie and the Bluegrass were aimed at the white South. This contrasts dramatically with the proliferation of missionary movements led by northern women who sought to educate and provide aid for the South's slave population.[128] Although many northern women traveled to St. Louis to work in the Western Sanitary Commission, virtually no white border state women assisted as teachers or aid providers for former slaves in either the border states themselves or the ex-Confederate South.[129] While the great moral cause for northern Christian women was the transformation of former slaves into educated citizens, the goal for border state women was the resuscitation of southern white society and the salvation of southern regional honor.

On one level the early pro-southern women's organizations resembled those appearing in the former Confederacy. Like women across the lower South, border state women of southern sympathies devoted much of their energies to the proper reburial of local Confederate soldiers and the assistance of Confederate soldiers recovering from wounds inflicted in the war.[130] In Paris, Kentucky, a "large number" of women met at a local cemetery in June 1866 to decorate with flowers and evergreens the graves of "brave sons of the South."[131] Given the regional context of these women's actions, coming on the heels of a bitterly divisive guerrilla war and carrying a barely concealed pro-Confederate sectional tone, their appearance in the border states suggests widespread community sanction of growing pro-southern orientation.

Making this transformation from pro-Unionism to southern solidarity even more remarkable was the large presence of ex-Union women in the movement. The wife of Lafayette County, Missouri, Unionist Richard C. Vaughan, for example, served on the Ladies' Southern Aid Society, which was founded in 1866 in Lexington, Missouri. Olivia Matthews, a manager in the Boone County aid society, was the daughter of Warren Woodson, a prominent Union general in central Missouri.[132] On the other hand, none of the women who appeared in the leadership of the wartime Union Ladies' Aid Society in Lexington served in the postwar southern Ladies' Aid Society of that town. Perhaps the membership of the Union Ladies' Aid Society was restricted to supporters of the Radical Party or to those who supported immediate emancipation, and none of them showed any sympathy for the plight of the white South after the war.

There is little available evidence describing the motives of women whose husbands and fathers had supported the Union during the war but who came around to support the southern aid movement after the war's conclusion. One possibility, which historian Amy Murrell Taylor explores, is that the women disagreed with the stances of their husbands; that is, they supported the Confederacy during the war, while their husbands, brothers, or fathers supported the Union.[133] But there is no evidence that women such as Richard C. Vaughan's wife or Warren Woodson's daughter had supported the Confederacy during the war. A more likely explanation is that the attitude of these former Unionist women reflected that of many Unionist men who grew disenchanted with the radical course of the Union war effort, especially the enlistment of African Americans into the army. Indeed, what the husbands and fathers of these Unionists had in common was that they all became ardent conservative Democrats following the war. Men such as Vaughan had been ardent Whigs right up through the 1860 election and remained staunchly loyal to the Union throughout the war. But Vaughan and many of his conservative Unionist cohorts immediately joined the Democratic Party in the shadows of Radical ascendancy. And in many cases they became the greatest advocates for the rights of disfranchised ex-Confederates under the new Radical regime in Missouri. If becoming a Democrat was the most potent way for conservative Unionist men to express their disappointment with the radicalization of the Union, joining the Southern Ladies' Aid Society movement was an equally powerful modality of political activism for former conservative Unionist women.

The mass of white conservatives in Little Dixie and the Bluegrass who supported the Union, or even remained neutral such as was possible, looked dubiously upon their own victory. They stood idly by as returning Confederates staffed the ranks of the reemergent Democratic Party of Kentucky;

an aborted Conservative Union third party quickly yielded to an inevitable union with the rebel Democracy. And in Missouri they apologized for and advocated on behalf of the most destructive guerrillas who had once terrorized them. They celebrated the deeds and venerated the honor of their wartime tormentors and fought vigorously for the restoration of the suffrage rights of those who once attempted to destroy the Union. But never did they publicly exalt the sacrifices of their own comrades-in-arms. They were ashamed of their cause. Conservative Unionists in central Missouri and Kentucky had become belated Confederates by 1870. And adding institutional power to belated Confederatism, ex–conservative Unionists such as Brutus Clay of Kentucky and Richard C. Vaughan of Missouri crossed over from the old Whig Party and joined their former partisan foes and battlefield enemies in a newfound Democratic solidarity. For them the Democratic Party stood as the only tool to protect white civilization and white supremacy from the onslaught of radical usurpations and, more important, black pretensions to racial equality.

But Democratic solidarity and belated Confederatism alone failed to answer the freedpeople's political charge. Only the use of violence, both organized and ad hoc, could restore white honor and prestige threatened once by black enlistment and now by black affectations of equality. White Regulator mobs chased African Americans out of small villages across central Kentucky, and to a lesser extent Missouri, and delivered summary violence against those who openly resisted white supremacy. Blacks who negotiated favorable sharecropping arrangements faced nighttime expulsion. And those who dared challenge the white monopoly on the formal reigns of power endured the most humiliating depredations. Chased and brutalized by whites, both actual and belated Confederates, blacks sought refuge in the larger towns of the Bluegrass and Little Dixie or in the neighboring states of Indiana, Kansas, and Ohio. This first migration blazed the trail followed later by Kansas Exodusters and in the twentieth century the Great Migration to the great industrial cities of the North and West.

White violence against African Americans in the postwar border states revealed the potency of the black challenge to white supremacy. Even without the vote, African Americans threatened white people's monopoly on civil and political authority and, so they feared, social and cultural authority as well. To white conservatives little stood between aspirations of civil and political equality, on the one hand, and miscegenation and black sexual predatoriness, on the other. After 1870, however, white conservatives faced the ultimate test of black political power. Passage of the Fifteenth Amendment introduced thousands of new black voters to the polls in Kentucky and Missouri and threatened to undermine the white supremacist consensus just as whites of the former Confederacy began their own campaign of "Redemption" in earnest.

CHAPTER 9

BLACK SUFFRAGE AND THE NEW POLITICAL ORDER

In August 1870 the *Harrodsburg People* newspaper denounced for a world audience the atrocity of black suffrage recently foisted upon the conservative white people of Kentucky: "The first Monday in August 1870 will be a day long remembered in the history of Kentucky. On that day, culminated in our State the series of outrages which within the last five years have been perpetrated upon the constitution of the United States and the liberties of the people. On that day took effect the fraudulent Amendment of the Constitution which in violation of the laws of Kentucky, forced to the polls a vast horde of men, utterly ignorant of the duties and responsibilities attached to the new position into which they had been thrust by the bayonet and by congressional corruption."[1]

As the *People* and other conservative Democrats had warned would happen, the election quickly turned into a general riot, with both black and white men killed in the usually quiet streets of Harrodsburg. As the editor disdainfully put it, after the "dark mass pressed toward the Court room" to register their votes, whites lined up alongside them, despite "the repulsive odor which, in such circumstances, always arises from the body of the negro."[2] And when a fight broke out inside the courtroom and spilled onto the street, "some drunks," including a "drunken white leader" named Lawrence, took advantage, and the fight became a general riot. As soon as the violence ensued, black men "summoned by the beating of a drum" were "fully equipped and prepared to fight in a few minutes."[3] The well-organized black mob threatened whites that if they didn't stop attacking black men, they would "burn down the town."[4] As a result of this violence, the conservative *People* moaned, the Democrats failed to "sweep the town ticket," as they had predicted.

The Election Day violence in Harrodsburg, Kentucky, resembled the sort of mayhem that often accompanied the polls in nineteenth-century America.[5] But as the *People* pointed out, this election was vastly different than those in the past. Not only were African Americans prepared to vote in this election, but they came armed and prepared for a fight that they knew would materialize. White conservatives both underestimated black organizational savvy and overestimated their own ability to maintain political—and so-cial—order in this central Kentucky town. The Fifteenth Amendment, which "thrust" equal manhood suffrage upon Kentucky, changed politics in the state forever.

Kentucky and its sister border state of Missouri experienced the Fifteenth Amendment in a fashion different from any other state in the Union. In the former Confederate states African Americans had voted regularly since passage of the congressional Reconstruction Acts in 1867. In most southern states blacks participated in at least three different votes by 1870 and in nearly all such states helped place the Republican Party in power. On the other side, northern states maintained various laws regarding black voting. Some, such as Massachusetts and New York, permitted black voting. Others, such as Connecticut and Indiana, refused it. But none of these northern states possessed a sizable black population; the highest percentage of African American voters in any northern state was 2.4 percent in Ohio.[6] Kentucky and Missouri—16.8 and 6.9 percent black, respectively—introduced a far greater sum of black voters to the polls for the first time in 1870.[7]

The Fifteenth Amendment was the result of national political developments and pressures and came about with only marginal contribution from the border states. Missouri's Radical political leaders supported the amendment, and Kentucky's Democrats opposed it, but neither of them held any significant say in the passage or ratification of the amendment in 1869 and 1870. But in both border states African Americans had long agitated for the right to vote and viewed ratification of the amendment as the result, in some way, of their own efforts. At the very least the political movement that advocated black suffrage in Missouri and Kentucky laid the organizational groundwork for a black Republican electoral movement once the amendment became law.

Once blacks became voters, white Democrats faced a dilemma. Although most Democrats accentuated their white supremacist claims to "purity" from the taint of black votes, many Democrats sought to obtain the electoral support of the new black voters. Republicans faced a similar internal divide.

Because of the persistence of a white Radical Republican Party, based in Missouri among the Germans of St. Louis and the small farmers of the Ozarks and in Kentucky among the eastern mountaineers and the merchants of the Ohio River towns and cities, white Republicans equivocated over the advent of black suffrage. Eventually, the Republican Party in both states openly solicited black voters and adopted the egalitarian rhetoric of the national Republican Party. This shift came only after some serious internal disagreement.

The Fifteenth Amendment altered the political culture surrounding elections in central Kentucky and central Missouri. But with a few exceptions, such as the Harrodsburg case, it did little to change the outcome of these elections. Blacks and whites both demonstrated in the first years following the Civil War that the ballot box was only one locus of power in the border state political culture. As before, institutional development, migration, labor strife, violence, and the cultural production of regional identity played an equally important role in determining political power as voting. Election outcomes certainly played a significant part in determining power at the grassroots level—decisions regarding patronage, civil rights laws, and school funding, for example, depended in large part on the outcome of elections at the local and state level. But for African Americans, a small minority of the border state population, the process of voting mattered as much as the outcome. The very presence of black voters, armed and organized to defend their right to vote, forced white Democrats to acknowledge black people's basic claims to the prerogatives of citizenship.

The Arrival of Manhood Suffrage

Just weeks before the United States secretary of state proclaimed ratification of the Fifteenth Amendment, the *Lexington (Mo.) Caucasian* published a vituperative editorial denouncing the prospect of black suffrage: "Nigger Equality. The Fifteenth Bedamnedment Certain to be 'Ratified.' Hell Just Ahead. The Only Way of Salvation. Rub in the Nigger! Official Equality the Watchword. Black the Winning Color for Congressmen and All Federal Officers."[8] Democrats across central Missouri and Kentucky nervously awaited the new "Bedamnedment" to the federal Constitution, which granted African Americans the right to vote for the first time. And just as white conservatives feared the political earthquake of black suffrage, African Americans anticipated the new amendment as the culmination of the radical promise of the Union Civil War effort. For white supporters of the Republican Party, the amendment's ratification posed a different set of challenges and possibilities: should they embrace the new supporters of the party or shun them in order to keep their white power base? Whatever the expectations of the new law, nobody viewed passage and ratification of the Fifteenth Amendment with indifference. For five years the people of Kentucky and Missouri had prepared for this day, with the political culture of the border states shaped to a large degree by their varying expectations.

Black Missourians lobbied for the right to vote as early as the state constitutional convention of January 1865. A National Convention of Colored Citizens of the United States formed the National Equal Rights League in December 1864 and explicitly rooted black assertions of political equality in their participation in the Union army. The foundational document declared: "While the devotion, the gallantry, and the heroism displayed by our sons, brothers and fathers at Port Hudson, Fort Wagner, Petersburg, New Market Heights . . . let us not fail to make every effort in our power to secure for ourselves and our children all those rights, natural and political, which belong to us as men and as native-born citizens of the United States of America . . . And who shall say we do not owe it to the noble men who represent us in the army and navy."[9] Seven black men in St. Louis formed a local branch of this organization in 1865, which they dubbed the Missouri Equal Rights League. The Executive Committee of this league included James Milton Turner, Moses Dickson, and others representing the merchant and laboring classes.[10] The league regularly held meetings throughout the state and offered petitions to the Missouri state constitutional convention as well as the state legislature. Most petitions reinforced their protest against "taxation without representation," a revolutionary discourse that linked the African American struggle for equal citizenship with the patriots of 1776.[11] National civil rights advocate John Mercer Langston joined the Missouri cause, delivering numerous rousing speeches to the state legislature and to audiences throughout the state. Perhaps most important was the inclusion of ordinary African Americans in the league petitions. Indeed, some of these petitions included signatures from thousands of African Americans, even in interior counties; Platte County on the state's western border offered 3,816 signatures alone.[12] Although the legislative record reveals no explicit evidence of petitions from Little Dixie, it is likely that blacks in Little Dixie joined their Platte County brethren and presented similar documents to Jefferson City. More important, the very process of obtaining signatures from scattered African Americans in rural central and western counties incorporated the black grassroots within the St. Louis–based Missouri Equal Rights League and the overall suffrage movement.

In Kentucky blacks pushed for suffrage rights through a series of state-wide organizations, though none with the potency of the Missouri Equal Rights League. The First Convention of the Colored Men of Kentucky, which met in March 1866, declared, "We claim each and every right and power guaranteed to any and all other American Citizens, including even that of suffrage, as naturally and legally belonging to us."[13] Although the same resolution tabled the suffrage demand for the moment, the convention made clear the aspirations of Kentucky's black community just three months after emancipation. Other high-profile conventions and gatherings reinforced the call for black suffrage. On July 4, 1867, several leading white radicals spoke at a "Colored People's Barbecue" in Lexington and told the crowd that either God or Congress would grant suffrage to black Kentuckians in due time.[14] Blacks formed special Republican Clubs in cities across Kentucky, including Lexington, and a proposed joint political organization with the white Republican Party.[15] A Negro State Central Committee of Lexington invited delegates from across Kentucky to assemble for a convention in late 1867 that would advocate black suffrage.[16] The Democrats in control of the Kentucky state legislature scoffed at these calls for black suffrage. But the black movement on behalf of suffrage did produce an important result. As with the Missouri petition movement, Kentucky black leaders organized petition drives throughout the Bluegrass countryside, obtaining signatures from thousands of ordinary African Americans lobbying Congress for passage of the Fourteenth and Fifteenth amendments.[17] This process helped nurture a formal, partisan political consciousness among the black masses and provided lessons for organizing later black Republican meetings in the Bluegrass hinterlands. The actions of the Missouri Equal Rights League and the various black Central State committees in Kentucky channeled grassroots pressure on state legislators between 1865 and 1870, just as the national Equal Rights League influenced the Radical Republicans in Congress to pass the Fourteenth and Fifteenth amendments. The momentum generated by this broad-based movement came to fruition just as the Fifteenth Amendment was officially ratified in March 1870.

Black suffrage advocates in Kentucky and Missouri prepared for the coming amendment in myriad ways. The first of these was to celebrate the amendment's passage and establish in the public square community approval of this critical governmental acknowledgment of citizenship. In a biracial celebration in Lexington, Missouri, hundreds gathered along the streets of the town and welcomed a procession with bands, black church Sunday schools, and many American flags. The participants and spectators from the town of Lexington and the surrounding county of Lafayette heard numerous speakers extolling the value of education and the role of black soldiers in the Civil War. As rainfall enveloped the event, a choir sang, "Abraham has spoken, all our chains are broken." The *Lexington Caucasian* offered a surprisingly positive portrayal of the event: "We but do the blacks simple justice when we say they acquitted themselves in a very creditable manner, both as to what was said and done."[18] The *Caucasian,* always quick to cite criminality or disorder among African Americans in general, may have emphasized the orderly behavior of the crowd in order to woo black votes for the coming referendum on rebel enfranchisement. But there is little doubt that the crowd acquitted itself with solemnity, a public performance calculated to demonstrate to both blacks and whites the gravity of the newly earned political equality. Just as important, the display of flags and banners helped to claim within public discourse the equation of patriotism with biracial suffrage.

Another amendment celebration took place in Versailles, Kentucky, and the conservative *Woodford Weekly* offered similarly faint praise for the orderliness of the attendees. With eight hundred men, women, and children from Woodford and "surrounding counties," attendees displayed numerous flags and banners throughout the town before moving to a grove on the outskirts for a general picnic.[19] As in the Missouri celebration, whites and blacks spoke to the crowd, referencing the courage of black soldiers in the Civil War. The conservative press understood the political significance of these celebrations, even if it did not always appreciate the motives. The *Kentucky Gazette* of Lexington remarked of another celebration in that city, "The purpose . . . was to convince the whites of their political persuasion, that they were many in number and ought to have a share in the offices, as well as to do the voting."[20] None of the three accounts described any blatant partisanship emerging from the amendment celebrations; if anything, they stressed the nonpartisan nature of the events and the willingness of blacks to "listen to all parties." Perhaps conservative Democrats still believed that African Americans could be wooed to flock to the Democracy, and the conservative press did not want to stand in the way.

Even before black Kentuckians and Missourians planned community celebrations of the new amendment, they devised formal electoral strategies for the coming campaigns. The nonpartisan nature of the Fifteenth Amendment celebrations revealed, at the very least, some choices within the black community regarding electoral strategy. They could give support to all political parties so that none could take them for granted, or they could cleave to the Radical Republicans, who had been most supportive of black suffrage. At a Fifteenth Amendment celebration in Lexington, Missouri, African Americans listened to white radicals offering divergent choices in the state elections ahead. Whereas some Radicals insisted that "the negroes . . . see to it that they vote for no man, unless they were fully in favor of the largest education of the people," other Radicals implored blacks to vote in favor of re-enfranchising "their former masters."[21]

But the vast preponderance of black political thought on the eve of suffrage favored the Republican Party and the most radical elements within it. A Negro State Convention met at Louisville in late February 1870 to praise imminent ratification of the Fifteenth Amendment, declaring, "We will affiliate with the Republican Party of progress and civilization, which has been the instrument in the hands of Providence, for the attainment by us of the blessings and privileges we enjoy."[22] This convention, with delegates from every county in the Bluegrass and most counties throughout the state, expressed the gendered militancy of black Kentuckians in the face of white Democratic intimidation: "We will treat with scorn and regard as an insult to our manhood any attempt from any source to influence our votes by threats of refusal to employ us as laborers and receive us as tenants, or by bribery or venality; and we do not regard any colored man who could be so influenced as worthy of our respect or friendship, or association."[23] For black Kentuckians the vote crystallized the relationship between full citizenship and manly resistance to white conservative and Democratic intimidation.

Black Kentuckians put their Republican allegiance into practice before final ratification. At a March 1870 Fayette County Republican Committee meeting, half of the delegates were black. Although the Fifteenth Amendment did not take effect until March 30, the March 14 meeting included African Americans from each of Lexington's four wards and four of Fayette County's six outer districts.[24] As the *Kentucky Gazette* noted, most of the black committeeman were preachers, selected to serve because of their "supposed influence over their flocks."[25] Perhaps most interesting, Henry King, Erasmus Wells and George Perry, black committee members from the first and fourth wards of Lexington, had served as delegates to the Kentucky State Colored Men's Convention in March 1866. For these men the long journey to black suffrage, first publicly envisioned in the months after emancipation, culminated on the eve of the Fifteenth Amendment's ratification with the mundane workings of Republican committee politics.

Several African Americans addressed a similar pre-ratification Republican meeting in Harrodsburg, Kentucky, in February 1870, which appointed delegates for the statewide Republican convention at Frankfort. The conservative Versailles newspaper reporting on the meeting in neighboring Mercer County noted that "Negros [sic] will be inspired with hatred and distrust of Democrats . . . the Democrats are his enemies and the Radicals are his only friends."[26] The paper also predicted that while whites will continue to control the Republican Party in Kentucky, the black man will be expected to do "his duty to help the party, which means to contribute from his scanty earnings to political documents, papers, preachers, etc."[27] As conservatives feared, African Americans would play a significant role in the state's Republican Party from the very beginning.

The political landscape in Missouri encouraged African Americans to view the Radical Republican Party with much more caution than in Kentucky.[28] After all, the Republican Party had failed to write black suffrage into the 1865 constitution and could not muster enough statewide support for the black suffrage referendum in 1868. Black Missourians had reason to doubt the commitment of the state's Radicals toward civil and political equality for African Americans. As soon as black Missourians attained the right to vote via the Fifteenth Amendment, the Republican Party split into Liberal and Radical factions over the proposed removal of the rebel disfranchisement provision in the state constitution.[29] With some of the earliest advocates of black suffrage such as B. Gratz Brown and Carl Schurz now firmly in the Liberal camp and with many Liberals advancing the appealing doctrine that there must be no proscriptions for voting based on either race or loyalty, many African Americans supported the Liberal party against the Radicals. Moses Dickson, a former AME minister and long-standing advocate for black suffrage and black education, strongly supported the Liberal position on enfranchisement in 1870.[30] Dickson, and national leaders such as Frederick Douglass counseled black Missourians to support the Liberals and their rebel re-enfranchisement policy because, even though the Liberals had formed an effective alliance with the hated Democratic Party, they feared that Democrats without the ballot would be more dangerous than if they could vote.[31] It was not until Missouri's African Americans grew utterly disgusted with Gratz Brown's Liberal administration after 1870 that black Missourians unified en masse behind the Radical Republican Party.

Still, there were many black Missourians who argued vociferously that the Radical wing of the Republican Party was the only suitable home for black Missourians when the state's black population first attained the right to vote. Typically, blacks voiced their support for the Radical wing by denouncing the rebel re-enfranchisement amendments. Daniel Cooper, chair of a mass meeting of blacks at the AME church in Glasgow, Howard County, declared, "Said amendments place the loyalty and patriotism of the colored man on a level with the disloyalty of the nation's enemies, who made a deadly thrust at the Federal heart within the last decade."[32] Chief among Missouri Radicals was James Milton Turner, the civil rights and education advocate and a teacher in Little Dixie for much of the late 1860s. Although black Missourians gained the right to vote in March 1870, their first opportunity to exercise their right came in the November 1870 gubernatorial vote and the constitutional referendum on rebel re-enfranchisement. And as black Liberals and Dickson urged blacks to support Gratz Brown and the Liberal ticket, Turner linked his opposition to rebel enfranchisement with his endorsement of the Radical ticket of Joseph McClurg. Turner toured the entire state throughout 1870 and vigorously rejected any link between black and rebel enfranchisement. Whereas some Liberals argued that the Republican Party's mission ended with the Fifteenth Amendment, Turner retorted, "I contend the mission of the party will not be complete until the word 'white' is stricken from the constitution of every State in this Union and all men placed on perfect equality before the law of the country."[33] The formerly Radical *St. Louis Democrat,* now a supporter of the Liberal ticket, quoted Turner as telling a train passenger: "I believe with Thomas Jefferson that every man who pays taxes should be allowed to vote. But I believe also . . . that every man who commits treason should be hung dead by the neck."[34] For Turner the real problem facing African Americans was the lukewarm commitment of the state's Radical party to black suffrage, education, and other rights. Adding former rebels back into the electoral fold would only hasten the demise of the state government's commitment to the rights of black Missourians. Turner may have irked much of the black and white Republican political establishment with his support of the increasingly unpopular McClurg administration, but he presciently assessed the downfall of Republicanism in the state after rebel enfranchisement.

While African Americans eagerly anticipated the Fifteenth Amendment, white Kentuckians and Missourians braced for a political earthquake. White divisions over how to approach the coming ratification had their roots in the immediate postwar partisan shakeout of the former Unionist coalition. Conservative Unionists who had migrated to the Democratic Party in the war's aftermath merely added the threat of black suffrage to their list of grievances with the course of "Unionism." Practical evidence of conservative Unionist rejection of black suffrage manifested itself in Missouri's 1868 referendum on black suffrage, in which Little Dixie voters led the way in opposition. Although all Little Dixie voters in the 1868 election were demonstrably Unionist during the Civil War and could take the oath of loyalty to that effect, they summarily rejected the black suffrage amendment. The amendment received support from 43 percent of all Missourians statewide, with most of its support in the arch Radical but mostly white Ozark region.[35] In Little Dixie, however, voters offered scant support for black suffrage. Howard County, a banner slave county of Little Dixie with one of the highest black populations in the state, gave only 5 percent support for the amendment. Callaway and Saline counties could not even register a vote because of fraud and violence at the ballot box. And Boone and Chariton counties offered support at 20 and 30 percent, respectively. Interestingly, voters in Lafayette and Cooper counties supported the measure to a greater extent—at 36 and 47 percent, respectively—even though both counties had once been strong proslavery hotbeds. The sizable German population in both counties and the influx of northerners after the Civil War probably explain the large support for black suffrage there.

Kentucky, of course, never submitted a black suffrage amendment to its voters, and virtually nobody within the state's white political community seriously considered it. To a large extent, white opposition to black suffrage and the Fifteenth Amendment in Kentucky followed a similar line as in Missouri. The conservative *Kentucky Gazette* wrote in 1867 that "this negro suffrage is a crime against society and an abomination in the sight of God and man, and will not only be resisted by every constitutional means, but is surely paving the way for a bloody war of races."[36] Threat to white civilization lay at the heart of conservative opposition. "The highest civilization the negro is capable of is to be a hewer of wood and a drawer of water to the white man. Emancipate him from this condition and he relapses into his native barbarism—enfranchise him and give him political equality with the white man, and he drags the latter down with him without the possibility of retarding the descent."[37] Fulton's conservative Unionist *Missouri Telegraph* reported in 1869 that the "war of the races" in the form of "terrorism" and a massive race riot had already begun in Washington, D.C., as a result of black suffrage there.[38] The newspaper implied that black suffrage in Missouri would herald a similar fit of riotous violence, anarchy, and terrorism.

White conservatives also rejected black suffrage on the grounds that it violated the very nature of the Republic. The *Telegraph* responded to radicals who echoed the Declaration of Independence and proclaimed, "All men are created equal," by asserting that the declaration was signed by men who represented white men only.[39] Others, such as the editor of the *Paris True Kentuckian,* protested the open-ended clause within the Fifteenth Amendment that authorized "appropriate legislation" to enforce the legislation.[40] Although this line of argument differed from the claim that the Declaration of Independence only applied to white men, it cited the views of the Founders to rebuke the new amendment. The editor of the *True Kentuckian* believed that the Constitution firmly placed all suffrage decisions within the hands of the states and that the new amendment would irreversibly alter that constitutional framework by allowing federal agents to interfere in state elections at whim. The amendment thus threatened the Founders' white supremacist construction of the Republic and the federal organization of that Republic that bolstered the principles of white supremacy.

Although Kentuckians and Missourians similarly feared the civilizational and constitutional threat of black suffrage, they revealed tactical differences between the two states. For Kentuckians the Fifteenth Amendment represented the formal introduction of one of the central tenets of Radical Reconstruction into the state for the first time. The state had already rebuffed federal efforts to enforce the Fourteenth Amendment's civil rights clauses, though it would grudgingly accept black testimonial rights in 1872. But white Kentuckians of all political stripes rejected black suffrage out of hand and viewed the Fifteenth Amendment as an unmitigated threat to the white, conservative Democratic political order that consolidated power in the first years after the Civil War. For Missourians, however, the Fifteenth Amendment was doubly offensive because it enfranchised blacks before white former rebels could vote again. The *Lexington Caucasian* mocked the new "Bedamnedment" and blasted the fundamental contradiction that lay at its heart: "Yes, the work is done! Shuffle your jay-bird heels; pat 'Juba'; and shout with barbaric delight, ye lousy, devil worshipping chattels of Carolina rice-plantations! Screech your beastly exultation, ye man-eating savages of Dahomey and Loango! Howl your ecstacy, ye vermin swarming, filth-reeking Hottentots! You're all citizens—voters—sovereigns—of the glorious 'American Republic'—While five hundred thousand WHITE MEN are disfranchised aliens!"[41] The *Missouri Telegraph* had denounced the state's proposal to grant suffrage to blacks in 1868 because, among other things, it refused to re-enfranchise white men who had once sympathized with the Confederacy.[42] It continued to hammer on this point throughout 1870. Conservative Democrats in Kentucky and Missouri both believed that the Fifteenth Amendment would severely damage the white Republic and the constitutional principles that undergird it. But Missouri conservatives especially despised the amendment because it explicitly granted suffrage rights to blacks while whites were still forbidden from voting—a terrifying and true example of "negro supremacy" sanctioned by the federal government and now by the Constitution itself.

There were, however, many white Democrats who acquiesced in the new world of biracial suffrage. In most cases this acquiescence proved tactical and short-lived, but it represented a sudden and shocking rhetorical twist in conservative sentiment. Perhaps most explicit was the *Lexington Caucasian,* which not only portrayed a Fifteenth Amendment celebration in a positive manner but even praised the overall conduct of black would-be voters. Just weeks after exclaiming, "Hell Just Ahead. The Only Way of Salvation. Rub in the Nigger!"[43] the *Caucasian* offered: "The negro has behaved himself far better than we had any right to expect of him under the circumstances through which he has passed. Far better. The love of liberty is inborn, in the black as well as white, and can scarcely be eradicated or lessened."[44] The newspaper reiterated its rejection of the amendment and heaped scorn upon white radicals who "forced upon the negro a privilege he never had or desired." But it stoically accepted the "fact that blacks are to vote, and will vote despite any captious opposition to it."[45] And it placed partisan hatred of radicalism over white supremacist unity by declaring conservative intentions to "vote for the negro whenever and wherever he is opposed by a radical alone, believing him to be more honest, if not more capable, than any of the radical tribe."[46] The *Caucasian* clearly believed that by praising the "behavior" of the African American community and proclaiming the permanence of black suffrage, it could woo black voters into the Democratic, or at least the Liberal, camp.

Other conservative newspapers optimistically projected that black voters would favor the Democrats because their "interests" dictated voting with their employers or at least that Democrats could convince black voters to that effect. The *Lexington Press* condemned blacks for letting Radicals influence them and wondered aloud why black voters would not support the ticket favored by their employers, "who provide aid and assistance to them better than Radical politicians."[47] The *Missouri Telegraph* claimed that in the former Confederate states, where blacks had been voting since 1867, "the Southern people will ultimately control the negro vote, and may use the Fifteenth Amendment to break the heads of its authors."[48] Considering how astute border state newspaper editorialists were regarding political behavior in the former Confederacy, where blacks shunned the Democratic Party from the moment of enfranchisement in 1867, it is surprising that the *Telegraph* would make such a naive remark. Perhaps the newspaper assumed that Missouri's black voters were unaware of the Republican allegiances of their compatriots in the lower South and could thus be swayed into siding with the Democratic Party. In response to Radical charges that the conservative paper had taken a "strange interest" in black voters, the *Telegraph* responded, "We know that a negro's vote will count as much as a white man's and if we can influence them to vote with us, we will most cheerfully do so."[49] Nevertheless, the Democratic Party made little more than symbolic efforts to woo black voters in Kentucky and Missouri, instead rallying virtually all white conservative and moderate voters under the banner of the White Man's Democracy.

For white border conservatives the Fifteenth Amendment represented the ultimate insult added to injury. The Fulton *Telegraph,* long one of the banner conservative Unionist newspapers in Little Dixie, placed the new amendment in perspective: "What the Fifteenth Amendment Has Cost: Two millions of precious lives! The destruction of nine thousand million dollars worth of property! The prostration of trade and commerce! The demoralization of the nation, with a mule rider for president."[50] To belated Confederates such as the editor of the *Missouri Telegraph,* the radical course of war and revolution simply wasted immeasurable amounts of property and countless human lives, all for a nefarious, unproven, and dangerous theory that directly betrayed the conservative basis of Union. In 1860 the *Telegraph,* like other conservative Unionist organs, had warned that civil war might lead to such an atrocious outcome. Conservatives caught between the anvil of Confederatism and the hammer of radicalism predicted the destruction of the white Republic that had prevailed since the American Revolution. To conservatives the Fifteenth Amendment represented the humiliating capstone of radical usurpation of the Union cause.

White border state Republicans expressed more division over the black suffrage question and the Fifteenth Amendment than did the Democrats. By 1870 Kentucky Republicans had assembled a viable local party apparatus in eastern Kentucky and in the northern cities along the Ohio River. Even in the Bluegrass heartland, Republicans garnered a respectable minority vote among the more staunch Union veterans, especially in the larger towns and cities such as Lexington and Danville. Kentucky Republicans' racial policies were considerably more conservative than those of the national Republican Party; during the 1865–66 legislative session Kentucky Republicans officially supported Andrew Johnson's conservative plan for Reconstruction, opposed black suffrage, and called for the removal of the Freedmen's Bureau from Kentucky.[51]

In Missouri the Republican Party embraced black civil rights and black suffrage more vigorously than in Kentucky. But even there, strong divisions with the state's party led to general opposition to black suffrage in 1865, mixed support for the black suffrage amendment in 1868, and a lukewarm embrace of the Fifteenth Amendment in 1870. There were three reasons Missouri's Republican Party eventually shifted its support in favor of black suffrage, even if incompletely. First, the national Republican Party embraced black suffrage in response to President Johnson's intransigence, and Missouri's Republican Party followed the national lead. Second, the party feared it would lose elections if it did not have black votes. And third, activists from the Missouri Equal Rights League applied grassroots pressure on the Missouri Republican Party to embrace black suffrage as concomitant with the party's radical ideology. The 1868 referendum on black suffrage ultimately failed, with Little Dixie leading the opposition, but the state's Republican Party, including both Radical and Liberal factions, uniformly accepted black suffrage two years before ratification of the Fifteenth Amendment. Some white Republican voters opposed the black suffrage referendum in 1868, but most of the opposition came from conservative Unionists centered in Little Dixie.

Black and white Kentuckians and Missourians prepared for Secretary of State Hamilton Fish to certify ratification of the Fifteenth Amendment in March 1870, knowing little of how this political temblor would shake border state politics. As blacks held large Fifteenth Amendment celebrations in small towns such as Versailles and Harrodsburg, Kentucky, and Lexington and Boonville, Missouri, whites reoriented their substantive and rhetorical positions to accommodate the changing times. Black Kentuckians and Missourians transformed partisan politics in the first two years after ratification of the Fifteenth Amendment. The time for celebration and preparation came to an end, and the task of constructing a formal biracial polity began.

Electoral Politics after the Fifteenth Amendment

On Saturday, April 2, 1870, just three days after Secretary of State Fish declared the Fifteenth Amendment officially ratified, voters in Danville, Kentucky, went to the polls to elect a slate of municipal officers. For the first time ever, the Republican Party swept the election, winning each and every office by an average majority of seventy-five votes.[52] African Americans, granted voting rights less than a week before the election, gave the Republicans the entire margin of victory; of more than two hundred black voters only two voted for the Democrats. In dozens of local, state, and national elections across the Bluegrass and Little Dixie after ratification of the Fifteenth Amendment, African American voters altered the partisan balance of power. Although blacks only made up about 20 percent of the Little Dixie population in 1870 and 39 percent in the Bluegrass, they demonstrated near unanimous support for the Republican Party.[53]

Black voters exerted the most influence in urban elections, such as that in Danville and in Lexington, Kentucky. In the November 1870 general election each of Lexington's four wards gave a majority to the Republican congressional candidate, even though surrounding rural portions of Fayette County lent its votes overwhelmingly to the Democrat. As was the case with Danville and Boyle County, Lexington's Republican Party had been active before the Fifteenth Amendment but never strong enough to win citywide. Table 9.1 shows Lexington's vote total by ward for 1867 and 1870. Although the offices up for election differed in each case, the party line style of voting makes comparisons valid across elections.

TABLE 9.1. Lexington, Kentucky, Electoral Results, March 1867 and November 1870

	March 1867	November 1870	Vote Increase
Ward 1 Dem.	153	263	110
Ward 1 Rep.	148	491	343
Margin of victory	5 (Dem.)	228 (Rep.)	233 to Rep.
Ward 2 Dem.	194	433	239
Ward 2 Rep.	110	456	346
Margin of victory	84 (Dem.)	23 (Rep.)	107 to Rep.
Ward 3 Dem.	173	481	308
Ward 3 Rep.	122	685	563
Margin of victory	51 (Dem.)	204 (Rep.)	255 to Rep.

TABLE 9.1. (*continued*)

	March 1867	November 1870	Vote Increase
Ward 4 Dem.	161	225	64
Ward 4 Rep.	110	344	234
Margin of victory	51 (Dem.)	119 (Rep.)	170 to Rep.
City total Dem.	681	1,402	721
City total Rep.	493	1,976	1,483
Margin of victory	188 (Dem.)	574 (Rep.)	762 to Rep.

Sources: 1867 results found in *Kentucky Gazette,* March 6, 1867. The 1870 results found in *Kentucky Gazette,* November 9, 1870. The 1867 election was purely for city officers, and the vote total listed is the result of the race for city mayor between J. T. Frazer (Dem.) and Bush (Rep.). The 1870 election included both city and congressional races, and the vote total reflects the returns for Congress between James B. Beck (Dem.) and William Brown (Rep.).

As the table demonstrates, both parties gained new voters between 1867 and 1870. Total voters increased from 1,174 in 1867 to 3,378 in 1870, a result of the overall rise in Lexington's population in the years following the war and the wider attention paid to a general November election versus a city election. But the different margin of increase suggests fundamental electoral changes afoot; Democrats increased their vote total by 105 percent, while Republicans increased theirs by 300 percent. The only plausible explanation is the presence of black voters in 1870. The Fifteenth Amendment added 762 new Republican voters to the Lexington city rolls. A closer look at the racial breakdown of each ward reveals the impact of black voters on the 1870 election. Table 9.2 shows the population by race for each Lexington ward in the 1870 census.

TABLE 9.2. Lexington, Kentucky, Population by Race, 1870

	White	Black	Black Percentage
Ward 1	1,723	1,607	48.2
Ward 2	2,432	1,895	43.7
Ward 3	1,985	2,478	55.5
Ward 4	1,489	1,191	44.4
City total	7,629	7,171	48.4

Source: Ninth Census, Population, 1870.

Only ward 3 had a black majority. As expected, ward 3 showed the highest increase in Republican support between 1867 and 1870. But ward 3 did not produce the highest Republican percentage in the 1870 election. Ward 1, with blacks constituting only 48.2 percent of the population, gave 65.1 percent of its votes to the Republican congressional candidate; ward 3 only produced a Republican majority of 58.7 percent. The Fifteenth Amendment thus produced uneven results across Lexington's four wards. Because of ward 1's pre-amendment Republican strength, Republicans secured a higher percentage of total votes in 1870 than did ward 3, which threw most of its support to the Democrats in 1867. Thus, in Lexington, as in Danville, Republicans secured citywide victories because of a sizable white minority vote in addition to the new black voters. This is particularly significant because in time some whites would in fact defect from the Republican Party, thus rendering the black vote powerless to affect elections even in the larger towns and cities.

Although most of the Republican gains took place in the cities and towns, some rural counties returned Republican victories thanks to the new black vote. Jessamine and Garrard counties, just south of Lexington, elected Republican county officers in the August 1870 election, causing the *Kentucky Gazette* to dub the southern Bluegrass area the "African district of Kentucky."[54] The *Gazette* understood the ramification of this outcome: "We cannot afford to have any 'negro holes' in this State, and this will surely be the case if the officers of any county owe their election entirely to the negroes as they have in Jessamine and Garrard."[55] The *Gazette* called for a purge of "illegal voters" from the pollbooks in order to restore Democratic rule to these counties. So threatening was the challenge from black voters that the *Gazette* demanded the state legislature reorganize county governments in order to strip power from localities that voted for Republicans based on black voters. But more important than the call for disfranchisement was the alarm with which the *Gazette* treated black-led electoral victories, even at the local level: "It is a great mortification to every body with a white face that this staunch little county should have been captured by the enemy . . . The Legislature, as a body of white gentlemen, cannot sit supinely by and permit so fair a section of this State to come under the dominion of the negroes and remain so."[56]

The *Gazette*, however, had little to worry about. By November 1870 every Bluegrass county solidly supported Democratic congressional candidate James Beck, including once black-majority Woodford County. Even Jessamine County, home of the "African District" from August 1870, delivered a Democratic majority in November that year.[57] The real question, then, is not why Lexington's four wards voted for Brown in the congressional election over Beck but why every precinct in Woodford County went for Beck, even though that county's black percentage mirrored that of Lexington.[58] The answer reflects the lack of pre-amendment Republican strength in Woodford County, the disorganized nature of rural Woodford County's black population following the Civil War, and the consequent inability of Woodford Republicans to mobilize black voters in black communities left behind. Woodford County had 5,829 slaves in addition to 114 free blacks in 1860 and was the only black majority county in Kentucky.[59] But by 1870 the black population had dropped by 36 percent.[60] The white population also declined but by much less (16 percent).[61] As in much of the Bluegrass countryside, the white and black population abandoned the hemp-based agricultural economy and headed for nearby towns and cities.[62] But the black exodus vastly surpassed white outflows, leaving behind an increasingly vulnerable and politically impotent black population.

Throughout Kentucky black influence on Republican politics depended largely on the level of support the Republican Party achieved before the Fifteenth Amendment. In every district, county, and city in the Bluegrass, a Republican Party competed for offices between 1865 and 1870. But the strength of the pre-amendment party varied. In rural communities with large black populations, such as outer Fayette County, Woodford County, and outer Boyle County, the all-white electorate almost unanimously supported the Democrats as early as 1867. Both the Conservative Union third party and the Republican Party exercised virtually no influence in these districts. But in the more urban districts such as Lexington, Danville, Nicholasville, and Lebanon, a viable Republican Party competed with Democrats right up to 1870. In these communities Republicans drew strength from benefactors of new commercial railroad ties northward to Cincinnati, Union army officers and veterans, and business leaders with contacts with the Lincoln and Grant administrations.[63] Nowhere did these elements produce a Republican majority before 1870, but they were strong enough to garner over a quarter of the vote in the Bluegrass. When the Fifteenth Amendment became law, black voters helped push some of these districts with existent Republican parties into power for the first time. In some places, such as rural Jessamine and Garrard counties, Republicans took over simply because the local Democratic Party had not yet organized itself (and in Garrard's case upland Unionists supported the Republicans along with their eastern mountain compatriots). But in the heavily black rural districts where the Democratic

Party consolidated political power shortly after the war—drawing from a large body of ex-Confederates and arch conservative Unionists—black voters had little impact on the election.

The real question, however, is whether or not white Republicans actually switched over to the Democracy in protest against the new Fifteenth Amendment. After all, as historian Thomas Owen has demonstrated, the pre-amendment Republican Party viewed itself as a staunchly white outfit, and "Kentucky's GOP was not to be a party of racial equality."[64] Did white-line Republicans abandon the Republican Party because of the newfound role of blacks in the party? Countywide election returns between 1870 and 1871 give a mixed answer. In some counties, notably Bourbon, Boyle, and Marion, the Democratic percentage of the final vote increased. But in other counties the Democratic percentage actually dropped from 1870 to 1871. Part of the explanation may have had to do with local organization and voter apathy; Democratic newspapers constantly warned against complacency, blaming close calls solely on Democratic voters' indifference. Indeed, Woodford County, which witnessed a massive drop in black population between 1860 and 1870 and which contributed to impressive Democratic victories across the county in November 1870, actually experienced a significant drop in the Democratic proportion of the vote in 1871. Some partisans blamed gubernatorial candidate Preston Leslie for failing to inspire Democrats to come to the polls the way they did in 1870 and in the previous gubernatorial race in 1867. Either way, the results are too inconclusive to suggest that white Republicans abandoned the party after passage of the Fifteenth Amendment.

Black Missourians participated in elections as early as April 1870, just as did black Kentuckians. But the electoral environment into which they entered hardly resembled Kentucky's. The Republican Party, the "natural home" for black voters, had split in half in the late 1860s over corruption in Jefferson City and ideological rigidity on the ex-rebel question. Although Republican leadership had accepted and advocated black suffrage as early as 1868, the party was not in a position to exploit the new black electorate until 1870, when the once-unified party found itself in weakened straits. By 1870 black voters offered little tonic to a struggling party that only five years earlier had rigged the state's new constitution to ensure a permanent Republican majority. Black voters split their own loyalties among Liberals and Radicals just as did white voters. Moreover, black voters accounted for a much smaller percentage of the electorate in Missouri than in Kentucky. The Fulton *Telegraph* asserted in May 1870 that Kentucky would introduce

39,261 new black voters to the polls, Maryland 28,522, and Missouri only about 21,000.[65] A split Missouri Republican Party stood to gain only slightly with the advent of black male suffrage.

Nevertheless, black voters participated in elections across Little Dixie with enthusiasm and changed the electoral calculus in at least a few local races. In Lafayette County, for example, the vote for the Republican candidate for Congress increased from 696 in 1868 to 1,000 in 1870, the Democrat earning 559 votes in 1868 and 859 in 1870.[66] Both parties gained approximately 300 new voters between 1868 and 1870. But the electoral environment in 1870 was vastly different, as reflected in the governor's race at the top of the ticket. Lafayette County supported Liberal and Democratic candidate B. Gratz Brown over Radical Republican Joseph McClurg by a 265-vote margin.[67] Widespread disaffection with Radical rule revealed itself in Lafayette County's refusal to support McClurg's Radical administration in its reelection campaign. Yet, while the county gave its majority to Brown, backed by both Liberals and Democrats, it continued to support the Republican congressional candidate by the same margin as it had in 1868. The only explanation for why the Republican maintained his 1868 margin of victory was the influx of black voters. Even as new black voters split their support between Liberal Brown and Radical McClurg, they demonstrated near unanimous support for the Republican congressional candidate George Smith. White voters who may have defected to the Democratic Party and supported the Democratic congressional candidate were easily replaced by new black voters committed to the Republican Party.

Black politics in post-amendment Missouri differed from Kentucky in three important ways. First, the Republican Party controlled Missouri's state government from 1865 to 1870, and the party's leadership had come around to support black suffrage as early as 1868. Although the party failed to secure black suffrage in the 1868 referendum, the state's political leadership openly accepted the prospect of black voters and, potentially, black officeholders. When black voters joined the fold in March 1870, they found a political establishment ready and willing to welcome them. As a result, the introduction of black voters into Missouri's electorate made fewer waves among white conservatives than in Kentucky. More problematic than black voters per se was the fact that former Confederates still could not vote. But with the re-enfranchisement amendment awaiting a vote in November 1870, even white conservatives could ignore the new black voters, knowing that their own day for "redemption" lay in the near future.[68]

The second difference lay in the divisions within Missouri's Republican Party. While Kentucky's Republican Party remained a beleaguered but united minority, Missouri's Republicans split into Radical and Liberal factions. Black Missouri voters joined a Republican Party beset with internal division over corruption, the test oath, and relations with the Grant administration. The Radical faction under Governor Joseph McClurg and the breakaway Liberal faction under B. Gratz Brown and Carl Schurz competed for the black vote in 1870. And black Missourians were split, supporting both Turner's Radical wing in opposition to rebel re-enfranchisement and the Liberal position favoring universal suffrage. By November 1872 nearly all black Missourians returned to the Republican (Radical) fold and voted for Grant over the Liberal-Democratic ticket of Greeley and Brown. But black voters did not return en masse to the rump Republican Party until after the crucial 1870 state poll.

The third important difference between the states was the prospect for rebel re-enfranchisement and the avalanche of support given to Missouri's Democratic Party by the new voters. Kentucky re-enfranchised ex-rebels as early as December 1865, allowing former Confederates to assume leadership positions within the Kentucky Democratic Party and the state by 1867. In Missouri former rebels were forbidden from voting until the referendum in 1870 restored them their voting rights. Anger at Confederate guerrillas, which once convinced the state's Unionist population to support the more draconian measures in the 1865 constitution, had worn off by the late 1860s. Only in a handful of regions, including the Ozarks, where hatred of the bushwhackers persisted, did support for disfranchisement remain strong. But once they gained access to the ballot box, former rebels and rebel sympathizers added more than seventy thousand new voters to the rolls, almost all of them Democrats. William Switzler, a conservative Unionist from Columbia exclaimed: "The fetters which were forged in 1865 by the DRAKE Convention have fallen from the wrists of seventy-five thousand white men, and the ballot is free. Infamous registry laws, odious test oaths, and venal and villainous registry officers will be known to our State no more forever."[69] Thus, just as African Americans gained the right to vote and added strength to the Republican Party then reeling under internal division, white former Confederates tipped the balance of power permanently in favor of the Democrats. Especially in the Little Dixie counties where Republican support was low even during the period of rebel disfranchisement, black voters did nothing to increase Republican power. There were, to put it simply, far more ex-rebel Democrats than black Republicans.

Just because black voters only marginally affected political races in Kentucky and Missouri did not mean Democrats and conservatives accepted their right to vote without a struggle. In fact, white conservatives employed a host of schemes to bribe, defraud, or intimidate black voters in the first years after the Fifteenth Amendment. Perhaps one of the most spectacular cases of fraud was in Danville, Kentucky, where blacks had already demonstrated the strength in April 1870 to turn the municipal government over to the Republicans. On April 1, 1871, the citizens of Danville headed to the polls to elect a slate of municipal officers. Between the previous election of November 1870 and the 1871 affair, Boyle County commissioners established a scheme to dampen black and Republican influence on the largest town in the county. The commissioners allowed Boyle County residents to establish town residence for election purposes by paying a small tax for each cemetery plot they owned in town.[70] This cemetery scheme was supposed to add enough white Democratic voters from the countryside to offset the large black vote within Danville. The effect was negligible, however. Table 9.3 shows the breakdown by race for each of the 1871 races for trustees, attorney, and assessor.

TABLE 9.3. April 1871 Municipal Election in Danville, Kentucky

Office	White Voters	Black Voters	Total Voters
Trustees (Dem.)	196	5	201
Trustees (Rep.)	56	217	273
Attorney (Dem.)	194	5	199
Attorney (Rep.)	54	217	271
Assessor (Dem.)	194	5	201
Assessor (Rep.)	58	217	275

Source: *Danville Advocate*, April 7, 1871. Seven trustees, or councilmen, ran for each party, and virtually no voters split their tickets. The figures for trustees' votes here are averages. For none of the individual trustee vote totals did the overall slate total differ by more than three votes. Democratic votes are italicized.

Seven Republican trustees defeated seven Democrats for the town council. Of the 222 black voters in the election, Republicans received the votes of 217, with only 5 going to the Democrats. Due to straight-ticket voting, black voters gave the same margin to Republican George C. Young in his race for city attorney and Republican H. B. Stanwood in his election for assessor. Of 252 white voters 58 sided with the Republicans.[71] The cemetery scheme failed to deliver the town to the Democrats.

The Democratic *Danville Advocate* was quick to defend the cemetery scheme by showing the dramatic rise in white Democratic votes. And indeed, compared to a municipal vote taken a year earlier, the white Democratic vote total had increased by fifty votes. The white Republican vote actually decreased by three votes over the same period. According to the *Advocate,* "It is fair to state . . . that the white Democratic vote was increased by a number of gentlemen who reside in the county and own Cemetery lots, voting under a late amendment to the town charter."[72] And surely the increased revenue from the cemetery tax scheme would help the town's treasury, the *Advocate* half-jokingly remarked. But the final result did little to lift the hearts of white Democrats in Danville. Black voters had permanently altered the town's political landscape, and whites would either have to adjust to Republican rule or convince the remaining fifty-six white Republicans to vote along racial lines and for the Democrats. White Democrats of Danville and Boyle County could not circumvent the Fifteenth Amendment.

But whites used violence in addition to fraud in order to consolidate Democratic control in both Kentucky and Missouri. Before 1870 white violence against blacks had more to do with overall assertions of black social autonomy than it did partisan politics. The Ku Klux Klan violence that afflicted every former Confederate state during Reconstruction had as one of its primary aims the removal of black Republican voters from the electorate and the reassertion of white Democratic rule. After 1870 Kentucky and Missouri whites began to use violence to intimidate black and white Republicans, just as the Ku Klux Klan had done in the former Confederate states in the three previous years. In Blackwater Township, Cooper County, Missouri, whites threatened black men in the community that if they voted for Grant and the Republicans in the 1872 election, they would be forcibly evicted from the area. Ten blacks defied the threat and voted the Republican ticket; in response, white night riders burned their schoolhouse.[73] But never did Ku Klux Klan or other paramilitary violence affect elections in the border the way it did in the former Confederate states. More common than night-riding political violence was Election Day mob activity of the sort that took place in Harrodsburg in August 1870. Similar Election Day "riots" occurred in Lancaster, Lexington, and Paris, Kentucky, between 1870 and 1872. And just as in the Harrodsburg case, African Americans came to the polls armed and prepared to fight for their right to vote.

The net electoral effect of the Fifteenth Amendment was marginal. In Missouri the Democrats catapulted to power in November 1870, thanks to the split between Liberals and Radicals in the Republican Party. Democrats tactfully endorsed Liberal B. Gratz Brown in the gubernatorial race and quickly exploited his win as a Democratic, not Liberal, victory. With the flood of tens of thousands of new former Confederate voters to the ballot box after the re-enfranchisement amendment passed overwhelmingly, Democrats safely assumed that they could manipulate Brown for their own ends. And they were proven correct, as Brown helped undo much of the Radical proscriptive measures of the 1860s and paved the way for a bona fide Democrat, Silas Woodson, to win the governorship in 1872.[74] The Fifteenth Amendment did nothing to stem the tide of Democratic "redemption" in Missouri.

In Kentucky Republicans did manage to gain control of some municipalities such as Danville and Lexington. And in some rural counties, including Jessamine and Garrard, Republicans briefly held power thanks to the new black voters. But Democrats retained their political hold on the Bluegrass region as a whole, winning every Bluegrass county in the 1871 gubernatorial race and the congressional races in 1870 and 1872. Horace Greeley, the joint Democrat-Liberal presidential candidate, easily won the Bluegrass region in 1872 as well. As in Missouri, the Fifteenth Amendment made little overall difference in electoral politics. Kentucky never experienced a "Radical Reconstruction" as a result of black voters the way virtually every former Confederate state did. Not only were there too few black voters to make a difference, but the Democratic Party had already reestablished hegemony in the state, especially in the Bluegrass, long before black voters came to the polls in 1870. Whereas in the former Confederacy Republicans could take advantage of a disorganized and potentially divided white population in order to build a majority with the help of black votes, Kentucky Republicans found Democratic strength completely consolidated by 1867, with the downfall of the Conservative Union third party movement. Kentucky Republicans accepted themselves to be a beleaguered minority, especially within the Bluegrass, and never honestly expected black voters to push them into power beyond a few urban districts. Like their Missouri counterparts, who restricted themselves to the southwestern Ozarks, Kentucky Republicans adjusted to life as an upland minority party, based in the eastern Appalachian counties and among German immigrants near Cincinnati. Black voters added to the rolls made very little difference in statewide elections for the next several decades. With the exception of brief interludes in the 1890s and 1920s, Democrats dominated Kentucky and Missouri politics until the 1970s.

Because the Fifteenth Amendment did so little to change the electoral picture in Kentucky and Missouri, it is tempting to cast the entire measure as irrelevant to border state political culture. After all, a primary function of elections is to offer the public a voice on who should control the government and what policies they should follow. If black voters were to have no net effect on the outcome in local political races in Kentucky and Missouri, what value did the Fifteenth Amendment really have? African Americans may not have turned the Bluegrass or Little Dixie into Republican strongholds, as blacks in the former Confederacy had done. But by participating in a civic process long denied them, black voters altered the political culture in other ways.

The Fifteenth Amendment's Political Significance

In June 1870 William J. Steele announced himself a Republican Party candidate for county judge in Woodford County. Steele was a prominent farmer and attorney from Versailles and declared himself to be "a Union man from the very start."[75] As a Republican candidate in the post–Fifteenth Amendment era, Steele sought support from Woodford County's sizable African American community. He spoke to a black audience at Versailles's "Colored Baptist Church" in March, before ratification of the amendment. Prominent black leaders in Versailles—including a blacksmith, Salem Waters; a carpenter, Aaron Searcy; a plasterer, Andrew Jackson; and the Reverend William Turpin—all spoke in favor of Steele's candidacy.[76] Each of these relatively wealthy members of the town's African American community eagerly anticipated voting for Steele after the Fifteenth Amendment's final ratification due at the end of the month.[77] But black support for Steele was far from universal. As the conservative Democratic *Woodford Weekly* pointed out, Steele was once a slaveholder and had held on to his slaves up to the bitter end in December 1865.[78] In fact, Steele owned twenty-three slaves in 1860, putting him in the census category of "planter," rare for a Kentuckian.[79] He then filed a claim for three hundred dollars per slave in an ill-fated postwar plan to recover fees from the federal government for Unionist masters who had lost their slaves to the Union army. And as recently as 1869, Steele had opposed black suffrage. Steele's sudden reversal was too convenient for the *Weekly*'s liking and also for many African Americans. Word reached the newspaper that black voters in Versailles planned a vigorous interrogation session with the Republican candidate, specifically targeting the inconsistency between Steele's suddenly radical positions on black testimony and suffrage and his opinions of just a few years earlier.[80] The *Weekly* "encouraged" this questioning and hoped black voters would see Steele not as a man of principle but as an opportunist who only embraced black suffrage and civil rights "because of circumstance."[81]

Moreover, William J. Steele feared black competition for the Republican seat. After hearing that a black man had announced his own candidacy for the position, Steele delivered a speech at nearby Midway, Kentucky, in which he reasserted his bona fide Republican credentials and implored African Americans not to split the Republican Party. Although an admitted former slaveholder—"I had niggers and lost them," he claimed—he framed his Republican position in terms of his unwavering support for the Union, his near martyrdom for it in pro-Confederate Woodford County, and his welcome association of the Union cause with that of black freedom: "I tell you that I have suffered for being a Union man and standing up for your rights. I have been persecuted for it and I have never faltered."[82] He even praised the honor of his former slaves who had joined the Union army: "I had nine niggers and four of them went into the Union army and made good and brave soldiers and I never faltered" in support for the Union.[83] Steele pledged to his black audience that he was not a belated Confederate like the thousands of other white slaveholders who had flocked to the Democratic Party after the Civil War. Rather, Steele was the rare breed of former slaveholder who embraced the radical logic of the Union cause—including black suffrage—even as his fellow slaveholders abandoned it. Because of the peculiar challenge of remaining loyal to the Union cause in a region filled with actual and belated Confederates, William J. Steele was as authentic a Radical Republican as African Americans in Woodford County were ever likely to find. Not even a black man could out-radical him, so he implored.

To conservatives, and to many African Americans, William J. Steele was the consummate "scalawag." He supported Kentucky's slaveholding regime and participated in it right up to the end, though he did claim to support the Union. Yet he took advantage of black votes in order to pursue his own career as a Republican county judge. Like the famed white Republicans in the former Confederate states, Steele came in for bitter attacks from both conservative Democrats, who challenged his loyalty to his race and class, and from African Americans, who questioned the authenticity of his support for black people. In post–Fifteenth Amendment Kentucky, William J. Steele was the first evidence that "Radical Reconstruction" had finally reached Woodford County.

But Steele's race is more important for what it says about the nature of political culture in post-amendment Kentucky. Never before had whites had to consider black opinion in a Kentucky election. And never before had Kentucky politicians felt the need to balance the new African American "base" of the Republican Party with the small cadre of moderate white Unionists. The uncertainty of electoral politics in the age of biracial suffrage encouraged conservatives, including the editor of the *Woodford Weekly,* to highlight embarrassing inconsistencies in Steele's record in order to jeopardize his support among the black population. Steele would end up losing his race as Democrats swept the county elections in August 1870. But white Democrats remained unsure of the outcome up to the very end.[84] Part of the reason for Democratic uncertainty lay in the changing demographics of Woodford County. In 1860 Woodford County was the only black-majority county in Kentucky, and white Democrats feared that this majority would inevitably lead to black Republican rule. These white conservatives did not know, however, that the black population had declined by over 36 percent between 1860 and 1870 and that blacks no longer formed a majority of the county's residents; the 1870 census results were not released until well after the election was completed. And for their part African Americans were not willing to support any candidate just because he represented himself as a Republican—despite the support Steele claimed from the skilled laboring elite among Versailles's blacks. Moreover, like the white population, Woodford County's blacks did not know that they no longer had a majority in the county and so felt emboldened to risk factional division within the Republican Party.

The Fifteenth Amendment did little to change the outcome of elections in Kentucky. And it did even less in Missouri, thanks to the near simultaneous re-enfranchisement of the state's former rebel population. But as the Steele case shows, the Fifteenth Amendment introduced new rhythms of political behavior and culture into border state public life that manifested itself in more ways than election results. For black Kentuckians and Missourians the amendment conferred the most important vestige of citizenship. And with it in hand blacks were unwilling to accept Republican candidates just because of their partisan affiliation. As in the majority-black states of the former Confederacy, black Kentuckians and Missourians were willing to insist upon Republican candidates who served the black community's demands, even if it risked splitting the party.[85] It was both a means and an end: a means to the protection of civil rights and the attainment of economic and social justice; and an end in representing male citizenship and the formation of a biracial republic.

Indeed, the story of black voting extended far beyond the simple mathematics of election races. As the Steele case demonstrated, African Americans were willing to run for office as well as to provide votes. With the Republicans in power, as was the case in Missouri through 1870, blacks demanded positions within the government itself. Perhaps the most prominent African American to serve Missouri's radical government was James Milton Turner, who advised the state superintendent of education and vigorously investigated the construction of black schools across Little Dixie. But more important and accessible to African Americans were positions within the Republican Party itself, as delegates, committee members, and leaders. In August 1870, for example, Radicals met in a Howard County party council meeting "without regard to color or previous condition."[86] Some notable black leaders, including reverends J. F. Jordan and Daniel Cooper, gave speeches to the meeting. Cooper was even favored for nomination for state representative in the district. Many other black men were appointed to committees, including the "respectable black man" Alex K. Herbert.[87] Other Republican meetings in Missouri and Kentucky placed black men on committees as well and often promised their black supporters a share of the offices. But neither blacks nor white conservatives took white Republican leaders at their word. The conservative *Missouri Telegraph* quoted black passersby at the Howard County meeting who commented, "If it is the object to give all the offices to the whites, and get the blacks to vote for them, then we are not in."[88] The *Danville Advocate* suggested that an upcoming district Republican meeting should give eight of the nine votes allotted to Boyle County to African Americans because black voters made up nearly the entire Republican voting population of the county.[89] The Democratic *Advocate* knew how unlikely it was that the district-wide Republican committee would allot 90 percent of the votes to blacks and so reveled in the opportunity to portray the Republicans as hypocrites. The Fulton *Telegraph* made a similar remark after the Callaway County Republican Party appointed only one black person to the Committee on Resolutions, when two-thirds of the Republican voters in the county were black.[90] Democrats egged on African Americans to demand the fruits of electoral office from white Republicans, knowing that such criticism hit on a legitimate sore spot among the black Republican electorate.

Blacks sought positions with the Republican Party for reasons other than mere patronage. They also hoped to steer party policy, especially on matters of vital importance to the black community. This was especially so in Kentucky, where the state's Republican Party had embraced racially conservative positions on suffrage and civil rights until shortly before the Fifteenth Amendment's ratification. It was the black testimony question, however, that allowed blacks to put the Kentucky Republican Party into a position of strength. Kentucky Republicans had endorsed changing the state's testimony law since 1866. But with the Democratic Party split over the testimony question in 1870, black pressure pushed the testimony issue to the top of the party's list of priorities and to the Republican Party's advantage.[91] By 1872 the Democratic Party supported changing the testimony law, granting black Republicans a major substantive and political victory.

Black Missourians and Kentuckians threatened to split or abandon the Republican Party if it failed to follow through on providing offices to them. A small minority of border state blacks aligned themselves with Democrats as a protest against the party ignoring the policy and patronage demands of the black voting base. In Missouri this was much more common as partisan lines blurred with the Republican split into Liberal and Radical factions. White Missouri conservatives promoted black supporters of the rebel re-enfranchisement amendment whenever possible, often in condescending terms that betrayed their true intent. Sam Casey, a self-described black Republican in Marshall, Missouri, printed a letter in the *Saline Progress* newspaper advocating passage of the rebel re-enfranchisement amendment. He also attacked the Republican Party for taking black votes for granted and for reserving all offices to whites while canvassing for black votes.[92] The *Caucasian* reproduced Casey's comments and entitled his remarks, "Sound Sense from a Darkey."[93] Charles Williams of Lexington, Missouri, penned a letter to the *Caucasian* asking blacks to "think twice" before voting for Radicals because it was the Radicals who refused to grant offices for blacks up to that point.[94] Neither of these cases reveals a substantive black conservatism within Little Dixie. In fact, the main charge here was that the so-called Radical Party was not radical enough and that blacks were willing to look elsewhere if their demands were not met.[95]

Although most black Kentuckians and Missourians who flirted with the Democratic or Liberal opposition did so to gain leverage with the Republican Party, some blacks openly courted the Democratic Party because they agreed with its ideological conservatism. The number of these genuine black Democrats was minuscule, however; in the Danville election, for example, 217 blacks voted the Republican ticket, and only 5 blacks supported the Democratic ticket. More important, the black community demonstrated a willingness to enforce Republican Party loyalty with violence, even against this tiny black Democratic minority. Ferdinand Robinson, an African American in Lexington, Kentucky, served as doorkeeper at a Fayette County Democratic meeting in 1871 and voted in the caucus.[96] Robinson was a mattress maker by trade and possessed two thousand dollars of property in 1870. His clientele probably included many prominent white Democrats, and the unusually high value of his real property for a black Lexingtonian likely explains Robinson's support for the Democratic Party.[97] In August 1871 the conservative *Kentucky Gazette* published a report that Robinson had been attacked and shot at by 18 black men.[98] After 5 black men were arrested, the *Gazette* threatened violence against black Radicals if they continued to attack black Democrats.[99] Although black Democrats were few and far between, they served a symbolic purpose in the larger political culture. For white conservatives black Democrats—especially wealthy ones—confirmed white prejudices that "the great majority of the negroes of this city are thriftless vagabonds."[100] But for African Americans black Democrats were guilty of treason against the community and were to be summarily ostracized and marginalized lest their influence undermine black solidarity in the face of hostile white Democrats.

The arrival of black suffrage also changed the context in which black and white people experienced and interpreted acts of violence. To white Democrats African Americans had become "demoralized" by the advent of suffrage, prone to violence against property holders at the behest of their white Radical instigators. In August 1870, shortly after black Versailles Republicans voted for William Steele, a "serious state of things" transpired in the town between blacks and whites. The immediate cause of the troubles was the striking of a black man by a white police officer's pistol.[101] Immediately afterward, black men formed armed pickets and guarded every road out of the town. The grainstacks of the policeman who had attacked the black man were burned, though a later report claimed that the burning resulted from a "private dispute."[102] Other blacks burned "barns, oats and haystacks" while on their "rampage."[103] Armed black men menaced white people who attempted to pass through the town. The blame for this state of affairs, according to the Democratic *Woodford Weekly,* fell squarely on the arrival of black suffrage. The *Weekly*'s editor complained, "This is the work of the Fifteenth Amendment; and these are the fruits of the Federal Government interfering in local affairs."[104] To the Democratic *Weekly* only black suffrage, advanced by the bugaboo of "external agents" who deigned to "interfere" in Versailles's local affairs, created the political climate that encouraged African Americans to organize themselves into armed units. More important, as Steven Hahn remarks, these highly militarized, organized acts of self-defense by the black population, which "acknowledged and responded to the dangers of collective action in the postemancipation South," also "lent visibility, order, and seriousness to the early efforts to define new forms of community."[105]

Black armed self-defense also took the form of attacks against white-owned land, and much of it occurred following the Fifteenth Amendment. The *Kentucky Gazette* cited a spasm of "negro incendiarism" across the Bluegrass countryside in early 1871 in which black individuals and gangs burned barns and destroyed fences.[106] But what white farmers described as "crime" meant something quite different to rural blacks facing deceitful landlords and white paramilitary gangs. For blacks pushed to the margins of survival by colluding landowners and Regulators, violent attacks against white property served as a form of leverage in the larger labor struggle, reminding whites that they did not possess total and complete power over their former slaves. Here is where seemingly isolated attacks against white property served the same political purpose as highly organized armed self-defense on Election Day or in defiance of white lynch mobs. In both cases African Americans demonstrated to white conservatives and to each other their unwillingness to accept either labor terms or suffrage restrictions without a fight. Through tense confrontations in the towns of the border states and nighttime attacks against white-owned property in the countryside, black Kentuckians and Missourians forged a political community on the basis of shared class goals.

For whites, however, these spates of property violence provoked an internal debate over the means of reestablishing control over the black laboring class. A Fayette County Farmers' Meeting held in response to the rash of barn burnings called for changes in the black testimony law as a way to encourage blacks to testify against fellow black perpetrators.[107] According to this moderate strategy, the spate of attacks and reprisals by the Ku Klux Klan only encouraged blacks to flee the countryside, leaving white farmers without labor for their hemp farms. Anything to calm the tensions in the countryside would benefit landowners, even if that meant acquiescing in the civil rights demands of blacks. Taking the opposite tack was the *Kentucky Gazette,* which stood willing to allow the Ku Klux Klan to take care of black saboteurs: "Our deliberate opinion is that nine-tenths of the country people look upon the Ku Klux as the best protection they have for their property, and as long as their property is in jeopardy and liable to be preyed upon, they will not discountenance or condemn Ku Kluxism."[108] The *Gazette* read into black "criminality" the makings of a class war and were determined to let the Ku Klux Klan fight the battles of the landowning class.

Whereas in the past white conservatives would chide blacks for failing to honor contracts or stay out of the towns and cities, now conservatives blamed black "misbehavior" on the Republican Party. The trope of the submissive Negro duped into confrontation and crime by his radical patrons dominated the political discourse of the former Confederacy in the late 1860s and early 1870s. Not surprisingly, white Democrats added the charge of radical "demagoguery" in Kentucky and Missouri once black voters went to the polls there as well. Blacks who attacked barns were blasted as Radical agents. Regulators and the Ku Klux Klan attacked blacks because they followed the advice of their Radical leaders. In many ways the assignation of blame for black violence on radicalism was only a continuation of the earlier charge that black crime would necessarily flow from emancipation itself. The conservative *Kentucky Gazette* commented in 1867: "The daily papers are filled with accounts of murders, robberies, rapes, and other outrages by negroes in this and other States. This is the necessary consequence of their emancipation and the attempted elevation of the negro to equality with the white race."[109] The implication of this claim was that blacks had not emancipated themselves but had been "placed" in a position of freedom and "equality with the white race." External radicals were to blame for this "unnatural" state of affairs shortly after the Civil War, and radicals were again to blame for black provocations after the Fifteenth Amendment. White Democrats thus minimized black agency, castigating them as unwitting savages unleashed by a devious clique of white interlopers. Black violence, even when it was "apolitical," took on a partisan hue in the post–Fifteenth Amendment era.

But there was some truth to the claim that the Fifteenth Amendment ushered in a different style of racial violence. It was on Election Day and in moments that followed such as in August 1870 in Versailles, where African Americans linked their willingness to use the ballot with their propensity to organize for armed self-defense. In Paris in 1871, after shots rang out between "a Democrat and a Republican" near the polls, "the negroes immediately rushed home and armed themselves with guns, etc., and came back."[110] On the same day in Lexington a more disorganized riot erupted, "a crowd, consisting almost altogether of negroes, broke in all directions, drew their pistols and commenced firing upon all white persons."[111] Earlier, in November 1870, a shootout ensued in Lancaster, Garrard County, when approximately seventy-five armed African Americans rushed out of the town square in pursuit of a fight with a mob of whites.[112] After a short melee in which "200 or 300 shots were fired," many black and white men were left gravely wounded. Naturally, the Democratic *Danville Advocate* claimed that "the negroes were put up to it by some of their Radical brethren."[113] The newspaper also took great pleasure in highlighting a white Radical who had abandoned his post shortly after telling the blacks to stand their ground. Like other conservatives, the *Advocate* pinned the blame for this incident on white Radicals, viewing black violence as a logical outcome of emancipation, equality, and suffrage.

The post-amendment era marked the first time since the Civil War that African Americans in Kentucky or Missouri had employed organized force in broad daylight—and the first time ever without leadership by white officers. Although they never developed formal militias like those that appeared in South Carolina or Mississippi, blacks organized and armed themselves for the inevitable Election Day violence. Election Day violence was certainly not a new phenomenon in the postwar border. For decades armed and often drunken men had prowled the polls, seeking a fight with political enemies. The Fifteenth Amendment's introduction of black voters to the Kentucky and Missouri electorate merely transformed the nature of Election Day violence and yielded some of the sensational "race wars" in the white imagination. In these general melees blacks reinforced community solidarity through arms, siding with one another in a racially unified phalanx. Alas, the Fifteenth Amendment did not just grant blacks the right to vote in elections. It also regularized the use of violence in public spaces previously reserved for whites. Indeed, the fact that blacks were armed at the polls was less remarkable to whites than that they were organized.

Black willingness to organize, arm, and fight also manifested itself after actual or supposed Ku Klux Klan attacks. In Danville in August 1871 dozens of black men followed the script laid out by the blacks of Versailles earlier in the year. They stood guard over the town's points of exit and conducted armed pickets of the entire area. The *Danville Advocate* complained, "On Sunday night formal military possession of the town was taken by a number of negroes."[114] The proximate cause of this mobilization was the threat by the Ku Klux Klan to capture a black man named Tom Jones from the jail and hang him for allegedly burning barns in neighboring Madison County. Danville's black community organized to protect Jones from a Ku Klux attack. Eventually, the black men were charged with rioting, and Jones was taken by train to Madison County for trial, without interference by the Ku Klux Klan. But rumors of the group's activity yielded a complete mobilization and organization of the town's black community in defense of one of its own members. Indeed, black men "stood guard" over the jail where the "rioters" were kept, preventing any further Ku Klux invasion.[115] Even though elections and the Fifteenth Amendment had nothing specifically to do with this incident, it is noteworthy that nothing of this sort had occurred in central Kentucky before the Fifteenth Amendment. And considering that the tactics used by blacks resembled those used during Election Day riots in places such as Lancaster and Harrodsburg, it is likely that the new political culture of biracial suffrage contributed to the incident. In short, black men relied on their Election Day experience to execute the picket and protection operations employed in defense of Tom Jones.

The Fifteenth Amendment ultimately had marginal consequences for border state electoral results. In Kentucky the Democratic Party was too strong to falter in the face of new black Republican voters. And in Missouri the more than seventy thousand former rebel voters added to the rolls just months after ratification of the Fifteenth Amendment vastly outweighed the new black voters. Much more important to Missouri electoral politics was the state constitutional amendment removing restrictions on voting rights for former rebels. Rebel re-enfranchisement made the Fifteenth Amendment a veritable nonissue in state politics. The great hubbub over black voting expressed by conservative newspapers such as the *Missouri Telegraph* and the *Lexington Caucasian* was in one sense overblown.

But black voting fundamentally altered the political culture of the border states in ways that went far beyond electoral politics. As members of the Republican Party, African Americans also made a claim for leadership and access to patronage. Black committeemen sparred with white business owners and railroad promoters for supremacy inside the party's councils. While white Republicans developed platforms that encouraged the immigration of German and Yankee laborers and the sale of bonds for railroads to every hamlet in the border interior, blacks demanded that state and local Republican parties push for equal funding for schools, testimony rights, and protection against the Ku Klux Klan. As a result, state Republican platforms reflected a mix of these demands, incongruous as they were. In many ways the tensions that developed between white and black Republicans resembled the kind of acrimonious relationships between the scalawags, carpetbaggers, and African Americans in the former Confederacy. But the political culture of Republicanism in the border states differed from the former Confederacy because a pre-amendment Republican Party had taken hold among many segments of the local white population. And because the black population never approached a majority, even in the formerly slave-rich areas such as Little Dixie or the Bluegrass, electoral logic forced black Republicans to acquiesce to the demands of the more conservative white business leaders in the Republican Party. The black base was too small to win in the border states, even at the local level.

By 1872 African Americans had finally achieved full citizenship rights in the border states. They sensed the precariousness of the ballot in light of white conservative hostility both within the border states and in the former Confederacy. They mobilized under arms to protect their right to vote, merging the individual act of casting a ballot with the communal expression of social power. In courthouse squares in towns such as Danville, Harrodsburg, and Versailles, Kentucky, and Boonville, Lexington, and Marshall, Missouri, blacks assembled en masse to cast ballots on Election Day and assert their presence in the expanded polity. As visible markers of citizenship, black voters reminded white conservatives of the new order every bit as publicly as did black soldiers who had stood guard over public places in the months after the Civil War. Although black voters in the border states could do little to influence election outcomes, especially in counties and districts dominated by conservative ex-Unionists and ex-Confederates, their performance of the ritual of voting, and martial defense of the right to that ritual, fundamentally transformed the white-dominated polity into a biracial republic.

CONCLUSION

The border states, a region that once symbolized for the nation the sectional comity and conservative Unionism that had held the United States together for over seventy years, represented by 1872 the sort of polarization that tore the nation apart during the Civil War and Reconstruction. Kentucky and Missouri had long represented the political and geographic center of American life. Citizens and political leaders embraced both slavery and Union for decades and viewed the future of the federal government and the local social order as inextricably bound through the constitutional compact. As late as 1862, conservative Unionists rebelled against the notion that the political order of old could no longer contain the sectional divisions between the free labor North and the plantation slavery–based South. But this traditional arrangement along the border between free and slave states faced two mutually reinforcing internal rebellions that ultimately toppled the old political, social, economic, and racial order. Confederates, including especially guerrillas, violently rejected continued loyalty to a Union that had become "hopelessly abolitionized" under Republican rule. In doing so, however, the Confederate uprising opened the way for a second and more radical rebellion among the slave population. Neither the border states nor America as a whole would ever be the same.

In a microcosm of national events the slave population would prove to be the real engine of political transformation during the Civil War and Reconstruction era as slaves exploited divisions among whites in the earliest months of war and pressed their way to the safety of Union lines and to military service under Union arms. Newly freed blacks then used their own experience in the Union army as a base for further claims to civil and political equality. But unlike in the victorious North, the mass of conservative

Unionists in the border states would not accept the social transformation of emancipation and Reconstruction. For white conservatives who cleaved to the federal flag in 1861 because they felt slavery would be best preserved within the Union, the employment of black soldiers signified the death of the "Union as it was, and the Constitution as it is." After the war ended in 1865, white Kentuckians and Missourians who had rejected the Confederate call in 1861 now symbolically rejected the Union they had fought to preserve. Subsequently, they collaborated with their wartime foes to create an incipient Lost Cause movement that would eventually find greater expression in the former Confederate states. Meanwhile, the remnants of guerrilla war continued to tear the border countryside asunder as gangsters and Regulators such as Skaggs's Men in Kentucky and the James Gang in Missouri terrorized the white and black Unionist population.

The purpose of this book is not simply to show how the political transformations at the heart of the Civil War and Reconstruction affected a largely ignored region but, rather, to set the entire period in a new light. The traditional narrative of America's greatest conflagration pits the free labor North against the plantation-dominated South. By approaching the prewar sectional conflict, the war itself, and the postwar Reconstruction struggle as a series of internal conflicts within the socially heterogeneous border states, and not just as a clash of fundamentally different societies, this study turns the Civil War and Reconstruction inside out.

Both the starting and ending points looked different in the middle belt of border states than they did in the free North or the plantation South. In 1860 Kentucky and Missouri were slave states, but even in their slaveholding heartlands of Little Dixie and the Bluegrass, they hardly resembled the lower South. The political culture that emerged from these sections, which ultimately dominated their respective states, embraced pragmatism over ideological inflexibility, tradition over revolutionary cant, and social diversity over plantation monoculture. People in central Missouri and central Kentucky considered themselves southerners, to be sure, but at the same time they defended their slave-based social order, they nurtured long-standing political, economic, and social relations with those in the North—especially in the more conservative states of the Old Northwest. Their political culture largely rejected the honor-laden discourse of southern militancy as well as the Free-Soil ideology of northern Republicans. Like conservative Democrats in Illinois, Indiana, and Ohio and Unionist Whigs in North

Carolina, Tennessee, and Virginia, border state whites sought every possible means to keep the "twin heresies" of abolitionism and secessionism at bay.

It is by defining politics broadly, to include not just elections and politicians—and efforts by African Americans to become voters and officeholders themselves—but also the myriad "collective struggles for socially meaningful power,"[1] that historians can appreciate the depth of political transformation in the border states. This is as true for the white population as it is for the slaves. As Steven Hahn has uncovered, slaves across the South created a cohesive politics based on social and kin ties that gave meaning to individual and collective struggles for autonomy and dignity.[2] This was true in Kentucky and Missouri, as it was in the lower South. But the social structure of border society, in which resident slaves, hired slaves, free blacks, white wage laborers, and children of landowners worked small farms together, revealed a unique form of slave politics that emerged in the border. Slaves in Kentucky and Missouri had fewer familial and social resources at their disposal than those living on larger plantations in the lower South. But their relatively high degree of mobility and proximity to the free North meant that their communication networks traversed wider swaths of land than in the more geographically circumscribed world of Deep South plantations.[3] In many ways border slaves' proximity to the free North gave them a special degree of revolutionary potential that slaves living in black-majority districts of the lower South never possessed. When war broke out, these widely dispersed slaves knew exactly what to do and what the war meant. And the whites of Kentucky and Missouri, whether they supported the Union or the Confederacy, understood perfectly well the threat their slaves posed in the event of civil war. Having lost control over the black laboring population and the national narrative of Union, postwar white conservatives in the border states formed new collectivities such as the reinvigorated Democratic Party and the Regulators to maintain what they deemed socially meaningful power.

The consequences of this political transformation could be felt far outside the border states and well into the late nineteenth century. The Lost Cause movement, which first found vital organizational support in Richmond in the 1870s and only flowered into a full-blown cultural assault on the northern victory in the 1890s, witnessed its first great expression in Kentucky and Missouri in the 1860s. Those conservative Kentuckians and Missourians, including former Unionists, who lionized John Hunt Morgan or William Clarke Quantrell in death and Jesse James in his postwar life demonstrated for the late-nineteenth-century South the power of commemorative narrative and martyrdom in recasting defeat into symbolic victory. Border violence also had a pedagogical effect for former Confederates across the South: when the northern Republicans stopped paying attention, they would let white southerners terrorize the black population and regain political power. Drawing lessons from Kentucky and Missouri in the late 1860s, Alabama, Georgia, and Tennessee employed methods of fraud, white political unity, and racial intimidation to "redeem" their states in 1870 and 1871. The border offered a salutary lesson on southern industrialization and renewal as well. Although Missouri thoroughly reinvented itself as a midwestern economy based on corn and wheat culture and on industry in St. Louis and Kansas City, it was Kentucky that showcased the "New South" for the progressive-minded in the former Confederacy. As historian C. Vann Woodward points out, Henry Watterson's *Louisville Courier-Journal* and the newly expanded Louisville and Nashville Railroad did more to remake the former Confederacy into an industrialized model than any other force within the old Confederacy itself.[4] As propagandist for the New and the Old South, the border led the way.

One historiographic consequence of this book is to complicate the notion of sectionalism itself. Historians from the Progressive school of Charles and Mary Beard right up to social historians such as Edward Ayers today have cast the sectional conflict and consequent Civil War as the outcome of two societies fundamentally at odds with one another over slavery.[5] In Ayers's masterful *Valley of the Shadow* project, which analyzes the fate of two counties only two hundred miles apart, the author concludes that "the North and South fought tenaciously in the political realm precisely because they were fighting over the spread of slavery's power."[6] Ayers offers a sophisticated version of the Progressive argument, noting that defenders of slavery embraced an "entire range of strategies from fervent Unionism to fervent secessionism" and that there is "little connection between slaveholding and political alignment in our Southern county."[7] Like Ayers, this book sees the relationship between slavery and political culture as affecting the "social and economic logic of local communities," and not as a broad-brush differentiation between "North" and "South."[8] Nevertheless, this book shows that had Ayers looked at the state lying between his two communities under study—Maryland—he would have uncovered an even more complex matrix of political actors and institutions, and social and economic forces, than in either free Pennsylvania or upper Confederate Virginia. The antebellum political culture and institutions of Maryland, for example, like those in Kentucky and

Missouri, tended to encourage national unity, not sectional militancy. The forces within Maryland political culture that broke down in 1861 reveal more about the national political crisis than do the ways in which Pennsylvanians and Virginians rallied to their respective flags with the outbreak of war.

Moreover, by viewing slavery as a national institution in which federally deputized slave catchers roamed the streets of Boston, and not merely as a sectional system limited to the South, this study takes Ayers's conclusions even further. After all, the fundamental conflict in Missouri and Kentucky did not embroil free labor advocates against defenders of slavery but, instead, drew two different defenders of slavery into open conflict with one another. Like the nation as a whole, the border states had thoroughly accepted slavery in 1860. The disagreements and consequent war resulted not over the supposed rightness or wrongness of slavery per se but over the various means through which different sections of American society sought to preserve and enhance it. The fundamental question for historians of sectionalism, then, is why did disagreements over the preservation of slavery—many of them dating back to the founding of the Republic—lead to secession and war, not why these differences existed in the first place.

It is my hope that this book furthers an emerging interest among scholars of the Civil War and Reconstruction in the border states, where ideological purity and sectional loyalty remained ever in doubt.[9] The story coming out of the border states complicates the existing historiography of the Civil War and Reconstruction in many ways, just as it foreshadows the historical narrative of the rest of the nation in the later nineteenth century. In some cases the border state picture—particularly the utter rejection of emancipation by white Unionists—completely refutes the national narrative of increasing white acceptance of radical Union war aims. In other ways the border simply reinforces our overall understanding of the sectional conflict, the war, slave emancipation, and Reconstruction. After all, conservative Unionists in Kentucky and Missouri failed at their primary mission: to preserve slavery, the Union, and peace. Sectional discord, with roots in the industrial North and the plantation South, proved too strong for conservative Unionists in the heartland to temper. In either case, however, the perspective of the middle third of the nation—home to a mass of small landholding whites and, in many localities, African Americans scattered on isolated farms—challenges the dominant sectional narrative of Civil War and Reconstruction and replaces it with a story of local struggles that reflect complex layers of loyalty and contradictory notions of the Republic.

NOTES

INTRODUCTION

1. H. A. Cook, Captain, 9th Missouri Cavalry, to Lieut., February 22, 1865, Letters Received, box 16, ser. 3537, District of North Missouri, United States Army Continental Commands, 1821–1920, Record Group 393/2 (hereafter cited as RG 393/2), National Archives, Washington, D.C.

2. *Central Kentucky Gazette* (Danville), December 26, 1866.

3. David Rice founded the First Presbyterian Church at Danville when the town served as the state's first capital. Rice advocated the prohibition of slavery in Kentucky's founding 1792 constitution. For his opinions regarding slavery at the Kentucky Constitutional Convention, see the pamphlet by David Rice, *Slavery Inconsistent with Justice and Good Policy Proved by a Speech Delivered in the Convention, Held at Danville, Kentucky* (New York: Isaac Collins, 1804).

4. *Paris (Ky.) Western Citizen,* May 10, 1861.

5. For other accounts of Reconstruction in Kentucky, see E. Merton Coulter, *Civil War and Readjustment in Kentucky* (Chapel Hill: University of North Carolina Press, 1926); Ross A. Webb, *Kentucky in the Reconstruction Era* (Lexington: University Press of Kentucky, 1979); and Thomas L. Connelly, "Neo-Confederatism or Power Vacuum: Post-War Kentucky Politics Reappraised," *Register of the Kentucky Historical Society* 64, no. 4 (October 1966): 257–69. Most recently, see Anne Marshall, *Creating a Confederate Kentucky: The Lost Cause and Civil War Memory in a Border State* (Chapel Hill: University of North Carolina Press, 2010). The literature on Civil War memory is one of the richest subfields in the study of the Civil War. The crowning work in this field is David W. Blight, *Race and Reunion: The Civil War in American Memory* (Cambridge: Harvard University Press, 2001).

6. J. Michael Rhyne, "Rehearsal for Redemption: The Politics of Racial Violence in Civil War–Era Kentucky," C. Ballard Breaux Conference Invited Lecture, Filson Historical Society (FHS), Louisville, Ky., May 19, 2001.

7. On Virginia's failure to approve a radical constitution—and later experiment with the Readjuster Party—see Jane Dailey, *Before Jim Crow: The Politics of Race in Postemancipation Virginia* (Chapel Hill: University of North Carolina Press, 2000); on Missouri's Radical constitution of 1865 and Radical rule thereafter, see William Parrish, *Missouri under Radical Rule, 1865–1870* (Columbia: University of Missouri Press, 1965), 14–35.

8. On black politics in the post–Civil War Deep South, see Michael W. Fitzgerald, *The Union League Movement in the Deep South: Politics and Agricultural Change during Reconstruction* (Baton

Rouge: Louisiana State University Press, 1989); Thomas Holt, *Black over White: Negro Political Leadership in South Carolina during Reconstruction* (Urbana: University of Illinois Press, 1979); Julie Saville, *The Work of Reconstruction: From Slave to Wage Laborer in South Carolina, 1860–1870* (Cambridge: Cambridge University Press, 1994); Edmund Drago, *A Splendid Failure: Black Politicians and Reconstruction in Georgia* (Baton Rouge: Louisiana State University Press, 1982); and John Rodrigue, *Reconstruction in the Cane Fields: From Slavery to Free Labor in Louisiana's Sugar Parishes, 1862–1880* (Baton Rouge: Louisiana State University Press, 2001). A general discussion of postwar black politics begins with W.E.B. Du Bois, *Black Reconstruction in America* (1935; rpt., New York: Touchstone Books, 1992); and includes much of Eric Foner, *Reconstruction: America's Unfinished Revolution, 1863–1877* (New York: Harper and Row, 1988). The most comprehensive analysis of postwar black politics is Steven Hahn, *A Nation under Our Feet: Black Political Struggles in the Rural South from Slavery to the Great Migration* (Cambridge: Belknap Press, 2003). Of the more general discussions the border states receive some passing mention but little to account for the black-minority nature of the population in that region. The best works on the upper South—Dailey, *Before Jim Crow;* and Elsa Barkley Brown, "Negotiating and Transforming the Public Sphere: African-American Political Life in the Transition from Slavery to Freedom," *Public Culture* 7 (Fall 1994): 107–46—deal primarily with either urban areas or black-majority districts within the upper South.

9. Barbara Fields, *Slavery and Freedom on the Middle Ground: Maryland during the Nineteenth Century* (New Haven: Yale University Press, 1985), xii.

10. One of the best discussions of this very old debate is from Thomas Bonner, "Civil War Historians and the 'Needless War' Doctrine," *Journal of the History of Ideas* 17, no. 2 (April 1956): 193–216. Marxian historians, in particular, tend to emphasize the fundamental social differences between the slaveholding South and the wage labor–based North. See esp. Eugene Genovese, *The World the Slaveholders Made: Two Essays in Interpretation* (New York: Vintage Books, 1969); and John Ashworth, *Slavery, Capitalism and Politics in the Antebellum Republic* (Cambridge: Cambridge University Press, 1995).

11. Perhaps no historian has grasped the significance of Jackson's southern militancy better than Christopher Phillips. See Christopher Phillips, *Missouri's Confederate: Claiborne Fox Jackson and the Creation of Southern Identity in the Border West* (Columbia: University of Missouri Press, 2000). For his more recent work on Judge William B. Napton, see Christopher Phillips and Jason L. Pendleton, eds., *The Union on Trial: The Political Journals of Judge William Barclay Napton, 1829–1883* (Columbia: University of Missouri Press, 2005).

12. Hahn, *A Nation under Our Feet,* 3; Ranajit Guha, *Elementary Aspects of Peasant Insurgency in Colonial India* (Delhi: Oxford University Press, 1983). For this definition I draw from Steven Hahn, who defines *politics* as "collective struggles for what might be termed socially meaningful power."

13. On the historiographic debate between those who argue for and against discontinuity between the antebellum and postbellum South, see C. Vann Woodward, *Origins of the New South* (Baton Rouge: Louisiana State University Press, 1951); and Jonathan Wiener, *Social Origins of the New South: Alabama, 1860–1885* (Baton Rouge: Louisiana State University Press, 1978).

14. There are, of course, some excellent studies on Missouri's guerrilla war. Probably the best is Michael Fellman, *Inside War: The Guerrilla Conflict in Missouri during the American Civil War* (New York: Oxford University Press, 1989). T. J. Stiles's study of the life and context of Jesse James adds to this informative canon of American guerrilla warfare. See T. J. Stiles, *Jesse*

James: Last Rebel of the Civil War (New York: Knopf, 2002). On Lincoln's response to the Missouri crisis, see Dennis K. Boman, *Lincoln and Citizens' Rights in Civil War Missouri: Balancing Freedom and Security* (Baton Rouge: Louisiana State University Press, 2011). Other important recent works on the Civil War's guerrilla conflict are Bryce D. Benedict, *Jayhawkers: The Civil War Brigade of James Henry Lane* (Norman: University of Oklahoma Press, 2009); Noel C. Fisher, *War at Every Door: Partisan Politics and Guerrilla Violence in East Tennessee, 1860–1869* (Chapel Hill: University of North Carolina Press, 1997); Thomas Goodrich, *Black Flag: Guerrilla Warfare on the Western Border, 1861–1865* (Bloomington: Indiana University Press, 1995); Brian D. McKnight, *Contested Borderland: The Civil War in Appalachian Kentucky and Virginia* (Lexington: University Press of Kentucky, 2006); Barton A. Myers, *Executing Daniel Bright: Guerrilla Violence in a Coastal Carolina Community, 1861–1865* (Baton Rouge: Louisiana State University Press, 2009); Phillip Shaw Paludan, *Victims: A True Story of the Civil War* (Knoxville: University of Tennessee Press, 1981); and Daniel Sutherland, *A Savage Conflict: The Decisive Role of Guerrillas in the American Civil War* (Chapel Hill: University of North Carolina Press, 2009).

15. The most comprehensive study of Little Dixie and its antebellum social structure is R. Douglas Hurt, *Agriculture and Slavery in Missouri's Little Dixie* (Columbia: University of Missouri Press, 1992).

16. Daniel W. Crofts, *Reluctant Confederates: Upper South Unionists in the Secession Crisis* (Chapel Hill: University of North Carolina Press, 1989). Crofts notes that most of those who supported the Union before the war but came to support the Confederacy after President Lincoln's troop call-up in April 1861 were residents of Middle Tennessee and the North Carolina and Virginia Piedmont. These "reluctant Confederates" were constantly goaded by West Tennesseans and Tidewater Virginians who supported secession immediately after Lincoln's election in December 1860. Hardcore Unionists, who never embraced the Confederacy, were mostly found in the Appalachian highlands of East Tennessee and western North Carolina and in the future state of West Virginia.

CHAPTER ONE

1. Eighth Census, 1860, Population MSS, intro., xxxv.

2. Barbara Jeanne Fields, *Slavery and Freedom on the Middle Ground: Maryland during the Nineteenth Century* (New Haven: Yale University Press, 1985). One notable difference between the "middle ground" of Maryland and that of Kentucky and Missouri was the sizable presence of free blacks in Maryland. Whereas nearly half the black population in Maryland was free by 1860, less than 10 percent of black Kentuckians or Missourians were free from bondage. Nevertheless, the farms that dotted the Little Dixie and Bluegrass countryside relied upon a mix of free and slave labor just as did those in southern Maryland and the Eastern Shore.

3. Coulter, *Civil War and Readjustment in Kentucky*, 8.

4. William Henry Perrin, *History of Fayette County, Kentucky* (Chicago: O. L. Baskin and Co., 1882), 761; Eighth Census, Slave Schedules, Fayette County, Ky., 1860.

5. T. Berry Smith and Pearl Sims Gehrig, *History of Chariton and Howard Counties, Missouri* (Topeka: Historical Publishing Co., 1923), 853–54; Seventh Census, Slave Schedules, Chariton County, Mo., 1850.

6. Eighth Census, Population MS, 1860, Callaway County, Mo., 13; Eighth Census, Slave MS, 1860, Callaway County, Bourbon Township, 6; the 1820 manuscript census of Millersburg,

Bourbon County, lists a Martin Baker with a 20-year-old male slave; see Fourth Census, Population MS, Bourbon County, Ky., 1820.

7. Smith and Gehrig, *History of Chariton and Howard Counties, Missouri*, 586–87; Eighth Census, Slave MS, Saline County, Mo., 1860.

8. David Hackett Fischer and James C. Kelly, *Bound Away: Virginia and the Westward Movement* (Charlottesville: University Press of Virginia, 2000), 216.

9. Ibid., 234. Fischer and Kelly quote Michael Tadman, *Speculators and Slaves: Masters, Traders and Slaves in the Old South* (Madison: University of Wisconsin Press, 1989), 247, who estimates that 40 percent of all slaves sent to the West from Virginia traveled with their masters.

10. Fischer and Kelly, *Bound Away*, 163. They attribute the term *portable planter* to Marian Winship. See her essay in Kenneth R. Bowling and Donald R. Kennon, eds., *The House and Senate in the 1790s: Petitioning, Lobbying, and Institutional Development* (Athens: Ohio University Press, 2002).

11. Since Frederick Jackson Turner advanced his famous frontier thesis in 1893, historians have debated whether or not westward migration to rural areas was the most prominent migratory pattern or whether movement from farms to cities was actually greater. A recent population study by Patricia Kelly Hall and Steven Ruggles corroborates Turner's general thrust—migration to western farms was extensive, especially in the early nineteenth century. The authors of this study also confirm that most westward migrants were not the poorest easterners but were primarily middling sorts. Yeomen, rather than landless farm laborers, likely constituted the greatest percentage of westward migrants to the Bluegrass and Little Dixie. Yet the growth of cities such as Lexington and small towns across central Kentucky and Missouri, filled with Virginians, also supports the charges of some of Turner's critics. See Patricia Kelly Hall and Steven Ruggles, "'Restless in the Midst of Their Prosperity': New Evidence on the Internal Migration of Americans, 1850–2000," *Journal of American History* 91, no. 3 (December 2004): 829–46.

12. Eighth Census, Population MS, Cooper County, Mo., 1860.

13. This is the central thesis in Phillips, *Missouri's Confederate: Claiborne Fox Jackson*.

14. Kentucky was originally part of a Virginia county known as Fincastle County. It was renamed Kentucky County and then split into three counties after 1780—Fayette, Jefferson, and Lincoln. Kentucky finally broke away from Virginia and joined the Union as the fifteenth state in 1792. Nearly all of the original white inhabitants in Kentucky traveled there via the Cumberland Gap in Virginia's southwestern corner.

15. Hazel Dicken-Garcia, *To Western Woods: The Breckinridge Family Moves to Kentucky in 1793* (Madison, N.J.: Fairleigh Dickinson University Press, 1991); Perrin, *History of Fayette County, Kentucky*, 756–59. According to the Eighth Census tabulation of earlier census aggregates, Kentucky's population grew from 73,077 in 1790 to 406,511 in 1810, a 556 percent increase in twenty years. Presumably, the first census captured Kentucky because statehood was imminent in 1792. Although most westward migrants were middling farmers, some were quite wealthy and sought to take advantage of a land speculation scheme originating in Virginia. For decades, however, most of those living on speculator land in Kentucky were not the speculators themselves but small farmers struggling to attain their own land. One such farmer on speculator land was Thomas Lincoln of Hardin County, father of Abraham Lincoln. See Lowell Harrison, *Lincoln of Kentucky* (Lexington: University Press of Kentucky, 2000).

16. Perrin, *History of Fayette County, Kentucky*, 640–42.

17. Eighth Census, Population MS, 1860. In the case of Kentucky, then, Turner's frontier thesis would have run its course. By 1860 migration drew people toward Kansas, Missouri, Texas, and the West and not to Kentucky.

18. Ibid.

19. Ibid.

20. I use the term *slave-based societies* to avoid the dichotomy of *slave societies* and *societies with slaves* as spelled out by Ira Berlin. Berlin describes "slave societies" in reference to large-scale plantation systems such as developed in the Deep South. His term *societies with slaves* refers to the more mixed slave-free systems that permeated the pre-Revolutionary North. But the leaders of "societies with slaves" expressed much more political and ideological ambiguity regarding slavery than did the slaveholders of Missouri or Kentucky. Thus, I use the term *slave-based societies* to describe Kentucky and Missouri, which fit neither of Berlin's models. See Ira Berlin, *Many Thousands Gone: The First Two Centuries of Slavery in North America* (Cambridge: Harvard University Press, 1998).

21. Frank L. Owsley, "The Pattern of Migration and Settlement on the Southern Frontier," *Journal of Southern History* 11, no. 2 (May 1945): 166.

22. Philip Morgan shows slaveholdings in Virginia to be much smaller than in South Carolina. See Philip D. Morgan, *Slave Counterpoint: Black Culture in the Eighteenth-Century Chesapeake and Lowcountry* (Chapel Hill: University of North Carolina Press, 1998).

23. The region of central Missouri is commonly referred to as the Boonslick because of a salt lick owned by Nathan Boone near the town of Arrow Rock in Saline County. Boonslick technically refers to the part of the Missouri River where Howard, Saline, and Cooper counties all meet. It is often used interchangeably with the term *Little Dixie,* however, to refer to the larger slaveholder-dominated region along the Missouri River. It does not usually include Lafayette, Chariton, or Callaway County, however, all three of which are included in Little Dixie for purposes of this study. See Hurt, *Agriculture and Slavery in Missouri's Little Dixie,* 2.

24. J. Winston Coleman, *Slavery Times in Kentucky* (Chapel Hill: University of North Carolina Press, 1940), 9–10.

25. In 1790, around the time of statehood, 11,830 slaves lived in Kentucky. See First Census of the United States, 1790.

26. In 1820, the year before Missouri was admitted into the Union 10,222 slaves lived in Missouri. Many of them lived in St. Louis, but the majority lived in Little Dixie. See Fourth Census of the United States, Slaves, 1820. William Freehling notes that the oft-overlooked debate over banning slave importation in 1808 invoked significant national debate, as did discussion of Louisiana's 1812 state constitution. Yet none of these issues roiled the nation's political fabric the way the Missouri controversy of 1820 did. See William Freehling, *The Road to Disunion: 1776–1854* (New York: Oxford University Press, 1990).

27. Fifth Census, Population MS, Howard County, Mo., 1830. The only Philip Turner in the 1820 census lived in Madison County, Ky., on the southeast edge of the Bluegrass and a very common origin for early Missouri settlers.

28. It is also noteworthy that none of the slaveholders in Pilot Grove Township were born in Missouri. As household heads, these slaveholders may have been too old to be born in Missouri.

29. Eighth Census, Population MS, 1860.

30. All data on Pilot Grove Township compiled from the Eighth Census, Population and Slave MSS, Cooper County, Mo., 1860.

31. *Boonville Observer,* November 3, 1860.

32. The reason for using this method is that the areas under study are the most heavily slave-based regions of the states. One would assume that less slave-based areas would produce higher rates of cereals and livestock and lower rates of staples versus the central regions, thus skewing the state totals in that direction. And considering that Kentucky and Missouri statewide produced reasonably mixed crops compared to the nation as a whole, analyzing the central slaveholding regions against state totals yields the extent to which high-slave areas maintained crop diversity.

33. One major reason for this is the low land requirements for cultivation of tobacco and hemp. Because only a minor portion of acreage of even the largest hemp and tobacco producers went toward staple production, it is no surprise that cereal production and livestock values would not be diminished. Compare this with cotton cultivation, for which production of that staple tended to drive out alternative crops, with the occasional exception of corn.

34. James F. Hopkins, *A History of the Hemp Industry in Kentucky* (Lexington: University Press of Kentucky, 1998), 39–64.

35. In some ways hemp breaking compared in labor intensity to the sugarcane harvest in Louisiana and the Caribbean. But the market for sugarcane was so much greater than hemp, and the process of harvesting and processing an acre of cane involved many more workers than were necessary to break an acre of hemp. Large numbers of laborers would not have helped to "speed up" the hemp breaking process the way it did the sugarcane harvest.

36. For a detailed discussion of livestock and non-staple crop production in Missouri, see Hurt, *Agriculture and Slavery in Missouri's Little Dixie,* 125–86.

37. Ibid.

38. See also *Williams' Lexington [Kentucky] Directory, City Guide, and Business Mirror,* vol. 1: *1859–60,* comp. C. S. Williams (Lexington: Hitchcock & Searles, 1859) (hereafter cited as *Lexington City Directory*).

39. Eighth Census, Slave MS, Fayette County, Ky., 1860; *Lexington City Directory.*

40. Eighth Census, Population MS, Fayette County, Ky., 1860; Slave MS, Fayette County, Ky., 1860. Ferguson's personal wealth is listed as $100,000, making her one of the richest women in Lexington. At 59 years of age Lucy was clearly the head of the household. A 29-year-old son lived on her estate as well.

41. Eighth Census, Slave MS, 1860. Bourbon County, Town of Millersburg, 29.

42. Deed Book no. 33, Mercer County Courthouse, Harrodsburg, Ky., June 30, 1860.

43. *Central City and Brunswicker,* Brunswick, Mo., December 31, 1859.

44. *Lexington Observer and Reporter,* October 20, 1860; see also *Lexington City Directory.*

45. Jonathan D. Martin, *Divided Mastery: Slave Hiring in the American South* (Cambridge: Harvard University Press, 2004).

46. Alexander Jeffrey, December 25, 1860, Promissory Notes, Microfilm Clift no. 481. University of Kentucky Special Collections (hereafter cited as UKSC).

47. Ibid., December 27, 1860.

48. G. Clay Smith to Uncle Brutus J. Clay, December 27, 1861, Covington, Ky., box 13, folder 88, Clay Family Papers, UKSC.

49. Eighth Census, Slave MS, Fayette, County, Ky., 1860; *Lexington City Directory.*

50. *Missouri Telegraph* (Fulton), January 4, 1861.

51. Keith C. Barton, "'Good Cooks and Washers': Slave Hiring and the Market in Bourbon County, Kentucky," *Journal of American History* 84, no. 2 (September 1997): 436–60.

52. Henry Clay Bruce, *The New Man: Twenty-nine Years a Slave, Twenty-nine Years a Free Man* (York, Pa.: P. Anstadt and Sons, 1895).

53. Perrin, *History of Fayette County, Kentucky*, 112.

54. Harriet Beecher Stowe sprinkled commentary regarding the mildness of Kentucky slavery compared to that in Louisiana throughout *Uncle Tom's Cabin*.

55. As in Maryland, Tennessee, and Virginia, Kentucky seriously considered gradual abolition of slavery in the early 1830s. Even though Kentucky legislators agreed in 1833 to retain the slave system, they hoped to preserve the small-scale nature of Kentucky slavery by banning the importation of new slaves into the state.

56. James Lane Allen, *The Blue Grass Region of Kentucky* (New York: Harper and Brothers, 1899), 52. Allen also quotes at length Stowe, who claimed: "Perhaps the mildest form of the system of slavery is to be seen in the State of Kentucky. The general prevalence of agricultural pursuits of a quiet and gradual nature, not requiring those periodic seasons of hurry and pressure that are called for in the business of more southern districts, makes the task of the negro a more healthful and reasonable one; while the master, content with a more gradual style of acquisition, had not those temptations to hard-heartedness which always overcome frail human nature when the prospect of sudden and rapid gain is weighed in the balance with no heavier counterpoise than the interests of the helpless and unprotected." Other abolitionists, including Frederick Douglass, echoed the claim that slavery in the upper South (Maryland in Douglass's case) was milder than in the Deep South. As will be discussed later, this is a curious position for abolitionists to assume considering that it ignores the special primacy of the interstate slave trade on the upper South slave system.

57. Ibid., 67.

58. Perry McCandless, *A History of Missouri*, vol. 2: *1820–1860* (Columbia: University of Missouri Press, 1972), 286.

59. Harold D. Tallant, *Evil Necessity: Slavery and Political Culture in Antebellum Kentucky* (Lexington: University Press of Kentucky, 2003).

60. On the southern obsession with honor, see Bertram Wyatt-Brown, *Southern Honor: Ethics and Behavior in the Old South* (New York: Oxford University Press, 1982).

61. George Fredrickson, *Black Image in the White Mind: The Debate on Afro-American Character and Destiny, 1817–1914* (New York: Harper and Row, 1971).

62. Leon Litwack, *North of Slavery: The Negro in the Free States, 1790–1860* (Chicago: University of Chicago Press, 1961); and Baker, *Affairs of Party*, 212–58.

63. White patrons were required under Kentucky law to post bond in court for manumitted blacks as insurance against potential criminal behavior by freed slaves. The bonding system ensured that white patrons kept a close eye on manumitted slaves. See Richard C. Brown, "The Free Blacks of Boyle County, Kentucky, 1850–1860: A Research Note," *Register of the Kentucky Historical Society* 87, no. 4 (Fall 1989): 431.

64. Ibid.

65. Harold Tallant cites a slew of central Kentuckians, including proslavery Charles Wickliffe and antislavery Robert J. Breckinridge, as fearing disorder with general emancipation. See Tallant, *Evil Necessity*, 59–90.

66. For a good account of German-Missourian sentiment regarding slavery and the slave labor system in general, see Steven Rowan, trans. and ed., *Germans for a Free Missouri: Translations from the St. Louis Radical Press, 1857–1862* (Columbia: University of Missouri Press, 1983), 124–25. Also see the introductory essay in this volume by James Neal Primm (3–45).

67. Phillips, *Missouri's Confederate*, 36–37.

68. For the definition of *household*, see Fox-Genovese, *Within the Plantation Household*, 31–32. As Fox-Genovese notes, the term *household* extends beyond personal family relationships. As such, it is possible for masters and mistresses to imagine the extension of paternalistic relationships to those who hire their slaves.

69. For a general description of slavery as a "way of life" based on the paternalistic prerogative, see the classic Ulrich Bonnell Phillips, *American Negro Slavery* (Baton Rouge: Louisiana State University Press, 1966), 291–308. For the most comprehensive analysis of slavery as a system characterized by paternalistic relations between slave and slaveholder, see Genovese, *Roll, Jordan, Roll*, 3–7.

70. Alexander Jeffrey, December 25, 1860, Promissory Notes, Microfilm Clift No. 481, Kentucky Historical Society, Frankfort (hereafter cited as KHS).

71. Allen, *Blue Grass Region of Kentucky*, 63.

72. Ibid., 52.

73. McCurry, *Masters of Small Worlds*, 18–19.

74. Martin, *Divided Mastery*, 17–19.

CHAPTER TWO

1. Glasgow *Weekly Times*, November 8, 1860.

2. Ibid.

3. These meetings took place in virtually every sizable southern community. For a sophisticated discussion of the rhetoric and resolutions of these meetings and related vigilance committees in South Carolina, see Stephanie McCurry, *Masters of Small Worlds: Yeoman Households, Gender Relations, and the Political Culture of the Antebellum South Carolina Low Country* (New York: Oxford University Press, 1995), 278–304.

4. *Glasgow Weekly Times*, December 6, 1860.

5. Ibid. Cockades were a form of hat used to symbolize one's political affiliation. The presence of these colorful emblems of secessionism at a Union meeting signaled a defiant rejection of the Union cause.

6. Personal liberty laws were passed by many northern states and offered freedom to any and all persons who set foot in those states. The object of these laws was to undermine the vigorous Fugitive Slave Act of 1850, which deputized northern citizens to return runaway slaves to southern masters. Southern states viewed personal liberty laws as a form of nullification of federal law. Northern states ironically made "states' rights" claims in defense of personal liberty laws. See esp. the famous Supreme Court case based in Wisconsin, *Abelman v. Booth*, which found these laws unconstitutional: *Abelman v. Booth*, 62 U.S. Supreme Court 506 (1858).

7. Alexander Stephens, quoted in Crofts, *Reluctant Confederates*, 116.

8. Quoted in ibid.,158.

9. Other southern Unionist strongholds were the wire grass region of Georgia, northwestern Virginia, the piney woods of Mississippi, the hilly region of western Arkansas, and the Ger-

man communities of south Texas. Not surprisingly, the eastern Appalachian area of Kentucky and the Ozark region of southwestern Missouri were Unionist strongholds as well.

10. For the best discussion of slavery and racial issues for the northern Democratic Party, see Jean H. Baker, *Affairs of Party: The Political Culture of Northern Democrats in the Mid-Nineteenth Century* (Ithaca: Cornell University Press, 1983). On anti-abolitionist mobs, see Leonard Richards, *"Gentlemen of Property and Standing": Anti-Abolitionist Mobs in Jacksonian America* (New York: Oxford University Press, 1970).

11. For the most extensive discussion of the importance of slavery in differentiating the social order in the North and South, see Edward Ayers, *Valley of the Shadow: Two Communities in the Civil War* (Charlottesville: Norton, 2000). On the distinction between the gendered "private sphere" of the free North and gender relations within slave households of the South, see Elizabeth Fox-Genovese, *Within the Plantation Household: Black and White Women of the Old South* (Chapel Hill: University of North Carolina Press, 1988). On the specific effect of slavery on labor relations in the South, see Ashworth, *Slavery, Capitalism and Politics in the Antebellum Republic*. On social relations in the lower North, see Nicole Etcheson, *The Emerging Midwest: Upland Southerners and the Political Culture of the Old Northwest, 1787–1861* (Bloomington: Indiana University Press, 1996). Even the most conservative regions of the lower North witnessed the creation of a gendered private-public sphere, developed a wage labor–based economic order, and did not feature slave patrols as a fundamental arbiter of public order.

12. Eugene Genovese, *Roll, Jordan, Roll: The World the Slaves Made* (New York: Pantheon Books, 1974), 5.

13. Lucian Pye and Sidney Verba, eds., *Political Culture and Political Development* (Princeton: Princeton University Press, 1965), 8–9.

14. *Boonville Observer*, September 22, 1860.

15. Richard Vaughan to Abiel Leonard, October 11, 1860, Lexington, Mo., folder 447, Leonard Papers C1013, Western Historical Manuscript Collection—State Historical Society of Missouri Joint Collection (hereafter cited as WHMC).

16. Harry A. Volz, "Party, State and Nation: Kentucky and the Coming of the American Civil War" (Ph.D. diss., University of Virginia, 1982), 22–25; and Michael Holt, *The Rise and Fall of the American Whig Party* (New York: Oxford University Press, 1999), 81.

17. John Vollmer Mering, *The Whig Party in Missouri* (Columbia: University of Missouri Press, 1967), 52–70. Mering also notes that Boone Countians overwhelmingly came from heavily Whig Madison County, Ky. Whigs tended to perform better where the population was more settled and businesses and agriculture both contributed to the area's economy. In many other parts of Missouri, including other Little Dixie counties, the base of wealth was almost universally agricultural, thus weakening the traditional pro-business Whiggish appeal.

18. Baker, *Affairs of Party*.

19. Benton would later break from western Democratic orthodoxy by embracing Free-Soilism, which would lead to a split in Missouri's Democratic Party in the 1850s. St. Louis Democrats remained loyal to the Bentonite wing of the party, while those in the Boonslick, following future Governor Claiborne Fox Jackson, formed the anti-Benton opposition.

20. For a general political history of antebellum Kentucky, see Lowell H. Harrison and James C. Klotter, *A New History of Kentucky* (Lexington: University Press of Kentucky, 1997), 109–24.

21. Louis Wright, *Culture on the Moving Frontier* (Bloomington: Indiana University Press, 1955), 46–80.

22. Phillips, *Missouri's Confederate,* 48.

23. Quote of Andrew Burnaby from ibid., 50, quoted by Breen, "Culture of Agriculture: The Symbolic World of the Tidewater Planter, 1760–1790," in *Saints and Revolutionaries: Essays in Early American History,* ed. David D. Hall, John M. Murrin, and Thad W. Tate (New York: Norton, 1983).

24. Even in Illinois, an apprenticeship system replicated slavery in all but name. When slaveholding settlers populated central Missouri in the 1810s and 1820s, much of the land north of the Ohio River was only beginning to be settled by New Englanders and New Yorkers as well as upland southerners.

25. This is the essence of Harold Tallant's thesis. See Tallant, *Evil Necessity.*

26. On Breckinridge as a truly reluctant Confederate, see William C. Davis, *Breckinridge: Statesman, Soldier, Symbol* (Baton Rouge: Louisiana State University Press, 1974). For Morgan's decision to enter the war on the side of the South, see James Ramage, *Rebel Raider: The Life of General John Hunt Morgan* (Lexington: University Press of Kentucky, 1986), 40–45.

27. John Hunt Morgan to Thomas Morgan, November 9, 1860, folder 5, Hunt-Morgan Papers, UKSC.

28. Thomas Morgan to Henrietta Morgan, n.d., Hunt-Morgan Papers, UKSC.

29. McCandless, *A History of Missouri,* vol. 2: *1820–1860,* 274. Davy Atchison, who called for southerners to send their sons to the Missouri-Kansas border to fight for slavery, repeatedly defended the "border ruffians" as men of property and education.

30. Many historians, including Perry McCandless in *A History of Missouri,* paint a portrait of Missouri politics as rent by extreme proslavery Democrats on one hand and increasingly abolitionist Republicans on the other. But by the end of the 1850s and the crucial 1860 gubernatorial election, conservatives gave the former Whig and staunch Unionist Sample Orr a majority of the vote in Boone, Callaway, and Saline counties and virtually split the vote between Orr and Claiborne Fox Jackson in the other counties of Little Dixie. Interestingly, Jackson was a lifelong Boonslicker, and Sample Orr was a virtual unknown from southwestern Missouri. In the 1856 race Little Dixie similarly supported local former Whig James S. Rollins by a substantial majority over the eventual victor, Robert Stewart. Proslavery, pro-southern extremists may have dominated the Democratic Party in late antebellum Missouri, but the white constituents of Missouri's most heavily slave-based region continually rejected these fire-eaters in favor of more moderate supporters of slavery and the Union.

31. Coulter, *Civil War and Readjustment in Kentucky,* 16–17. The bulk of Lexington's hemp trade went to the South, especially to cotton planters. But its horses were known throughout the country as the finest stock and were in high demand in the South and the Northwest.

32. Before the late 1840s all central Missouri tobacco was sold in lower South ports such as New Orleans. The establishment of major tobacco processing facilities in St. Louis, as well as in Missouri River towns such as Glasgow, allowed Missourians to trade tobacco upriver to Illinois and Iowa and, via the Great Lakes, to the Northeast. See Hurt, *Agriculture and Slavery in Missouri's Little Dixie.*

33. On Mary Todd Lincoln and her Kentucky childhood, see Jean H. Baker, *Mary Todd Lincoln: A Biography* (New York: Norton, 1987).

34. On Lincoln's relationship to his state of birth, see Harrison, *Lincoln of Kentucky.*

35. Eighth Census, Population MS, 1860, 616–17. Data compiled and presented in Coulter, *Civil War and Readjustment in Kentucky,* 13.

36. Quoted in ibid., 15.

37. Ibid.

38. Eighth Census, Slave MS, 1860.

39. *Boonville Observer,* December 8, 1860.

40. *Glasgow Times,* January 5, 1860.

41. Eric Foner, *Free Soil, Free Labor, Free Men: The Ideology of the Republican Party Before the Civil War* (New York: Oxford University Press, 1970).

42. *Glasgow Weekly Times,* March 29, 1855, quoted in Christopher Phillips, *Missouri's Confederate,* 187. Phillips uses the extension of this quote, in which the *Times* warns against calling all political opponents by these epithets, as an example of the generally moderate nature of central Missouri public opinion. I completely agree with Phillips on this point.

43. On southerners who hoped to expand a southern slave empire into Central America, with filibusterers at the vanguard, see Robert May, *Manifest Destiny's Underworld: Filibustering in Antebellum America* (Chapel Hill: University of North Carolina Press, 2004). See also James McPherson, *Battle Cry of Freedom* (New York: Ballantine Books, 1988), 78–116.

44. This was also true in the eastern border states such as Maryland and Virginia. On the politics of the Fugitive Slave Act during the 1850s, see Stanley Harrold, *Border War: Fighting over Slavery before the Civil War* (Chapel Hill: University of North Carolina Press, 2010).

45. *Paris (Ky.) Western Citizen,* February 1, 1861.

46. See speech by Kentucky senator Garrett Davis in *Paris (Ky.) Western Citizen,* March 22, 1861.

47. Author unknown, *History of Howard and Cooper Counties, Missouri* (St. Louis: National Historical Co., 1883), 271.

48. G. W. Miller to Abiel Leonard, December 16, 1860, Jefferson City, Mo., folder 449, Leonard Papers C1013, WHMC.

49. A. Leonard to Reeves Leonard, March 26, 1861, Oakwood, Mo., folder 452, Leonard Papers C1013, WHMC.

50. *Paris (Ky.) Western Citizen,* February 1, 1861.

51. *Missouri Telegraph,* November 23, 1860.

52. Ibid.

53. *Paris (Ky.) Western Citizen,* February 1, 1861.

54. *Ibid.*

55. Ibid.; *Missouri Telegraph,* November 23, 1860; *Glasgow Times,* December 6, 1860.

56. Yancey was such a dangerous ideologue that Jefferson Davis sent him to Europe as a Confederate commissioner. Yancey repeatedly denounced the government of the Confederate States of America (CSA) in the same manner in which he blasted the United States.

57. *Lexington Observer and Reporter,* July 21, 1860.

58. *Boonville Observer,* August 11, 1860.

59. *Glasgow Times,* February 7, 1861.

60. *Paris (Ky.) Western Citizen,* March 22, 1861.

61. *Missouri Telegraph,* November 23, 1860.

62. *Paris (Ky.) Western Citizen,* June 7, 1861.

63. As Christopher Phillips notes in *Missouri's Confederate,* however, many Missourians gradually eschewed the mantle of Jackson as the party adopted a more southern identity in the 1850s. Nevertheless, most Democratic meetings in Missouri proudly invoked Old Hickory and

his defense of Union in 1831. See, e.g., *Boonville Observer,* September 22 and August 11, 1860. George Robertson of Lexington, Ky., explicitly praised Andrew Jackson for quashing secession in 1833. See *Lexington Observer and Reporter,* November 26, 1860.

64. The *Paris (Ky.) Western Citizen* commented upon a conservative Unionist speech by Garrett Davis that it "reminded us of the days of Webster." Daniel Webster was not only a famous orator but also a nationally respected conservative Whig who had a great following in the South despite his New England heritage. Indeed, Massachusetts's Edward Everett, the vice presidential nominee with John Bell on the Constitutional Union ticket of 1860, regularly associated himself with the philosophy and politics of Daniel Webster.

65. *Lexington Observer and Reporter,* October 20, 1860.

66. *Paris (Ky.) Western Citizen,* September 7, 1860.

67. *Missouri Telegraph,* March 1, 1861.

CHAPTER THREE

1. *Boonville Observer,* January 19, 1861. The constitutional amendments at the heart of the Crittenden Compromise would have extended the Missouri Compromise line (36 degrees, 30 minutes) to the West Coast; explicitly forbade the U.S. Congress from abolishing slavery; protected slavery in the District of Columbia, so long as Maryland and Virginia still had slavery; prevented Congress from regulating the interstate slave trade; given the Fugitive Slave Act constitutional protection; and made these amendments "unamendable" in the future. See *Congressional Globe,* December 18, 1860, for the full text of the Crittenden Compromise.

2. Emergency organizations in the Deep South often referred to themselves as "Minute Men" as well. See, e.g., Charles Dew, *Apostles of Disunion* (Charlottesville: University Press of Virginia, 2001), 69, for mention of John Preston's Minute Men of Columbia, S.C.

3. According to the 1860 Census, all named officers at the meeting lived in Saline Township, Cooper County, Mo. A comprehensive listing of soldier records does not positively identify any of the participants except James H. Chandler, the secretary of the Minute Men. James H. Chandler is listed in the 2nd Missouri Cavalry (Confederate). It is more likely that the other members of the meeting ended up in pro-Confederate bushwhacker gangs not accounted for in the official records. See "Military Records: Civil War Service Records," *Ancestry.com,* Provo, Utah, 2002, disc 1.

4. *Boonville Observer,* February 2, 1861.

5. Charles Colcock Jones was a highly influential Georgia proslavery minister who delivered numerous high-profile sermons in defense of slavery as a uniquely Christian institution.

6. James Shannon, *An Address Delivered before the Pro-Slavery Convention of the State of Missouri on Domestic Slavery,* held in Lexington, Mo., July 13, 1855 (St. Louis: Republican Book and Job Office, 1855), 24.

7. Words capitalized in the original, underscoring the shocking tone of such a remark as early as 1855 and in as northerly a locale as Lexington, Mo.

8. Shannon, *Address,* 27.

9. In fact, Shannon's case resembled many of the Deep South secession commissioners who invoked the specter of race war and the degradation of the white race in the event of black Republican rule. While other border secessionists similarly worried about servile insurrection

and race war—especially after John Brown's raid—few made explicit appeals to threats against white supremacy at the center of their secessionist arguments. See Dew, *Apostles of Disunion,* 51–58, for a discussion of Deep South white supremacist rhetoric from Alabama commissioners sent to the border states.

10. Robert E. Shalhope, *Sterling Price: Portrait of a Southerner* (Columbia: University of Missouri Press, 1971), 122. Shalhope demonstrates that while Price sympathized with the proslavery cause on racial and social grounds, he remained a Jacksonian to the end. He considered Thomas Hart Benton and Stephen Douglas some of his greatest political allies, even when he disagreed with their positions. During the tempestuous period surrounding Benton's reelection campaign, Claiborne Fox Jackson's famous "Jackson Resolutions" (actually penned by Judge Napton) demanded Senator Benton take a militant stance on slavery in the territories. Although sympathetic to the content of the Jackson Resolutions, Price rallied Chariton County forces to the defense of Benton himself, who Price felt was being unfairly maligned. Moreover, unlike the rest of the Boonslick Democracy that controlled state politics in Missouri and obsessed over the slavery issue, Price continued to place opposition to soft money and government spending at the center of his political philosophy.

11. Ibid., 116. Price would remain a conservative Unionist until the Lyon crackdown in June 1861, when he took the Missouri State Guard into the service of the Confederacy. Price became the highest-ranking military official from Missouri and led the entire Confederate army in the state.

12. *Glasgow Times,* January 5, 1860.

13. John Hope Franklin, *The Militant South, 1800–1861* (Cambridge: Harvard University Press, 1956), 80–95.

14. *Kentucky Tribune* (Danville), February 8, 1861; *Paris (Ky.) Western Citizen,* May 10, 1861. These militias are not to be confused with the proliferating Home Guards who fought for the Union cause after the Kentucky State Guard vacated the state in September 1861. In Missouri more formalized state militia would replace the fleeing state guards after vacating Missouri in late 1861. Later chapters address the political significance of these wartime Home Guards and militias in greater detail.

15. *Lexington Kentucky Statesmen,* June 1, 1860.

16. Mary E. Wharton and Ellen F. Williams, eds. *Peach Leather and Rebel Gray: Diary and Letters of a Confederate Wife* (Lexington: Helicon Co., 1986), 10.

17. J. Winston Coleman, *Lexington during the Civil War* (Lexington: Commercial Printing Co., 1938), 9.

18. Perrin, *History of Fayette County, Kentucky,* 448–49.

19. Ibid., 444. For John Hunt Morgan's prewar life, and especially his obsession with southern conceptions of manhood and honor, see James A. Ramage, *Rebel Raider: The Life of General John Hunt Morgan* (Lexington: University Press of Kentucky, 1986), 18–39.

20. Wm. B. Richardson to Mr. Morgan, May 22, 1861, New Orleans, box 15, folder 9, Hunt-Morgan Papers, UKSC.

21. Charles B. Dew, *Apostles of Disunion: Southern Secession Commissioners and the Causes of the Civil War* (Charlottesville: University Press of Virginia, 2001), 43.

22. Napton, *Past and Present of Saline County, Missouri,* 138. The meeting was held December 26, 1859.

23. Ibid., 145. The meeting was held December 15, 1860.

24. The Breckinridge platform called for a slave code in all territories, and the future Crittenden Compromise included the disavowal of personal liberty laws and constitutional protection of slavery in the states.

25. *Louisville Courier,* March 21, 1861, quoting a mass meeting resolution in Lexington, Ky.

26. Ibid., March 20, 1861, quoting resolutions of a southern rights meeting in Paris, Bourbon County, Ky.

27. Ibid.

28. Ibid., March 21, 1861.

29. Ibid., April 9, 1861. Following Lincoln's election Kentucky's political parties realigned according to the sectional crisis at hand. Former advocates of Stephen Douglas and John Bell generally coalesced around the new, dominant Union Democratic Party. Supporters of Breckinridge and more militant pro-South activists in the Bell camp renamed themselves the States' Rights Party. The States' Rights Party convention selected delegates to the forthcoming Border Slave States Conference for May 4. Once Virginia seceded on April 17, the Kentucky State's Rights Party withdrew its candidates, allowing Unionists to dominate the border state conference. When Kentucky sided with the Union in September 1861, the States' Rights Party was renamed the Peace Democratic Party. With so many members of the States' Rights Party leaving the state to join the Confederate army and the Union army applying pressure on secessionist sympathizers—especially on Election Day—the Union Democrats dominated Kentucky politics until the end of the war.

30. *Paris (Ky.) Western Citizen,* April 12, 1861.

31. Phillips, *Missouri's Confederate,* 193, quoting Napton Diary, folder 1, 50–51, Missouri Historical Society. Napton goes on to suggest that the "North regards it as a point of honor to persist, so it is merely a point of honor upon which we split." But Christopher Phillips highlights the significance of the pronoun *we,* placing Missouri squarely on the southern side of the honor equation.

32. The banner was placed in Neshoba County, Miss. Originally cited in *Eastern Clarion,* November 14, 1860; quoted in William L. Barney, *The Secessionist Impulse: Alabama and Mississippi in 1860* (Tuscaloosa: University of Alabama Press, 1974), 190.

33. *Charleston Mercury,* November 9, 1860, quoted in the *Semi-Weekly Mississippian* and cited in Barney, *Secessionist Impulse,* 232.

34. *Kentucky Statesman,* August 28, 1860, quoted in in Coulter, *Civil War and Readjustment in Kentucky,* 23 n. 21.

35. Napton, *Past and Present of Saline County, Missouri,* 146–47. Note that the term *Conditional Unionists* was used to describe an ad hoc political party in the race for the sovereignty convention. Some Conditional Unionists did, in fact, condition their Unionism on the maintenance of a policy of nonaggression at Washington, but many other so-called Conditional Unionists remained loyal throughout. Unconditional Unionists were most prominent in St. Louis and among the German population throughout the state.

36. Coulter, *Civil War and Readjustment in Kentucky,* 29–30.

37. The *Louisville Courier* was the most prominent secessionist newspaper in Kentucky or Missouri. It regularly reprinted articles from local pro-secessionist papers such as the *Woodford Pennant* and the *Lexington Statesman.* Unfortunately, no copies of these Bluegrass area newspapers remain. In Missouri virtually no major newspaper actively supported secession prior to

Fort Sumter, even though the governor and the legislature desperately yearned for a chance to take Missouri out of the Union.

38. Democrats, especially those in the pro-Breckinridge wing of the party, lampooned Constitutional Unionist supporters of Bell for advancing no principles and no solutions to the sectional crisis.

39. *Louisville Courier,* April 9, 1861.

40. See quote by Senator Garrett Davis about the "Canada line" in *Paris (Ky.) Western Citizen,* March 22, 1861.

41. Ibid.

42. Confederate states sent special secession commissioners into each of the border states in early 1861 in order to convince them to join the new nation. Alabama sent S. F. Hale to Kentucky for this purpose. See Dew, *Apostles of Disunion,* 51–57.

43. *Official Records,* ser. 4, vol. 1, p. 14.

44. I use the term *original secessionist* in a border state context only. Because virtually none of these secessionists openly demanded secession prior to Lincoln's election, they would hardly qualify as "original secessionists" when measured against the likes of Robert Barnwell Rhett, Edmund Ruffin, and William Lowndes Yancey. But within Kentucky and Missouri they formed the vanguard of the secessionist movement in the weeks after the November 1860 election.

45. Phillips, *Missouri's Confederate,* 235.

46. Ibid.

47. Eighth Census, Population MS, 1860; Eighth Census, Slave MS, 1860.

48. *Louisville Courier;* Eighth Census, Population MS, 1860; Eighth Census, Slave MS, 1860.

49. This is the finding of a study of secessionists in Alabama and Mississippi as well. Young, upwardly mobile attorneys and small planters were the most avid supporters of secession, while older, more established planters tended to hold out for the Union as late as practicable. See William L. Barney, *The Secessionist Impulse: Alabama and Mississippi in 1860* (Tuscaloosa: University of Alabama Press, 1974).

50. Amy Murrell Taylor concludes that younger people tended to gravitate toward the secessionist cause, while many of their own parents remained loyal to the Union. This was partly a result of economic self-interest, as young men hoped to capitalize on the slave system, but it also reflected the decades of compromise and sectional reconciliation that their elders had witnessed. While older farmers in Kentucky and Missouri fondly remembered Henry Clay's heroic defense of Union in 1850, younger upstarts viewed sectional politics more cynically. See Amy Murrell Taylor, *The Divided Family in Civil War America* (Chapel Hill: University of North Carolina Press, 2005), 13–34.

51. George Rawick, interview with Bert Mayfield, *The American Slave: A Composite Autobiography* (Westport, Conn.: Greenwood, 1972), vol. 16.

52. Ibid., interview with Aunt Harriet Mason, 31.

53. In both cases Kentucky and Missouri slave codes predated statehood, and both were heavily influenced by Virginia's slave code. Missouri's first slave code was the Territorial Slave Law of 1804, and Kentucky's first code copied Virginia's upon statehood in 1792. Later revisions to the Kentucky and Missouri codes were mostly minor, with a few exceptions. Kentucky banned the importation of slaves in 1833 and repealed the non-importation ban in the new constitution of 1851. And Missouri did not ban the teaching of reading and writing to slaves until 1847. Both codes defined slaves as chattel property, with no rights to own property them-

selves. And recognizing the peril of surrounding free soil, both codes provided strict punishment for whites who transported slaves throughout the state without the master's permission. Also, in both states slaveholders could manumit their slaves so long as they posted bond. Pressure in the late antebellum era, however, restricted the rights of slaveholders to manumit their slaves within Kentucky or Missouri. See Harrison Trexler, *Slavery in Missouri, 1804–1865* (Baltimore: Johns Hopkins Press, 1914), 57–81, for a good summary of slave law in Missouri. For Kentucky's slave code and the various complications with respect to its enforcement, see Ivan E. McDougle, *Slavery in Kentucky, 1792–1865* (Westport, Conn.: Negro Universities Press, 1918), 30–70.

54. Kentucky's 1851 constitution required free blacks to leave the state unless bonded by their former masters. See Stanton, *Revised Statutes of Kentucky*. Missouri passed a law banning education of blacks, slave or free, in 1847 in response to abolitionist fears. Localities across Missouri passed more stringent curfew laws and increased the pay for slave patrols in the 1850s as well. For these changes in Missouri law, see Gary R. Kremer, Lorenzo J. Greene, and Antonio F. Holland, *Missouri's Black Heritage*, rev. ed. (Columbia: University of Missouri Press, 1993), 38–40.

55. *Glasgow Times*, January 5, 1860.

56. *Missouri Telegraph* (Fulton), April 5, 1861.

57. Glen Hardeman, August 1, 1855, Saline County, Mo., folder 32, Receipts, C3655, WHMC.

58. Joseph Northcutt printed advertisements in every Lexington newspaper. For an example of a transaction settled in outer Fayette County, see "Joseph Northcutt Slave Bill of Sale," September 6, 1859, KHS.

59. Thomas Jones to Mr. John Stout, November 13, 1860, Midway, Ky., David S. G. Silcock Collection, KHS.

60. William Switzler, *History of Boone County, Missouri* (St. Louis: Western Historical Co., 1882), 393 "Prices of Slaves in 1859." For another Boone County sale of a similar nature, see Sheriff's Sale C2846, "Sheriff's Sales! At the May Term of the Circuit Court of Boone County, Mo., 1861," WHMC.

61. *Glasgow Times*, October 20, 1859.

62. Rawick, interview with Delicia Patterson, *American Slave*, 11:270–76.

63. J. W. George to Calvin Morgan, January 11, 1861, New Orleans, box 15, folder 7, Hunt-Morgan Papers, UKSC.

64. Marion B. Lucas, *A History of Blacks in Kentucky*, vol. 1: *From Slavery to Segregation, 1760–1891* (Frankfort: Kentucky Historical Society, 1992), 99. Marion Lucas notes that these figures are estimations, but they are the most commonly agreed upon number for overall sale from Kentucky.

65. Michael Tadman, *Speculators and Slaves: Masters, Traders, and Slaves in the Old South* (Madison: University of Wisconsin Press, 1989), 302.

66. Ibid.

67. The myth of border slavery's mildness received sanction from contemporaries as well as later observers. Even Frederick Douglass wrote that slavery in Maryland was milder than in the Deep South, and Harriet Beecher Stowe's juxtaposition of Kentucky and Louisiana slave life dramatized the supposed contrast even more explicitly. Late-nineteenth-century writers such as James Lane Allen added to the myth in his cultural survey of Bluegrass life. Allen, like most nineteenth-century observers, associated close relationships between individual slaves

and their masters as evidence of the "humaneness" of upper South slavery. Presumably, the image of large gangs of blacks implied a degree of brutality unto itself, regardless of the offsetting possibilities for vibrant slave community life on the larger slave plantations. Even modern scholars tend to accept the myth, though with the qualification that all slave systems were bad. In Marion Lucas's otherwise excellent survey of Kentucky's black history, e.g., he remarks, "To state that slaves fared better under Kentucky's slave system as compared to that of the Deep South does not exonerate the evil of both systems." Lucas, *History of Blacks in Kentucky*, 1:43. But this caveat does injustice to the uniquely brutal component of Kentucky—and Missouri by extension—slavery, the prominence of the Deep South slave trade, and the resulting decimation of slave family and community life. Ironically, the small-scale farms and flexibility of border South slavery rendered slaves the greatest cruelty of all by further circumscribing and sundering slave community and family life. Closeness to the master was hardly the slave's idea of humanity. One exception to this historiographic pattern is Barbara Fields, who specifically excoriates small-scale slavery and slave hiring for its community- and family-breaking effects. See Fields, *Slavery and Freedom on the Middle Ground*, 25–26. A more recent acknowledgment of the unique cruelties faced by Missouri's small-scale slaves comes from Diane Mutti-Burke, *On Slavery's Border: Missouri's Small Slaveholding Households, 1815–1865* (Athens: University of Georgia Press, 2010).

68. Lorenzo J. Greene, *Missouri's Black Heritage*, rev. ed., 43.

69. For local reaction to the Hopkinsville plot, see Wallace-Starling Family Diaries, KHS, in which Ellen Kenton McGaughey Wallace reveals the community's terrified response to the planned insurrection.

70. Coleman, *Slavery Times in Kentucky*, 88–92; *Louisville Courier*, August 14, 1848, quoted in J. Blaine Hudson, *Fugitive Slaves and the Underground Railroad in the Kentucky Borderland* (Jefferson, N.C.: McFarland and Co., 2002), 137.

71. Tallant, *Evil Necessity*, 146.

72. Hudson, *Fugitive Slaves*, 49.

73. *Randolph Citizen*, August 9, 1855, quoted in Harriet C. Frazier, *Runaway and Freed Missouri Slaves and Those Who Helped Them, 1763–1865* (Jefferson, N.C.: McFarland and Co., 2004), 101.

74. Hudson, *Fugitive Slaves*; Frazier, *Runaway and Freed Missouri Slaves*.

75. Hudson, *Fugitive Slaves*, 74–75.

76. Frazier, *Runaway and Freed Missouri Slaves*, 112–13.

77. Rawick, interview with George Henderson, *American Slave*, vol. 16, Garrard County, 7. The old wagon route to Madison, Ind.—the nearest crossing point on the Ohio River—would have been eighty miles. The current road US 421 roughly traces what was likely the same route from Versailles, Woodford County, to Madison, Ind.

78. On the Anti-Slavery League, see Hudson, *Fugitive Slaves*, 25.

79. Ibid., 162.

80. *Glasgow Times*, November 17, 1859.

81. Margaret O'Brien, "Slavery in Louisville during the Antebellum Period: 1820–1860" (M.A. thesis, University of Louisville, 1979), 130, quoted in Frazier, *Runaway and Freed Missouri Slaves*, 82.

82. Thomas Morgan to "Mother," April 29, 1861, box 15, folder 8, Hunt-Morgan Papers, UKSC.

83. *Glasgow Weekly Times*, November 17, 1859.

84. Rawick, interview with Mary Belle Dempsey. *American Slave,* 16:33.

85. *Missouri Telegraph* (Fulton), November 2, 1860. As this case demonstrates, large-scale lynch mobs aimed at African Americans appeared long before the late nineteenth century.

86. *Boonville Observer,* November 11, 1860. The article quotes the *Fulton (Mo.) Vox Populi.* Unfortunately, no issues of that newspaper survive.

87. *Paris (Ky.) Western Citizen,* September 1, 1860. The ultimate fate of the slave is unknown.

88. Ebenezer Stedman, *Bluegrass Craftsman: Being the Reminiscences of Ebenezer Hiram Stedman, Papermaker, 1808–1885,* ed Frances L. S. Dugan and Jacqueline P. Bull (Lexington: University Press of Kentucky, 1959). Discussed in greater detail in Tallant, *Evil Necessity,* 65.

89. Bruce, *New Man,* 67.

90. Hahn, *Nation under Our Feet,* 16.

91. Diane Mutti Burke, "On Slavery's Borders: Slavery and Slaveholding on Missouri's Farms, 1821–1865" (Ph.D. diss., Emory University, 2004), 205.

92. Hahn, *Nation under Our Feet,* 17.

93. General Affidavit, December 26, 1889, Chariton County, Mo., folder 2487, Benecke Family Collection C3825, WHMC.

94. Mechal Sobel, *Trabelin' On: The Slave Journey to an Afro-Baptist Faith* (Westport, Conn.: Greenwood, 1979), 333.

95. Bennett H. Young, *A History of Jessamine County, Kentucky* (Louisville: Courier-Journal Job Printing, 1898), 198–99.

96. *Paris (Ky.) Western Citizen,* April 6, 1860.

97. Mechal Sobel, *Trabelin' On,* 335–36.

98. There is little quantitative data to back this claim up, but in one comprehensive study of runaways the preponderance of runaways to family members was overwhelming, even in the border states. See John Hope and Loren Schweniger Franklin, *Runaway Slaves: Rebels on the Plantation* (New York: Oxford University Press, 1999), 113.

99. Rawick, , interview with Aunt Harriet Mason, *American Slave,* 31.

100. *Lexington Observer and Reporter,* August 7, 1844, cited in Lucas, *History of Blacks in Kentucky,* 27.

101. For a typical annual hire agreement, see John Stout, January 1, 1849, Woodford County, Ky., David S. G. Silcock Collection, KHS.

102. Alexander Jeffrey, December 27, 1860, Promissory Notes, Microfilm Clift No. 481, KHS.

103. Broadside, December 26, 1861, Danville, Ky., Property of Calvin Fackler, 53M44, UKSC.

104. Broadside, July 12, 1859, Lexington, Ky., J. Winston Coleman Papers, UKSC.

105. Frazier, *Runaway and Freed Missouri Slaves,* 91. The Missouri law of 1845 offered a graduated pay scale akin to the Kentucky broadside notices. Slaves aged 20 years and older and captured outside the state garnered a greater award than those younger than 20 and caught inside Missouri.

106. Hahn, *Nation under Our Feet,* 1–10. This is one of the central themes of Hahn's book.

CHAPTER FOUR

1. *Paris (Ky.) Western Citizen,* June 28, 1861.

2. Parrish, *History of Missouri,* 3:22. According to historian Christopher Phillips, this infamous quote may in fact be apocryphal. Thus I add the qualifier *allegedly.*

3. *Paris (Ky.) Western Citizen,* November 1, 1861.

4. For a discussion of deliberations in the Kentucky legislature regarding neutrality, see Coulter, *Civil War and Readjustment in Kentucky,* 55.

5. *Brunswicker* (Brunswick, Mo.), May 17, 1861 (hereafter cited as *Brunswicker*).

6. The most extensive discussion of slave emancipation in the border states, Berlin et al.'s *Slaves No More,* argues that slavery did not really fall apart until black troop mobilization in 1864. But if the commentary of local whites and the completely collapsing price of slaves is any indication, slavery had effectively died well before large-scale black enlistment. As this, and the following chapter, makes clear, however, the imminent destruction of slavery by mid-1863 did not mean that white owners or white society willingly obliged. See Ira Berlin et al., *Slaves No More: Three Essays on Emancipation and the Civil War* (New York: Cambridge University Press, 1992), 63.

7. *Paris (Ky.) Western Citizen,* April 12, 1861.

8. Ibid.

9. *Louisville Journal,* April 15, 1861.

10. Napton, *Past and Present of Saline County, Missouri,* 146–47.

11. Coulter, *Civil War and Readjustment in Kentucky,* 35–56.

12. Throughout the spring of 1861 secessionists from Tidewater Virginia, eastern North Carolina, southwest Tennessee, and eastern Arkansas applied pressure on wavering conservative Unionists in Piedmont North Carolina and Virginia, middle Tennessee, and central Arkansas. Lincoln's troop decision tipped the balance in these already tense legislatures and conventions toward secession. Nowhere in Kentucky or Missouri did a prewar secession movement match that in the plantation belts of Arkansas, North Carolina, Tennessee, or Virginia. See Crofts, *Reluctant Confederates,* for a detailed account of the secession crisis in those states. For pressure within supposedly pro-Confederate Tennessee strongholds, see also Derek Frisby, "The Vortex of Secession: West Tennesseans and the Rush to War," in *Sister States, Enemy States: The Civil War in Kentucky and Tennessee,* ed. Kent T. Dollar, Larry H. Whiteaker, and W. Calvin Dickinson (Lexington: University Press of Kentucky, 2009).

13. Coulter, *Civil War and Readjustment in Kentucky,* 38.

14. Phillips, *Missouri's Confederate,* 245.

15. *Glasgow Times,* May 2, 1861.

16. Ibid., December 6, 1860.

17. Ibid.

18. William Parrish, *Turbulent Partnership: Missouri and the Union, 1861–1865* (Columbia: University of Missouri Press, 1963), 26. Parrish mistakenly cites Congressman John B. Clark of Howard County as having shifted his allegiance because of Camp Jackson. In fact, in a letter written to the *Central City and Brunswicker* on April 24, 1861, Clark denounced in vitriolic terms Lincoln's troop call-up; in the coming Civil War there was no question of loyalty for him: "Being of the South let us be with the South in such a conflict if come it must." Clark had been swayed by Lincoln's election to support the Confederacy long before Camp Jackson. See ibid., May 4, 1861.

19. A close reading of the *Louisville Daily Courier* between April 12 and April 30 reveals a paucity of secession meetings across Kentucky. The *Courier* was the most adamantly secessionist newspaper in Kentucky and paraded every instance of support for secession whenever possible. Many secession meetings did indeed occur throughout the state, including in Bluegrass counties such as Bourbon and Fayette. But the number of these meetings paled in comparison

to the number of Union or neutrality meetings over the same period, including in the Blue-grass. Not surprisingly, the *Courier* did not mention these events.

20. *Paris (Ky.) Western Citizen,* May 10, 1861.

21. *Glasgow Weekly Times,* June 14, 1861.

22. *Missouri Telegraph* (Fulton), April 19, 1861.

23. *Louisville Journal,* April 15, 1861.

24. *Missouri Telegraph* (Fulton), April 19, 1861.

25. *Brunswicker,* May 17, 1861.

26. *Paris (Ky.) Western Citizen,* April 19, 1861.

27. Switzler, *History of Boone County, Missouri,* 408.

28. *Brunswicker,* May 4, 1861.

29. Ibid.

30. *Paris (Ky.) Western Citizen,* May 10, 1861. This writer, pseudonymed "Kentuckian," wrote this letter to the *Cincinnati Enquirer,* and the *Paris (Ky.) Western Citizen* reprinted it. The same author penned the comments about preserving "peace, liberty and order."

31. *Lexington Observer and Reporter,* October 19, 1861.

32. Secessionists, for their part, cited numerous violations of neutrality by the Federal government, including the establishment of an enlistment center at Camp Dick Robinson in Garrard County and facilitation of the Union blockade of the Confederacy at Louisville. Yet none of these actions compared to open, armed invasion of the state as General Polk had launched in the far southwestern reaches of Kentucky. Polk's invasion was designed as a preemptive strike to secure the bluffs along the Mississippi River and the mouths of the Cumberland and Tennessee rivers and to protect the Tennessee capital at Nashville. For a discussion of violations of neutrality in the summer of 1861, see Coulter, *Civil War and Readjustment in Kentucky,* 88–107.

33. *Paris (Ky.) Western Citizen,* October 4, 1861.

34. Ibid.

35. In 1861 Confederate troops in Missouri were almost entirely Missourian, with the exception of Texan general Ben McCulloch. In 1864 Sterling Price's invasion of the state involved mostly Missourians. In Kentucky Polk's command included some Kentuckians, but this was primarily a central CSA offensive. Missourians could claim that their homes were threatened by pro-Confederate guerrillas and by Sterling Price's army, but the notion that a foreign, invading foe stood at the door of the state simply did not resonate with Unionist Missourians the way it did with Unionist Kentuckians.

36. James McPherson, *For Cause and Comrades* (New York: Oxford University Press, 1997), 95–97.

37. Ibid., 18.

38. *Paris (Ky.) Western Citizen,* May 10, 1861.

39. Ibid., June 7, 1861.

40. Ibid., July 12, 1861.

41. *Missouri Telegraph* (Fulton), September 6, 1861.

42. Mark K. Douglas, *Soldiers, Secesh and Civilians: Compiled Records of Callawegians in the War of the Rebellion* (Fulton, Mo.: Jones Republic Press, 2001), 175.

43. N. G. Markham to Eunice, October 25, 1862, Lexington, Ky., NG Markham Papers MSS 4, M345, FHS.

44. Ibid.

45. Historian E. Merton Coulter argues that the Bluegrass provided minimal support for the Union, with only 16 percent of eligible men joining the Union army. He does not provide data, however, on how many joined the Confederate army. Although more white men undoubtedly fought for the South than the Union in many Bluegrass counties, Coulter probably overstates Confederate strength because the vast majority of Bluegrass men fought for neither side. As William Freehling points out, Kentucky provided a stunningly low rate of military service to either side in the Civil War. Assuming Confederate domination based on low Union military numbers belies the more common practice of staying home and fending off attacks from whichever direction they came. See Coulter, *Civil War and Readjustment in Kentucky,* 124; on Kentucky's low rate of participation, see William Freehling, *The South versus the South: How Anti-Confederate Southerners Shaped the Course of the Civil War* (Oxford: Oxford University Press, 2001), 72–73.

46. Coulter, *Civil War and Readjustment in Kentucky,* 114.

47. The remaining newspapers tread carefully in their criticism of the Lincoln administration, which most of the Unionist papers found far too radical for border state consumption.

48. Parrish, *Turbulent Partnership,* 86. The provisional government ruled Missouri until January 1865, when a new government was elected. The provisional government under Hamilton Gamble, and later Willard Hall, was the only state government in United States history to be established by a body not designed for that purpose. The convention that created the provisional government was the same one that insisted upon Missouri's loyalty to the Union in February 1861. Immediately, President Lincoln recognized the provisional government as official, even though many within Missouri would question its legitimacy throughout the war. The test oath was a critical component for the new government as it helped rid all loyalists to the old Jackson regime. For the entire process of establishing the provisional government, see ibid., 33–47.

49. Ibid., 78.

50. Phillips and Pendleton, *Union on Trial,* 185. Unfortunately, the collected journals of Napton do not include the period during which Napton decided to refuse the oath.

51. On loyalty oaths in Kentucky, see Harrison and Klotter, *New History of Kentucky,* 205–6.

52. Following Price's retreat from Jefferson City and Boonville in June 1861, he retreated to the southwestern corner of the state. At Wilson's Creek near Springfield, Price's forces defeated the Federals and killed General Lyon on August 10. The MSG, with support from Arkansas Confederates, then headed north to the Missouri River to recruit new members for the Confederate cause. This campaign culminated in the successful siege of Lexington, Mo., in September 1861. But following Price's capture of that important river town, Federal forces drove Price back to the South, leaving thousands of potential Confederate recruits behind Union lines again. Union forces eventually drove Price's army into Arkansas, defeating it decisively at Pea Ridge in early March 1862. Price never seriously threatened Missouri again until a desperate last-ditch invasion in the summer of 1864.

53. There were actually seven total Union militia organizations raised in Missouri during and after the Civil War. Predominantly German Home Guards in St. Louis chased the Jackson administration out of Jefferson City in June 1861. In August Provisional Governor Gamble attempted to convert the Home Guards into permanent organizations called the "Six-Month Militia." In February 1862 Gamble sought a new financing mechanism for the militia and so created the Missouri State Militia (MSM), funded by the Federal government and staffed with

ten thousand men across the state. Gamble maintained authority over the MSM, which served as the most potent Union fighting force in the state against large-scale invasion and guerrilla attacks. But ten thousand men were not enough to keep the peace, so in July 1862 Gamble authorized the creation of the part-time Enrolled Missouri Militia (EMM), which would only be called up in emergencies. Later in the war Missouri governors created a Provisional Enrolled Missouri Militia (an offshoot of the EMM, composed of full-time soldiers), a Provisional Enrolled Militia to stave off Price's invasion in 1864, and finally a Missouri Militia that served the new Radical administration of Governor Thomas Fletcher after March 1865. For more on Missouri militias, see Parrish, *Turbulent Partnership*, 79-81, 92-95. A good summary of Missouri militia activity by Kirby Ross, "Federal Militia in Missouri," can be found online at *Civil War St. Louis*, www.civilwarstlouis.com/militia/federalmilitia.htm#3.%20Missouri%20State%20Militia, posted January 16, 2004.

54. *History of Howard and Cooper Counties, Missouri* (St. Louis: National Historical Co., 1883), 272-73.

55. Frances Peter, a Unionist from Lexington, Ky., remarked on numerous instances in her diary of the "secesh ladies" sowing uniforms for the rebels. Many of the secessionist women congregated at the home of John Hunt Morgan's wife. See John David Smith and William J. Cooper, eds., *A Union Woman in Civil War Kentucky: The Diary of Frances Peter* (Lexington: University Press of Kentucky, 2000), 11.

56. *Paris (Ky.) Western Citizen*, October 25, 1861.

57. For examples of women's volunteer activity in Bourbon County, see *Paris (Ky.) Western Citizen*, November 1, 8, 15, 22, and throughout 1862. Nearly every issue of the *Western Citizen* described in detail the activities of women's Union organizations.

58. Ibid., November 1, 1861.

59. Smith and Cooper, *Union Woman in Civil War Kentucky*, 56-88.

60. Ibid., 37.

61. October 28, 1862, Lexington, Ky., Miscellaneous Documents, FHS.

CHAPTER FIVE

1. *Paris (Ky.) Western Citizen*, January 18, 1861.

.2. Many conservatives pointed to Lincoln's First Inaugural Address as evidence that he would not use force against the South. His commitment to protect Federal property remained worrisome to conservatives and proved decisive after April 12.

3. Crofts, *Reluctant Confederates*, 104-6. Crofts refers to most Unionists in these states as "ultimatumists" or "anticoercionists."

4. *History of Saline County, Missouri* (St. Louis: Missouri Historical Co., 1881), 276-77.

5. Stephanie McCurry highlights the gendered terms of protection that Confederates across the South used during the secession crisis and the war. See Stephanie McCurry, *Confederate Reckoning* (Cambridge: Harvard University Press, 2010).

6. Mary E. Wharton and Ellen F. Williams, eds., *Peach Leather and Rebel Gray: Bluegrass Life and the War, 1860-1865* (Lexington: Helicon Co., 1986), 87.

7. Bragg's failure to raise substantial troop numbers in his 1862 invasion of Kentucky marked one of the Confederacy's greatest disappointments. Hoping to raise as many as fifty thousand troops, Bragg yielded only about three thousand. He cited lukewarm support for the

Confederacy (and an alarming loss of men who were not to be replaced by hoped-for Kentucky replacements) as a reason to abandon the state after the Battle of Perryville on October 8, 1862. The political timing for Bragg's invasion proved disastrous too. In the summer of 1862 Unionism had established itself across Kentucky as the dominant force, and the Federal government's slave policy still held the rights of loyal slaveholders inviolable. Had Bragg's invasion occurred in 1863, after emancipation had become a stated war aim, the outcome might have been different. After the Battle of Perryville, however, the Confederacy never seriously threatened Kentucky again. On Perryville and Bragg's decision to leave for Tennessee, see Kenneth Noe, *Perryville: This Grand Havoc of Battle* (Lexington: University Press of Kentucky, 2001), 313–15.

8. See discussion in chap. 1.

9. It is notoriously difficult to estimate the overall loyalties of a particular region because enlistment records did not list the hometown or county of the enlistee. Also, many pro-Confederates enlisted outside Kentucky and in the far reaches of southwestern Missouri, making it especially difficult to identify Confederate soldiers with their place of origin. Contemporary observers concluded that much of the Bluegrass countryside supported the Confederacy, often at a rate of two to one or higher. The same rate applied in Little Dixie. Some of these observations are colored by the biases of those who recount them; not surprisingly, many former Unionists made the exact opposite estimation, granting wartime Unionism a much larger place than actually existed. Another complication is the presence of the draft after 1863, which forced thousands of formerly neutral—or even passively pro-Confederate men—from central Missouri and Kentucky into the Union army. Also, loyalty oaths required for any public service in the latter phase of the war encouraged many people to lie about their earlier sympathies. In Wharton and Williams, *Peach Leather and Rebel Gray,* 94, the editors cite an adjutant general's report listing twice as many Confederate enlistees as Unionists in the inner Bluegrass. There are numerous problems with these reports, however, as many Kentuckians left the state to join both armies before the report's beginning date. Nevertheless, it is reasonable to conclude that the voluntary affiliations of a majority of rural white people in central Missouri and Kentucky tended toward the South after the war began. But Unionists did not form an insignificant portion of the population in any county.

10. Perrin, *History of Fayette County, Kentucky,* 449–50.

11. Eighth Census, Population MS, 1860. Income for soldiers or their parents whenever available; roster appears in Perrin, *History of Fayette County, Kentucky,* 449–50.

12. There were seventy-four members of the Chasseurs in 1860. See ibid., 449–50.

13. Eighth Census, Slave MS, 1860; Eighth Census, Population MS, 1860. I use median slave ownership to eliminate the small number of very large slaveholdings. As expected, the average slaveholding was also much higher for Confederates than it was for Unionists by a margin of 12.75 to 3.2.

14. By *owned* I mean a member of a family whose household head owned slaves. In many cases Chasseurs were 18 years old and possessed no property or slaves of their own. But their fathers were substantial property and slaveholders. Because these young men grew up in households with slaves, I count them along with those listed in the census as slaveholders. Neal McCann, e.g., owned forty-four slaves. His three sons listed in the McCann household in the 1860 census—Thomas, Howard, and Rube—are considered owners of forty-four slaves as well. After all, each son experienced alike the ownership of forty-four slaves.

15. The one non-slaveholding Confederate Chasseur, J. B. Steves, was born in Pennsylvania. His participation in the Confederate cause was unusual, but not unheard of, for a northern native.

16. To compile the data for this sample, I used the comprehensive "Soldiers, Secesh and Civilians: Compiled Records of Callawegians in the War of the Rebellion," by Mark K. Douglas. I sampled every twentieth name for Confederates and Unionists and matched them against the 1860 Federal Population and Slave Census. See Mark K. Douglas, *Soldiers, Secesh and Civilians: Compiled Records of Callawegians in the War of the Rebellion* (Fulton, Mo.: Jones Republic Press, 2001); Eighth Census, Population MS, 1860; Eighth Census, Slave MS, 1860.

17. In many ways this conclusion seems obvious. But it is very difficult to quantify the social basis of Civil War loyalty in most locales because most comprehensive Civil War military records do not list the home county, township, or town of the individual soldier. Moreover, differing rates of loyalty over larger rural districts may obscure many local considerations, including the decisions of kin and neighbors. The Lexington Chasseurs provide stronger evidence for the social basis of loyalty because they drew their membership from the same geographic region and had once maintained strong social relations across the eventual loyalty divide.

18. Unionists within the Confederacy faced a similar challenge as they rejected their states' course as well as the new nation to which their state had attached.

19. Martha Jones to "My Father," December 21, 1862, Edgewood, Ky., folder 1, Jones Family Papers, MS A J78, FHS.

20. *Missouri Telegraph* (Fulton), December 6, 1861.

21. Price's reference to "Hessians" undoubtedly served a double meaning. First, the strongest Unionists in Missouri were German immigrants. Second, Price felt that these Germans were mere "mercenaries" of Radical congressman Frank Blair and the Lincoln government. The term *Hessian* delegitimized the Union cause by associating it with treachery. The usage of *Jay-Hawker,* in reference to Kansas Free-Soilers and abolitionists under Charles Jennison's command, likewise served to delegitimize the Union cause by associating it with "foreign" (non-Missouri) abolitionism. Indeed, "jayhawking" regiments and German-run militia and Union military companies caused considerable damage to pro-Confederate property throughout the war. But many conservative Unionists also figured in the mix. Prominent Little Dixie Unionists such as Odon Guitar, James Rollins, and William Switzler could never be tainted with the "Hessian" or "Jay-Hawker" charge, even though soldiers under their command and influence also cracked down on pro-Confederates across Missouri.

22. Richard Franklin Bensel, *The American Ballot Box in the Mid-Nineteenth Century* (Cambridge: Cambridge University Press, 2004), 282–85. Similarly, Union supporters were always "loyal" or "for the Union" and never "for the North."

23. Martha Jones to "My Father," December 21, 1862, Edgewood, Ky., folder 1, Jones Family Papers, MSS A J78, FHS.

24. *Glasgow Times*, January 10, 1861.

25. Switzler, *History of Boone County, Missouri,* 435. In other examples of plummeting slave prices in central Missouri, slaves at the Philip Robertson estate were sold for prices between $48.50 and $211 in January 1864. See Smith and Gehrig, *History of Chariton and Howard Counties, Missouri,* 189. In a slave deed dated September 1863, prime-age male slaves sold for an average of $211. See *Howard County Advertiser,* September 3, 1863.

26. The *Paris (Ky.) Western Citizen* noted that the average price for slaves in a recent central Kentucky auction in 1860 was $1,200. That average includes elderly and very young slaves,

who sold for much less. See ibid., January 20, 1860. One Kentucky slave trader advertiser claimed that he would pay between $1,200 and $1,250 for "No. 1 young men" and $850 to $1,000 for "No. 1 young women" in 1853. See Broadsides, July 2, 1853, Lexington, Ky., J. Winston Coleman Papers, UKSC. It is very likely that slave prices in 1860 had risen even higher than in 1853, especially with the high demand for slaves in the burgeoning cotton market in the Deep South.

27. The Emancipation Proclamation of January 1, 1863, did not apply in Kentucky and Missouri, and slavery legally survived in both states until 1865. Thus, the veritable death of slavery before that time requires explanation beyond Federal slave policy and the movement of Union troops into heavy slave areas.

28. Berlin et al., *Slaves No More*, 63.

29. Bruce, *New Man*, 99–100.

30. Ibid., 100.

31. Affective relationships, or relationships through marriage, linked black people every bit as strongly as blood ties. See Herbert Gutman, *The Black Family in Slavery and Freedom, 1750–1925* (New York: Vintage Books, 1976), 201–2, for a discussion of affective kinship networks.

32. Bruce, *New Man*, 100.

33. Ibid.

34. For a good overall discussion of Federal slave policy in Missouri during the Civil War, see Parrish, *Turbulent Partnership*. Also see Ira Berlin et al., *The Destruction of Slavery, Freedom:* A Documentary History of Emancipation (Cambridge: Cambridge University Press, 1985), 395–412. For a general account of emancipation in Kentucky and relationships between the Federal and state governments, see Victor B. Howard, *Black Liberation in Kentucky: Emancipation and Freedom, 1862–1884* (Lexington: University Press of Kentucky, 1983); Coulter, *Civil War and Readjustment in Kentucky*; and Berlin et al., *Destruction of Slavery*, 493–518.

35. Beriah Magoffin resigned as Kentucky governor in August 1862 and was replaced by James F. Robinson.

36. *Missouri Telegraph* (Fulton), March 7, 1862.

37. April 15, 1862, box 4 W-197, Letters Received, ser. 2786, Department of the Missouri Office of PMG, NA [C-199]. Bracketed items indicate source also found at the Freedmen and Southern Society Project, College Park, Md.

38. Ibid.

39. L. Irvine to Susan Grigsby, December 17, 1862, Traveller's Rest, Ky., folder 175, Grigsby Family Papers, MSS A/G 857, FHS.

40. Bruce, *New Man*, 103.

41. Ibid.

42. Ibid., 99.

43. For a good discussion of changes in army-slave relations during the 1862 invasion, see Howard, *Black Liberation in Kentucky*, 12–28.

44. Markham to "Dear Wife and Boy," April 13, 1863, Lebanon, Ky., FL2, NG Markham Papers, MSS A M345, FHS.

45. Wharton and Williams, *Peach Leather and Rebel Gray*, 94.

46. Ibid., 117.

47. It is possible that slaves in eastern Texas or the interior of Alabama could have yielded that much money in the summer of 1863.

48. Benjamin Jones to "Brother," January 12, 1864, Camp near Chattanooga, Tenn., Miscellaneous Documents, FHS.

49. *Howard County Advertiser*, September 3, 1863.

50. *History of Howard and Cooper County, Missouri* (St. Louis: Missouri Historical Co., 1883), 285.

51. Francis Lieber, a German legal theorist and professor at Columbia College in New York, helped General Henry Halleck codify the laws of war in Missouri and in the United States generally. His code dealt specifically with guerrilla warfare, the proper limits of counterinsurgency, and the rights of property, civilians, and prisoners. The "Lieber Instructions" later influenced the Hague and Geneva conventions on warfare. For Lieber's 1863 code, see D. Schindler and J. Toman, *The Laws of Armed Conflicts* (Martinus Nihjoff, 1998), 3–23. Lieber's original code is titled "Instructions for the Government of Armies of the United States in the Field (Lieber Code)," issued April 24, 1863.

52. *Paris (Ky.) Western Citizen*, July 29, 1861.

53. Ibid.

54. Bodley to "Brother," October 27, 1862, Lexington, Ky., FL 69, Bodley Family Papers, C, FHS. Confederate troops occupied Lexington from September 1 until the beginning of October, during which time they required citizens to trade in Confederate currency. Confederates were forced to leave the state after the Battle of Perryville on October 8. By late October, the time of Bodley's letter, Lexington was safely in Union hands, and Confederate currency had been outlawed. There is no telling when the incident in question occurred, though Bodley clearly viewed the payment of merchandise and horses with Confederate currency as akin to theft.

55. Broadsides, October 2, 1862, Lexington, Ky., J. Winston Coleman Papers, UKSC.

56. Union provost marshals had the responsibility to enforce this assessment. The plan proved to be deeply unpopular and ineffective because it alienated many neutral civilians, and Union commander Henry Halleck eventually dropped it. See Fellman, *Inside War*, 94–95.

57. *History of Lafayette County, Missouri* (St. Louis: Missouri Historical Co., 1881), 286–87.

58. Fellman, *Inside War*, 159.

59. Both Unionist and Confederate Missourians regularly referred to pro-Confederate guerrillas as "bushwhackers."

60. Sanford Bullock to General Guitar, September 9, 1863, Fayette, Mo., folder 8, Odon Guitar Collection, C1007, WHMC. Historian Michael Fellman interprets this intriguing letter differently. For him "here is the agony of a young man caught between his desire for vengeance growing from personal rage and his desire to live in a lawful 'civilization.'" Fellman is correct in identifying the dual pressures of guerrilla war on civilians: toward personal revenge on one hand and appeal to the dictates of a "modern army" and legal procedure on the other. More interesting for purposes of understanding the breakdown of conservative Unionism in the countryside was Bullock's reference to "extermination" and the desire to see one hundred rebels killed for every Union man's death. For Bullock the entire rebel community had to pay the ultimate price, and there is little reason to believe Bullock was not speaking in earnest. Indeed, legalized mass reprisals became more and more commonplace in modern warfare than in previous conflicts. See Fellman, *Inside War*, 63–65.

61. The 1860 census lists Sanford Bullock in Chariton County as a day laborer, born in Ohio. His brother Isaac Bullock, born in New York, was probably the one killed by guerrillas. Isaac's wife, Elizabeth, made destitute by the guerrilla murder of Isaac, was born in Kentucky. It is not surprising that Isaac and Sanford would support the Union, given their northern births.

Isaac's marriage to a Kentucky woman suggests the mixed regional heritage of many Missouri families in the Civil War. None of the Bullocks owned slaves, according to the slave census. See Eighth Census, Population MS, 1860.

62. Letters Sent, 1862, vol. 225, ser. 3372, District of Central Missouri, 393/2, NA.

63. Unionists jailed many wives and sisters of guerrillas in an effort to coax them to turn in their husbands and brothers. These actions against pro-Confederate women only hardened the Confederate perception that Unionists had no respect for white womanhood.

64. R. Leonard to "Lieutant.," July 8, 1863, Hd Quarters Detachment 9th Cav, Fayette, Mo., folder 464, Abiel Leonard Papers, C1013, WHMC.

65. Poindexter's raid involved Missouri State Guard captain John Poindexter, who, with fifteen hundred men, raided north central Missouri, looking for Confederate recruits. Poindexter's men opened jails in Columbia and released Confederates. They tried to burn the offices of the *Statesman*, a Unionist newspaper, and they dragged a U.S. flag through the streets of Columbia. See Switzler, *History of Boone County, Missouri*, 421–22.

66. Reprinted in *Central City and Brunswicker*, October 2, 1862.

67. William S. Bryan and Robert Rose, *History of the Pioneer Families of Missouri, with Numerous Sketches, Anecdotes, Adventures, Etc., Relating to Early Days in Missouri* (St. Louis: Bryan, Brand and Co., 1876).

68. Dibble Memo to Gamble, n.d., box 1, folder 2, RG 3, Governor Gamble Papers, Missouri State Archives.

69. According to historian Mark K. Douglas's extensive analysis of Callaway County loyalties, at least 470 white men in the county served the Union cause. See Douglas, *Soldiers, Secesh, Civilians.*

70. Smith, *Union Woman in Civil War Kentucky.*

71. Letters Sent, 1862, vol. 225, ser. 3372, District of Central Missouri, RG 393/2, NA.

72. Bruce, *New Man,* 103.

73. *Central City and Brunswicker,* February 12, 1863.

74. For a general discussion of Missouri's emancipation debate, see Parrish, *Missouri under Radical Rule,* 123–48.

75. "General Orders No. 35," December 24, 1862, Orders and Circulars, ser. 44, Headquarters, Department of the Missouri, RG 94, NA.

76. Berlin et al., *Destruction of Slavery,* 409.

77. *Lexington Observer and Reporter,* November 26, 1862.

78. Robert L. Stanton, *The Church and the Rebellion* (1864; rpt., Freeport, N.Y.: Books for Libraries Press, 1971), 358.

CHAPTER SIX

1. Linda Kerber, *No Constitutional Right to Be Ladies* (New York: Hill and Wang, 1998), 241.

2. On postwar racial violence, see esp. George C. Rable, *But There Was No Peace: The Role of Violence in the Politics of Reconstruction* (Athens: University of Georgia Press, 1984). He discusses the Memphis and New Orleans riots of 1866 among other acts of violence, both of which involved partisan politics and working-class tensions between blacks and Irish. Leon Litwack, *Been in the Storm So Long* (New York: Vintage Books, 1979); Allen W. Trelease, *White Terror: The Ku Klux Klan Conspiracy and Southern Reconstruction* (Baton Rouge: Louisiana State University

Press, 1971); Hannah Rosen, *Terror in the Heart of Freedom: Citizenship, Sexual Violence, and the Meaning of Race in the Postemancipation South* (Chapel Hill: University of North Carolina Press, 2008); and Scott Reynolds Nelson, *Iron Confederacies: Southern Railways, Klan Violence, and Reconstruction* (Chapel Hill: University of North Carolina Press, 1999). On racial violence in postwar Kentucky, see George C. Wright, *Racial Violence in Kentucky: Lynchings, Mob Rule, and "Legal Lynchings," 1865–1940* (Baton Rouge: Louisiana State University Press, 1990) 19–60; and J. Michael Rhyne, "'The Whole Family Driven Away': Regulators, Politics, and the Assault on Black Households in Post-Emancipation Kentucky," paper presented at Southern Historical Association Annual Conference, Baltimore, 2002.

3. The best general discussion of Missouri's Radical regime between the Drake constitution of 1865 and the election of the Democratic Woodson administration in 1872 is Parrish, *Missouri under Radical Rule.* Charles Drake chaired the constitutional committee that drafted the strict 1865 constitution barring all rebels and rebel sympathizers from voting, holding office, or even performing significant civilian services such as teaching, preaching the Gospel, or practicing law. In 1870, with the anger of guerrilla war fading into distant memory and the state entering a more vigorous period of capitalist expansion, Liberal Republican dissidents under B. Gratz Brown and Carl Schurz successfully pushed for a general enfranchisement amendment to the constitution. With Brown elected governor in 1870, the Radical period effectively came to an end, though many Liberals hoped that newly enfranchised former rebels would reward their new benefactors in their more conservative wing of the Republican Party. Sadly for the Liberals, rebels turned immediately to the old Democratic Party, electing Silas Woodson to the governor's mansion in 1872. Democrats proceeded to dominate the state's political scene for the next hundred years, placing Missouri squarely in the solid South.

4. Ironically, a state constitutional amendment in 1870 pushed by dissident Liberal Republicans was passed that enfranchised both African Americans and former rebels, thus equating both as similarly anathema elements in the postwar political order. As a result, the number of re-enfranchised whites vastly outnumbered the new black voters, thus establishing Democratic Party hegemony in Missouri for a century. On black political campaigns for enfranchisement, see Gary Kremer, *James Milton Turner and the Promise of America: The Public Life of a Post–Civil War Black Leader* (Columbia: University of Missouri Press, 1991).

5. On civil and legal rights for blacks in Kentucky, see Howard, *Black Liberation in Kentucky,* 130–76. Howard notes that African Americans agitated for civil and legal rights immediately after emancipation. But the conservative Kentucky government utterly ignored their demands.

6. Eighth Census, Population and Slave MSS, 1860. In the Deep South slaveholdings averaged 12.7 slaves per holding.

7. On the declining hemp industry after the Civil War, see Hopkins, *History of the Hemp Industry in Kentucky,* 193–219.

8. Where white landowners still required farm help, they turned to white immigrants. Especially in central Missouri, where a larger German and Irish population already lived, wage-earning immigrants easily replaced the labor once performed by slaves. Kentucky landowners had less luck in attracting immigrants, largely because the antebellum immigrant population was concentrated in Louisville and not the Bluegrass. Nevertheless, the collapse of the hemp industry rendered the more arduous tasks once performed by slaves obsolete. In both Little Dixie and the Bluegrass the loss of black farm labor caused minimal distress for landowners, especially when compared to the crisis facing former planters in the lower South.

9. By contrast, slavery in the eastern border states of Maryland and Delaware was in decline, as half the black population of Maryland was free in 1860, as was 90 percent of Delaware's black population. Surplus slaves in Kentucky and Missouri were sent en masse to the lower South in the lucrative Mississippi River slave trade.

10. Peter Bruner, *A Slave's Adventures toward Freedom. Not Fiction, but the True Story of a Struggle* (1918; rpt., Chapel Hill: University of North Carolina Press, 2000), 43. Camp Nelson was situated along the Kentucky River in southern Jessamine County, about twenty miles south of Lexington.

11. Ibid., 33.

12. Ibid., 43.

13. For an excellent documentary history of Camp Nelson, see Richard D. Sears, *Camp Nelson, Kentucky: A Civil War History* (Lexington: University Press of Kentucky, 2002).

14. Elijah P. Marrs, *Life and History of the Rev. Elijah P. Marrs, First Pastor of Beargrass Baptist Church* (Louisville: Bradley and Gilbert Co., 1885), 22.

15. The Militia Act, passed on July 17, 1862, "authorized to receive into the service of the United States, for the purpose of constructing intrenchments, or performing camp service or any other labor, or any military or naval service for which they may be found competent, persons of African descent." See *United States, Statutes at Large* (Washington, D.C.: Government Printing Office, 1937). "Treaties, and Proclamations of the United States of America, vol. 12" (Boston, 1863), 597–600. While free blacks joined the U.S. military in the latter part of 1862, slaves did not really join the military en masse until after the Emancipation Proclamation. Nevertheless, some slaves did enter military service before that time, even if they were mostly used for labor and construction purposes. See Berlin et al., *Slaves No More,* 189–233.

16. See *Official Records of the War of the Rebellion* (hereafter cited as *Official Records*), ser., 3, vol. 5, 138. For a full tabulation of enlistment rates, see Berlin et al., *Slaves No More,* 203. In Tennessee 39 percent of the state's eligible slave population also joined the military, though at a rate a few tenths of a percent less than Missouri. The state with the highest raw total of black recruits was Louisiana, with 24,052, which constituted 31 percent of the state's eligible black male population.

17. The recruitment totals listed in the Bureau of Colored Troops only reflect those "credited" to each state, not necessarily the number actually emerging from those states.

18. Berlin et al., *Slaves No More,* 203. This is especially true because only 126 black people lived in Kansas in 1860.

19. Out of 930 eligible recruits, 600 joined the Union army. *History of Howard and Cooper County, Missouri* (St. Louis: Missouri Historical Co., 1883), 278–82. Howard County's 37 percent slave percentage was highest in the state; in total numbers Lafayette County to the west of Howard had a higher number.

20. Only 4.5 percent of all black Kentuckians were free in 1860. In Missouri only 3 percent of the black population was free. See Joseph C. G. Kennedy, *Eighth Census* (Washington, D.C.: Government Printing Office, 1864), 181 and 285.

21. O'Connor to Schofield, December 7, 1863, Letters Received, box 10, O-111, ser. 2593, Department of the Missouri, RG 393, NA.

22. *Howard County Advertiser,* January 15, 1864.

23. According to the slave census, John R. White owned seventy-six slaves in 1860. See *Eighth Census, Slave MS, 1860.*

24. *Missouri Telegraph* (Fulton), February 26, 1864.

25. *Paris (Ky.) Western Citizen,* March 11, 1864.

26. *Official Records,* ser. 3, 4:233–34, issued by Thomas Fairleigh, acting assistant adjutant-general on behalf of General Burbridge.

27. Dickson to Sidell, May 26, 1864, Letters Received, box 2, ser. 3967, Assistant Adjutant Provost Marshal General for Kentucky (hereafter cited as KY AAPMG), RG 110, NA.

28. It is possible that a local official in Boyle County notified slaves that all could enlist, even though official restrictions were not removed until early June 1864. In this case the rumor of unrestricted slave enlistment mattered more than the actual change in policy.

29. *Official Records,* ser. 3, 4:429–30.

30. Sears, *Camp Nelson, Kentucky,* xxxviii–xxxix.

31. *Danville Tribune,* August 4, 1864, reprinted in *Lexington National Unionist,* August 9, 1864.

32. Boyle County had 3,714 total black inhabitants in 1860. Using the same ratio of male, military-age to total population (17.7 percent) as in Berlin et al., *Slaves No More,* the number of militarily eligible African Americans in Boyle County was 659. Of these 275 constitute 42 percent.

33. In Kentucky 95.5 percent of all African Americans were enslaved in 1860. In Missouri 97 percent of all African Americans were enslaved. See Eighth Census, Population and Slave MSS, 1860.

34. Mass slave escapes were not unknown in antebellum Kentucky. See chap. 3 for an example of mass runaway plots in the antebellum Bluegrass.

35. Bruce, *New Man,* 99–100.

36. *Paris (Ky.) Western Citizen,* June 16, 1865.

37. Ibid., October 27, 1865. Many black soldiers were removed to Texas, however, as a way to placate white conservatives.

38. *History of Lafayette County, Missouri* (St. Louis: Missouri Historical Co., 1881), 294.

39. For a general discussion of Missouri provisional governor Hamilton Gamble's view of the war and the Union cause, see William Parrish, *Turbulent Partnership: Missouri and the Union, 1861–1865* (Columbia: University of Missouri Press, 1963); and Dennis K. Boman, *Lincoln's Resolute Unionist: Hamilton Gamble, Dred Scott Dissenter and Missouri's Civil War Governor* (Baton Rouge: Louisiana State University Press, 2006). Gamble was never actually elected governor but was assigned to the position by a state convention after the elected governor, Claiborne Fox Jackson, attempted to take the state out of the Union in 1861. Gamble was succeeded by another conservative, Willard P. Hall, in 1864, upon Gamble's death. Following passage of the new radical constitution, Thomas Fletcher was elected in 1865. For Kentucky the best account of Governor Thomas Bramlette's views of the war remains E. Merton Coulter, *Civil War and Readjustment in Kentucky* (Chapel Hill: University of North Carolina Press, 1926), 189–214. Bramlette was elected governor in 1863 and served until 1867. Prior to Bramlette's administration, a secessionist, Beriah Magoffin, governed the state from 1859 to 1862, and following his resignation James F. Robinson served until 1863.

40. Missouri and Kentucky are far from the only historical examples of slaves and masters fighting in a war on the same side. In the Cuban wars of independence, particularly the Ten Years' War between 1868 and 1878, slaves in the eastern Oriente Province regularly fought alongside slaveholders for Cuban independence. In the Cuban case, however, the white insurgent leaders differed over the propriety of emancipation. Early insurgents supported emanci-

pation as the best tool to gain soldiers for the cause. But as the Spanish colonial administration successfully deployed the discourse of race war and the specter of Saint-Domingue, later insurgents distanced themselves from both general emancipation and the use of Afro-Cubans as soldiers. For an excellent discussion of this case, see Ada Ferrer, *Insurgent Cuba: Race, Nation, and Revolution, 1868–1898* (Chapel Hill: University of North Carolina Press, 1999). In central Missouri and Kentucky virtually no white Unionists embraced general emancipation or slave-soldiers as a means to put down the rebellion until several years into the Civil War. And even then, support for such revolutionary measures remained tepid at best.

41. Ada Ferrer, *Insurgent Cuba: Race, Nation, and Revolution, 1868–1898* (Chapel Hill: University of North Carolina Press, 1999). But in the case of Cuba slaveholders promised freedom in return for military service and ultimately viewed the insurrection as a testing ground for general emancipation.

42. After publication of Du Bois's *Black Reconstruction in America* in 1935, the current narrative painting black soldiery as a fight against the master class begins with Dudley Cornish, *The Sable Arm: Negro Troops in the Union Army, 1861–1865* (New York: Longmans, Green and Co., 1956); and continues with Ira Berlin et al., *Slaves No More;* and John David Smith, ed., *Black Soldiers in Blue: African American Soldiers in the Civil War Era* (Chapel Hill: University of North Carolina Press, 2002). On black soldier recruitment in Kentucky, see John David Smith, "The Recruitment of Negro Soldiers in Kentucky, 1863–1865," *Register of the Kentucky Historical Society* 72 (October 1974): 364–90. Black soldiers' accounts portray black enlistment in a similar light.

43. *Howard County Advertiser,* January 29, 1864.

44. Bruce, *New Man,* 103.

45. See Robert Durden, *The Gray and the Black: The Confederate Debate on Emancipation* (Baton Rouge: Louisiana State University Press, 1972); Bruce Levine, *Confederate Emancipation: Southern Plans to Free and Arm Slaves during the Civil War* (Oxford: Oxford University Press, 2005); and also James McPherson, *Battle Cry of Freedom* (New York: Ballantine Books, 1988), 831–38. While some Confederate commanders such as General Patrick Cleburne openly floated the possibility of arming slaves for the Confederacy, Confederate civilian leaders were aghast at the prospect. Most famously, Georgian Howell Cobb remarked that slaves could not become good soldiers because if they did, "our whole theory of slavery is wrong." For Cobb's quote, see *Official Records,* ser. 4, 3:1009–10. The Confederate Congress ultimately authorized the employment, though not emancipation, of black soldiers, but by that point the war was in its closing hour.

46. On midwestern acquiescence to black enlistment, see V. Jacque Voegeli, *Free but Not Equal: The Midwest and the Negro during the Civil War* (Chicago: University of Chicago Press, 1967). On postwar assessment of black troop performance and support for Radical Republicanism in one state, see Robert Dykstra, *Bright Radical Star: Black Freedom and White Supremacy on the Hawkeye Frontier* (Cambridge: Harvard University Press, 1993).

47. W. S. King, Lt. Col. 35th MA Infantry, to Wm. Whiting, Solicitor War Department, March 12, 1864, Lexington, Ky., Letters Received, K-66, Provost Marshal General Office, RG 110, NA.

48. *Paris (Ky.) Western Citizen,* March 18, 1864.

49. *Lexington Observer and Reporter,* March 11, 1864, reprinted in *Paris Western Citizen,* March 18, 1864. There is no extant copy of Wolford's speech, only the *Observer and Reporter's* paraphrase of it.

50. *Paris (Ky.) Western Citizen,* March 18, 1864.

51. Bramlette himself had been one of the most outspoken critics of black enlistments and had even fanned the flames of violent resistance to it. In January 1864 he wrote to General Boyle regarding black recruiting: "No such recruiting will be tolerated here. Summary justice will be inflicted upon any who attempt such unlawful purpose." See *ibid.,* January 29, 1864.

52. W. S. King, Lt. Col. 35th MA Infantry, to Wm. Whiting, Solicitor War Department, March 12, 1864, Lexington, Ky., Letters Received, K-66, Provost Marshal General Office, RG 110, NA.

53. Ibid.

54. Fidler to Sidell, June 9, 1864, Letters Received, box 2 F-178, ser. 3967, KY AAPMG, RG 110, NA.

55. Ibid. The letter describes James and Jasper Edwards as "boys," though it is unclear if the term refers to actual children or was the standard, diminutive term used by white Kentuckians to refer to all black men.

56. J. Winston Coleman, *Slavery Times in Kentucky* (Chapel Hill: University of North Carolina Press, 1940), 247. Coleman cites a Boyle County, Ky., slave with "both ears slightly cropped." The citation comes from a runaway advertisement and suggests that the ear cropping was a result of an earlier runaway attempt. For commentary on Coleman's useful but outdated study of slavery in Kentucky, see John David Smith, "'To Hue the Line and Let the Chips Fall Where They May': J. Winston Coleman's Slavery Times in Kentucky Reconsidered," *Register of the Kentucky Historical Society* 103 (Fall 2005): 691–726.

57. Neither McMann nor Burns appear in the 1860 census. If they had lived in the area for any considerable time, they would have been required to serve as patrollers. James Fidler, Union army official at Lebanon, believed that McMann was the only assailant, even though Burns was arrested too. Regarding Kentucky slave patrol law, custom, and social makeup, see Coleman, *Slavery Times in Kentucky,* 96–97. The slave code neither demanded nor prohibited bodily mutilation in the enforcement of runaway laws. Patrollers maintained full authority to exact whatever punishment they deemed necessary, as long as they did not materially diminish the value of the slave.

58. Cornell to Sanderson, March 28, 1864, Letters Received, box 1, C-258, ser. 2786, Office of Provost Marshal General, Department of the Missouri, RG 393/2, NA.

59. *Lexington National Unionist,* October 4, 1864.

60. The 1860 census lists a man from Midway, Woodford County, named Joseph Maddox. He was a wagon maker and a relatively small property holder. He did not own any slaves, according to the slave schedules. There are no other entries for the name "Maddox" in Woodford County. See Eighth Census, Population MS, 1860; and Eighth Census, Slave MS, 1860.

61. The constitutional convention formally abolished slavery in Missouri on January 11, 1865.

62. Russell to Fisk, February 21, 1865, Letters Received, box 16, ser. 3537, District of North Missouri, 393/2, NA.

63. Major A. H. Bowen to Brigadier General J. S. Brisbin, September 25, 1865, Letters Received, B-549 1865, ser. 2173, Department of Kentucky, RG 393, NA [C-4336].

64. The *Paris True Kentuckian,* 1865, reprinted the article from the *Lexington Observer and Reporter.*

65. The most powerful quote comes from General George H. Thomas, a conservative Unionist from Virginia and commander of the Army of the Cumberland, who declared, "Gentlemen,

the question is settled; negroes will fight." Thomas long doubted the propriety of black soldiers. Cornish, *Sable Arm*, 261.

66. Evidence from dozens of such attacks in the postwar period demonstrates that Union military perception of ex-rebel leaders participating in racial violence largely matched reality. See, e.g., R. E. Johnston, Bvt. Col. USV Lt Col VRC, Chf Supt Lex Sub Dist, to John Ely, Bvt. Brig. Gen Vols and Chf Lex Sub Dist, September 30, 1867, Lexington, Ky., Letters Sent, vol. 2 (123), Kentucky Assistant Commissioner, Record Group 105, Bureau of Refugees, Freedmen, and Abandoned Lands, National Archives Microfilm Publication (hereafter cited as NA Microfilm) M1904, reel no. 98, for a claim that former rebels led most antiblack mobs.

67. A. H. Bowen, the officer who reported the Danville Shooting Affray, was the superintendent for recruitment of colored troops in central Kentucky. It is not clear where Bowen originated from, though the 1860 census lists a 25-year-old A. H. Bowen from Cerro Gordo, Iowa. Tellingly, he trusted the word of a black man as equal to that of a white. See Eighth Census, MS Census, 1860.

68. R. E. Johnston, Bvt. Col. USV Lt Col VRC, Chf Supt Lex Sub Dist, to John Ely, Bvt. Brig. Gen Vols and Chf Lex Sub Dist, September 5, 1866, Lexington, Ky., Letters Sent, vol. 1 (122), KY AC BRFAL, RG 105, NA Microfilm M1904 reel no.98. The Freedmen's Bureau established a presence in Kentucky but not in Missouri. The bureau justified its operations in Kentucky because of the state's refusal to accept black testimony in courts. On the role of the Freedmen's Bureau in Kentucky, see Howard, *Black Liberation in Kentucky*.

69. *Central Kentucky Gazette*, October 31, 1866, reprinted from the *Lebanon Kentuckian*.

70. Between 1864 and 1867 a handful of newspapers in central Kentucky advanced the cause of Radical Reconstruction, supporting the Freedman's Bureau and the Civil Rights bill as well as the congressional Reconstruction Acts (even though they did not apply in Kentucky). The *Central Kentucky Gazette, Lexington National Unionist,* and *Lebanon Kentuckian* fit this mold. By mid-1867 all remaining Radical newspapers had disappeared, replaced entirely with conservative newspapers such as the *Danville Advocate* (which still exists today) and the *Lexington Gazette*. For more on southern Republican newspapers, see Richard Abbott and John W. Quist, eds., *For Free Press and Equal Rights: Republican Newspapers in the Reconstruction South* (Athens: University of Georgia Press, 2004).

71. *Kentucky Gazette*, July 11, 1866.

72. Mid-nineteenth-century lynching apologists did not employ the same language of "white womanhood" used by lynching advocates at the turn of the twentieth century. But the sentiment offered by conservative newspapers unmistakably suggests protection of white women as a legitimate cause for mob violence. In one telling example a *Missouri Telegraph* (Fulton) article defends mob law against a black man accused of raping a white woman as "deserving." But in reference to a different incident the newspaper excuses the lack of mob law against a white man accused of raping a black woman because the victim was a "strumpet" and the assailant was "just drunk." Nevertheless, Kentuckians and Missourians did not employ generalized terms such as *white womanhood* the way that lynching apologists later would. See ibid., September 10, 1869. On lynching and gender in late-nineteenth-century America, see Jane Dailey, Glenda Gilmore, and Bryant Simon, eds., *Jumpin' Jim Crow: Southern Politics from Civil War to Civil Rights* (Princeton: Princeton University Press, 2001), 140–61; and Glenda Gilmore, *Gender and Jim Crow: Women and the Politics of White Supremacy in North Carolina, 1896–1920* (Chapel Hill: University of North Carolina Press, 1996).

73. *Paris True Kentuckian*, April 5, 1866.

74. *Weekly Brunswicker,* March 30, 1867.

75. In addition to the *Weekly Brunswicker,* the *Saline Progress* described the incident, which was reprinted in the *Lexington Caucasian and Express,* March 30, 1867.

76. For an example of conservative Unionists' rejection of postwar radicalism, see *Weekly Brunswicker,* March 23, 1867. In response to the recent Military Reconstruction Act, the newspaper proclaimed itself opposed to "corrupt and unscrupulous assumptions of power exercised by the dominant party in this State; the implacable enemy of the new Dogmas of the Radical Party, as represented by the tyrannical majority in Congress."

77. *Lexington Caucasian* April 25, 1866.

78. Ibid., September 26, 1866. J. M. Julian, editor of the *Caucasian,* was not a Union supporter during the war. In a bid to draw support from the large base of disaffected conservative Unionists in central Missouri, however, he portrayed himself and his allies as "conservative Union" men in the war's aftermath.

79. A Radical editor in 1868 observed the editor of the *Weekly Caucasian* returning from the site of a lynching of a white man. The victim had been a rebel soldier but had vowed to bear witness against fellow rebels who tried to vote illegally in Missouri elections. Worse than a Radical or even a black man, the victim was a turncoat. Nevertheless, the presence of the editor of the *Caucasian* at the lynching suggests his approbation of mob violence to solve "community" problems. See *Boonville Weekly Eagle,* August 1, 1868, reprinting a story from the *Lexington Register.*

80. *Lexington Caucasian* May 16, 1866. Radical Republican supporters of black education were ambivalent about racial segregation in the classroom. Most white Radicals believed that black and white children should attend different schools and should integrate only in cases where blacks formed a tiny minority of the community. The law requiring a separate black school in districts with more than twenty black pupils reflects this attitude. Hermann was almost entirely white, and so the handful of black children would have attended school with whites, thus prompting the outcry about black students in white schools. But as historian Robert Morris has shown, white radicals within the northern Freedmen's Aid movement also expressed ambivalence regarding integrated education across the South. He cites one particularly intriguing example in which white Kentucky radical John Fee protested the segregation of black teachers and pupils at Camp Nelson. See Robert C. Morris, *Reading, 'Riting, and Reconstruction: The Education of Freedmen in the South, 1861–1870* (Chicago: University of Chicago Press, 1976), 126.

81. As historian George C. Rable notes in his analysis of the 1866 riot in Memphis, the newspapers played a significant role in stoking racial tensions, with a particular emphasis on the problem of black soldiers. See Rable, *But There Was No Peace,* 37, citing *Memphis Daily Avalanche,* January 4, 1866.

82. See Bertram Wyatt-Brown, *Southern Honor: Ethics and Behavior in the Old South* (New York: Oxford University Press, 1982).

83. As Steven Hahn points out, the fear of "negro rule" in the Reconstruction era was not unwarranted in much of the South, especially in states and localities where African Americans constituted a majority. See Steven Hahn, *A Nation under Our Feet: Black Political Struggles in the Rural South from Slavery to the Great Migration* (Cambridge: Belknap Press, 2003), 237–49. But in Kentucky and Missouri the black percentage never approached such Deep South centers of slavery as the Mississippi Delta or the South Carolina Low Country. Kentucky's Woodford County was the only county in either Kentucky or Missouri to have a slave majority in 1860,

and even there the percentage of the population enslaved was only 52 percent. With no chance to form a black political majority at the county level within the Bluegrass and Little Dixie, "negro rule" would have been virtually impossible in the border states.

84. White mobs often cloaked their extralegal activities with pseudo-legalisms and "solemn" regard for an alternative form of due process. A series of letters appeared in various Kentucky newspapers in late 1866 from "Judge Lynch," which detailed meticulous proceedings prior to the hanging of blacks and white Union men. See December 8, 1866, Letters Received, box 6, ser. 2173, Department of Kentucky, RG 393/1, NA.

85. William Freehling notes that Kentucky contributed fewer white troops to either side of the Civil War than any other state. With the draft in full effect and no option for emancipation available, African Americans filled the state's quota at a higher rate than elsewhere. See William Freehling, *The South versus the South: How Anti-Confederate Southerners Shaped the Course of the Civil War* (New York: Oxford University Press, 2001).

86. Virginia's black population also dropped, but the census data for 1860 includes the region that became West Virginia in 1863.

87. Ninth Census, Population Statistics, 1870. Note that the white population of Kentucky and Missouri continued to rise between 1860 and 1870, including in the central counties of the Bluegrass and Little Dixie.

88. The data for Kansas City is actually Jackson County, which was increasingly dominated by Kansas City. St. Louis City and St. Louis County were part of the same administrative district until 1876. The higher rate of black emigration from Missouri's central counties may be a reflection of the chaotic nature of guerrilla war in that region. The rapid rise of guerrilla activity across central Missouri in late 1861 drove a significant portion of blacks and whites to flee the region. By the end of the war, however, most whites returned to their Little Dixie homes, as new immigrants from northerly states and from Germany arrived en masse to settle in radicalized Missouri. African Americans who had fled to Iowa, Kansas, Kansas City, and St. Louis had little incentive to return to central Missouri. On social changes and northern immigration in postwar Missouri, see David Thelen, *Paths of Resistance: Tradition and Dignity in Industrializing Missouri* (New York: Oxford University Press, 1986).

89. On black movement into and around the South after emancipation, see Litwack, *Been in the Storm So Long*, 292–335. A fair number of blacks in the border states moved to the larger towns and cities within the border states, including Kansas City, Lexington, Louisville, and St. Louis. Fayette County, Ky., home of the city of Lexington, was the only Bluegrass county to experience a sizable increase in black population between 1860 and 1870. On former slaves' exodus to the upper Midwest states of Iowa, Minnesota, and Wisconsin after the Civil War, see Leslie Schwalm, *Emancipation's Diaspora: Race and Reconstruction in the Upper Midwest* (Chapel Hill: University of North Carolina Press, 2009).

90. *Lexington Weekly Caucasian and Express*, August 24, 1867.

91. For bushwhackers returning runaway slaves to their owners, see April 25, 1865, General Orders, vol. 383-942, District of Central Missouri, ser. 3367, RG 393/2, NA. In response Major Davis issued General Order No. 7, declaring that any former slaveholder who threatens his former slaves will be charged with aiding the bushwhackers.

92. The "Proclamations of Judge Lynch" appeared in numerous Kentucky newspapers from late 1866 until 1868. See, e.g., *Central Kentucky Gazette*, February 27, 1867; and *Kentucky Gazette*, November 24, 1866.

93. The Freedmen's Bureau in Kentucky operated criminal courts in order to prosecute whites guilty of abusing former slaves. The excuse for the bureau's presence in a Union state was Kentucky's refusal to admit black testimony in court. With civil courts in suspension on matters involving African Americans, white conservatives bitterly complained that the federal government had "usurped" the proper state authority.

CHAPTER SEVEN

1. August 22, 1865, Danville, Ky., D-37, Registered Letters Received, ser. 3329, Tennessee Assistant Commissioner (hereafter cited as TN AC), RG 105, NA [A-6106].

2. Ibid.

3. Ibid.

4. Bourne to Johnston, March 26, 1867, J-426, Registered Letters Received, ser. 1068, Kentucky Assistant Commissioner (hereafter cited as KY AC), RG 105 KY AC, NA [A-4375].

5. H. G. Thomas, Bvt. Brig. Genl. USA, Chf. Subassistant Commissioner Danville District, to Ben Runkle, Bvt. Colonel, April 14, 1868, Danville, Ky., Letters Sent, vol. 1 (100), KY AC, RG 105, NA Microfilm M1904, reel no. 94, NA.

6. R. E. Johnston, Bvt. Col. USV Lt Col VRC, Chf Supt Lex Sub Dist, to Ben Runkle, Bvt. Col. and Chf Supt State Ky., May 1, 1868, Lexington, Ky., Letters Sent, vol. 3 (124), KY AC, RG 105, NA Microfilm M1904, reel no. 99, NA.

7. Howard, *Black Liberation in Kentucky*, 160, quoting *National Anti-Slavery Standard,* November 4, 1865.

8. S. Thompson to "Cousin," May 20, 1865, Georgetown, Ky., Webber-Lewis Family MSS A W372/2, FHS.

9. Richard D. Sears, *Camp Nelson, Kentucky: A Civil War History* (Lexington: University Press of Kentucky, 2002), xlvi–xlvii.

10. For a good discussion of the Kentucky laws on education and their effect on taxation and unequal distribution of educational resources, see Howard, *Black Liberation in Kentucky,* 163–66.

11. The law decentralized all schooling, not just black schools, but the effect on black education was especially deleterious.

12. John Ely, Bvt. Brig Gen'l USV Chief Supt of State of Ky., Circular No. 8, September 26, 1866, Louisville, Ky., General Orders and Circulars, vol. 36, KY AC, RG 105, NA Microfilm M1904, reel no. 48.

13. Ibid.

14. R. E. Johnston, Bvt. Col. USV Lt Col VRC, Chf Supt Lex Sub Dist, to Ben Runkle, Bvt. Col. and Chf Supt State Ky., November 2, 1868 Lexington, Letters Sent, vol. 4 (125), KY AC, RG 105, NA Microfilm M1904, reel no. 99.

15. Ibid.

16. Levi Burnett, Bvt. Captain, U.S. Army, A.A.A. Genl, to Josias R. King, Lieut., Sub Asst. Commr., March 30, 1868, Lebanon, Ky., Letters Received, KY AC, RG 105, NA Microfilm M1904, reel no. 97.

17. H. G. Thomas, Bvt. Brig. Genl. USA, Chf. Subassistant Commissioner Danville District, to Ben Runkle, Bvt. Colonel, March 6, 1868, Danville, Ky., Letters Sent, vol. 1 (100), KY AC, RG 105, NA Microfilm M1904, reel no. 94.

18. Ibid., March 31, 1868.

19. Ibid., March 6, 1868.

20. Ibid., April 14, 1868.

21. Ibid., July 31, 1868.

22. *Kentucky Gazette,* April 17, 1869.

23. Ibid.

24. Ibid., October 16, 1869.

25. Henry Sullivan Williams, "The Development of the Negro Public School System in Missouri," *Journal of Negro History* 5, no. 2 (April 1920): 138.

26. W. Sherman Savage, "The Legal Provisions for Negro Schools in Missouri from 1865 to 1890," *Journal of Negro History* 16, no. 3 (July 1931): 309.

27. *Laws of the State of Missouri,* Adjourned Session, 23rd General Assembly, 191.

28. Savage, "Legal Provisions," 310–12.

29. N. H. Parker, *Missouri as It Is in 1867* (Philadelphia, 1867), 53.

30. Williams, "Development of the Negro Public School System," 142.

31. The Freedmen's Bureau's agent S. A. Feely played an important role in initiating an investigation into Missouri's failure to follow through on its commitment to black education. But the bureau played little role beyond that.

32. Kremer, *James Milton Turner,* 27–39.

33. Ibid., 30, quoting Turner to Seely, October 23, 1869, Registered Letters Received, vol. 2, 1867–69, RG 105, BRFAL, NA.

34. White objections to black teachers were not restricted to Missouri. In every southern state white conservatives and radicals alike objected to the presence of black teachers, especially in the earlier years of Reconstruction. Morris, *Reading, 'Riting, and Reconstruction,* 88–91. After 1868, however, white radicals embraced black teachers as necessary for the sustenance of black education. White conservatives continued to object to both white radical and black teachers throughout the late nineteenth century.

35. Kremer, *James Milton Turner and the Promise of America,* 31.

36. Ibid., 33, quoting Turner to Sealy, November 9, 12, 1869, BRFAL.

37. Ibid., 35.

38. Ibid., 38.

39. *Boonville Eagle,* quoted in *Missouri Telegraph* (Fulton), August 12, 1870. The *Telegraph* relayed this quote in an attempt to discredit Turner among white people. The *Telegraph* feared that Turner would deliver twenty thousand black votes to defeat a measure that would remove disfranchisement provisions against former rebels. The newspaper cited various sources testifying to Turner's "dishonesty." The paper called him an "intriguing demagogue—devoid of honesty, with a private character not above reproach."

40. Kremer, *James Milton Turner and the Promise of America,* 38.

41. *Proceedings of the First Convention of Colored Men of Kentucky, Held in Lexington, March the 22d, 23d, 24th and 26th, 1866 with the Constitution of the Kentucky State Benevolent Association.* (Louisville: Civill and Calvert, Printers, 1866) 24 (hereafter cited as *Proceedings*).

42. Ibid., 24.

43. Of those speaking against the amendment their home counties were Boyle, Fayette, Garrard, Jefferson, Scott, and Woodford, all of which, except Jefferson, are within the Bluegrass. Those speaking in favor of the amendment hailed from Henry, Franklin, Kenton, McCracken, and Shelby. Franklin County, home to the state capital, lies on the outer edge of the Bluegrass.

44. *Proceedings*, 9.

45. Ibid., 9.

46. Ibid., 10.

47. Although most blacks in the border states rejected the myth of upper South racial "mild-ness," some prominent black leaders advanced this trope in the national discourse. Most no-tably, Frederick Douglass, in his autobiography, highlighted the "unusually" rough treatment accorded him on Maryland's Eastern Shore while in slavery. Perhaps Douglass's own experience in the free North led him to accept the general abolitionist framework depicting the Deep South as more "cruel" toward blacks than the upper South. See Frederick Douglass, *My Bond-age, My Freedom* (New York: Penguin Classics, 2003), 62.

48. *Acts of Kentucky*, 1866, 38–39. For an extensive discussion of the "Negro Testimony Controversy," see Howard, *Black Liberation in Kentucky*, 130–45. Howard claims that the black convention held at Lexington was in some respect a response to the legislature's failure to provide testimony rights. But nowhere in the proceedings of the convention do the delegates specifically cite this issue (132).

49. Ibid., 135. The earlier *Ex Parte Milligan* case ruled that military tribunals were unconstitu-tional. It is unclear if the *Milligan* case applied to the former Confederate states still under mili-tary occupation and unrepresented in Congress. According to Paul Cimbala, there was consider-able disagreement over this matter between Freedmen's Bureau commissioner Oliver Howard and the Georgia assistant commissioner. At President Johnson's insistence Howard dropped the matter and simply referred cases involving African Americans to federal court in accordance with the Civil Rights Act. See Paul Cimbala, *Under the Guardianship of the Nation: The Freedmen's Bureau and the Reconstruction of Georgia, 1865–1870* (Athens: University of Georgia Press, 1997), 260 n. 106.

50. *William Roberts (Col'd) v. Thomas Outten*, July 13, 1865, Lexington, Ky., Records of the Office of the Judge Advocate General Court Martial Case Files MM2633, RG 153.

51. *Paris True Kentuckian*, July 29, 1868. Goodloe was the only judge to accept black testi-mony and did so under the auspices of the federal Civil Rights Act. No other Kentucky judge recognized the constitutionality of the act and so disregarded it in favor of Kentucky's state prohibition against black testimony. Only ratification of the Fourteenth Amendment would convince Kentucky state judges to pay any attention to the federal government's position on black testimony.

52. J. W. Cardwell to Col. W. H. Coyl, Registered Letters Received, F-18 (1866), KY AC ser. 1068, NA [A-6026].

53. Fisk to Ely, February 13, 1866, Registered Letters Received, F-18, ser. 1068, KY AC, KY AC, RG 105, [A-6026]; February 1866, ser. 1068, KY AC, KY AC, RG 105, [A-6026].

54. Ibid.

55. Johnston to Bourne, Lexington Chf. Supt, April 30, 1867, Unregistered Letters Received, ser. 1186, NA [A-6026].

56. *Kentucky Gazette*, November 2, 1867.

57. Ibid. The writer of the letter to the *Clark County Democrat*, cited in the *Gazette*, men-tioned these complaints immediately after describing the black secret societies, thus suggest-ing a causal relationship in the author's mind between secret societies and black dishonesty and failure to adhere to contracts.

58. Howard, *Black Liberation in Kentucky*, 139; quoting *Elyria Independent Democrat*, May 1, 1867.

59. *Louisville Courier,* August 2, 1867.

60. Ibid., June 12, 1867.

61. *Kentucky Gazette,* July 13, 1867.

62. *Louisville Courier,* October 26, 1867.

63. *Kentucky Gazette,* November 2, 1867.

64. The resolutions of the meeting appeared in numerous national newspapers, including the *Chicago Tribune.* See *Chicago Tribune,* November 28, 1867.

65. Ibid., November 28, 1867.

66. *Louisville Courier,* January 25, 1866.

67. Ibid.

68. Howard, *Black Liberation in Kentucky,* 148.

69. R. E. Johnston to W. R. Bourne, May 30, 1867, Letters Received, BRFAL, RG 105.

70. Thomas Louis Owen, "The Formative Years of Kentucky's Republican Party, 1864–1871" (Ph.D. diss., Lexington: University of Kentucky, 1981), 166–68.

71. The term *grasstops* carries many meanings. One critic of modern social movements notes that elites who fund and align themselves with movements that they support like to call themselves "grasstops." Thus, they give an imprimatur of mass support to a cause that relies upon elite sanction. See Tony Proscio, *When Words Fail: How the Public Interest Becomes Neither Public nor Interesting* (New York: Edna Clark McDowell Foundation, 2005). I mean the term differently to refer to dynamics *within* communities, wherein elite members of certain communities play a dominant role in the organization, funding, and execution of social activism on that community's behalf.

72. Interview with Will Oats, Mercer County, in Rawick, *The American Slave* (hereafter cited as *Slave Narratives*), 16.

73. Paulding County, Ohio, interview with Kisey McKimm, in ibid., 16:64–65.

74. Unknown to H. G. Thomas, Bvt. Brig. Genl, Chf Subt Dist Commissioner, May 25, 1868, Lebanon, Ky., Letters Sent, vol. 117, KY AC, RG 105, NA Microfilm M1904, reel no.97.

75. *Kentucky Gazette,* January 13, 1869.

76. Ibid., January 27, 1869.

77. Ibid., January 13, 1869.

78. Ibid.

79. Ibid., January 27, 1869.

80. R. E. Johnston, Bvt. Col. USV Lt Col VRC, Chf Supt Lex Sub Dist, to John Ely, Bvt. Brig. Gen Vols and Chf Lex Sub Dist, July 4, 1867 Lexington, Ky., Letters Sent, vol. 2 (123), KY AC, RG 105, NA Microfilm M1904, reel no. 98.

81. Ibid., June 30, 1866, vol. 1 (122).

82. Ibid., August 1, 1867, vol. 2 (123).

83. R. E. Johnston, Bvt. Col. USV Lt Col VRC, Chf Supt Lex Sub Dist, to C. C. Rogers, Esq., December 26, 1867 Georgetown, Ky., Letters Sent, vol. 3 (124), RG 105, KY AC, NA Microfilm M1904, reel no. 99. In a letter to Kentucky chief superintendent Ben Runkle, Johnston elaborated on the case a bit. The white man in question, Mr. C. C. Rogers, had driven Coleman off his land at the end of the year without paying him anything and threatened to kill him if he returned to his place. Johnston noted that "a number of farmers in Scott County," just northwest of Lexington, also refused to pay crop shares to their field hands and that this particularly egregious case would be a perfect example of fraud and brutality to highlight for the federal

courts. See R. E. Johnston, Bvt. Col. USV Lt Col VRC, Chf Supt Lex Sub Dist, to Ben Runkle, Bvt. Col. and Chf Supt State Ky., January 23, 1868 Lexington, Ky., Letters Sent, vol. 3 (124), KY AC, RG 105, NA Microfilm M1904, reel no. 99.

84. Ibid., March 1, 1868.

85. H. G. Thomas, Bvt. Brig. Genl. USA, Chf. Subassistant Commissioner Danville District, to Ben Runkle, Bvt. Colonel, July 31, 1868 Danville, Ky., Letters Sent, vol. 2 (101), KY AC, RG 105, NA Microfilm M1904, reel no. 94.

86. Martha Hodes notes that the Ku Klux Klan across the South assaulted black men for "insults to white ladies." In most cases these charges could not be substantiated, but their mortal power intimidated African Americans. See Martha Hodes, *White Women, Black Men: Illicit Sex in the 19th Century* (New Haven: Yale University Press, 1997), 168. Leon Litwack remarks that these sorts of symbolic acts of "insolence," especially toward white women, drew particularly harsh responses from whites because they represented the most basic consequence of emancipation: "social equality." See Litwack, *Been in the Storm So Long,* 255–61.

87. Laura Edwards has identified the common practice among wealthy southern whites in the Reconstruction era of accusing blacks of sexual crimes as a cover for class and racial grievances. This was especially true of many accusations of rape, but it also applied to more symbolic attacks such as "insulting a lady." As for rape, "it became a convenient vehicle through which to debate the ways race and class would shape civil rights and the exercise of power through institutional channels." See Laura Edwards, *Gendered Strife and Confusion: The Political Culture of Reconstruction* (Urbana: University of Illinois Press, 1997), 12–13.

88. Parrish, *Missouri under Radical Rule, 1865–1870,* 111.

89. Ibid., 109.

90. In Davis Township, Lafayette County, e.g., only two out of ninety-eight black adults owned any land. Ninth Census, Population MS, 1870.

91. *Boone County Journal,* February 18, 1870.

92. Chaplain A. Wright to Sprague, Letters Received, August 2, 1865, Missouri-Arkansas District, BRFAL, RG 105, NA.

93. John Ely, Bvt. Brig Gen'l USV Chief Supt of State of Ky., Circular No. 1, January 24, 1867, Louisville, General Orders and Circulars, vol. 36, RG 105, KY AC, NA Microfilm M1904, reel no. 48.

94. Palmer to B. F. Bullen, mayor of Paris, Letters Sent, ser. 2164, vol. 1, DKy, 229–32, Department of Kentucky, RG 393, NA [C4315]. This quote is a paraphrase of the mayor's remarks as written by General John Palmer.

95. See *Kentucky Gazette,* August 4 and September 8, 1869, for evidence of white Farmers' Clubs meetings that demanded Chinese laborers "who are willing to work and can stand the heat."

96. Of the dozens of Freedmen's Bureau letters and newspaper articles commenting on the turmoil in the countryside, none cited a particular labor leader by name. Bureau reports and letters listed the names of blacks assaulted for various activities, including refusal to acquiesce in the terms of their landlords (such as Harry Lewis), but nowhere does the bureau cite the names of leaders of this labor struggle. Considering the tendency of both radicals in the bureau and conservatives in the border state press to highlight the activities of "representative colored men" (even if for different purposes), I conclude that the leadership in the countryside was largely unknown to the white community. It is for that reason that I differentiate between the

"grassroots" actors on the farms, trading in subterranean communication networks out of the purview of the white landlord class, and the "grasstops" of "representative colored men" who presided over civil and political rights conventions in the larger cities.

97. I do not mean to imply that these black elites were utterly disconnected from the grassroots or that their class position estranged them from the demands and aspirations of the rural black masses. Many of these elites were preachers and skilled craftsmen with significant moral authority in the black community. But these ties were considerably stronger in urban communities such as Lexington and Danville, Ky., and Columbia and Lexington, Mo., than they were in the countryside. And the stated goals of the various black conventions in the border states never addressed the labor demands of those living in rural areas.

98. President Lincoln used the term *new birth of freedom* in his Gettysburg Address.

CHAPTER EIGHT

1. *Weekly Brunswicker,* July 18, 1868.

2. Ibid.

3. For an example of white supremacist campaign slogans, see Baker, *Affairs of Party,* 254.

4. A statement issued by leaders of a Colored Men's Border State Convention held in 1869 listed the states that had already granted voting rights to blacks, including each and every former Confederate state. See *Missouri Telegraph* (Fulton), January 22, 1869.

5. *Kentucky Gazette,* January 27, 1869.

6. Ibid., September 11, 1867.

7. Ibid.

8. Richard Vaughan to Abiel Leonard, October 11, 1860 Lexington, Mo., folder 447, Leonard Papers C1013, WHMC.

9. Ibid., November 12, 1860 Lexington, Mo., folder 448, Leonard Papers C1013, WHMC.

10. *History of Lafayette County, Missouri* 294. This volume notes that the incident was the first time that black militiamen had ever made an appearance in Lafayette County.

11. Coulter, *Civil War and Readjustment in Kentucky,* 274.

12. Stephen Douglas ran a strong second to Lincoln in every northern state and ran a respectable third place in Delaware, Kentucky, Maryland, and Virginia. But only in Missouri did Douglas eke out a victory.

13. Governor Magoffin welcomed John P. Hale from Alabama to speak to the Kentucky legislature, though he politely rejected the offer of secession. See Dew, *Apostles of Disunion,* 51–57.

14. Coulter, *Civil War and Readjustment in Kentucky,* 170.

15. *Congressional Globe,* 38 Cong., 1st sess. (1863–64), pt. 4 and app., 71, quoted in Coulter, *Civil War and Readjustment in Kentucky,* 174.

16. Robert Breckinridge, uncle of Confederate general and former Democratic presidential nominee John C. Breckinridge, actually chaired the Republican National Convention at Baltimore in 1864. See ibid., 181–82.

17. *National Unionist* (Lexington, Ky.), June 27, 1865. See also the *National Unionist* on June 30, 1865, for more detail on Shanklin's speech in a debate with Unconditional Unionist candidate Speed Fry. Shanklin eventually defeated Fry by a wide margin in the 1866 election.

18. *Paris (Ky.) Western Citizen,* June 9, 1865.

19. Ibid., June 16, 1865.

20. *National Unionist* (Lexington, Ky.), July 11, 1865. In both cases the governors conceded that slavery had already died and that it was futile to pretend otherwise.

21. One of the first former Confederates to win state office was Confederate colonel Hart Gibson, elected to the legislature from Woodford County in 1866.

22. Chester H. Rowell, *A Historical and Legal Digest of All the Contested Election Cases in the House of Representatives of the United States from the First to the Fifty-Sixth Congress, 1789–1901* (Washington, D.C.: Government Printing Office, 1901), *Switzler v. Anderson* case. A congressional investigation disagreed on the merits of this charge because it was not specific enough, but the plaintiff offered evidence that the Callaway election judge was intimidated into not enforcing the Registration Law vigorously.

23. *Lexington Caucasian*, June 27, 1866.

24. Parrish, *Missouri under Radical Rule*, 116–18. Ironically, when a state referendum was offered to the people in 1868 that would have enfranchised the state's African Americans, voters in the Ozarks registered the highest level of support.

25. I have previously defined the ability of African Americans to disfranchise their former masters as a "negative franchise." This concept makes sense in the zero-sum world of post-1865 Missouri politics, in which conservative disfranchisement meant more to Radical success than increased Radical Republican votes. See Aaron Astor, "The Negative Franchise: Race, Radicalism, and the Registration Law in Post–Civil War Chariton County, Missouri," paper delivered at the Southern Historical Association Annual Conference, Atlanta, November 5, 2005.

26. *Griffin v. Salisbury*, November 6, 1866, folder 2204, Contested Election, Benecke Family Collection C3825, WHMC.

27. *Lexington Caucasian*, June 27, 1866.

28. Ibid., July 11, 1866. This statement was delivered by the head of the Washington Township Johnson Club in Lafayette County.

29. Wealthy farmers in Missouri may have lost their lands partly due to a war-related financing scheme gone awry as well. See esp. Mark Geiger, "Indebtedness and the Origins of Guerrilla Violence in Civil War Missouri," *Journal of Southern History* 75, no. 1 (February 2009): 49–82.

30. Edward L. Gambill, *Conservative Ordeal: Northern Democrats and Reconstruction* (Ames: Iowa State University Press, 1981).

31. *Kentucky Gazette*, August 3, 1867.

32. Richard Vaughan to Abiel Leonard, November 12, 1860 Lexington, Mo., folder 448, Leonard Papers C1013, WHMC.

33. *Lexington Caucasian*, June 15, 1867.

34. *Kentucky Gazette*, January 16, 1867.

35. Ibid., October 23, 1867.

36. Coulter, *Civil War and Readjustment in Kentucky*.

37. *Central Kentucky Gazette*, June 19, 1867.

38. *Kentucky Gazette*, March 6, 1867.

39. *Central Kentucky Gazette*, May 8, 1867.

40. Ibid.

41. *Central Kentucky Gazette*, January 3, 1868.

42. *Kentucky Gazette*, July 27, 1867.

43. On the life and career of William Preston, see Peter Sehlinger, *Kentucky's Last Cavalier: General William Preston, 1816–1887* (Lexington: University Press of Kentucky, 2004).

44. Coulter, *Civil War and Readjustment in Kentucky,* 290–91. Governor Bramlette and the coalition of Democrats and Conservative Unionists removed all legal disabilities against Confederates in a series of acts in late 1865 and early 1866. Governor Bramlette felt that with the war over, there was no reason for the "continued punishment" of those who had lost the war.

45. *Weekly Brunswicker,* November 28, 1868.

46. *Kentucky Gazette,* July 20, 1867.

47. Although most of the property was returned to former masters, some of it remained in black ownership for decades following the Civil War. Moreover, there was no way for border state conservatives to know, at the height of Radical Reconstruction, that the land would eventually be returned to its original white owners.

48. *Kentucky Gazette,* April 21, 1869.

49. Ibid., February 26, 1868.

50. *Lexington Caucasian,* December 7, 1867.

51. *Kentucky Gazette,* August 24, 1867.

52. Hodes, *White Women, Black Men,* 166–67. Others who have examined the gendered charge of "social equality" in the Reconstruction era include Edwards, *Gendered Strife and Confusion;* Victoria E. Bynum, *Unruly Women: The Politics of Social and Sexual Control in the Old South* (Chapel Hill: University of North Carolina Press, 1992); Nell Irvin Painter, "'Social Equality,' Miscegenation, Labor, and Power," in *The Evolution of Southern Culture,* ed. Numan Bartley (Athens: University of Georgia Press, 1988); Forrest G. Wood, *Black Scare: The Racist Response to Emancipation and Reconstruction* (Berkeley: University of California Press, 1968); and Litwack, *Been in the Storm So Long,* 255–61.

53. *Missouri Telegraph,* June 4, 1869.

54. Hodes, *White Women, Black Men,* 167.

55. Ibid.

56. *Missouri Telegraph,* September 3, 1869.

57. Stiles, *Jesse James: Last Rebel of the Civil War,* 323–25.

58. Ibid., 165. Stiles offers the best analysis of Jesse James's postwar career as a robber and, as the title suggests, the "last rebel" of the Civil War. Stiles refutes earlier historians who tried to depoliticize James's activities by highlighting the effective neo-Confederate propaganda campaign carried out between James and *Kansas City Times* editor John N. Edwards.

59. Danville supported a Radical newspaper until 1867, when the editor consolidated it with a Frankfort paper. The disappearance of the radical *Central Kentucky Gazette* in 1867 adds further evidence that radicalism had virtually ceased to exist in what was once one of central Kentucky's most solidly Unionist towns.

60. The "Proclamation from Judge Lynch" appeared in the *Louisville Courier* on February 21, 1867.

61. *Central Kentucky Gazette,* July 17, 1867.

62. Norton to Runkle, September 1, 1867, Letters Received, box 6, ser. 2173, Department of Kentucky, RG 393(1).

63. *Central Kentucky Gazette,* September 11, 1867.

64. Norton to Runkle, September 1, 1867, box 6, Letters Received, ser. 2173, Department of Kentucky, RG 393(1).

65. Scott Reynolds Nelson maps Klan activity in South Carolina along railroad routes as well. See Nelson, *Iron Confederacies.* Federal captain W. R. Roume believed that Regulators also

used the railroad. See W. R. Roume, Capt. VRC, Bvt. Maj., to R. E. Johnston, Bvt. Col., Chf. Supt. Lex Sub Dist, June 9, 1867, Danville, Ky., Letters Sent, vol. 3 (102), KY AC, NA Microfilm M1904, reel no. 94; H. G. Thomas, Bvt. Brig. Genl. USA, Chf. Subassistant Commissioner Danville District, to Ben Runkle, Bvt. Colonel, April 30, 1868, Danville, Ky., Letters Sent, vol. 1 (100), KY AC, RG 105, NA Microfilm M1904, reel no. 94.

66. R. E. Johnston, Bvt. Col. USV Lt Col VRC, Chf Supt Lex Sub Dist, to John Ely, Bvt. Brig. Gen Vols and Chf Lex Sub Dist, July 4, 1867, Lexington, Ky., Letters Sent, vol. 2 (123), KY AC, NA Microfilm M1904, reel no. 98.

67. Ibid.

68. *Central Kentucky Gazette,* February 27, 1867.

69. Ben P. Runkle, Bvt. Col. U.S. Army, Chief Supd., to John Ely, Bvt. Brig Gen'l USV Chief Supt of State of Ky, June 20, 1868, Louisville, Ky., Inspection Reports, KY AC, RG 105, NA Microfilm M1904, reel no. 48.

70. *Kentucky Gazette,* July 24, 1867.

71. The *Advocate* account and the radical story from the *Frankfort Commonwealth* were reprinted in the *Kentucky Gazette,* August 3, 1867.

72. J. Michael Rhyne wrote a perceptive essay on the Bridgewater murder and memory in modern Kentucky. See J. Michael Rhyne, "The Whole Family Driven Away," *Ohio Valley History* 1 (2001).

73. *Boonville Weekly Eagle,* January 23, 1869.

74. *Lexington Caucasian,* April 25, 1868.

75. *Boonville Weekly Eagle,* July 4, 1868.

76. Hahn, *Nation under Our Feet,* 267.

77. Hahn notes that the Klan and its localized offspring appeared across the South "in response not so much to black enfranchisement as to the mass mobilization of freedpeople by the Union League and the Republican party and to the failure of Democrats and Conservatives to attract or compel substantial black support." Ibid., 268. This is only partially true in Kentucky, as the Union League's activities were negligible in the Bluegrass, and the Republican Party never seriously threatened Democratic rule in the region. It is more applicable in Missouri, however, where white Radical Republicans controlled the entire state apparatus, and the Ku Klux Klan, among other organizations, appeared to counteract the power of the Radicals and their militias. Hahn also differentiates between immediate postwar paramilitary bands of white "regulators" and "scouts," tasked with enforcing farm labor discipline in the immediate aftermath of emancipation. The Kentucky Regulators embodied a sort of combination between the immediate postwar regulators found throughout the South and the more symbolically conscious Ku Klux Klan that generally appeared a year or so later in the former Confederate states.

78. Martha Hodes, "The Sexualization of Reconstruction Politics: White Women and Black Men in the South after the Civil War," *Journal of the History of Sexuality* 3, no. 3 (1993): 402–17.

79. Hodes, *White Women, Black Men,* 176.

80. Ibid., 148. As Hodes points out, the Ku Klux Klan played a leading role in violently enforcing sexual boundaries, especially those involving wealthy white women.

81. H. G. Thomas, Bvt. Brig. Genl. USA, Chf. Subassistant Commissioner Danville District, to Ben Runkle, Bvt. Colonel, March 31, 1868 Danville, Ky., Letters Sent, vol. 1 (100), KY AC, RG 105, NA Microfilm M1904, reel no. 94. As Hodes points out, these sorts of relationships between black men and "low" white women were not uncommon in the postwar South. Class

played the most important role here in determining the level of white community outrage toward these forms of "miscegenation." See Hodes, *White Women, Black Men*, 148. Victoria Bynum and Laura Edwards have also uncovered the extent to which interracial sexual relationships existing among blacks and poor whites. See Bynum, *Unruly Women*, 10; and Edwards, *Gendered Strife and Confusion*, 16, for a discussion of the ways in which white elites ambivalently dealt with poor white "prostitutes" accused of sexual relations with black men.

82. Ibid.

83. Bynum, *Unruly Women*, 7.

84. Ben P. Runkle, Bvt. Col. US Army, Chief Supd., to John Ely, Bvt. Brig Gen'l USV Chief Supt of State of Ky., June 20, 1868, Louisville, Inspection Reports, KY AC, RG 105, NA Microfilm M1904, reel no. 48.

85. R. E. Johnston, Bvt. Col. USV Lt Col VRC, Chf Supt Lex Sub Dist, to Ben Runkle, Bvt. Col. and Chf Supt State Ky., March 31, 1868 Lexington, Letters Sent, vol. 3 (124), KY AC, RG 105, NA Microfilm M1904, reel no. 99. It is noteworthy that political meetings of black elites in Lexington during this time were not attacked. Perhaps whites felt that the black leaders in Lexington were sufficiently removed from the more "radical" lower-class blacks of the countryside and that they posed no real threat.

86. Many historians have found struggles over autonomy at the core of racial violence throughout the postwar South. See Litwack, *Been in the Storm So Long;* Rable, *But There Was No Peace;* Steven V. Ash, *Middle Tennessee Society Transformed, 1860–1870: War and Peace in the Upper South* (Baton Rouge: Louisiana State University Press, 1988); and Hahn, *Nation under Our Feet*.

87. R. E. Johnston, Bvt. Col. USV Lt Col VRC, Chf Supt Lex Sub Dist, to Ben Runkle, Bvt. Col. and Chf Supt State Ky., July 31, 1868 Lexington, Letters Sent, vol. 3 (124), KY AC, RG 105, NA Microfilm M1904, reel no. 99.

88. This is where border state violence most differs from that affecting the lower South. In the early postwar period known as "Presidential Reconstruction," in which ex-Confederate states established Black Codes enforcing rigid labor discipline, violence targeted blacks unwilling to work the plantations as well as those blacks accused of "insolence" in the face of white authority. Once Radical Reconstruction took hold in 1867, more formalized organizations such as the Ku Klux Klan emerged, and they devoted their energies primarily toward the destruction of the new Republican ascendancy. See Hahn, *Nation under Our Feet*, 266–68. Thus, as Allen Trelease comments, the Klan became a "terrorist arm of the Democratic party." Trelease, *White Terror*, xlvii. Other historians of the former Confederacy have identified a similar progression in racial violence, from labor and social control to partisan intimidation, though never did the Klan abandon labor and social control as a raison d'être. See Ted Tunnell, *Crucible of Reconstruction: War, Radicalism, and Race in Louisiana, 1862–1877* (Baton Rouge: Louisiana State University Press, 1984), 153–57; Charles L. Flynn, *White Land, Black Labor: Caste and Class in Late Nineteenth-Century Georgia* (Baton Rouge: Louisiana State University Press, 1983), 29–56; and more generally, Nelson, *Iron Confederacies*, 95–138.

89. *Kentucky Gazette*, August 8, 1868.

90. Ibid., September 9, 1868.

91. *Lexington Weekly Register*, October 12, 1871.

92. Ibid.

93. *Kentucky Gazette*, March 2, 1867.

94. *Weekly Brunswicker*, October 5, 1867.

95. Lexington *Caucasian,* October 4, 1867.

96. Kentucky *Gazette,* April 25, 1868.

97. LeeAnn Whites, *The Civil War as a Crisis in Gender: Augusta, Georgia, 1860–1890* (Athens: University of Georgia Press, 1995), 160–98. Interestingly, Whites identifies the formation of the Ladies' Memorial Association in Augusta, Ga., in 1875, much later than in Kentucky or Missouri. David Blight, however, has uncovered local women's memorial associations in the former Confederacy as early as 1866. See Blight, *Race and Reunion,* 77. But Blight does not really identify a coherent Lost Cause movement until 1873 at the earliest. As a formal, national movement, Blight is correct. But the highly publicized memorialization activities of pro-Confederate Kentucky and Missouri women from 1866 on suggest a high degree of political coherence from that early date.

98. *Missouri Telegraph* (Fulton), July 23, 1869.

99. *Kentucky Gazette,* April 24, 1867.

100. *Paris True Kentuckian,* November 18 and December 2, 1868.

101. *Danville Advocate,* February 24, 1871.

102. Ibid., November 24 and December 1, 1871.

103. *Missouri Telegraph* (Fulton), November 17, 1871.

104. *Lexington Caucasian,* October 14, 1871.

105. *Lexington Weekly Register,* October 12, 1871.

106. Albert Castel, "Order No. 11 and the Civil War on the Border," *Missouri Historical Review* 57, no. 4 (July 1963): 357–68.

107. *Central Missouri Advertiser,* March 27, 1869.

108. *Boonville Weekly Eagle,* September 5, 1868.

109. Anne Marshall, "A Manifest Aversion to the Union Cause: The Lost Cause and Civil War Memory in Kentucky," paper presented at the American Historical Association conference, Philadelphia, January 5, 2006.

110. A similar memorial was built much later at Camp Nelson National Cemetery.

111. *Paris True Kentuckian,* July 7, 1867. Unfortunately, the newspaper printed none of Williams's speech. Williams, however, was the most fervid advocate for the memorialization of black soldiers in the nineteenth century. At the dedication ceremony for the African American Civil War Memorial in Washington, D.C., in 1997, the keynote speaker noted that the memorial's unveiling was the fulfillment of George Washington Williams's lifelong dream.

112. *Missouri Telegraph* (Fulton), January 14, 1870.

113. Blight, *Race and Reunion.*

114. Marshall, "Manifest Aversion to the Union Cause."

115. Contemporary political battles in Kentucky and Missouri reveal the continuing Confederate narrative. In one of the most haunting chapters of *Confederates in the Attic* Tony Horwitz describes the near worship of Jefferson Davis in western Kentucky and the total identification with the Confederate battle flag. See Tony Horwitz, *Confederates in the Attic: Dispatches from the Unfinished Civil War* (New York: Vintage Books, 1998). In Missouri Congressman Richard Gephardt drew heavy criticism from neo-Confederate groups in January 2003 for advocating the lowering of the Confederate flag over the Confederate Soldier's Home at Higginsville in Lafayette County. See Scott Charton, "Gephardt Wants Missouri Confederate Flag Pulled Down," *Associated Press,* January 14, 2003. Former attorney general John Ashcroft, of southwestern Missouri, also provoked a firestorm in 2001 when news of his 1998 interview with the

neo-Confederate newspaper *Southern Partisan,* in which he praised the group for "setting the record straight" on the Confederate cause, caught the attention of the larger media. See Alicia Montgomery, "Ashcroft Whistles Dixie," *Salon,* January 3, 2001. Ironically, Ashcroft hails from the most Unionist portion of Missouri.

116. Blight, *Race and Reunion,* 2.

117. *Lexington Caucasian,* June 20, 1866.

118. Ibid., June 27, 1866.

119. Carol Faulkner, *Women's Radical Reconstruction: The Freedmen's Aid Movement* (Philadelphia: University of Pennsylvania Press, 2004).

120. *Howard County Advertiser,* March 29, 1866.

121. Ibid.

122. Ibid.

123. *Paris (Ky.) Western Citizen,* October 25, 1861.

124. *Glasgow Times,* February 14, 1861; *Paris (Ky.) Western Citizen,* November 1 and December 20, 1861.

125. The first northern women's aid association to arrive in the Civil War–era South was a group that called itself "Gideon's Band" and served as educators and missionaries in South Carolina's Sea Islands in November 1861. As Carol Faulkner argues, women's abolitionist organizations combined feminism, religious obligation, and Victorian conceptions of dependence. See Faulkner, *Women's Radical Reconstruction,* 10.

126. J. Williams to Susan Grigsby, January 5, 1863, FL176, Grigsby Family Papers MSS A/G 857, FHS.

127. *History of Lafayette County, Missouri,* 335.

128. Faulkner, *Women's Radical Reconstruction.*

129. Wartime aid to the Western Sanitary Commission was not uncommon, however. Women in Fayette, Mo., held a "Grand Festival" to benefit the Western Sanitary Commission in 1864. But after the war's completion, no word of similar aid to women's Union organizations appears in private correspondence or newspapers in the border states. On the Fayette meeting, see *Howard County Advertiser,* March 11, 1864.

130. Whites, *Civil War as a Crisis in Gender,* 160–98.

131. *Lexington Gazette,* June 30, 1866.

132. Eighth Census, Population MS, 1860; *Howard County Advertiser,* March 29, 1866.

133. Amy Elizabeth Murrell, *The Divided Family in Civil War America* (Chapel Hill: University of North Carolina Press, 2005).

CHAPTER NINE

1. *Woodford Weekly,* August 12, 1870, reprinting the article from the *Harrodsburg (Ky.) People.*

2. Ibid.

3. Ibid.

4. Ibid.

5. For an extensive discussion of Election Day activity around the ballot box, including violence, see Bensel, *American Ballot Box in the Mid-Nineteenth Century.*

6. Ninth Census, Population MS, 1870, 5.

7. Ibid.

8. *Lexington Caucasian,* February 26, 1870. The necessary twenty-nine states ratified the amendment by February 3, 1870. But New York subsequently withdrew its ratification, and Secretary of State Hamilton Fish did not certify ratification until Georgia assented to the amendment in March. Fish offered his official certification on March 30, 1870, proclaiming the amendment a part of the Constitution. The first African American to vote under it did so in New Jersey on March 31, 1870.

9. *Liberator,* December 23, 1864.

10. Margaret L. Dwight, "Black Suffrage in Missouri, 1865–1877" (Ph.D. diss., University of Missouri, Columbia, 1978), 50.

11. Ibid.

12. Ibid., 53.

13. *Proceedings of the First Convention of Colored Men of Kentucky,* March 22, 23, 24, and 26, 1866, Lexington (Louisville: Civill and Calvert Printing, 1866), 24.

14. Howard, *Black Liberation in Kentucky,* 150.

15. Owen, "Formative Years of Kentucky's Republican Party," 51.

16. Howard, *Black Liberation in Kentucky,* 152.

17. R. E. Johnston to W. R. Bourne, May 30, 1867, BRFAL, RG 105.

18. *Lexington Caucasian,* May 7, 1870.

19. Woodford *Weekly,* May 13, 1870.

20. *Kentucky Gazette,* April 20, 1870.

21. *Lexington Caucasian,* May 7, 1870.

22. *Paris True Kentuckian,* March 2, 1870.

23. Ibid.

24. *Kentucky Gazette,* March 16, 1870.

25. Ibid.

26. *Woodford Weekly,* February 25, 1870.

27. Ibid.

28. In Missouri it is particularly important to denote the "Radical" Republican Party as the "Radicals" because the party split into Radical and Liberal factions. Both Radicals and Liberals thought of themselves as Republicans, though most Missourians—whether Radical Republicans, Liberal Republicans, or Democrats—simply referred to the Radical wing as the "Radical Party." In Kentucky the Republican Party never split into Liberal and Radical factions.

29. B. Gratz Brown and Carl Schurz introduced a motion in the state Republican Party convention in 1870 providing "universal enfranchisement and universal amnesty." This motion, which would have committed the state's Republican Party toward removal of the 1865 disfranchisement clauses, was voted down by a 349–342 margin. Following defeat of the measure, 250 supporters of the motion walked out of the convention, declared themselves the new Liberal Republican Party, and nominated Brown for governor against the radical nominee James McClurg. See John Lalor, ed., *Cyclopædia of Political Science, Political Economy, and the Political History of the United States by the Best American and European Writers* (New York: Maynard, Merrill and Co., 1881), 2:320.14.

30. Dwight, "Black Suffrage in Missouri, 1865–1877," 140.

31. Ibid. Most likely, Douglass feared that continued disfranchisement of former rebels would yield Klan-style violence in Missouri.

32. *Missouri Telegraph* (Fulton), June 24, 1870.

33. *Missouri Democrat*, April 12, 1870. A peculiarity in Missouri politics was the names of its most prominent St. Louis–based newspapers. The *Missouri Democrat* was a staunchly Republican newspaper, though it did support the liberal Republicans and the re-enfranchisement amendment in 1870. The *Missouri Republican* was a conservative Democratic newspaper, though it supported the Union throughout the war and used much less vituperative language than the *Lexington Caucasian*.

34. *Missouri Democrat*, August 2, 1870.

35. For a compilation of county votes on the 1868 suffrage amendment, see Dwight, "Black Suffrage in Missouri, 1865–1877," 97–100. It would be rash to suggest that white supremacist feelings among Ozark Unionists had subsided by 1868; nevertheless, Ozark Unionists who had suffered grievously from bushwhacker violence during the war pragmatically supported black suffrage as a way to bolster the state's Radical party.

36. *Kentucky Gazette*, August 24, 1867.

37. Ibid.

38. *Missouri Telegraph* (Fulton), June 11, 1869.

39. Ibid., March 26, 1869.

40. *Paris True Kentuckian*, March 9, 1870.

41. *Lexington Caucasian*, April 16, 1870.

42. *Missouri Telegraph* (Fulton), July 9, 1869.

43. *Lexington Caucasian*, February 26, 1870.

44. Ibid., April 30, 1870.

45. Ibid.

46. Ibid.

47. Quote printed in the *Danville Advocate*, July 28, 1871.

48. *Missouri Telegraph* (Fulton), January 28, 1870.

49. Ibid., April 29, 1870.

50. Ibid., September 2, 1870.

51. Hambleton Tapp and James C. Klotter, *Kentucky: Decades of Discord, 1865–1900* (Frankfort: Kentucky Historical Society, 1977), 14.

52. *Kentucky Gazette*, April 6, 1870.

53. Ninth Census, Population MS, 1870, 43.

54. *Kentucky Gazette*, August 10, 1870.

55. Ibid.

56. Ibid. It is noteworthy that the *Gazette* never called for the reorganization of local governments where white Republicans were a majority. What bothered the *Gazette* was not simply the presence of a viable Republican Party, which had established dominance among the mostly white southeastern mountain counties, but the role that African Americans played in pushing the Republican Party over the top.

57. *Danville Advocate*, November 11, 1870.

58. The 1870 census shows a black population at roughly 48 percent of the total for Lexington and 46.5 percent for Woodford County. See Ninth Census, Population MS, 148.

59. There were only 5,276 whites in Woodford County. See ibid., 32.

60. The black population dropped from 5,943 to 3,825, a loss of 2,118.

61. The white population in Woodford County in 1870 was 4,415.

62. Garrard, Jessamine, and Mercer counties also lost aggregate population between 1860 and 1870. Bourbon, Boyle, and Marion counties remained almost constant between 1860 and 1870; considering normal population growth, there must have been a surplus emigration from these counties as well. Only Lexington's Fayette County increased by a sizable total between 1860 and 1870. See Ninth Census, Population MS, 32.

63. Owen, "Formative Years of Kentucky's Republican Party, 1864–1871," 61.

64. Ibid., 69.

65. *Missouri Telegraph* (Fulton), *Telegraph,* May 6, 1870.

66. For election return information in Lafayette County, see *Lexington Caucasian,* November 1870; and *Weekly Brunswicker,* November 28, 1868.

67. Brown was nominated by both the Liberal Republican Party, commonly called the "Liberal Party," and the Democratic Party in 1870.

68. With opposition to the re-enfranchisement so weak in the Missouri press and among the electorate, conservatives remained confident that the amendment would pass overwhelmingly. They were correct in their assumption, as support for the amendment, and the combined Liberal and Democratic ticket superseded that of the anti-amendment and Radical forces by a ratio of 104,771 to 62,854, or more than 40,000 votes. See Lalor, *Cyclopedia of Political Science,* 2:320.14.

69. *Missouri Statesman,* December 2 and 9, 1870. Quoted in Parrish, *Missouri under Radical Rule,* 309. Parrish attributes the collapse in support for the disfranchisement provisions to heavy-handedness by the Radicals of the McClurg administration, corruption in Jefferson City, and the healing power of time, which rendered disfranchisement no longer palatable by 1870.

70. The state supreme court actually invalidated the original ordinance allowing those with family members buried in the town cemetery to declare residency. After the court invalidated this plan, the commissioners established an ordinance allowing county residents to purchase one-inch-wide strips of land in the cemetery in order to establish residency in the town.

71. The shortfall in white attorney vote totals probably reflects split tickets in which voters crossed out the name of the Republican and added in another name or left it blank.

72. *Danville Advocate,* April 7, 1871.

73. *Boonville Eagle,* April 5, 1872.

74. The Democratic tide culminated in 1875 with the creation and ratification of a new conservative state constitution that repudiated all of the residual disfranchising elements of the 1865 constitution. The 1875 constitution did not limit black civil or voting rights, as "Redemption" constitutions in the lower South had done.

75. The Ninth Census lists Steele as possessing forty-eight thousand dollars in real property. See Ninth Census, Population MS, 1870; *Woodford Weekly,* June 24, 1870.

76. On the occupations of Waters, Searcy, and Turpin, see Ninth Census, Population MS, 1870.

77. *Woodford Weekly,* March 18, 1870.

78. Ibid., March 18, 1870.

79. Eighth Census, Slave MS, 1860. As many as ten of Steele's male slaves were of military age during the later part of the Civil War.

80. *Woodford Weekly,* June 10, 1870.

81. Ibid., July 20, 1870. The *Weekly* actually compares Steele to President Lincoln, in hopes that showing both men to be creatures of "circumstance" would render them not worthy of black people's adulation.

82. Ibid., June 24, 1870.

83. Ibid. The Eighth Census shows Steele as possessing twenty-three slaves, not nine. He is probably referring, however, to military-age black slaves, which was much closer to nine.

84. *Woodford Weekly*, August 12, 1870. The Democratic *Weekly* believed the Democrats had swept the ticket because many black voters decided not to bother voting and that the "Radicals didn't really support them."

85. The classic work examining black factional divides during Reconstruction is Thomas Holt, *Black over White*. More recently, Michael Fitzgerald examined factionalism within the urban setting of Mobile, Ala. See Michael Fitzgerald, *Urban Emancipation: Popular Politics in Reconstruction Mobile, 1860–1890* (Baton Rouge: Louisiana State University Press, 2002). Justin Behrend explores black factionalism in the Natchez District of Mississippi and Louisiana and concludes that black political divisions were a logical outcome in a black-majority district. That blacks in Woodford County likely thought they lived in a black-majority district confirms Behrend's thesis. See Justin Behrend, "Building Democracy from Scratch: African American Politics and Community in the Postemancipation Natchez District" (Ph.D. diss., Northwestern University, 2006), chap. 4.

86. *Missouri Telegraph* (Fulton), August 12, 1870.

87. Although Herbert's name does not appear in the 1870 census, he was likely a skilled craftsman or small business owner. When conservative newspapers referred to black men as "respectable," they usually meant so both as a class identification and a statement of the man's unwillingness to ruffle the racial feathers of the community. This is similar to what Nell Irvin Painter identifies as the propensity of whites to refer to "representative colored men." See Nell Irvin Painter, *Exodusters: Black Migration to Kansas after Reconstruction* (New York: Norton, 1976), 53.

88. *Missouri Telegraph* (Fulton), August 12, 1870.

89. *Danville Advocate*, August 19, 1870. The *Advocate*'s calculation was probably accurate. In the April 1871 election blacks constituted 80 percent of the Republican vote in Danville alone. Considering the consolidation of white support for the Democratic Party in rural Boyle County, it is likely that black voters made up roughly 90 percent of all Republican voters in the county.

90. *Missouri Telegraph* (Fulton), February 23, 1872.

91. *Danville Advocate*, May 26, 1871. The Republican Party platform blasted the Democratic legislature for a variety of reasons. Second on the list, after refusal to crack down against the Ku Klux Klan, was the refusal of the state to allow blacks to testify in court.

92. There was a fair amount of truth to this charge. Blacks held a handful of positions on Republican committees but far less than their share of the Republican electorate would warrant. Tensions between black and white Republicans over offices were common in every southern state. As Steven Hahn points out, bond requirements and differing class demands between northern and southern white Republicans and black Republicans weakened the overall Republican Party. See Hahn, *Nation under Our Feet*, 249–59.

93. *Lexington Caucasian*, September 17, 1870.

94. Ibid., October 22, 1870.

95. Democrats across the lower South employed the same charge, highlighting the refusal of white-run Republican parties to grant offices to blacks and charging white Republicans with hypocrisy. The purpose of these campaigns was only partially to lure blacks over to the Democratic Party. After all, Democrats had no desire to give blacks offices in either the border or

lower South. But Democrats hoped to sow enough dissent within Republican ranks to cause a schism that they could exploit.

96. *Kentucky Gazette,* May 6, 1871.

97. Ninth Census, Population MS, 1870.

98. This sort of violent enforcement of black Republican loyalty was quite common throughout the South. In one particularly egregious case in Mississippi, a group of black men threatened to castrate another black man if he voted for the Democrats. See Behrend, "Building Democracy from Scratch," chap. 5. For the role that black women played in enforcing Republican loyalty, see Elsa Barkley Brown, "Negotiating and Transforming the Public Sphere: African-American Political Life in the Transition from Slavery to Freedom," *Public Culture* 7 (Fall 1994): 107–46.

99. *Kentucky Gazette,* August 10, 1871.

100. Ibid.

101. *Woodford Weekly,* August 3, 1870.

102. See ibid., August 12, 1870, for the "correction."

103. *Kentucky People,* August 12, 1870.

104. *Woodford Weekly,* August 3, 1870.

105. Hahn, *Nation under Our Feet,* 174–75.

106. *Kentucky Gazette,* February 8, 1871.

107. Ibid., February 15, 1871.

108. Ibid., February 8, 1871.

109. Ibid., August 24, 1867.

110. *Danville Advocate,* August 11, 1871.

111. Ibid.

112. Ibid., November 11, 1870.

113. Ibid.

114. Ibid., September 1, 1871.

115. Ibid., September 8, 1871.

CONCLUSION

1. Hahn, *Nation under Our Feet,* 3.

2. Ibid.

3. This is not to suggest that slaves on large plantations had no contact outside their own neighborhoods. Indeed, many of these slaves arrived via the interstate slave trade from the upper South, and a fair number continued to be sold to the newer cotton regions of the Southwest. Nevertheless, the size of lower South plantations suggests a richer and deeper set of social and kin relationships within individual plantations than would have been possible among the smallholdings of the border states.

4. C. Vann Woodward, *Origins of the New South* (Baton Rouge: Louisiana State University Press, 1951), 6–7.

5. Charles Beard, *The Rise of American Civilization* (New York: Macmillan Press, 1927).

6. Edward Ayers and William G. Thomas III, *Valley of the Shadow Project,* www.vcdh.virginia.edu/AHR/, "The Differences Slavery Made: A Close Analysis of Two American Communities."

7. Ayers differentiates his approach from James McPherson, who, according to Ayers, offers an argument with "no gradations" that is "built around fundamental and far-reaching

differences between the sections." See Ayers, *Valley of the Shadow*, review of James McPherson's *Ordeal by Fire: The Civil War and Reconstruction* (New York: Knopf, 1982), http://jefferson.village.virginia.edu:8090/xslt/servlet/ramanujan.XSLTServlet?xml=/vcdh/xml_docs/ahr/article.xml&xsl=/vcdh/xml_docs/ahr/article.xsl&section=context&area=context_entries&piece=&list=&item=mcpherson-ordeal.

8. Ibid.

9. There is a fair degree of scholarship in progress focusing on Kentucky and Missouri. For ongoing and recently completed dissertations on Kentucky, see Adrian Buser "Borderlines in the Bluegrass: The Elite White Women of Kentucky during the Civil War" (Indiana University); J. Michael Crane, "Slavery on the Edge of 'Freedom': Kentucky in the 19th Century" (Vanderbilt University); Luke Harlow, "From Border South to Solid South: Religion, Race, and the Making of Confederate Kentucky, 1830–1880" (Rice University); Helen Hoguet Lacroix, "A Head with the Union, a Heart with the South: Race, Labor, and Politics in Kentucky's Bluegrass Region, 1865–1900" (University of Wisconsin, Madison); Patrick Lewis, "'Master for Loyalty's Sake': Benjamin F. Buckner, Proslavery Unionism, and Civil War Kentucky" (University of Kentucky); and J. Michael Rhyne, "Rehearsal for Redemption: Violence in the Post-War Lexington Sub-District" (University of Cincinnati); and Matthew Stanley, "'No More Shall the Winding Rivers Be Red': War, Reunion, and Identity in Nineteenth Century Middle America" (University of Cincinnati). For recently completed dissertations on Missouri, see Diane Mutti Burke, "On Slavery's Borders: Slavery and Slaveholding on Missouri's Farms, 1821–65" (Emory University); Kevin Butler, "The Creation of African American Christianity: Slavery and Religion in Antebellum Missouri" (University of Missouri, Columbia); and Mark Geiger, "Missouri's Hidden Civil War: Financial Conspiracy and the End of the Planter Elite, 1861–65" (University of Missouri, Columbia).

BIBLIOGRAPHY

PRIMARY SOURCES

Parker, N. H. *Missouri as It Is in 1867.* Philadelphia, 1867.

Proceedings of the First Convention of Colored Men of Kentucky, Held in Lexington, March the 22d, 23d, 24th and 26th, 1866 with the Constitution of the Kentucky State Benevolent Association. Louisville: Civill and Calvert, Printers, 1866.

Rice, David. "Slavery Inconsistent with Justice and Good Policy Proved by a Speech Delivered in the Convention, Held at Danville, Kentucky." New York: Isaac Collins, 1804.

Shannon, James. *An Address Delivered before the Pro-Slavery Convention of the State of Missouri on Domestic Slavery.* Held in Lexington, Mo., July 13, 1855. St. Louis: Republican Book and Job Office, 1855.

Williams' Lexington [Kentucky] Directory, City Guide, and Business Mirror, vol. 1: 1859–60, comp. C. S. Williams. Lexington: Hitchcock and Searles, 1859.

ARCHIVAL AND GOVERNMENT DOCUMENTS

KENTUCKY STATE ARCHIVES

County Records

Stanton, Richard H. *Revised Statutes of Kentucky.* Cincinnati: Robert Clarke and Co., 1860.

MISSOURI STATE ARCHIVES

Governor Fletcher Papers

Governor Gamble Papers

Laws of the State of Missouri, Adjourned Session. 23rd General Assembly

NATIONAL ARCHIVES

Record Group 94: Army Adjutant General's Office
Record Group 105: Bureau of Refugees, Freedmen, and Abandoned Lands
Record Group 110: Provost Marshal File
Record Group 393: United States Army Continental Commands, 1821–1920

OFFICIAL RECORDS OF THE WAR OF THE REBELLION

Military Records: Civil War Service Records," *Ancestry.com,* Provo, Utah, 2002, disc 1.
United States Decennial Population and Agricultural Census

OTHER SOURCES

Abelman v. Booth, 62 U.S. Supreme Court 506, 1858.
Congressional Globe
Cooper County Deed Book, Boonville, Mo.
Freedmen and Southern Society Project.
Mercer County Deed Book, Harrodsburg, Ky.
Record Group 105—Selected documents at University of Maryland, College Park.
United States Statutes at Large. Washington, D.C.: Government Printing Office, 1937.

MANUSCRIPT COLLECTIONS

FILSON HISTORICAL SOCIETY

Bodley Family Papers
Grigsby Family Papers
Jones Family Papers
Markham Papers
Miscellaneous Documents

JOINT COLLECTION OF THE STATE HISTORICAL SOCIETY OF MISSOURI AND THE WESTERN HISTORICAL MANUSCRIPT COLLECTION

Beineke Family Collection
Glen Hardeman Papers
Leonard Family Papers
Odon Guitar Papers

KENTUCKY HISTORICAL SOCIETY

David Sillcock Family Papers
Wallace-Stirling Diary

UNIVERSITY OF KENTUCKY SPECIAL COLLECTIONS

Alexander Jeffrey Papers
Broadside Collection
Clay Family Papers
Hunt-Morgan Papers
J. Winston Coleman Papers

NEWSPAPERS

KENTUCKY

Central Kentucky Gazette (Danville)
Danville Advocate
Kentucky Gazette (Lexington)
Kentucky People (Harrodsburg)
Kentucky Statesman (Frankfort)
Kentucky Tribune (Danville)
Kentucky Yeoman (Frankfort)
Lebanon Weekly Standard
Lexington National Unionist
Lexington Observer and Reporter
Lexington Statesman
Louisville Commercial
Louisville Courier
Louisville Journal
Paris True Kentuckian
Paris Western Citizen
Woodford Pennant
Woodford Weekly

MISSOURI

Boonville Observer
Boonville Weekly Eagle
Central City and Brunswicker (Brunswick)
Glasgow Herald
Howard County Advertiser
Lexington Caucasian
Lexington Weekly Express
Marshall Democrat Missouri Statesman (Columbia)
Missouri Telegraph (Fulton)
Randolph Citizen

St. Louis Democrat
St. Louis Republican

OTHER NEWSPAPERS

Chicago Times
Chicago Tribune
Cincinnati Commercial
Cincinnati Enquirer
Cincinnati Gazette
Liberator
New York Herald
New York Tribune
Washington Globe

ELECTRONIC SOURCES

Indexed United States Manuscript Census Records (stored online). Provo, Utah: *Ancestry.com*, 2000.

Ross, Kirby. "Federal Militia in Missouri, *Civil War St. Louis*, www.civilwarstlouis .com/militia/federalmilitia.htm#3.%20Missouri%20State%20Militia, posted January 16, 2004.

SECONDARY SOURCES

BOOKS AND DISSERTATIONS

Abbott, Richard, and John Quist, eds. *For Free Press and Equal Rights: Republican Newspapers in the Reconstruction South.* Athens: University of Georgia Press, 2004.

Allen, James Lane. *The Blue Grass Region of Kentucky.* New York: Harper and Brothers, 1899.

Ash, Steven V. *Middle Tennessee Society Transformed, 1860–1870: War and Peace in the Upper South.* Baton Rouge: Louisiana State University Press, 1988.

Ashworth, John. *Slavery, Capitalism and Politics in the Antebellum Republic.* Cambridge: Cambridge University Press, 1995.

Ayers, Edward. *Valley of the Shadow: Two Communities in the Civil War.* Charlottesville: Norton, 2000.

Baker, Jean H. *Affairs of Party: The Political Culture of Northern Democrats in the Mid-Nineteenth Century.* Ithaca: Cornell University Press, 1983.

———. *Mary Todd Lincoln: A Biography.* New York: Norton Press, 1987.

Barney, William L. *The Secessionist Impulse: Alabama and Mississippi in 1860.* Tuscaloosa: University of Alabama Press, 1974.

Bartley, Numan, ed. *The Evolution of Southern Culture.* Athens: University of Georgia Press, 1988.

Beard, Charles. *The Rise of American Civilization.* New York: Macmillan, 1927.

Behrend, Justin. "Building Democracy from Scratch: African American Politics and Community in the Postemancipation Natchez District." Ph.D. diss., Northwestern University, 2006.

Benedict, Bryce. *Jayhawkers: The Civil War Brigade of James Henry Lane.* Norman: University of Oklahoma Press, 2009.

Bensel, Richard Franklin. *The American Ballot Box in the Mid-Nineteenth Century.* Cambridge: Cambridge University Press, 2004.

Berlin, Ira. *Many Thousands Gone: The First Two Centuries of Slavery in North America.* Cambridge: Harvard University Press, 1998.

Berlin, Ira, Barbara Fields, Thavolia Glymph, Joseph Reidy, and Leslie Rowland. *The Destruction of Slavery. Freedom:* A Documentary History of Emancipation. Cambridge: Cambridge University Press, 1985.

Berlin, Ira, Barbara J. Fields, Steven F. Miller, Joseph P. Reidy, and Leslie S. Rowland. *Slaves No More: Three Essays on Emancipation and the Civil War.* New York: Cambridge University Press, 1992.

Berlin, Ira, Joseph P. Reidy, and Leslie S. Rowland, eds. *Freedom's Soldiers: The Black Military Experience in the Civil War.* Cambridge: Cambridge University Press, 1998.

Blight, David W. *Race and Reunion: The Civil War in American Memory.* Cambridge: Harvard University Press, 2001.

Boman, Dennis. *Abiel Leonard, Yankee Slaveholder, Eminent Jurist, and Passionate Unionist.* Lewiston, N.Y.: Edwin Mellen Press, 2002.

———. *Lincoln and Citizens' Rights in Civil War Missouri: Balancing Freedom and Security.* Baton Rouge: Louisiana State University Press, 2011.

———. *Lincoln's Resolute Unionist: Hamilton Gamble: Dred Scott Dissenter and Missouri's Civil War Governor.* Baton Rouge: Louisiana State University Press, 2006.

Bowling, Kenneth R., and Donald R. Kennon, eds. *The House and Senate in the 1790s: Petitioning, Lobbying, and Institutional Development.* Athens: Ohio University Press, 2002.

Brown, Richard C. *A History of Danville and Boyle County Kentucky, 1774–1992.* Danville, Ky.: Bicentennial Books, 1992.

Bruce, Henry Clay. *The New Man: Twenty-Nine Years a Slave, Twenty-Nine Years a Free Man.* York, Pa.: P. Anstadt and Sons, 1895.

Bruner, Peter. *A Slave's Adventures toward Freedom, Not Fiction, but the True Story of a Struggle.* 1918. Reprint. Chapel Hill: University of North Carolina Press, 2000.

Bryan, William S. and Robert Rose. *History of the Pioneer Families of Missouri, with Numerous Sketches, Anecdotes, Adventures, Etc. Relating to Early Days in Missouri.* St. Louis: Bryan, Brand and Co., 1876.

Bynum, Victoria E. *Unruly Women: The Politics of Social and Sexual Control in the Old South.* Chapel Hill: University of North Carolina Press, 1992.

Cimbala, Paul. *Under the Guardianship of the Nation: The Freedmen's Bureau and the Reconstruction of Georgia, 1865–1870.* Athens: University of Georgia Press, 1997.

Coleman, J. Winston. *Lexington during the Civil War.* Lexington: Commercial Printing Co., 1938.

———. *Slavery Times in Kentucky.* Chapel Hill: University of North Carolina Press, 1940.

Cornish, Dudley Taylor. *The Sable Arm: Black Troops in the Union Army, 1861–1865.* 1956. Reprint. Lawrence: University Press of Kansas, 1987.

Coulter, E. Merton. *Civil War and Readjustment in Kentucky.* Chapel Hill: University of North Carolina Press, 1926.

Crofts, Daniel W. *Reluctant Confederates: Upper South Unionists in the Secession Crisis.* Chapel Hill: University of North Carolina Press, 1989.

Dailey, Jane. *Before Jim Crow: The Politics of Race in Postemancipation Virginia.* Chapel Hill: University of North Carolina Press, 2000.

Davis, William C., *Breckinridge: Statesman, Soldier, Symbol.* Baton Rouge: Louisiana State University Press, 1974.

Dew, Charles B. *Apostles of Disunion.* Charlottesville: University Press of Virginia, 2001.

Dicken-Garcia, Hazel. *To Western Woods: The Breckinridge Family Moves to Kentucky in 1793.* Madison, N.J.: Fairleigh Dickinson University Press, 1991.

Dollar, Kent T., Larry H. Whiteaker, and W. Calvin Dickinson, eds. *Sister States, Enemy States: The Civil War in Kentucky and Tennessee.* Lexington: University Press of Kentucky, 2009.

Douglas, Mark K. *Soldiers, Secesh and Civilians: Compiled Records of Callawegians in the War of the Rebellion.* Fulton, Mo.: Jones Republic Press, 2001.

Douglass, Frederick. *My Bondage, My Freedom.* New York: Penguin Classics, 2003.

Drago, Edmund. *A Splendid Failure: Black Politicians and Reconstruction in Georgia.* (Baton Rouge: Louisiana State University Press, 1982.

Du Bois, W.E.B. *Black Reconstruction in America.* 1935. New York: Touchstone Books, 1992.

Dugan, Frances L. S., and Jacqueline P. Bull, eds. *Bluegrass Craftsman: Being the Reminiscences of Ebenezer Hiram Stedman, Papermaker, 1808–1885.* Lexington: University Press of Kentucky, 1959.

Durden, Robert. *The Gray and the Black: The Confederate Debate on Emancipation.* Baton Rouge: Louisiana State University Press, 1972.

Dykstra, Robert. *Bright Radical Star: Black Freedom and White Supremacy on the Hawkeye Frontier.* Cambridge: Harvard University Press, 1993.

Edwards, Laura. *Gendered Strife and Confusion: The Political Culture of Reconstruction.* Urbana: University of Illinois Press, 1997.

Etcheson, Nicole. *Bleeding Kansas: Contested Liberty in the Civil War Era.* Lawrence: University Press of Kansas, 2006.

———. *The Emerging Midwest: Upland Southerners and the Political Culture of the Old Northwest, 1787–1861*. Bloomington: Indiana University Press, 1996.

Faulkner, Carol. *Women's Radical Reconstruction: The Freedmen's Aid Movement*. Philadelphia: University of Pennsylvania Press, 2004.

Fellman, Michael. *Inside War: The Guerilla Conflict in Missouri during the American Civil War*. New York: Oxford University Press, 1989.

Ferrer, Ada. *Insurgent Cuba: Race, Nation, and Revolution, 1868–1898*. Chapel Hill: University of North Carolina Press, 1999.

Fields, Barbara Jeanne. *Slavery and Freedom on the Middle Ground: Maryland during the Nineteenth Century*. New Haven: Yale University Press, 1985.

Fischer, David Hackett, and James C. Kelly. *Bound Away: Virginia and the Westward Movement*. Charlottesville: University Press of Virginia, 2000.

Fisher, Noel C. *War at Every Door: Partisan Politics and Guerrilla Violence in East Tennessee, 1860–1869*. Chapel Hill: University of North Carolina Press, 1997.

Fitzgerald, Michael W. *The Union League Movement in the Deep South: Politics and Agricultural Change during Reconstruction*. Baton Rouge: Louisiana State University Press, 1989.

———. *Urban Emancipation: Popular Politics in Reconstruction Mobile, 1860–1890*. Baton Rouge: Louisiana State University Press, 2002.

Flynn, Charles L. *White Land, Black Labor: Caste and Class in Late Nineteenth-Century Georgia*. Baton Rouge: Louisiana State University Press, 1983.

Foner, Eric. *Free Soil, Free Labor, Free Men: The Ideology of the Republican Party before the Civil War*. New York: Oxford University Press, 1970.

———. *Reconstruction: America's Unfinished Revolution, 1863–1877*. New York: Harper and Row, 1988.

Fox-Genovese, Elizabeth. *Within the Plantation Household: Black and White Women of the Old South*. Chapel Hill: University of North Carolina Press, 1988.

Franklin, John Hope. *The Militant South, 1800–1861*. Cambridge: Harvard University Press, 1956.

Franklin, John Hope, and Loren Schweniger. *Runaway Slaves: Rebels on the Plantation*. New York: Oxford University Press, 1999.

Frazier, Harriet C. *Runaway and Freed Missouri Slaves and Those Who Helped Them, 1763–1865*. Jefferson, N.C.: McFarland and Co., 2004.

Fredrickson, George. *Black Image in the White Mind: The Debate on Afro-American Character and Destiny, 1817–1914*. New York: Harper and Row, 1971.

Freehling, William. *The Road to Disunion: 1776–1854*. New York: Oxford University Press, 1990.

———. *The South versus the South: How Anti-Confederate Southerners Shaped the Course of the Civil War*. Oxford: Oxford University Press, 2001.

Gambill, Edward L. *Conservative Ordeal: Northern Democrats and Reconstruction*. Ames: Iowa State University Press, 1981.

Genovese, Eugene. *Roll, Jordan, Roll: The World the Slaves Made.* New York: Pantheon Books, 1974.

———. *The World the Slaveholders Made: Two Essays in Interpretation.* New York: Vintage Books, 1969.

Gerteis, Louis. *Civil War St. Louis.* Lawrence: University Press of Kansas, 2001.

Gilmore, Glenda. *Gender and Jim Crow: Women and the Politics of White Supremacy in North Carolina, 1896–1920.* Chapel Hill: University of North Carolina Press, 1996.

Gilmore, Glenda, and Bryant Simon, eds. *Jumpin' Jim Crow: Southern Politics from Civil War to Civil Rights.* Princeton: Princeton University Press, 2001.

Glatthaar, Joseph T. *Forged in Battle: The Civil War Alliance of Black Soldiers and White Officers.* Baton Rouge: Louisiana State University Press, 2000.

Goodrich, Thomas. *Black Flag: Guerrilla Warfare on the Western Border, 1861–1865.* Bloomington: Indiana University Press, 1995.

Greene, Lorenzo J., Antonio Holland, and Gary Kremer. *Missouri's Black Heritage: Revised Edition.* Columbia: University of Missouri Press, 1993.

Gutman, Herbert. *The Black Family in Slavery and Freedom, 1750–1925.* New York: Vintage Books, 1976.

Hahn, Steven. *A Nation under Our Feet: Black Political Struggles in the Rural South from Slavery to the Great Migration.* Cambridge: Belknap Press, 2003.

———. *The Political Worlds of Slavery and Freedom.* Cambridge: Harvard University Press, 2009.

Hall, David D., John M. Murrin, and Thad W. Tate, eds. *Saints and Revolutionaries: Essays on Early American History.* New York: Norton, 1984.

Harrold, Stanley. *Border War: Fighting over Slavery before the Civil War.* Chapel Hill: University of North Carolina Press, 2010.

Harrison, Lowell H., and James C. Klotter. *A New History of Kentucky.* Lexington: University Press of Kentucky, 1997.

Harrison, Lowell. *Lincoln of Kentucky.* Lexington: University Press of Kentucky, 2000.

History of Howard and Cooper Counties, Missouri. St. Louis: National Historical Co., 1883.

History of Howard and Cooper County, Missouri. St. Louis: Missouri Historical Co., 1883.

History of Lafayette County, Missouri. St. Louis: Missouri Historical Co., 1881.

History of Saline County, Missouri. St. Louis: Missouri Historical Co., 1881.

Hodes, Martha. "The Sexualization of Reconstruction Politics: White Women and Black Men in the South after the Civil War." *Journal of the History of Sexuality* 3, no. 3 (1993): 402–17.

———. *White Women, Black Men: Illicit Sex in the Nineteenth-Century South.* New Haven: Yale University Press, 1997.

Holt, Michael. *The Rise and Fall of the American Whig Party.* New York: Oxford University Press, 1999.

Holt, Thomas. *Black over White: Negro Political Leadership in South Carolina during Reconstruction.* Urbana: University of Illinois Press, 1979.

Hopkins, James F. *A History of the Hemp Industry in Kentucky.* Lexington: University Press of Kentucky, 1951.

Horwitz, Tony. *Confederates in the Attic: Dispatches from the Unfinished Civil War.* New York: Vintage Books, 1998.

Howard, Victor B. *Black Liberation in Kentucky: Emancipation and Freedom, 1862–1884.* Lexington: University Press of Kentucky, 1983.

Howe, Daniel Walker. *The Political Culture of the American Whigs.* Chicago: University of Chicago Press, 1979.

Hudson, J. Blaine. *Fugitive Slaves and the Underground Railroad in the Kentucky Borderland.* Jefferson, N.C.: McFarland and Co., 2002.

Hurt, R. Douglas. *Agriculture and Slavery in Missouri's Little Dixie.* Columbia: University of Missouri Press, 1992.

Johnson, Walter. *Soul by Soul: Life inside the Antebellum Slave Market.* Cambridge: Harvard University Press, 2001.

Kerber, Linda. *No Constitutional Right to Be Ladies.* New York: Hill and Wang, 1998.

Kremer, Gary. *James Milton Turner and the Promise of America: The Public Life of a Post–Civil War Black Leader.* Columbia: University of Missouri Press, 1991.

Lalor, John, ed. *Cyclopedia of Political Science, Political Economy, and the Political History of the United States by the Best American and European Writers,* vol. 2. New York: Maynard, Merrill, and Co., 1881.

Launius, Roger D. *Alexander William Doniphan: Portrait of a Missouri Moderate.* Columbia: University of Missouri Press, 1997.

Levine, Bruce. *Confederate Emancipation: Southern Plans to Free and Arm Slaves during the Civil War.* Oxford: Oxford University Press, 2005.

Litwack, Leon. *Been in the Storm So Long.* New York: Vintage Books, 1979.

———. *North of Slavery: The Negro in the Free States, 1790–1860.* Chicago: University of Chicago Press, 1961.

Lorenzo J. Greene, Gary R. Kremer, and Antonio F. Holland. *Missouri's Black Heritage: Revised Edition.* Columbia: University of Missouri Press, 1993.

Lucas, Marion B. *A History of Blacks in Kentucky,* vol. 1: *From Slavery to Segregation, 1760–1891.* Frankfort: Kentucky Historical Society, 1992.

Marrs, Elijah P. *Life and History of the Rev. Elijah P. Marrs, First Pastor of Beargrass Baptist Church.* Louisville: Bradley and Gilbert Co., 1885.

Marshall, Anne. *Creating a Confederate Kentucky: The Lost Cause and Civil War Memory in a Border State.* Chapel Hill: University of North Carolina Press, 2010.

Martin, Jonathan D. *Divided Mastery: Slave Hiring in the American South.* Cambridge: Harvard University Press, 2004.

Masur, Kate. *An Example for All the Land: Emancipation and the Struggle over Equality in Washington, D.C.* Chapel Hill: University of North Carolina Press, 2010.

May, Robert. *Manifest Destiny's Underworld: Filibustering in Antebellum America.* Chapel Hill: University of North Carolina Press, 2004.

McCandless, Perry. *A History of Missouri,* vol. 2: *1820–1860.* Columbia: University of Missouri Press, 1972.

McCurry, Stephanie. *Confederate Reckoning: Power and Politics in the Civil War South.* Cambridge: Harvard University Press, 2010.

———. *Masters of Small Worlds: Yeoman Households, Gender Relations, and the Political Culture of the Antebellum South Carolina Low Country.* New York: Oxford University Press, 1995.

McDougle, Ivan. *Slavery in Kentucky, 1792–1865.* Westport, Conn.: Negro Universities Press, 1918.

McGee, James E. *Guide to Missouri Confederate Units, 1861–1865.* Fayetteville: University of Arkansas Press, 2008.

McKnight, Brian D. *Contested Borderland: The Civil War in Appalachian Kentucky and Virginia.* Lexington: University Press of Kentucky, 2006.

McPherson, James. *Battle Cry of Freedom.* New York: Ballantine Books, 1988.

———. *For Cause and Comrades.* New York: Oxford University Press, 1997.

———. *The Negro's Civil War: How American Felt and Acted during the War for the Union.* New York: Vintage Press, 2003.

Mering, John Vollmer. *The Whig Party in Missouri.* Columbia: University of Missouri Press, 1967.

Morgan, Philip D. *Slave Counterpoint: Black Culture in the Eighteenth-Century Chesapeake and Lowcountry.* Chapel Hill: University of North Carolina Press, 1998.

Morris, Robert. *Reading, 'Riting, and Reconstruction: The Education of the Freedmen in the South, 1861–1870.* Chicago: University of Chicago Press, 1976.

Murrell, Amy Elizabeth. "The Divided Family in Civil War America, 1860–1870." Ph.D. diss., University of Virginia, Charlottesville, 2001.

Mutti-Burke, Diane. *On Slavery's Border: Missouri's Small Slaveholding Households, 1815–1865.* Athens: University of Georgia Press, 2010.

Myers, Barton A. *Executing Daniel Bright: Race, Loyalty, and Guerrilla Violence in a Coastal Carolina Community, 1861–1865.* Baton Rouge: Louisiana State University Press, 2009.

Napton, William B. *Past and Present of Saline County, Missouri.* Indianapolis: B. F. Bowen and Co., 1910.

Nelson, Scott Reynolds. *Iron Confederacies: Southern Railways, Klan Violence, and Reconstruction.* Chapel Hill: University of North Carolina Press, 1999.

Noe, Kenneth. *Perryville: This Grand Havoc of Battle.* Lexington: University Press of Kentucky, 2001.

Oertel, Kristen Tegtmeier. *Bleeding Borders: Race, Gender, and Violence in Pre–Civil War Kansas.* Baton Rouge: Louisiana State University Press, 2009.

Owen, Thomas Louis. "The Formative Years of Kentucky's Republican Party, 1864–1871." Ph.D. diss., University of Kentucky, Lexington, 1981.

Painter, Nell Irvin. *Exodusters: Black Migration to Kansas after Reconstruction.* New York: Norton, 1976.

Paludan, Phillip Shaw. *Victims: A True Story of the Civil War.* Knoxville: University of Tennessee Press, 1981.

Parrish, William. *A History of Missouri,* vol. 3: *1860–1875.* Columbia: University of Missouri Press, 1973.

———. *Missouri under Radical Rule, 1865–1870.* Columbia: University of Missouri Press, 1965.

———. *Turbulent Partnership: Missouri and the Union, 1861–1865.* Columbia: University of Missouri Press, 1963.

Penningroth, Dylan. *The Claims of Kinfolk: African American Property and Community in the Nineteenth-Century South.* Chapel Hill: University of North Carolina Press, 2002.

Perrin, William Henry. *History of Fayette County, Kentucky.* Chicago: O. L. Baskin and Co., 1882.

Phillips, Christopher. *Missouri's Confederate : Claiborne Fox Jackson and the Creation of Southern Identity in the Border West.* Columbia: University of Missouri Press, 2000.

Phillips, Christopher, and Jason L. Pendleton, eds. *The Union on Trial: The Political Journals of Judge William Barclay Napton, 1829–1883.* Columbia: University of Missouri Press, 2005.

Phillips, Ulrich Bonnell. *American Negro Slavery.* Baton Rouge: Louisiana State University Press, 1966.

Potter, David. *Lincoln and His Party in the Secession Crisis.* New Haven: Yale University Press, 1942.

Proscio, Tony. *When Words Fail: How the Public Interest Becomes Neither Public nor Interesting.* New York: Edna Clark McDowell Foundation, 2005.

Pye, Lucian, and Sidney Verba, eds. *Political Culture and Political Development.* Princeton: Princeton University Press, 1965.

Rable, George C. *But There Was No Peace: The Role of Violence in the Politics of Reconstruction.* Athens: University of Georgia Press, 1984.

Ramage, James. *Rebel Raider: The Life of General John Hunt Morgan.* Lexington: University Press of Kentucky, 1986.

Rawick, George. *The American Slave: A Composite Autobiography.* Westport, Conn.: Greenwood, 1972.

Richard, Leonard. *"Gentlemen of Property and Standing": Anti-Abolitionist Mobs in Jacksonian America.* New York: Oxford University Press, 1970.

Rockman, Seth. *Scraping By: Wage Labor, Slavery, and Survival in Early Baltimore.* Baltimore: Johns Hopkins University Press, 2008.

Rodrigue, John. *Reconstruction in the Cane Fields: From Slavery to Free Labor in Louisiana's Sugar Parishes, 1862–1880.* Baton Rouge: Louisiana State University Press, 2001.

Rosen, Hannah. *Terror in the Heart of Freedom: Citizenship, Sexual Violence, and the Meaning of Race in the Postemancipation South.* Chapel Hill: University of North Carolina Press, 2008.

Rowan, Steven, trans. and ed. *Germans for a Free Missouri: Translations from the St. Louis Radical Press, 1857–1862.* Columbia: University of Missouri Press, 1983.

Rowell, Chester H. *A Historical and Legal Digest of all the Contested Election Cases in the House of Representatives of the United States from the First to the Fifty-Sixth Congress, 1789–1901.* Washington, D.C.: Government Printing Office, 1901

Saville, Julie. *The Work of Reconstruction: From Slave to Wage Laborer in South Carolina, 1860–1870.* Cambridge: Cambridge University Press, 1994.

Schindler, D., and J. Toman. *The Laws of Armed Conflicts.* The Hague: Martinus Nihjoff, 1998.

Schwalm, Leslie. *Emancipation's Diaspora: Race and Reconstruction in the Upper Midwest.* Chapel Hill: University of North Carolina Press, 2009.

Sears, Richard D. *Camp Nelson, Kentucky: A Civil War History.* Lexington: University Press of Kentucky, 2002.

Sehlinger, Peter J. *Kentucky's Last Cavalier: General William Preston, 1816–1887.* Fayetteville: University of Arkansas Press, 2008.

Shalhope, Robert E. *Sterling Price: Portrait of a Southerner.* Columbia: University of Missouri Press, 1971.

Smith, John David, ed. *Black Soldiers in Blue: African American Troops in the Civil War Era.* Chapel Hill: University of North Carolina Press, 2002.

Smith, John David, and William Jr. Cooper, eds. *A Union Woman in Civil War Kentucky: The Diary of Frances Peter.* Lexington: University Press of Kentucky, 2000.

Smith, T. Berry, and Pearl Sims Gehrig. *History of Chariton and Howard Counties, Missouri.* Topeka: Historical Publishing Co., 1923.

Sobel, Mechal. *Trabelin' On: The Slave Journey to an Afro-Baptist Faith.* Westport, Conn.: Greenwood Press, 1979.

Stanton, Robert L. *The Church and the Rebellion.* 1864. Reprint. Freeport, N.Y.: Books for Libraries Press, 1971.

Stiles, T. J. *Jesse James: Last Rebel of the Civil War.* New York: Knopf, 2002.

Sutherland, Daniel. *A Savage Conflict: The Role of Guerrillas in the American Civil War.* Chapel Hill: University of North Carolina Press, 2009.

Switzler, William. *History of Boone County, Missouri.* St. Louis: Western Historical Co., 1882.

Tadman, Michael. *Speculators and Slaves: Masters, Traders, and Slaves in the Old South.* Madison: University of Wisconsin Press, 1989.

Tallant, Harold D. *Evil Necessity: Slavery and Political Culture in Antebellum Kentucky.* Lexington: University Press of Kentucky, 2003.

Tapp, Hambleton, and James C. Klotter. *Kentucky: Decades of Discord, 1865–1900.* Frankfort: Kentucky Historical Society, 1977.

Taylor, Amy Murrell. *The Divided Family in Civil War America*. Chapel Hill: University of North Carolina Press, 2005.

Thelen, David. *Paths of Resistance: Tradition and Dignity in Industrializing Missouri*. New York: Oxford University Press, 1986.

Trefousse, Hans L. *Carl Schurz: A Biography*. Knoxville: University of Tennessee Press, 1982.

Trelease, Allen W. *White Terror: The Ku Klux Klan Conspiracy and Southern Reconstruction*. Baton Rouge: Louisiana State University Press, 1971.

Trexler, Harrison. *Slavery in Missouri, 1804–1865*. Baltimore: Johns Hopkins Press, 1914.

Tunnell, Ted. *Crucible of Reconstruction: War, Radicalism, and Race in Louisiana, 1862–1877*. Baton Rouge: Louisiana State University Press, 1984.

Voegeli, Jacque. *Free but Not Equal: The Midwest and the Negro during the Civil War*. Chicago: University of Chicago Press, 1967.

Webb, Ross A. *Kentucky in the Reconstruction Era*. Lexington: University Press of Kentucky, 1979.

Wharton, Mary E., and Ellen F. Williams, eds. *Peach Leather and Rebel Gray: Bluegrass Life and the War, 1860–1865*. Lexington: Helicon Co., 1986.

Whites, LeeAnn. *The Civil War as a Crisis in Gender: Augusta, Georgia, 1860–1890*. Athens: University of Georgia Press, 1995.

Wiener, Jonathan. *Social Origins of the New South: Alabama, 1860–1885*. Baton Rouge: Louisiana State University Press, 1978.

Wood, Forrest G. *Black Scare: The Racist Response to Emancipation and Reconstruction*. Berkeley: University of California Press, 1968.

Woodward, C. Vann. *Origins of the New South*. Baton Rouge: Louisiana State University Press, 1951.

Wright, George C. *Life behind a Veil: Blacks in Louisville, Kentucky, 1865–1930*. Baton Rouge: Louisiana State University Press, 1985.

———. *Racial Violence in Kentucky: Lynchings, Mob Rule, and "Legal Lynchings," 1865–1940*. Baton Rouge: Louisiana State University Press, 1990.

Wright, Louis. *Culture on the Moving Frontier*. Bloomington: Indiana University Press, 1955.

Wyatt-Brown, Bertram. *Southern Honor: Ethics and Behavior in the Old South*. New York: Oxford University Press, 1982.

Young, Bennett H. *A History of Jessamine County, Kentucky*. Louisville: Courier-Journal Job Printing, 1898.

ARTICLES AND PAPERS

Anderson, Kristen L. "German Americans, African Americans, and the Republican Party in St. Louis, 1865–1872." *Journal of American Ethnic History* 28 (Fall 2008): 34–51.

Barton, Keith C. "'Good Cooks and Washers' Slave Hiring and the Market in Bour-
    bon County, Kentucky." *Journal of American History* 84, no. 2 (September 1997):
    436–60.
Bonner, Thomas. "Civil War Historians and the 'Needless War' Doctrine." *Journal of
    the History of Ideas* 17, no. 2 (April 1956): 193–216.
Brown, Elsa Barkley. "Negotiating and Transforming the Public Sphere: African-
    American Political Life in the Transition from Slavery to Freedom." *Public Culture*
    7 (Fall 1994): 107–46.
Brown, Richard C. "The Free Blacks of Boyle County, Kentucky, 1850–1860: A Research
    Note." *Register of the Kentucky Historical Society* 87, no. 4 (Fall 1989): 426–38.
Buser, Adrian. "Borderlines in the Bluegrass: The Elite White Women of Kentucky
    during the Civil War." Ph.D. diss., Indiana University, Bloomington, ongoing.
Butler, Kevin. "The Creation of African American Christianity: Slavery and Religion
    in Antebellum Missouri." Ph.D. diss., University of Missouri, Columbia, ongoing.
Castel, Albert. "Order No. 11 and the Civil War on the Border." *Missouri Historical
    Review* 57, no. 4 (July 1963): 357–68.
Charton, Scott. "Gephardt Wants Missouri Confederate Flag Pulled Down." *Associated
    Press,* January 14, 2003.
Cheek, Christen Ashby. "Memoirs of Mrs. E. B. Patterson: A Perspective on Danville
    during the Civil War." *Register of the Kentucky Historical Society* 92, no. 4 (Fall 1994):
    347–99.
Christensen, Lawrence O. "Carr W. Pritchett and the Civil War Era in Glasgow and
    Fayette." *Missouri Historical Review* 103, no. 1 (October 2008): 41–55.
Connelly, Thomas L. "Neo-Confederatism or Power Vacuum: Post-War Kentucky
    Politics Reappraised." *Register of the Kentucky Historical Society* 64, no. 4 (Octo-
    ber 1966): 257–69.
Copeland, James. "Where Were the Kentucky Unionists and Secessionists?" *Register
    of the Kentucky Historical Society* 71, no. 4 (October 1973): 344–63.
Crane, J. Michael. "'Slavery on the Edge of Freedom': Kentucky in the 19th Century."
    Ph.D. diss., Vanderbilt University, 2009.
Dwight, Margaret L. "Black Suffrage in Missouri, 1865–1877." Ph.D. diss., University
    of Missouri, Columbia, 1978.
Efford, Allison Clark. "Race Should Be as Unimportant as Ancestry: German Radicals
    and African American Citizenship in the Missouri Constitution of 1865." *Missouri
    Historical Review* 104, no. 3 (April 2010): 138–58.
Frizzell, Robert W. "Southern Identity in Nineteenth-Century Missouri: Little Dixie's
    Slave Majority Areas and the Transition to Midwestern Farming." *Missouri His-
    torical Review* 99, no. 3 (April 2005): 238–60.
Geiger, Mark. "Indebtedness and the Origins of Guerrilla Violence in Civil War Mis-
    souri." *Journal of Southern History* 75, no. 1 (February 2009): 49–82.

———. "Missouri's Hidden Civil War: Financial Conspiracy and the End of the Planter Elite, 1861–65." Ph.D. diss., University of Missouri Press, Columbia, 2006.

Gerber, Richard Allen. "Carl Schurz's Journey from Radical to Liberal Republican: A Problem in Ideological Consistency." *Mid America* 82, nos. 1–2, (2000): 71–99.

Gienapp, William E. "Abraham Lincoln and the Border States." *Journal of the Abraham Lincoln Association* 13 (1992): 13–46.

Hall, Patricia Kelly, and Steven Ruggles. "'Restless in the Midst of Their Prosperity': New Evidence on the Internal Migration of Americans, 1850–2000." *Journal of American History* 91, no. 3. (December 2004): 829–46.

Harris, Theodore H. H. "Creating Windows of Opportunity: Isaac E. Black and the African American Experience in Kentucky, 1848–1914." *Register of the Kentucky Historical Society* 98, no. 2 (2000).

Hood, James Larry. "The Union and Slavery: Congressman Brutus J. Clay of the Bluegrass." *Register of the Kentucky Historical Society* 75, no. 3 (July 1977): 214–21.

Kempker, Erin. "The Union, the War, and Elvira Scott." *Missouri Historical Review* 95, no. 3 (April 2001): 287–301.

Lacroix Hoguet, Helen. "A Head with the Union, a Heart with the South: Race, Labor, and Politics in Kentucky's Bluegrass Region, 1865–1900." Ph.D. diss., University of Wisconsin, Madison, 2010.

Lewis, Patrick A. "'All Men of Decency Ought to Quit the Army': Benjamin F. Buckner, Manhood, and Proslavery Unionism in Kentucky." *Register of the Kentucky Historical Society* 107, no. 4 (Fall 2009).

Martin, James B. "Black Flag over the Bluegrass: Guerrilla Warfare in Kentucky, 1863–1865." *Register of the Kentucky Historical Society* 86, no. 4 (Fall 1988): 352–75.

Montgomery, Alicia. "Ashcroft Whistles Dixie." *Salon*, January 3, 2001.

Mutti-Burke, Diane. "On Slavery's Border: Slavery and Slaveholding on Missouri's Farms, 1821–1865." Ph.D. diss., Emory University, 2004.

O'Brien, Margaret. *Slavery in Louisville during the Antebellum Period: 1820–1860.* Master's thesis, University of Louisville, 1979.

Owsley, Frank L. "The Pattern of Migration and Settlement on the Southern Frontier." *Journal of Southern History* 11, no. 2 (May 1945): 147–76.

Rhyne, J. Michael. "'A Murderous Affair in Lincoln County': Politics, Violence, and Memory in a Civil War Era Kentucky Community." *American Nineteenth Century History* 7, no. 3 (2006): 337–59.

———. "Rehearsal for Redemption: The Politics of Racial Violence in Civil War–Era Kentucky." C. Ballard Breaux Conference Invited Lecture at the Filson Historical Society, May 19, 2001.

———. "'The Whole Family Driven Away': Regulators, Politics, and the Assault on Black Households in Post-Emancipation Kentucky." Paper presented at the Southern Historical Association Annual Conference, Baltimore, 2002.

Savage, W. Sherman. "The Legal Provisions for Negro Schools in Missouri from 1865 to 1890." *Journal of Negro History* 16, no. 3 (July 1931): 309–21.

Smith, John David. "E. Merton Coulter, the 'Dunning School,' and *The Civil War and Readjustment in Kentucky*." *Register of the Kentucky Historical Society* 86, no. 1 (Winter 1988): 52–69.

———. "The Recruitment of Negro Soldiers in Kentucky, 1863–1865." *Register of the Kentucky Historical Society* 72, no. 4 (October 1974): 691–726.

———. "Slavery Ideology and the Underground Railroad in Kentucky: A Review Essay." *Register of the Kentucky Historical Society* 101, nos. 1–2 (Winter–Spring 2003): 93–108.

———. "'To Hue the Line and Let the Chips Fall Where They May': J. Winston Coleman's Slavery Times in Kentucky Reconsidered." *Register of the Kentucky Historical Society* 103, no. 4 (Fall 2005): 147–76.

Smith, Krista. "Slaveholders vs. Slaveholders: Divided Kentuckians in the Secession Crisis." *Register of the Kentucky Historical Society* 97, no. 4 (Fall 1999): 375–402.

Stegmeier, Mark J. "Abraham Lincoln and the Danville Farmer: The President-Elect Discusses Policy with a Kentuckian." *Register of the Kentucky Historical Society* 106, nos. 3–4 (Summer–Fall 2008): 409–32.

Volz, Harry A. "Party, State and Nation: Kentucky and the Coming of the American Civil War." Ph.D. diss., University of Virginia, 1982.

Vorenberg, Michael. "The Era of the Oath Reconsidered: Race, Religion, and Citizenship in the Civil War Era." Lecture given at the Northwestern University School of Law, November 3, 2003.

Waldrep, Christopher. "Memory, History, and the Meaning of the Civil War." *Register of the Kentucky Historical Society* 102, no. 3 (Summer 2004): 383–402.

Webb, Ross A. "'The Past Is Never Dead, It's Not Even Past': Benjamin P. Runkle and the Freedmen's Bureau in Kentucky, 1866–1870." *Register of the Kentucky Historical Society* 84, no. 4 (Fall 1986): 343–59.

Wharton, Mary E., and Ellen F. Williams, eds. *Peach Leather and Rebel Gray: Diary and Letters of a Confederate Wife*. Lexington: Helicon Co., 1986.

Williams, Henry Sullivan. "The Development of the Negro Public School System in Missouri." *Journal of Negro History* 5, no. 2 (April 1920).

Williams, Kenneth H., and James Russell Harris. "Kentucky in 1860: A Statistical Overview." *Register of the Kentucky Historical Society* 103, no. 4 (Fall 2005): 743–64.

INDEX

Note: Italic page numbers refer to figures and tables.

abolitionism: and black education, 146; conversion of Unionism to, 90; extremism of, 8, 33, 34, 36, 43, 47; and jayhawking, 272n21; in Kentucky, 19, 34, 40; and "mildness" of slavery, 255n56; and Republican Party, 53; and slave runaways, 68, 69, 70; as threat to racial order, 9, 29; white conservative Unionists opposed to, 35, 43–44, 48, 54, 75, 83, 109, 121, 132

African Americans: children, 134, 150, *150*, 152, 193; and conventions, 153–55, 158–59, 189, 285n43, 286n48, 287n64; and criminality, 185–86, 213, 239, 240; elites, 147–48, 155, 160, 165–66, 287n71, 289n97, 293n85; emigration from countryside, 8, 142–43, 164–65, 225, 238, 283nn88–89; families of, 5, 121, 134, 138–39, 144–45, 158, 202; kin and social networks of, 4, 36–37, 64–65, 69, 71, 105, 128, 130–31, 143, 166, 245, 273n31; and manhood, 158–59, 214; militias of, 171, 186, 240, 289n10; social autonomy of, 4, 5, 36–37, 66, 70, 72, 74, 166, 192–93, 230, 293n86. *See also* black citizenship; black education; black political collectivities; black soldiers; black suffrage; free blacks; racial equality; slave families; slave hiring; slave politics; slave resistance; slavery; slaves

agrarianism, 184, 185

Allen, James Lane, 28, 29, 31, 255n56, 264–65n67

American Missionary Association (AMA), 151, 152

American Revolution, rhetoric of, 49, 86, 159, 211

Anderson, "Bloody" Bill, 115, 199

Arkansas, 78, 82, 93, 267n12, 269n52

Atchison, David R., 36, 41, 54, 258n29

Ayers, Edward, 246–47, 300–301n7

Baker, Martin, 16, 17

Beard, Charles, 246

Beard, Mary, 246

Beck, James, 182, 224, 225

Behrend, Justin, 299n85

Bell, John, 35, 37–38, 47, 50, 172–73, 262n29, 263n38

Benton, Thomas Hart, 39, 172–73, 257n19, 261n10

Berlin, Ira, 104–5, 111, 253n20, 267n6

Bingham, George Caleb, 197–98

black citizenship: and black education, 147; and black elites, 160, 165, 166, 287n71; and black enlistment in Union army, 124, 125, 129, 144; conceptions of, 152, 167, 169; development of, 3–4; and Fifteenth Amendment passage, 212–13, 214, 234–35; in Kentucky, 7; meaning of, 10; racial order threatened by, 2; and racial violence, 5, 11, 122, 135–45, 170, 190–92, 194, 230, 238–41, 288n86, 293n88; and sharecropping, 161–62

black education: funding for, 146, 147–53, 241; and legislation, 147, 150, 151, 284n11; politics of, 146–54, 160; and racial violence, 190–92; school census for, 150, *150*, 152; and school